THE SEVEN DEADLY SINS

nakaba suzuki presents

8

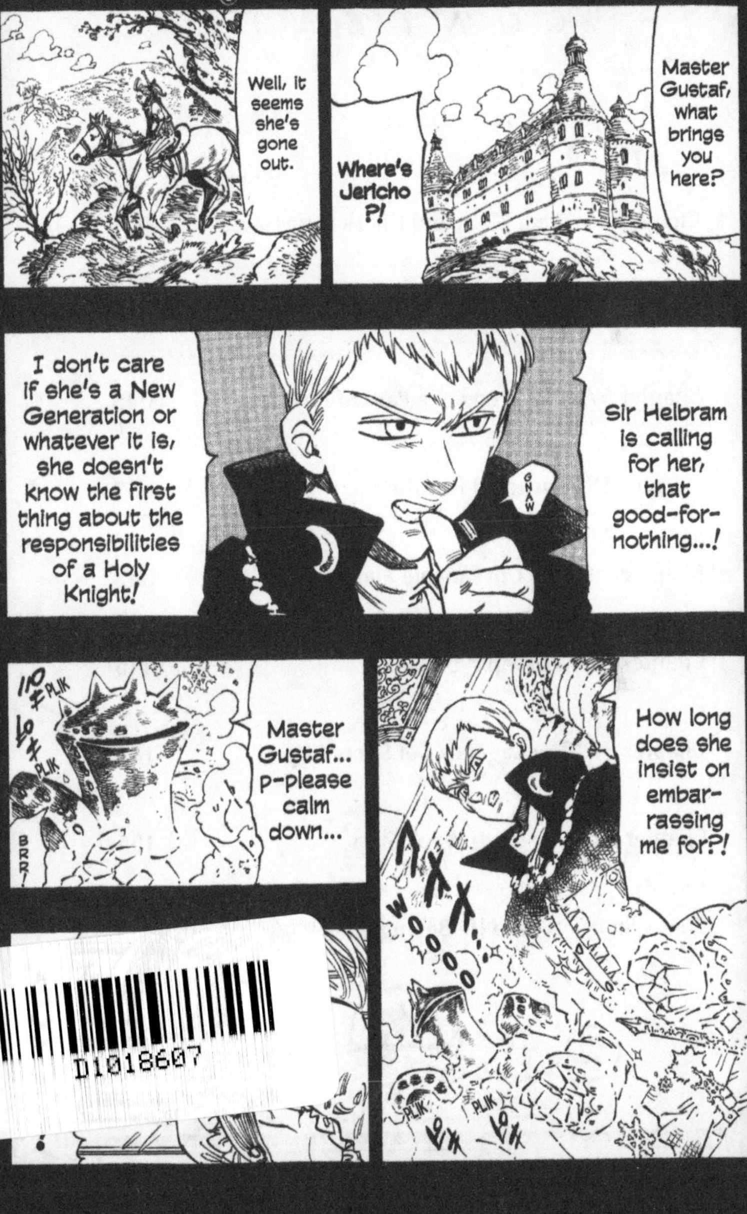
Master Gustaf, what brings you here?
Where's Jericho?!
Well, it seems she's gone out.
Sir Helbram is calling for her, that good-for-nothing...!
GNAW
I don't care if she's a New Generation or whatever it is, she doesn't know the first thing about the responsibilities of a Holy Knight!
How long does she insist on embarrassing me for?!
WOOOO...
PLIK
PLIK
Master Gustaf... p-please calm down...
PLIK
PLIK
BRR!

CONTENTS

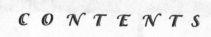

BOAR HAT

The Seven Deadly Sins

THE SEVEN DEADLY SINS

the seven deadly sins
tale·55

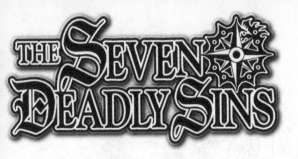

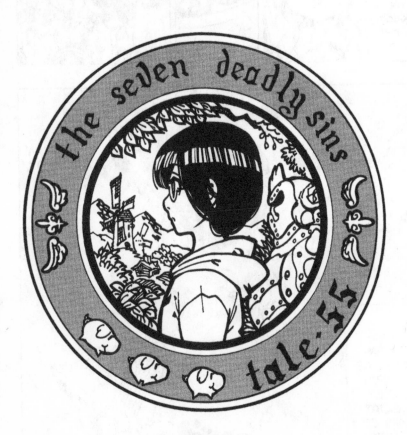

Chapter 55 - That Man, And His Heartlessness

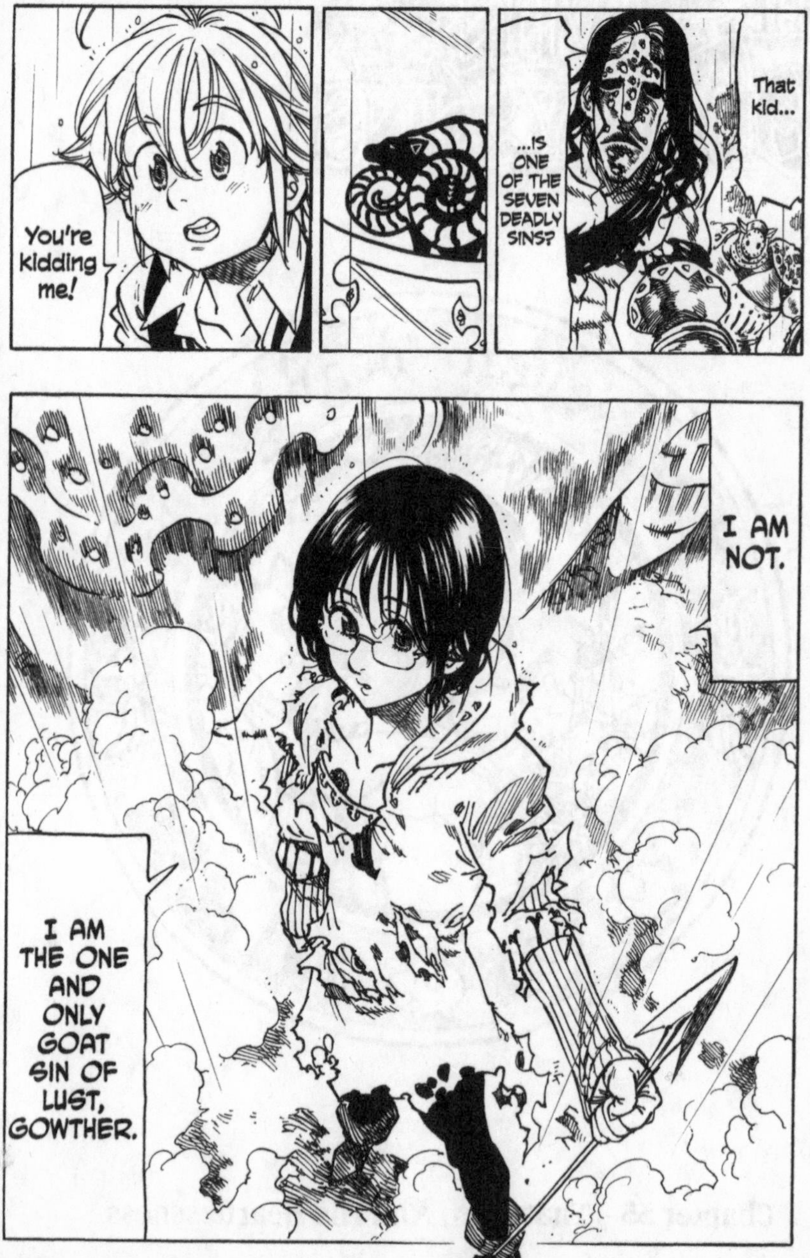
That kid...
...IS ONE OF THE SEVEN DEADLY SINS?
You're kidding me!
I AM NOT.
I AM THE ONE AND ONLY GOAT SIN OF LUST, GOWTHER.

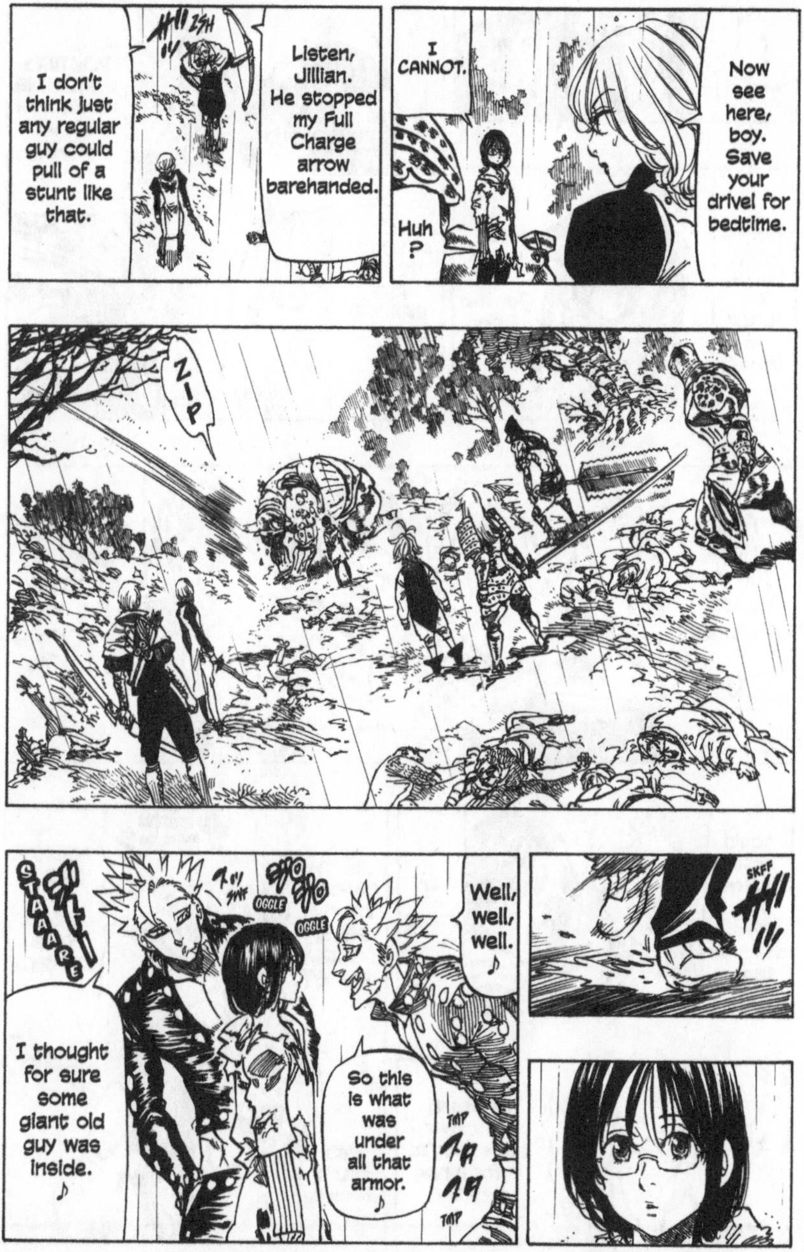
Now see here, boy. Save your drivel for bedtime.
I CANNOT.
Huh?
Listen, Jillian. He stopped my Full Charge arrow barehanded.
ZSH
I don't think just any regular guy could pull of a stunt like that.
ZIP
SKFF
Well, well, well. ♪
OGGLE
OGGLE
SNF
STAAARE
So this is what was under all that armor. ♪
TMP
TMP
I thought for sure some giant old guy was inside. ♪

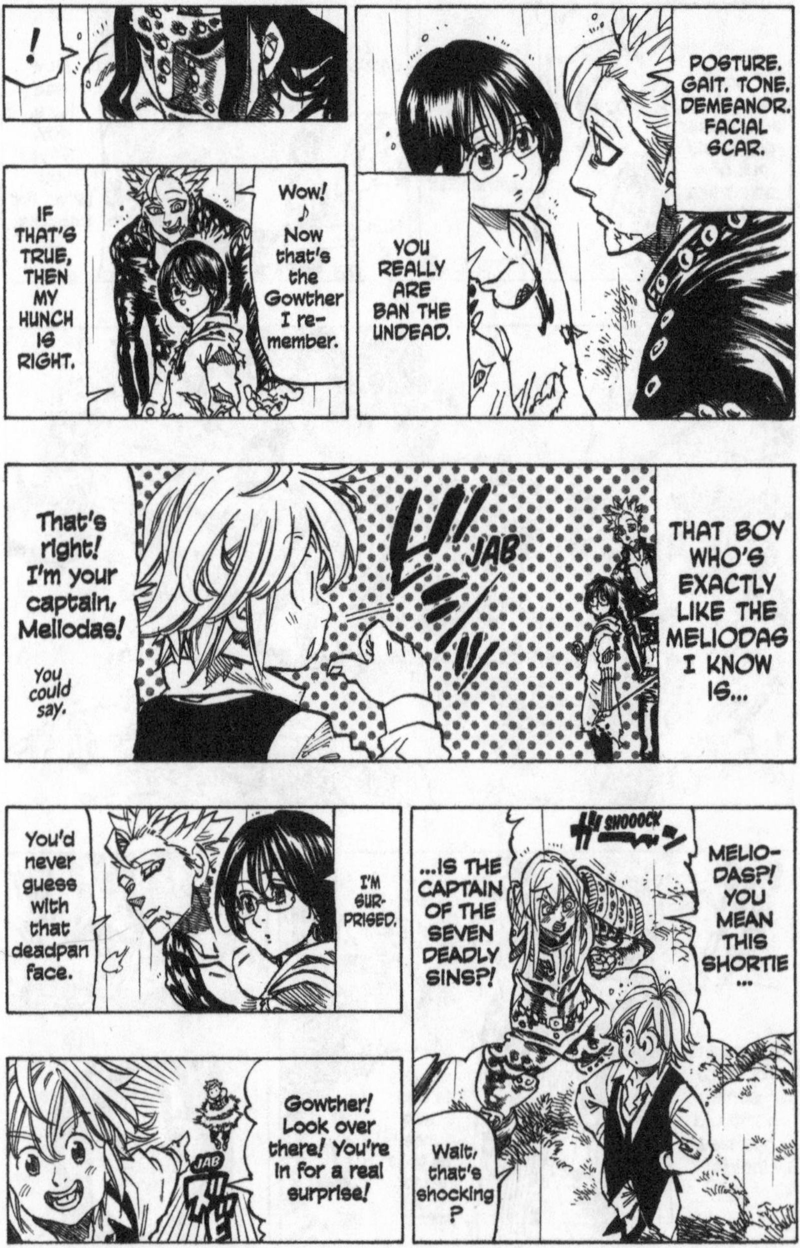
POSTURE. GAIT. TONE. DEMEANOR. FACIAL SCAR.
YOU REALLY ARE BAN THE UNDEAD.
!
Wow! ♪ Now that's the Gowther I re-member.
IF THAT'S TRUE, THEN MY HUNCH IS RIGHT.
THAT BOY WHO'S EXACTLY LIKE THE MELIODAS I KNOW IS...
JAB
That's right! I'm your captain, Meliodas!
You could say.
MELIO-DAS?! YOU MEAN THIS SHORTIE ...
SHOOOCK
...IS THE CAPTAIN OF THE SEVEN DEADLY SINS?!
Wait, that's shocking?
I'M SUR-PRISED.
You'd never guess with that deadpan face.
Gowther! Look over there! You're in for a real surprise!
JAB

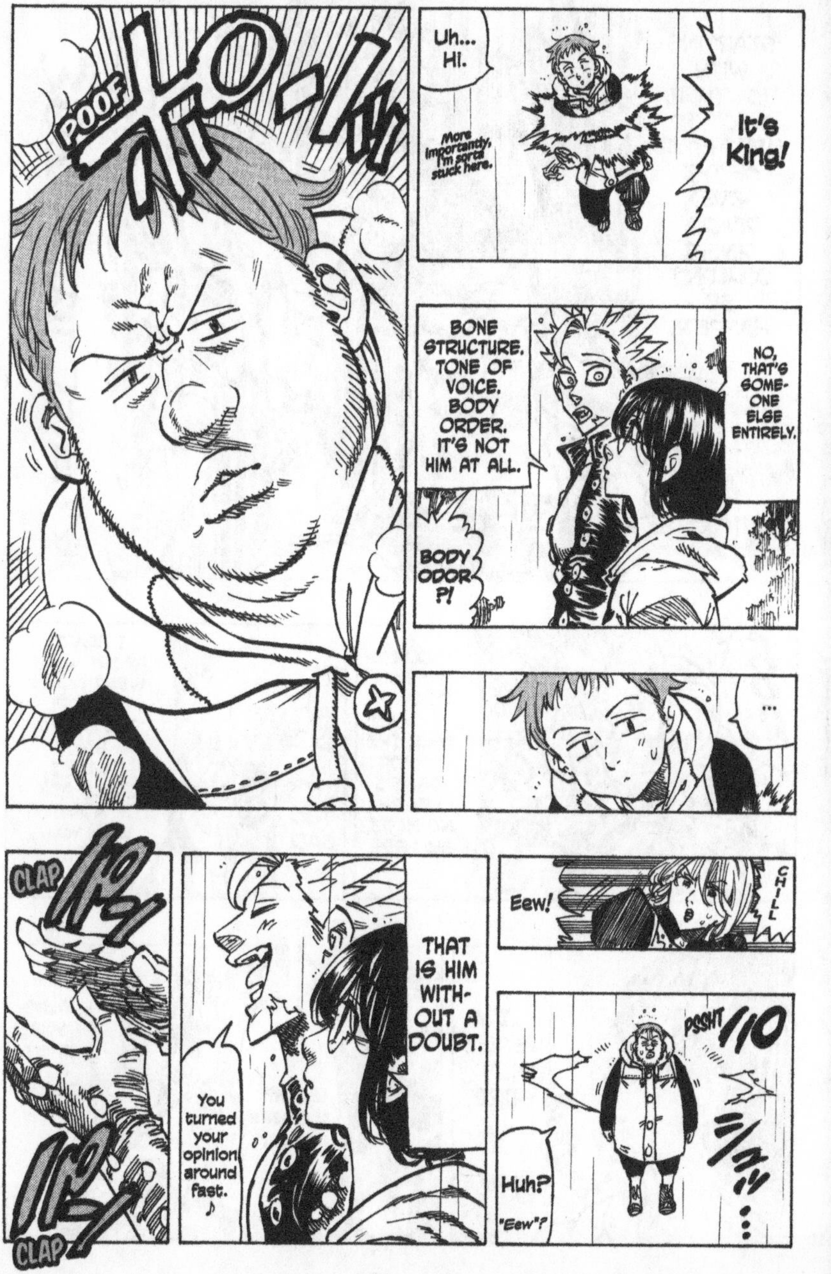
It's King!
Uh... Hi.
More importantly, I'm sorta stuck here.
NO, THAT'S SOME-ONE ELSE ENTIRELY.
BONE STRUCTURE. TONE OF VOICE. BODY ORDER. IT'S NOT HIM AT ALL.
BODY ODOR?!
...
POOF
CHILL
Eew!
PSSHT
Huh?
"Eew"?
THAT IS HIM WITH-OUT A DOUBT.
You turned your opinion around fast. ♪
CLAP
CLAP

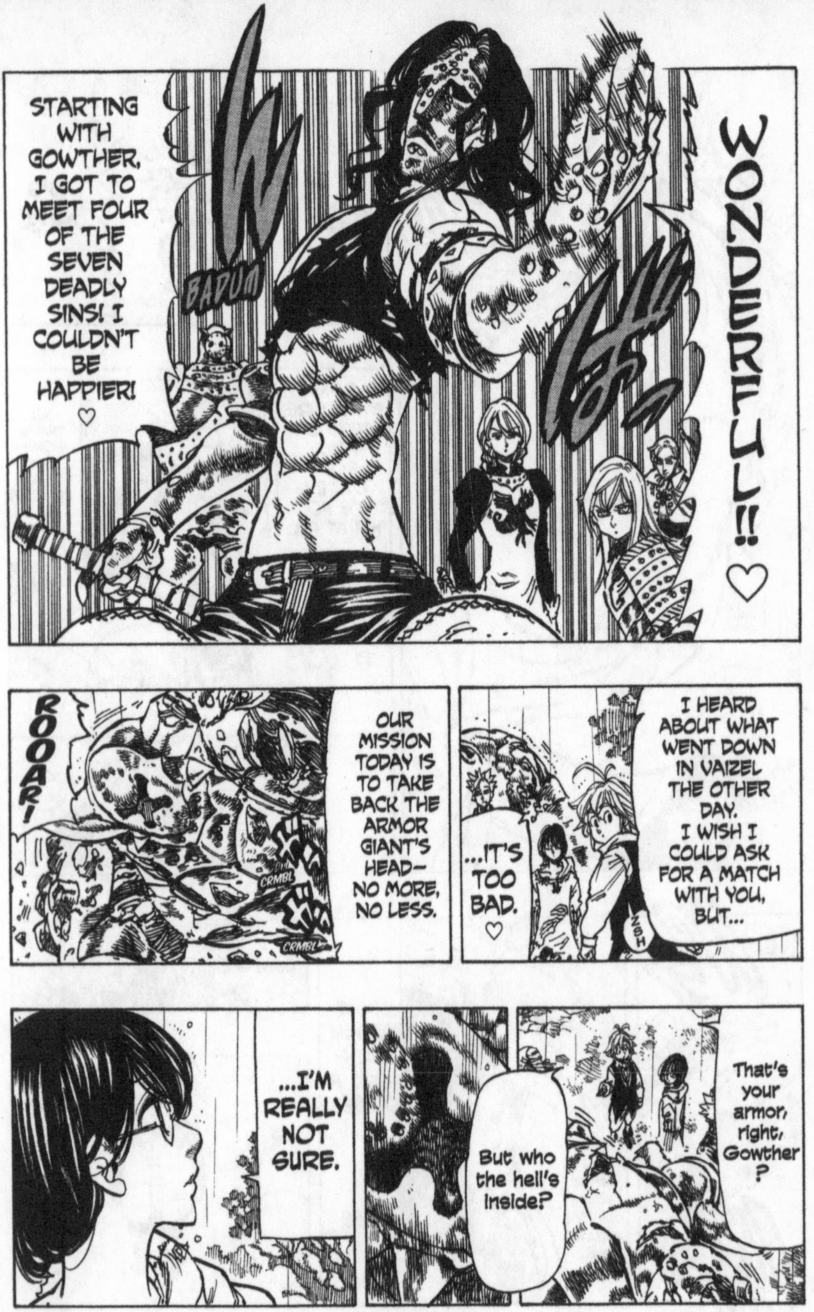
WONDERFUL!! ♡
STARTING WITH GOWTHER, I GOT TO MEET FOUR OF THE SEVEN DEADLY SINS! I COULDN'T BE HAPPIER! ♡
BADUM
I HEARD ABOUT WHAT WENT DOWN IN VAIZEL THE OTHER DAY. I WISH I COULD ASK FOR A MATCH WITH YOU, BUT...
ZSH
...IT'S TOO BAD. ♡
OUR MISSION TODAY IS TO TAKE BACK THE ARMOR GIANT'S HEAD— NO MORE, NO LESS.
ROOAR!
CRMBL
CRMBL
That's your armor, right, Gowther?
But who the hell's inside?
...I'M REALLY NOT SURE.

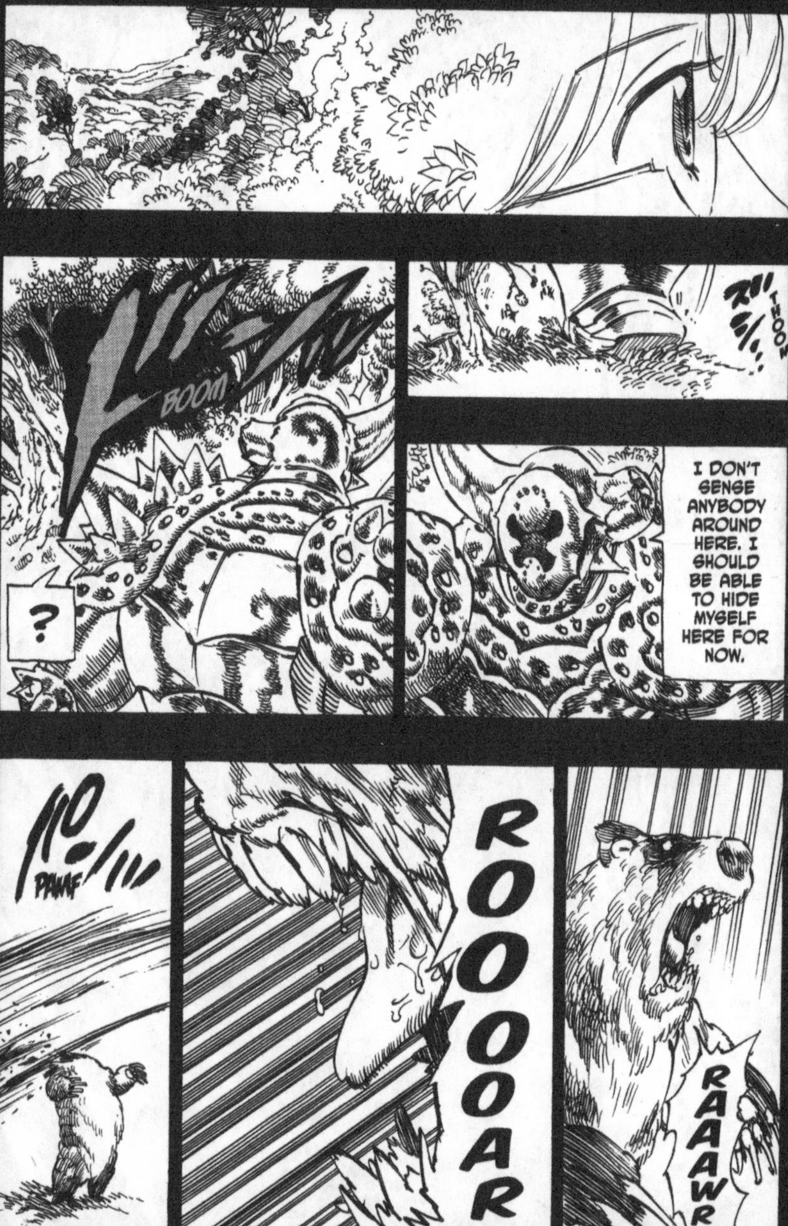
THOOM
I DON'T SENSE ANYBODY AROUND HERE. I SHOULD BE ABLE TO HIDE MYSELF HERE FOR NOW.
BOOM
?
RAAAWR
ROOOOAR
PWAF

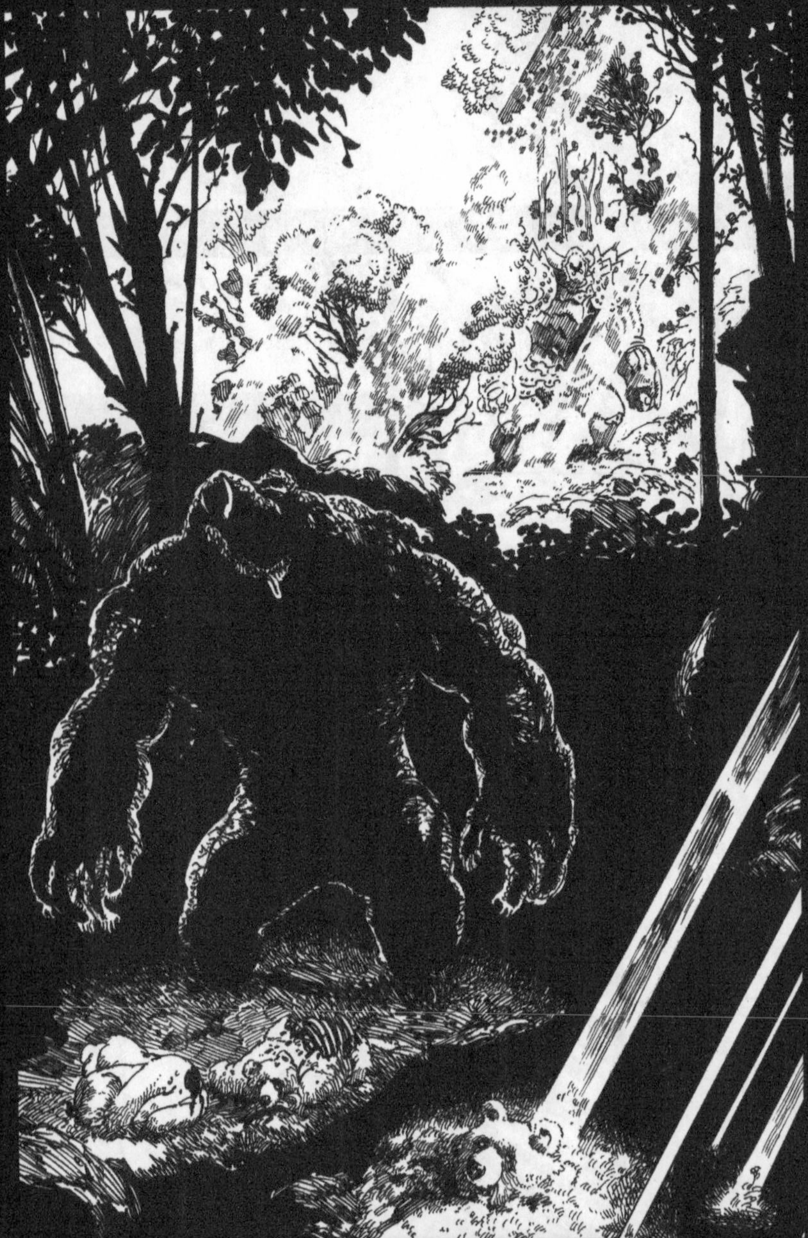

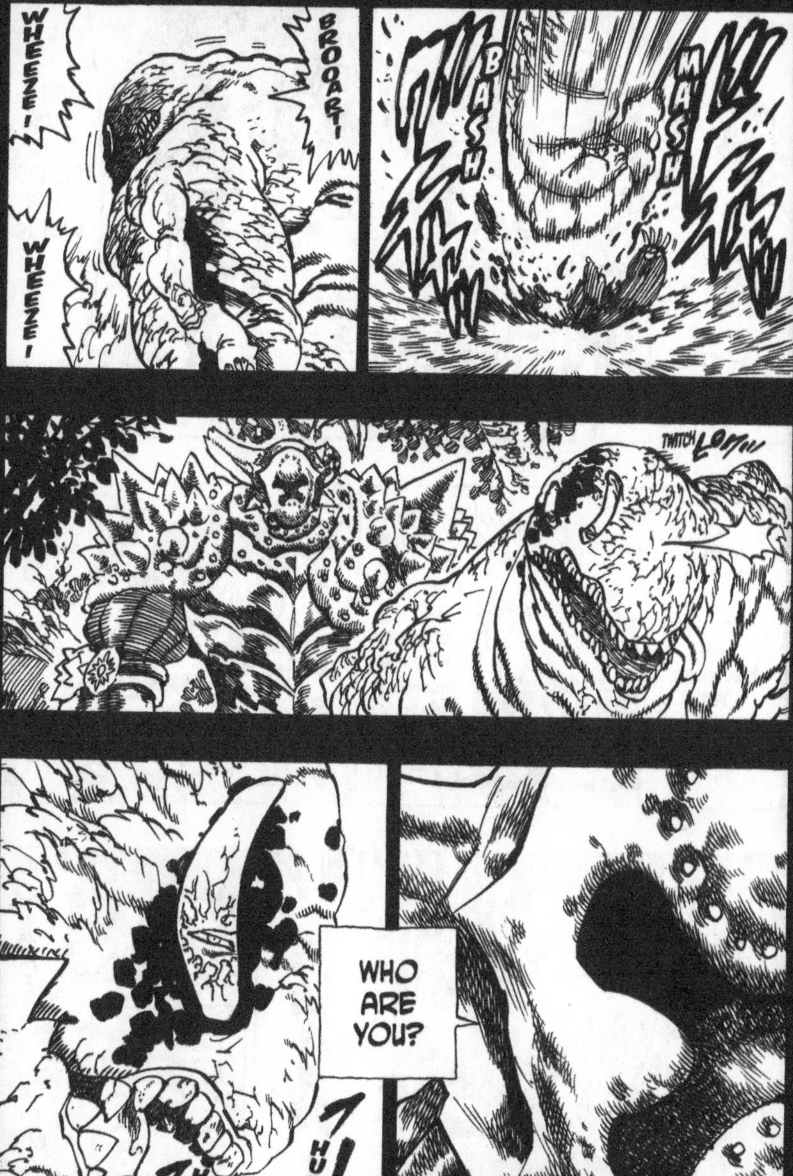
MASH
BASH
BROOART!
WHEEZE!
WHEEZE!
TWITCH
WHO ARE YOU?
HUFF!
HUFF!

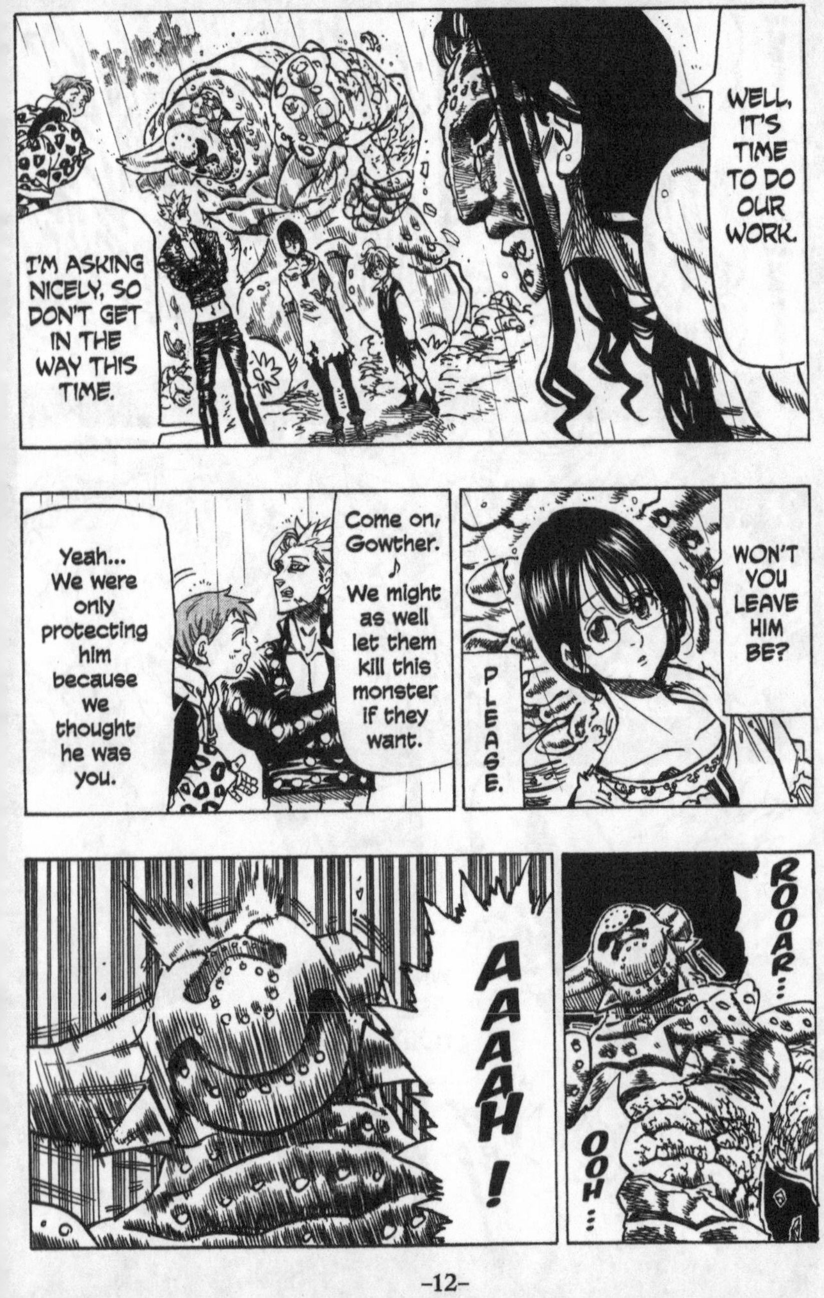
WELL, IT'S TIME TO DO OUR WORK.
I'M ASKING NICELY, SO DON'T GET IN THE WAY THIS TIME.
WON'T YOU LEAVE HIM BE?
PLEASE.
Come on, Gowther. ♪ We might as well let them kill this monster if they want.
Yeah... We were only protecting him because we thought he was you.
ROOAR...
OOH...
AAAAH!

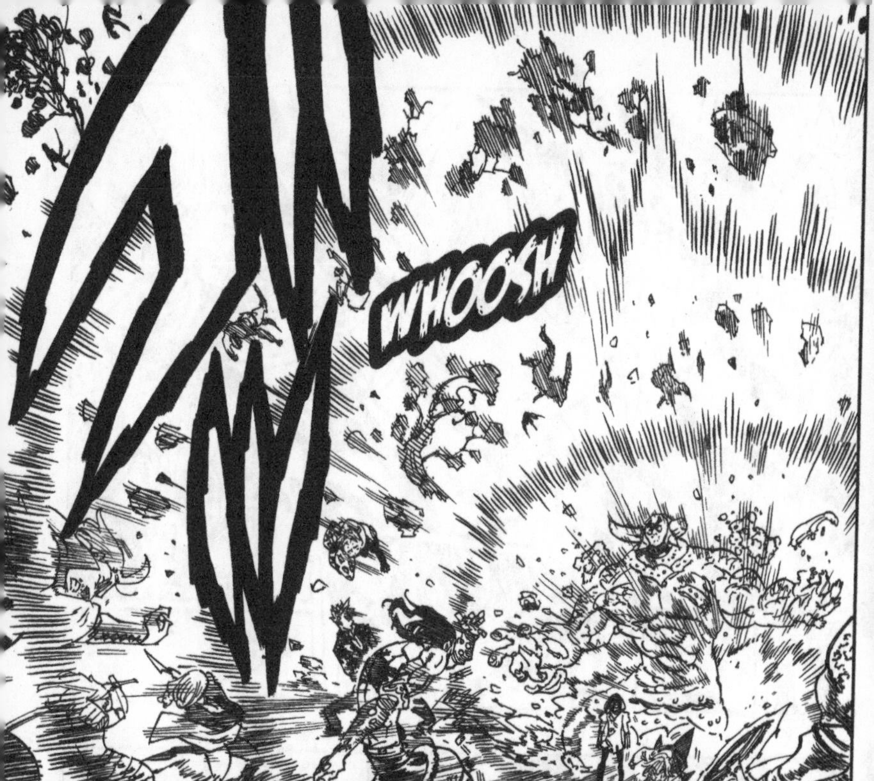
WHOOSH
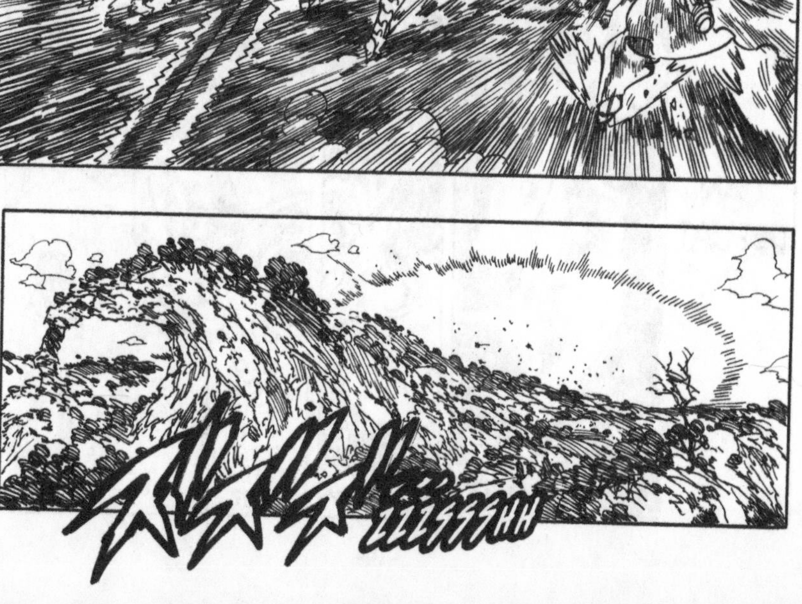
ZZZSSSHH

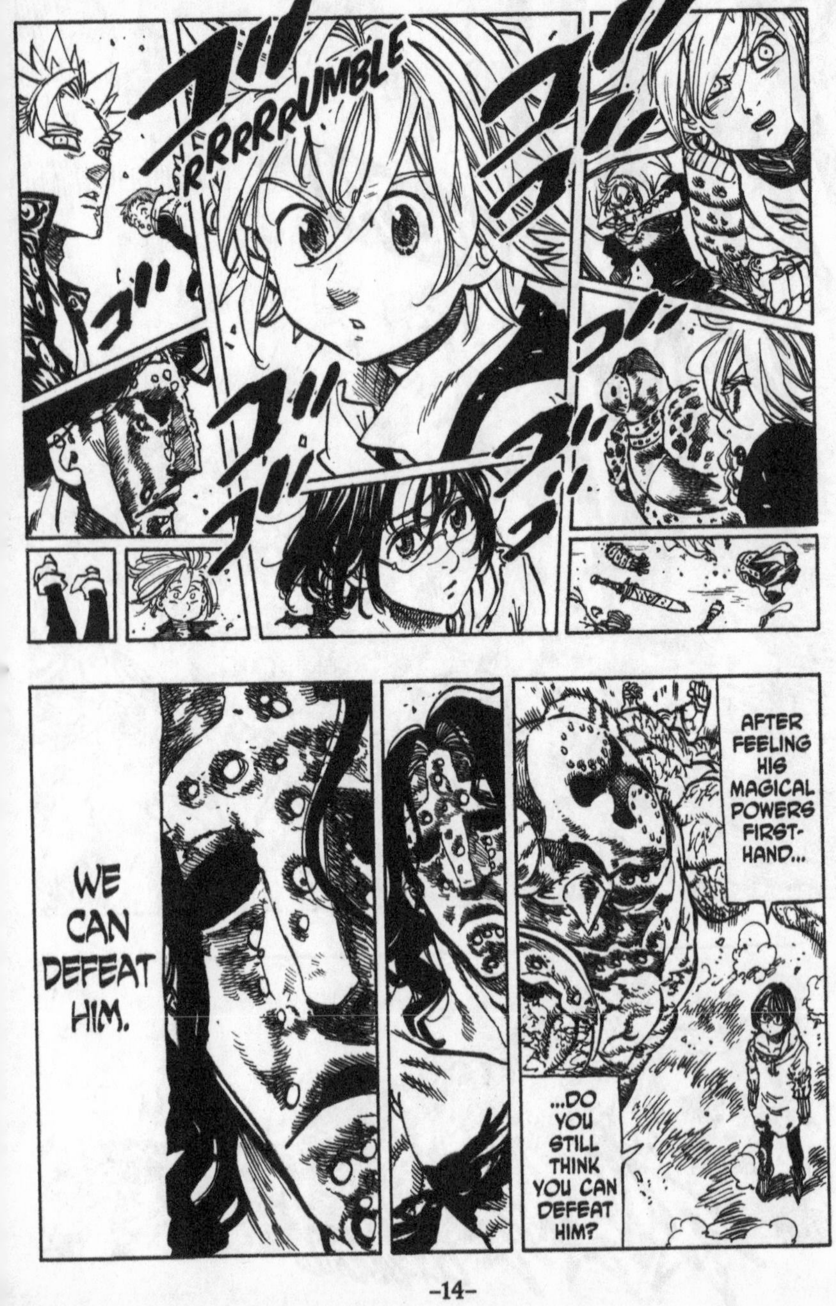
RRRRRUMBLE
AFTER FEELING HIS MAGICAL POWERS FIRST-HAND...
...DO YOU STILL THINK YOU CAN DEFEAT HIM?
WE CAN DEFEAT HIM.

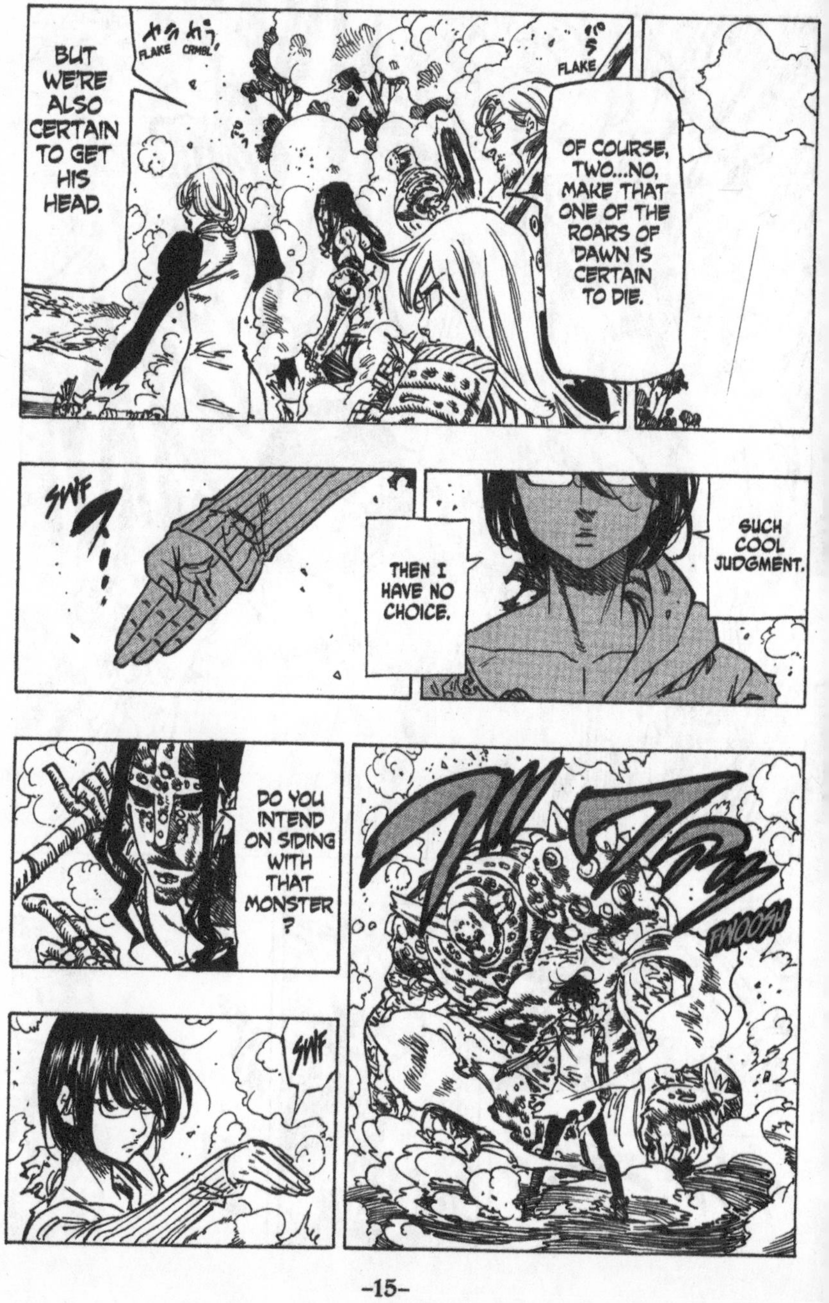
FLAKE
OF COURSE, TWO...NO, MAKE THAT ONE OF THE ROARS OF DAWN IS CERTAIN TO DIE.
FLAKE CRMBL
BUT WE'RE ALSO CERTAIN TO GET HIS HEAD.
SUCH COOL JUDGMENT.
THEN I HAVE NO CHOICE.
SWF
FWOOSH
DO YOU INTEND ON SIDING WITH THAT MONSTER?
SWF

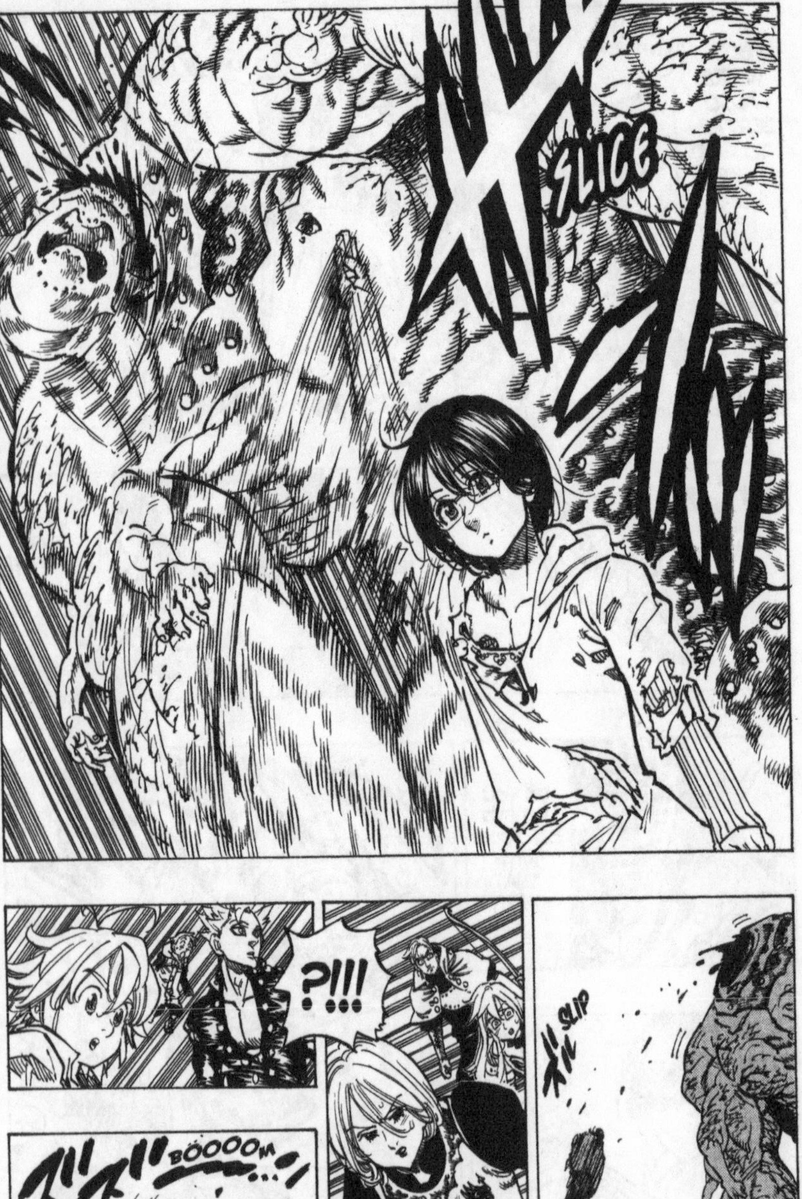
SLICE
ズル
SLIP
?!!!
ズ!!ズ!!
BOOOOM..!

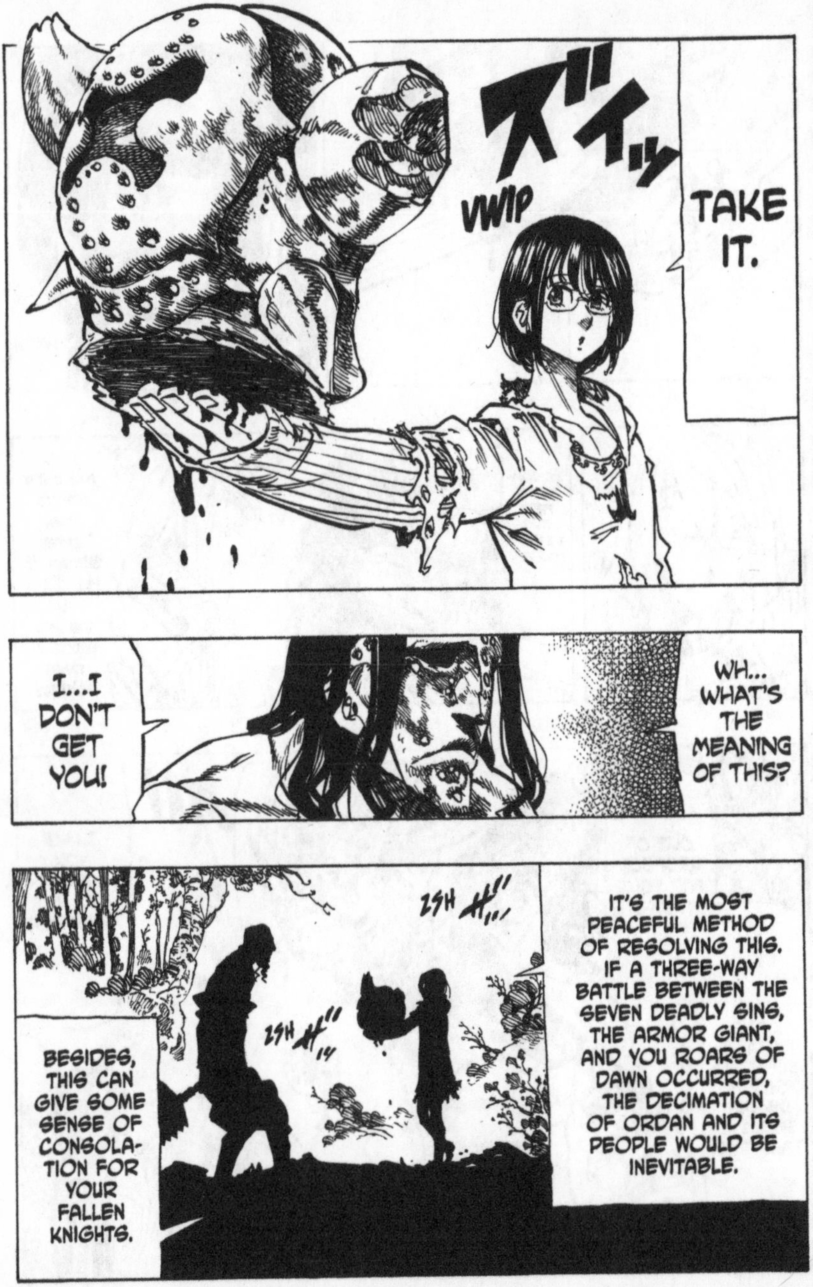
ズイッ
VWIP
TAKE IT.
WH... WHAT'S THE MEANING OF THIS?
I...I DON'T GET YOU!
ZSH
IT'S THE MOST PEACEFUL METHOD OF RESOLVING THIS. IF A THREE-WAY BATTLE BETWEEN THE SEVEN DEADLY SINS, THE ARMOR GIANT, AND YOU ROARS OF DAWN OCCURRED, THE DECIMATION OF ORDAN AND ITS PEOPLE WOULD BE INEVITABLE.
ZSH
BESIDES, THIS CAN GIVE SOME SENSE OF CONSOLA-TION FOR YOUR FALLEN KNIGHTS.

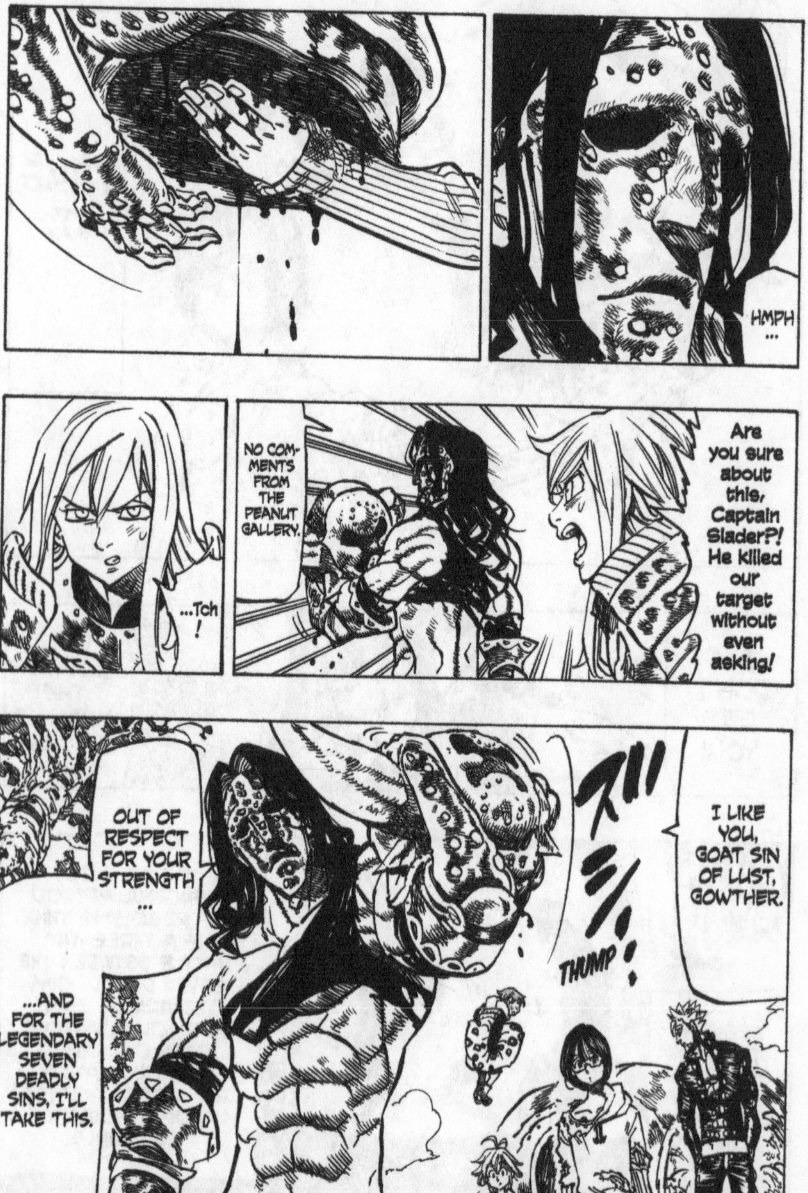
HMPH...
Are you sure about this, Captain Slader?! He killed our target without even asking!
NO COMMENTS FROM THE PEANUT GALLERY.
...Tch!
I LIKE YOU, GOAT SIN OF LUST, GOWTHER.
THUMP!!
OUT OF RESPECT FOR YOUR STRENGTH...
...AND FOR THE LEGENDARY SEVEN DEADLY SINS, I'LL TAKE THIS.

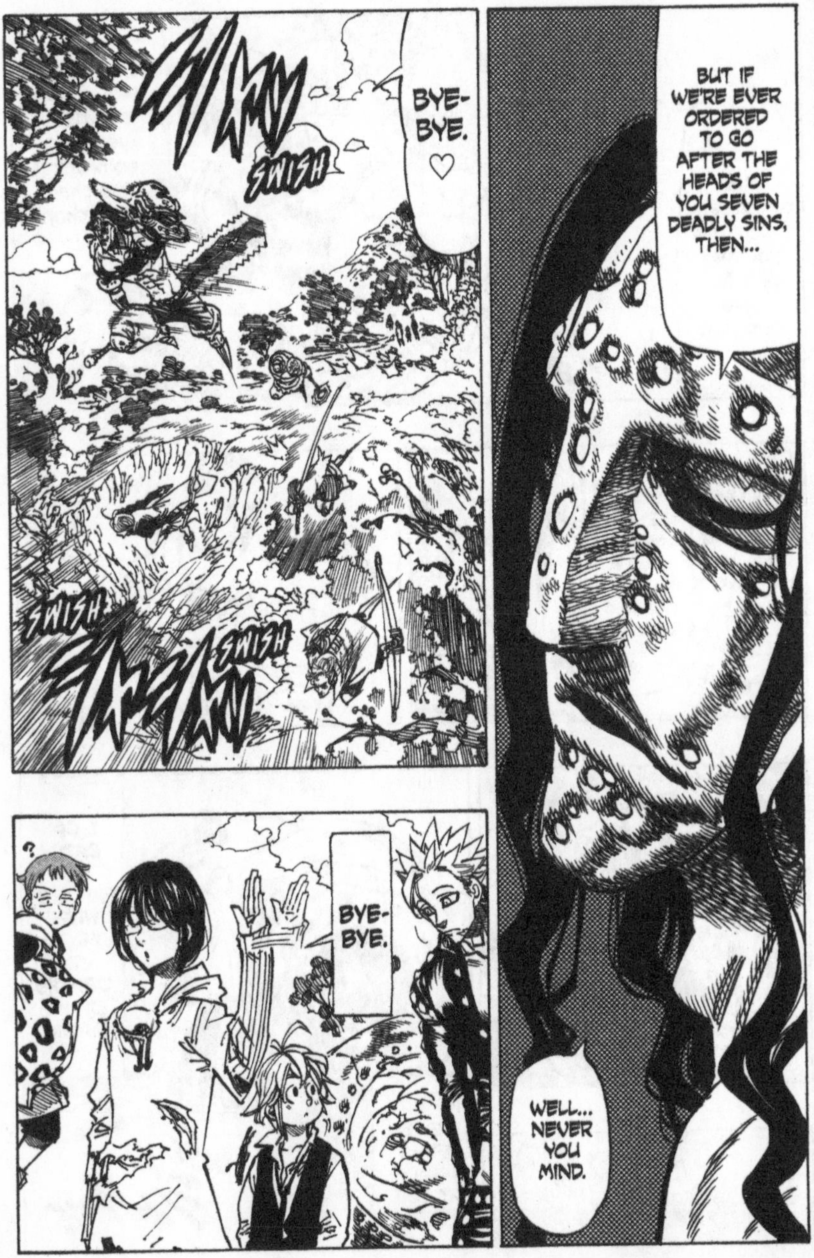
BUT IF WE'RE EVER ORDERED TO GO AFTER THE HEADS OF YOU SEVEN DEADLY SINS, THEN...
WELL... NEVER YOU MIND.
BYE-BYE. ♡
SWISH
SWISH
SWISH
BYE-BYE.

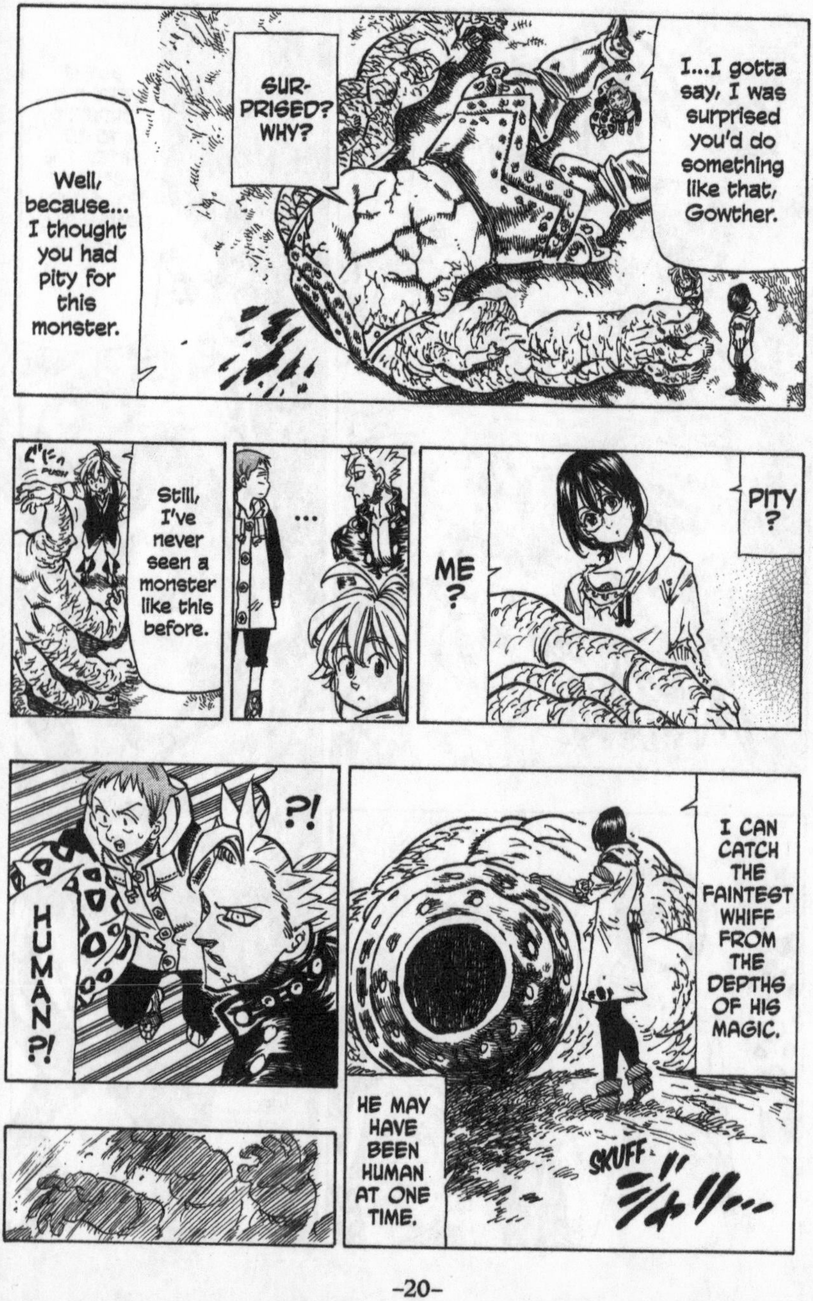
I...I gotta say, I was surprised you'd do something like that, Gowther.
SUR-PRISED? WHY?
Well, because... I thought you had pity for this monster.
PITY?
ME?
...
PUSH
Still, I've never seen a monster like this before.
I CAN CATCH THE FAINTEST WHIFF FROM THE DEPTHS OF HIS MAGIC.
HE MAY HAVE BEEN HUMAN AT ONE TIME.
SKUFF
?!
HUMAN?!

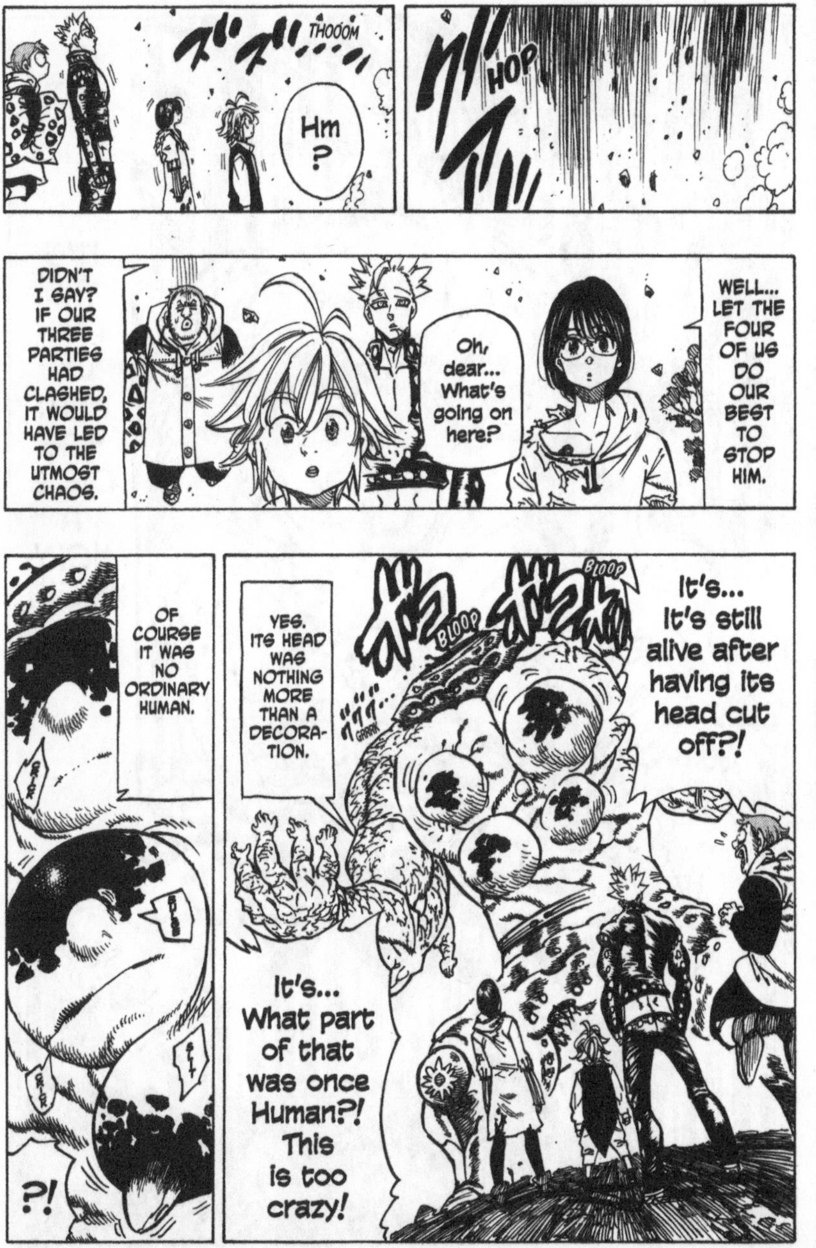
HOP
THOOOM
Hm?
WELL... LET THE FOUR OF US DO OUR BEST TO STOP HIM.
Oh, dear... What's going on here?
DIDN'T I SAY? IF OUR THREE PARTIES HAD CLASHED, IT WOULD HAVE LED TO THE UTMOST CHAOS.
BLOOP
BLOOP
It's... It's still alive after having its head cut off?!
YES. ITS HEAD WAS NOTHING MORE THAN A DECORATION.
GRRRK
It's... What part of that was once Human?! This is too crazy!
OF COURSE IT WAS NO ORDINARY HUMAN.
CRICK
CRICK
?!

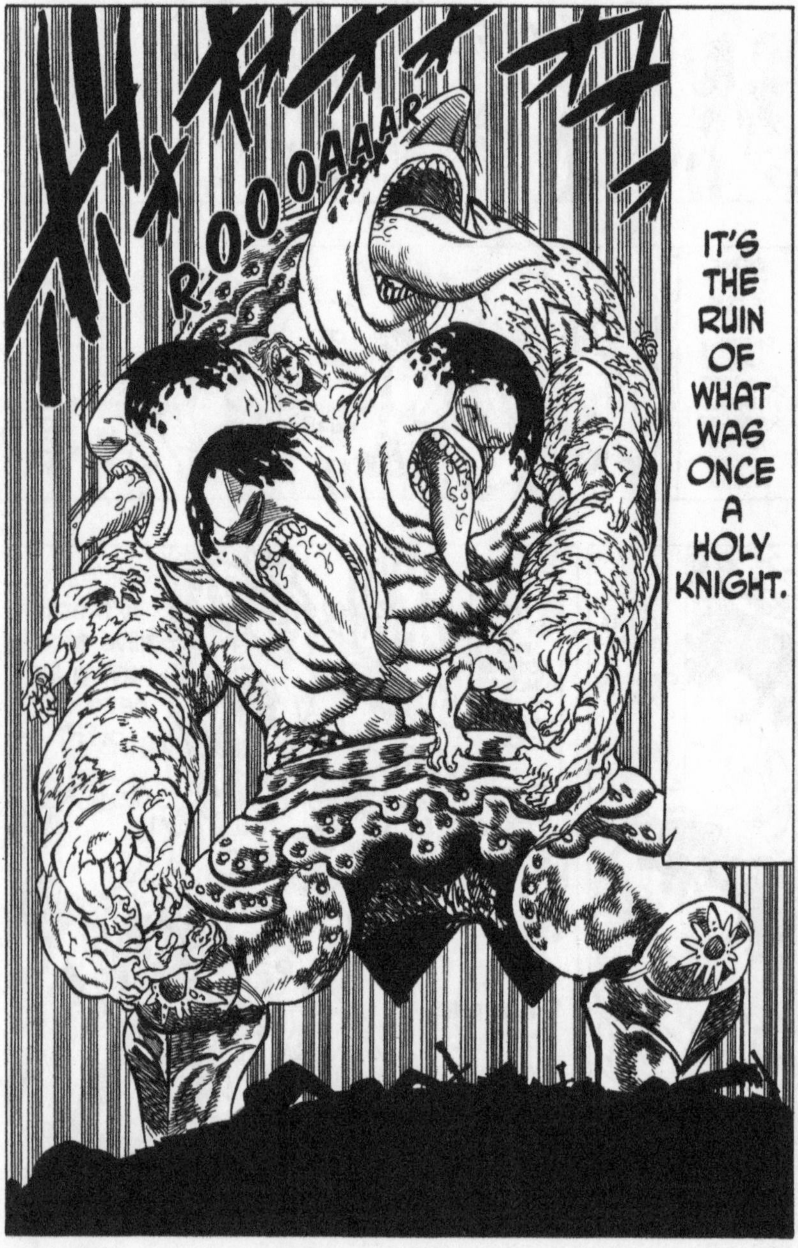
ROOOAAAR
IT'S THE RUIN OF WHAT WAS ONCE A HOLY KNIGHT.

Chapter 56 - Unholy Knight

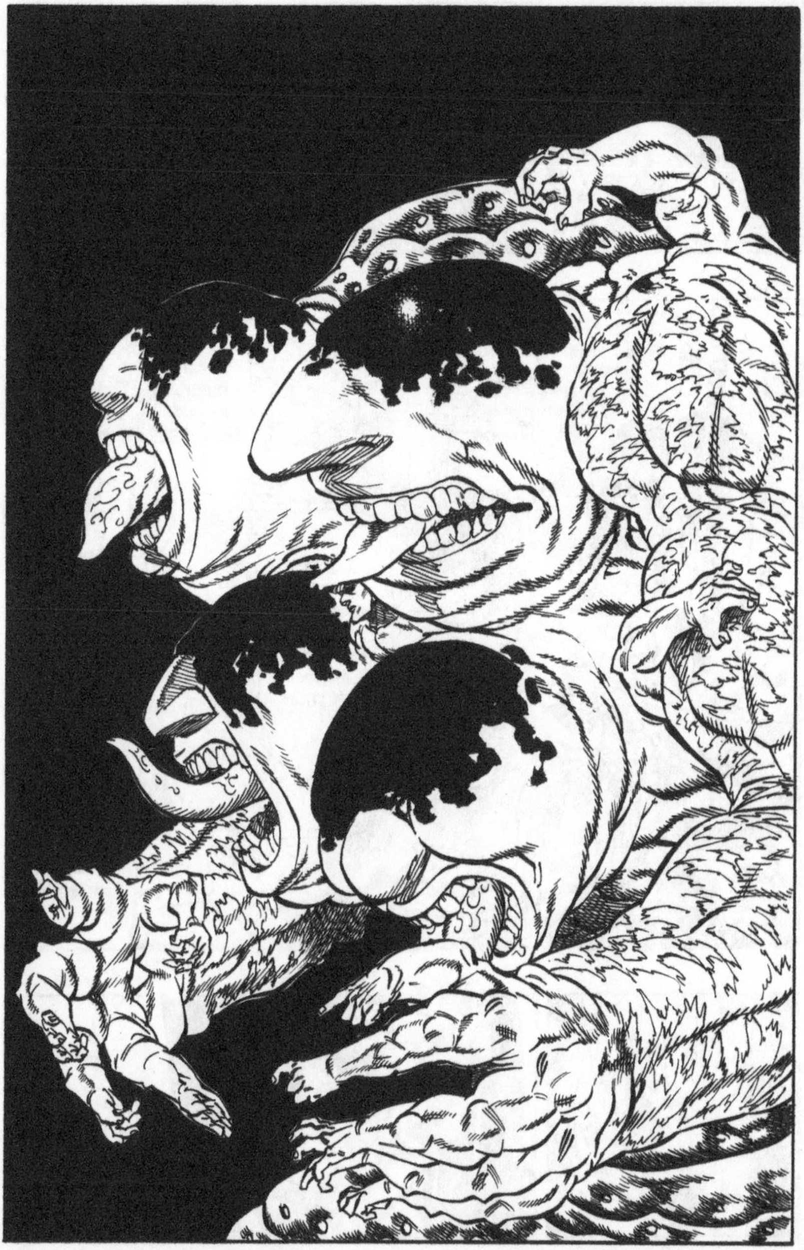

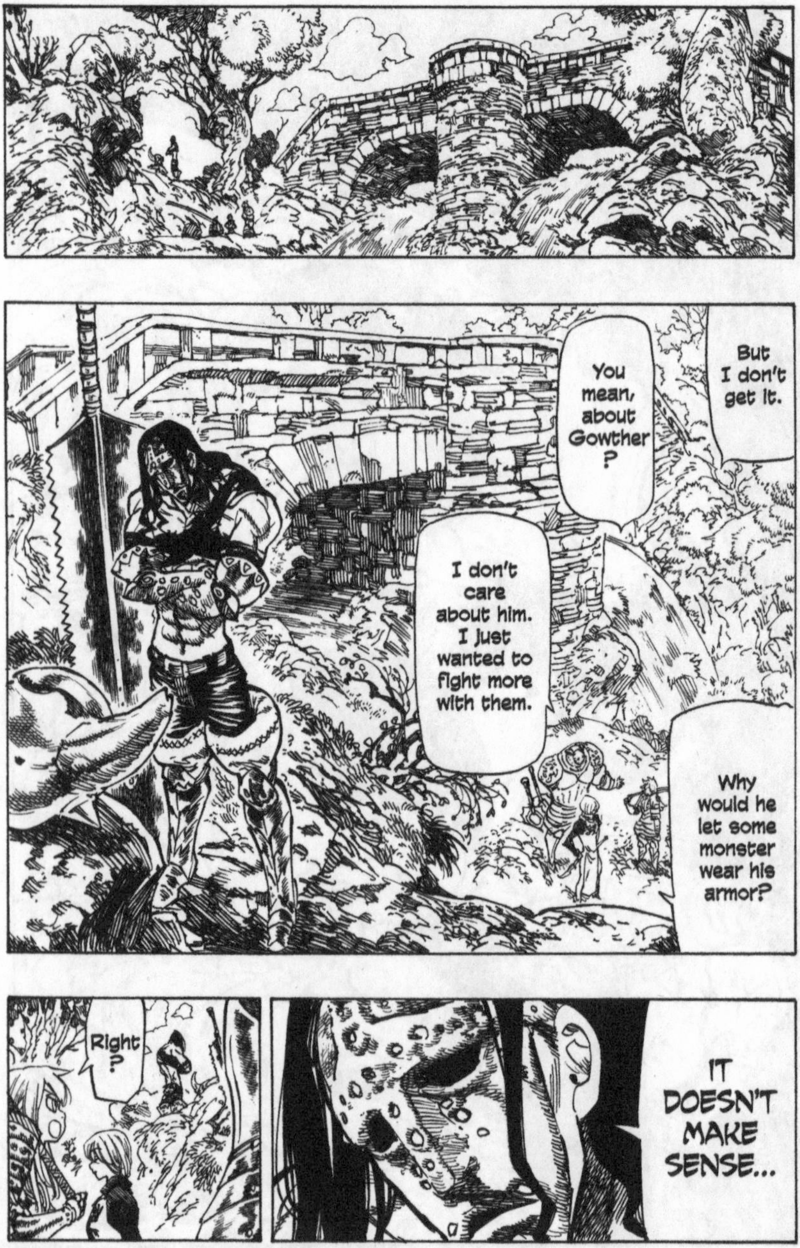

But I don't get it.
You mean, about Gowther?
I don't care about him. I just wanted to fight more with them.
Why would he let some monster wear his armor?
IT DOESN'T MAKE SENSE...
Right?

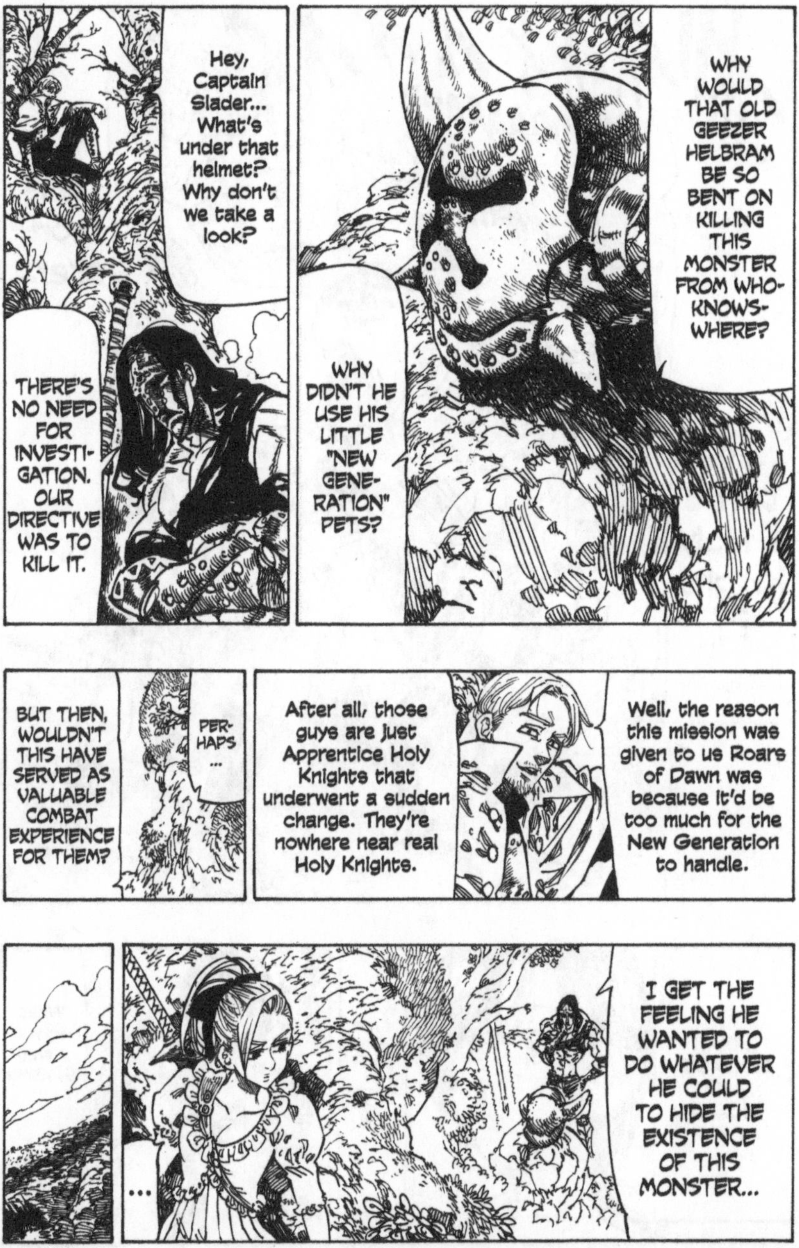
WHY WOULD THAT OLD GEEZER HELBRAM BE SO BENT ON KILLING THIS MONSTER FROM WHO-KNOWS-WHERE?
WHY DIDN'T HE USE HIS LITTLE "NEW GENERATION" PETS?
Hey, Captain Slader... What's under that helmet? Why don't we take a look?
THERE'S NO NEED FOR INVESTIGATION. OUR DIRECTIVE WAS TO KILL IT.
Well, the reason this mission was given to us Roars of Dawn was because it'd be too much for the New Generation to handle.
After all, those guys are just Apprentice Holy Knights that underwent a sudden change. They're nowhere near real Holy Knights.
PERHAPS...
BUT THEN, WOULDN'T THIS HAVE SERVED AS VALUABLE COMBAT EXPERIENCE FOR THEM?
I GET THE FEELING HE WANTED TO DO WHATEVER HE COULD TO HIDE THE EXISTENCE OF THIS MONSTER...
...

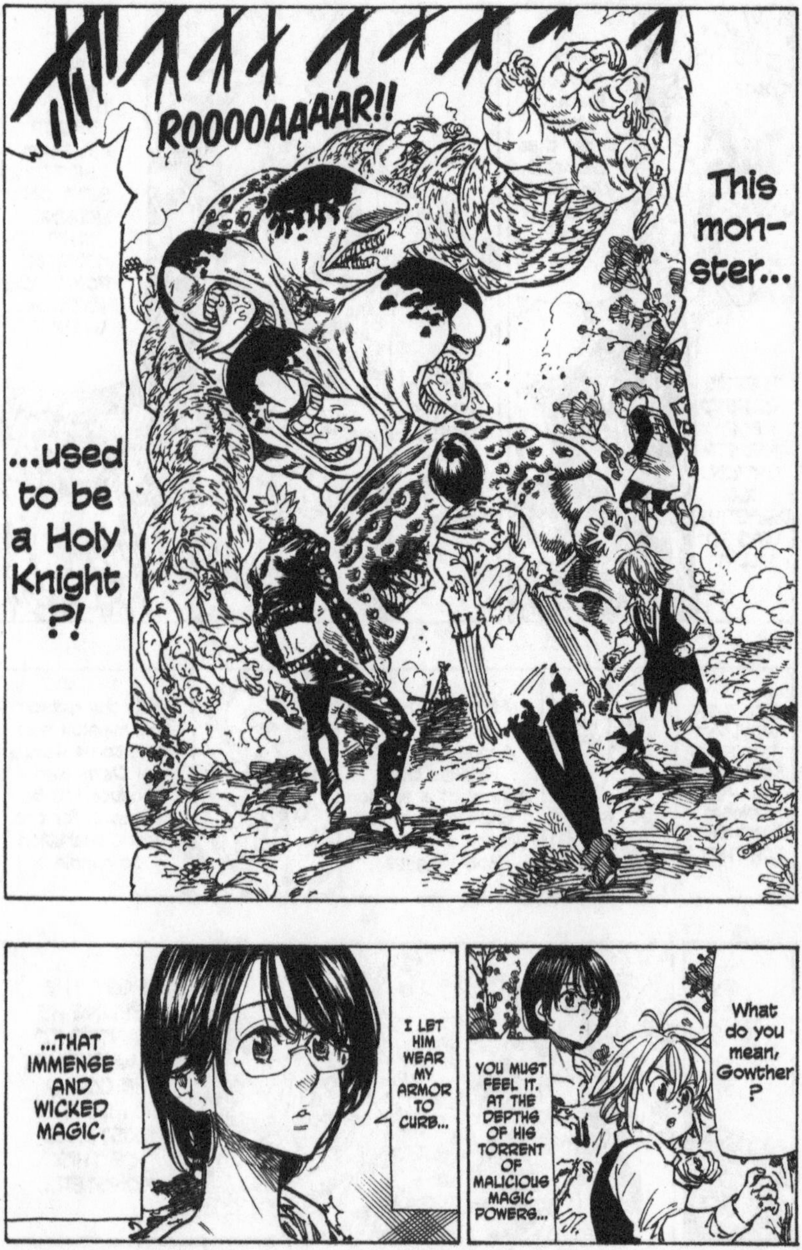
ROOOOAAAAR!!
This monster...
...used to be a Holy Knight?!
What do you mean, Gowther?
YOU MUST FEEL IT. AT THE DEPTHS OF HIS TORRENT OF MALICIOUS MAGIC POWERS...
I LET HIM WEAR MY ARMOR TO CURB...
...THAT IMMENSE AND WICKED MAGIC.

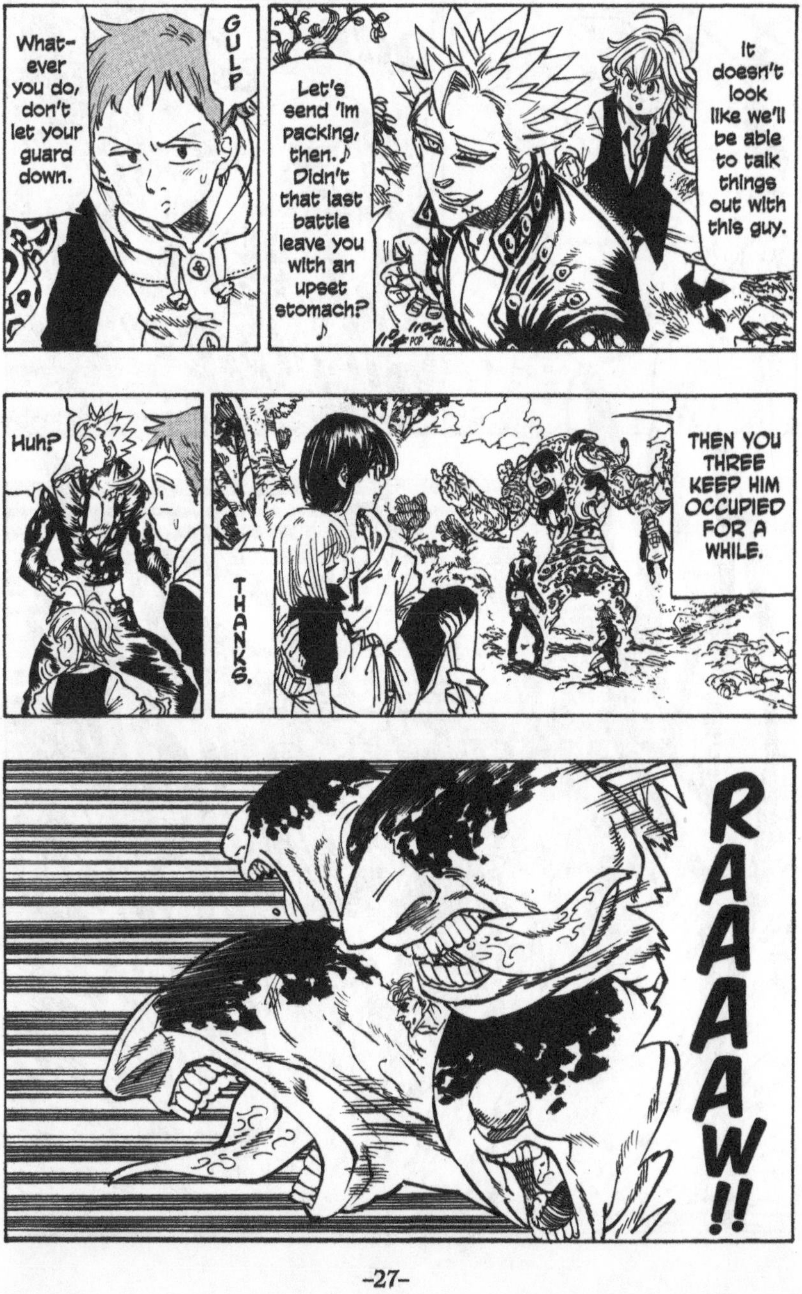
It doesn't look like we'll be able to talk things out with this guy.
Let's send 'im packing, then.♪ Didn't that last battle leave you with an upset stomach?♪
POP
CRACK
GULP
Whatever you do, don't let your guard down.
THEN YOU THREE KEEP HIM OCCUPIED FOR A WHILE.
THANKS.
Huh?
RAAAAAW!!

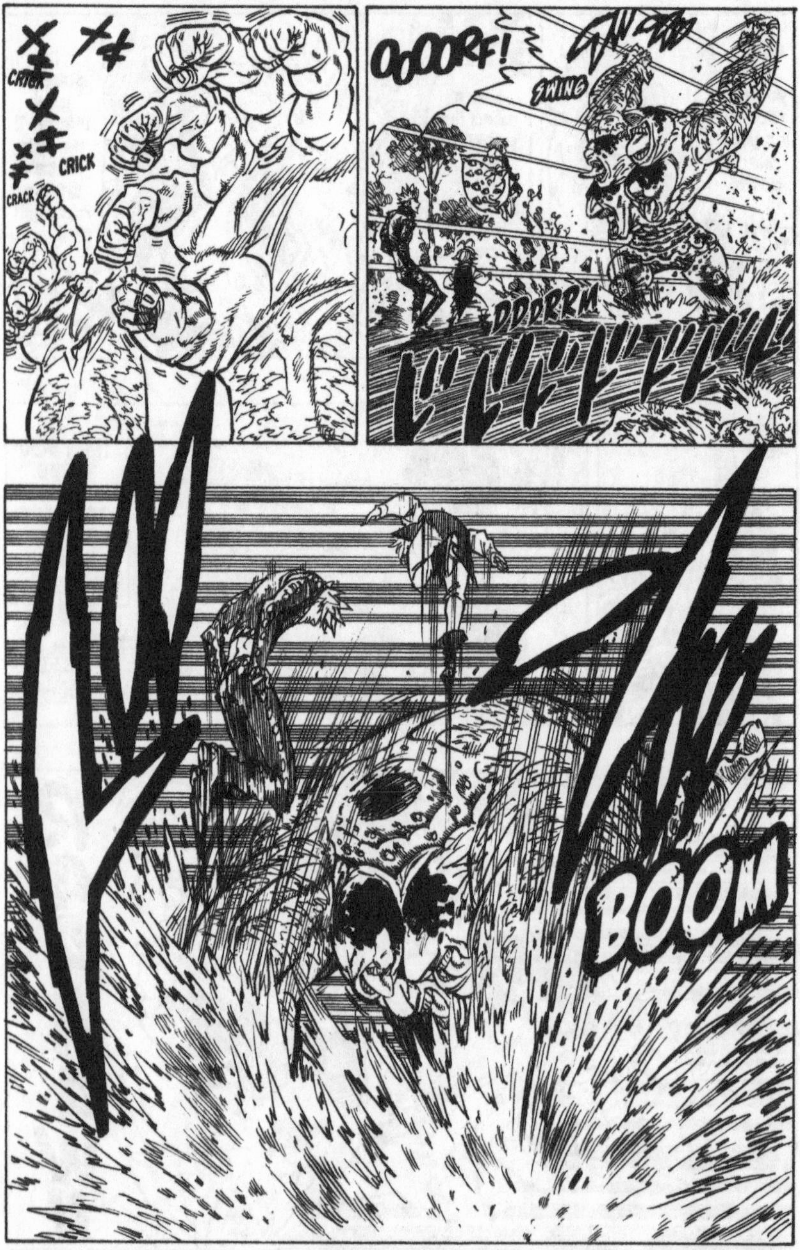
OOOORF!
SWING
DDDRRRM
CRICK
CRICK
CRACK
BOOM

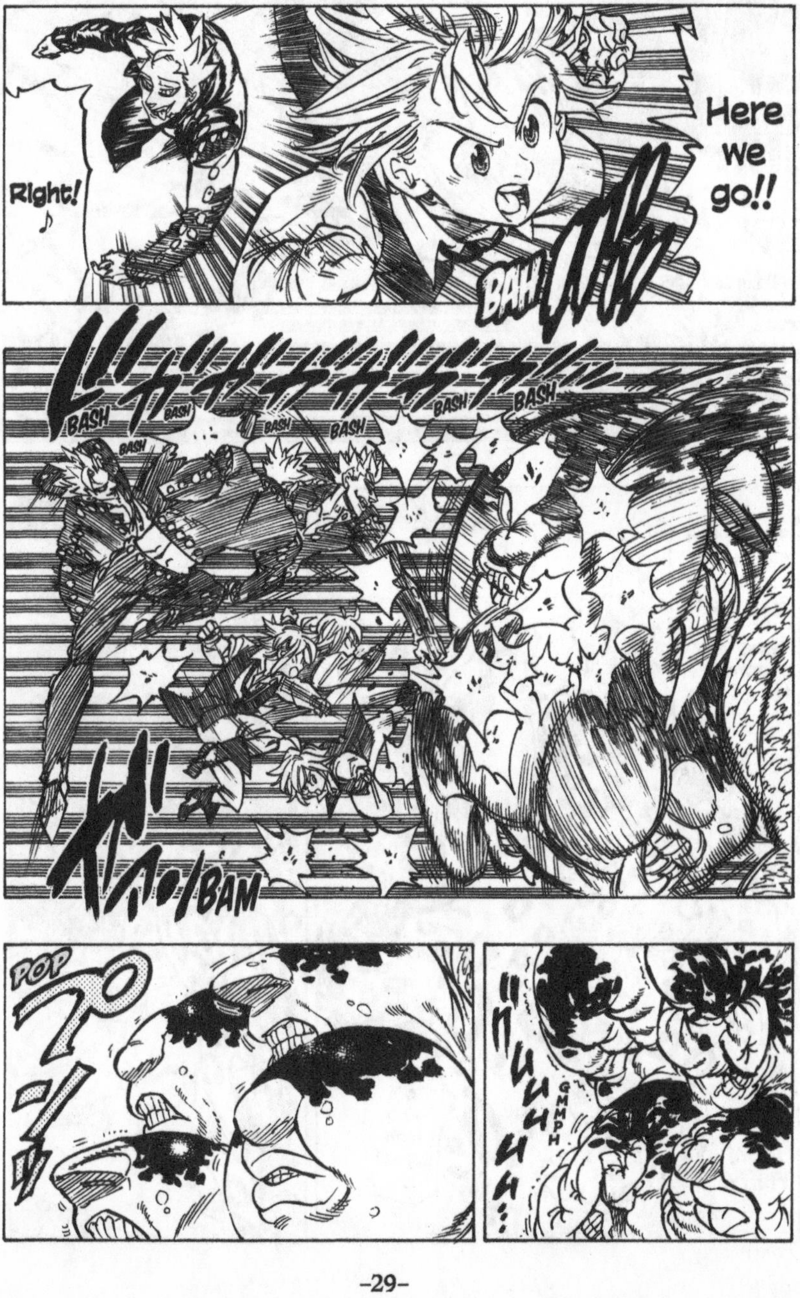
Here we go!!
BAH
Right! ♪
BASH
BASH
BASH
BASH
BASH
BASH
BASH
BAM
GMMPH
POP

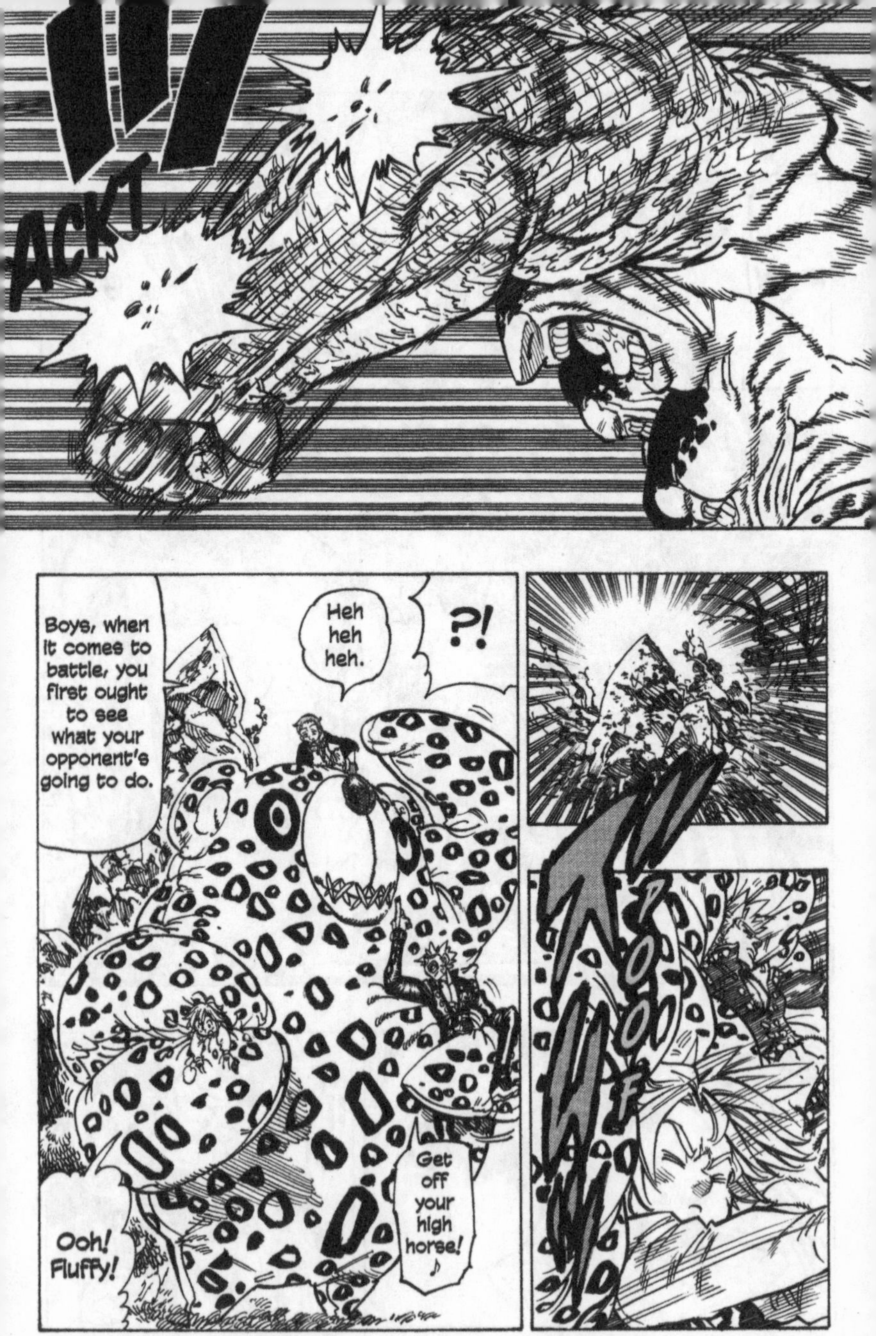
ACK!
WHOOOF
?!
Heh heh heh.
Boys, when it comes to battle, you first ought to see what your opponent's going to do.
Get off your high horse! ♪
Ooh! Fluffy!

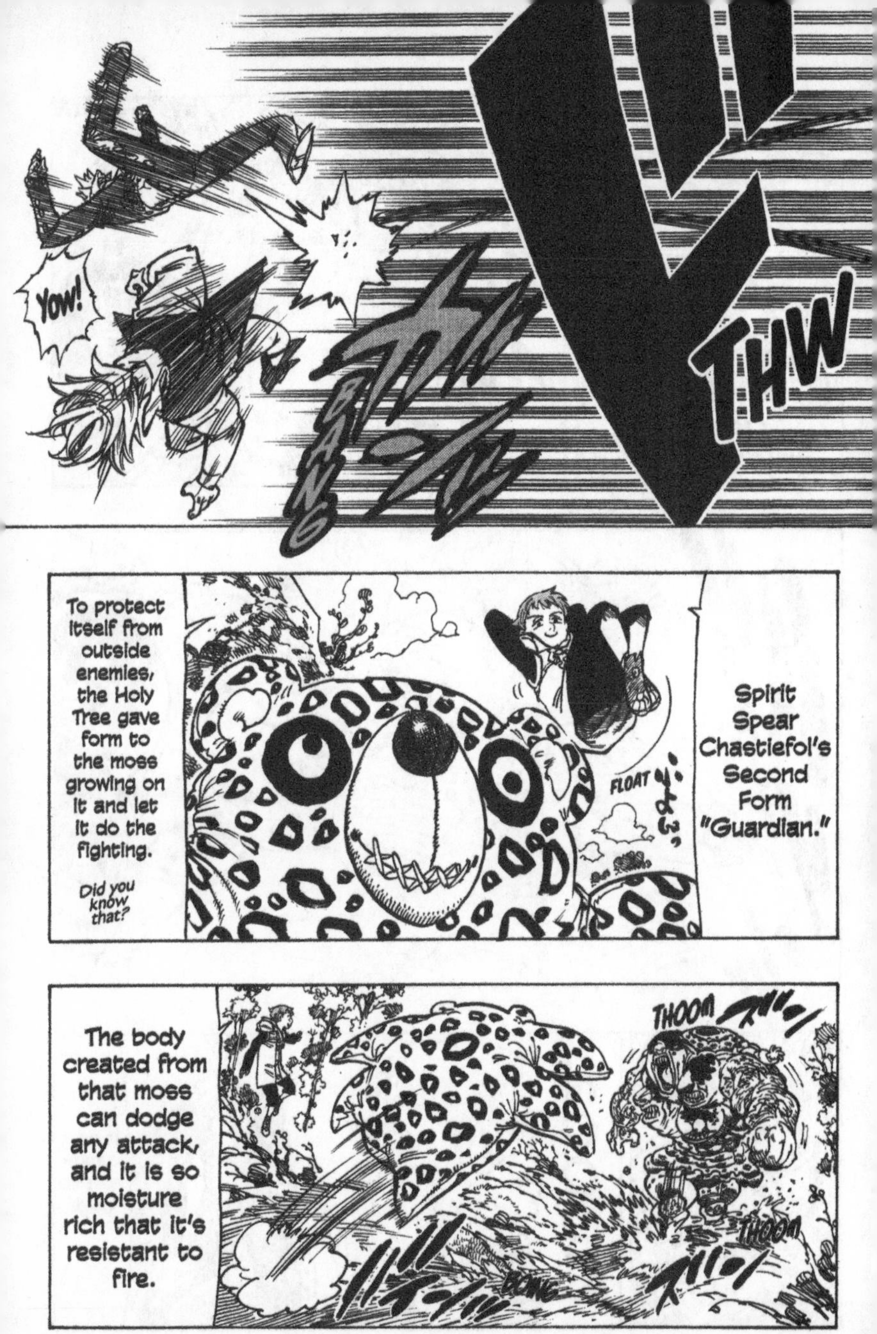
THW
BANG
YOW!
Spirit Spear Chastiefol's Second Form "Guardian."
FLOAT
To protect itself from outside enemies, the Holy Tree gave form to the moss growing on it and let it do the fighting.
Did you know that?
THOOM
THOOM
BOING
The body created from that moss can dodge any attack, and it is so moisture rich that it's resistant to fire.

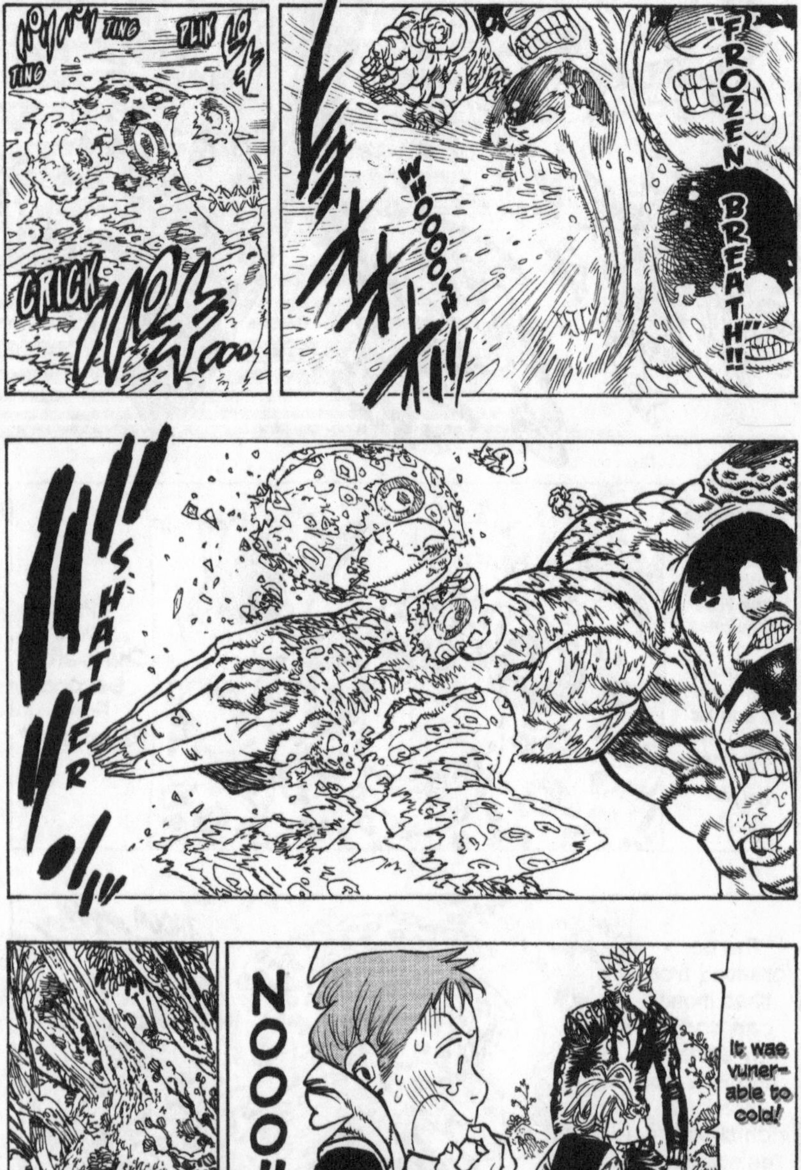
"FROZEN BREATH"!!
WHOOOOOSH
PLINK
TING
TING
CRICK
SHATTER
It was vuner-able to cold!
NOOOO!!

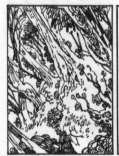

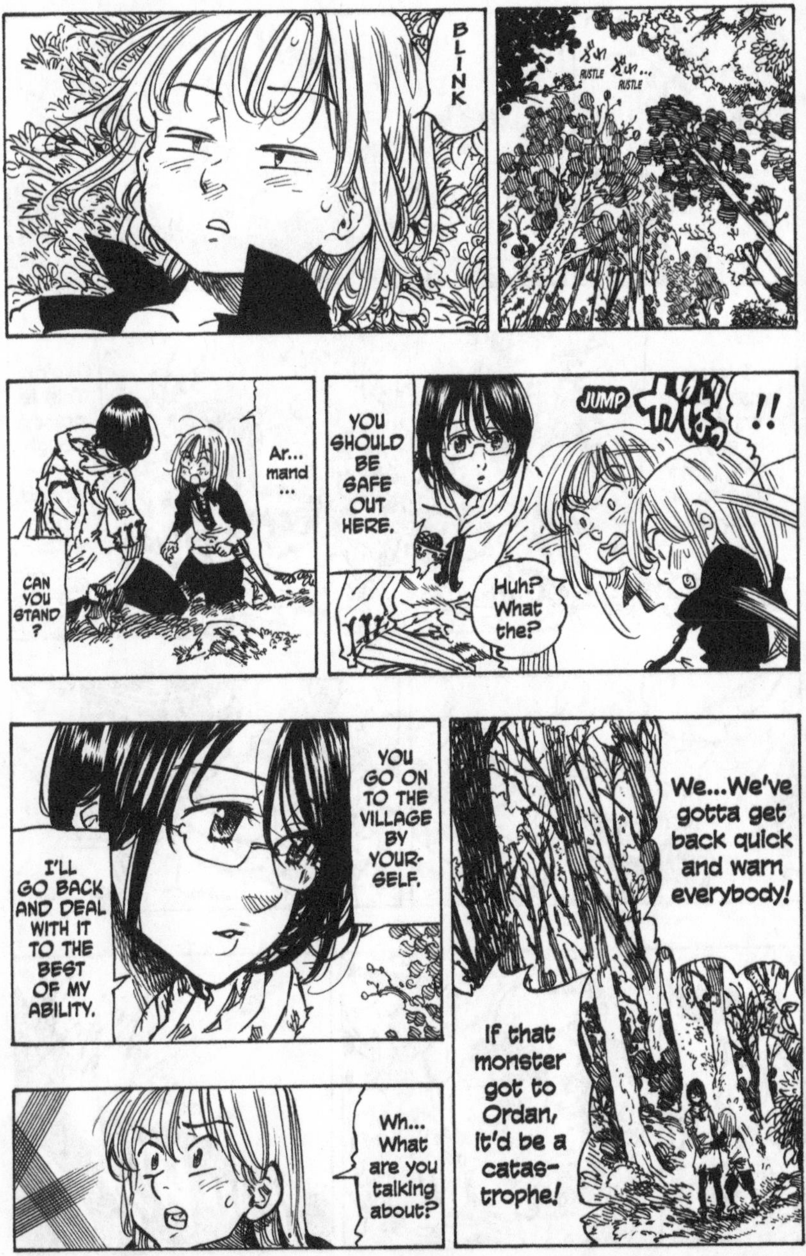

RUSTLE
RUSTLE
BLINK
JUMP
!!
YOU SHOULD BE SAFE OUT HERE.
Huh? What the?
Ar... mand...
CAN YOU STAND?
We...We've gotta get back quick and warn everybody!
If that monster got to Ordan, it'd be a catas-trophe!
YOU GO ON TO THE VILLAGE BY YOUR-SELF.
I'LL GO BACK AND DEAL WITH IT TO THE BEST OF MY ABILITY.
Wh... What are you talking about?

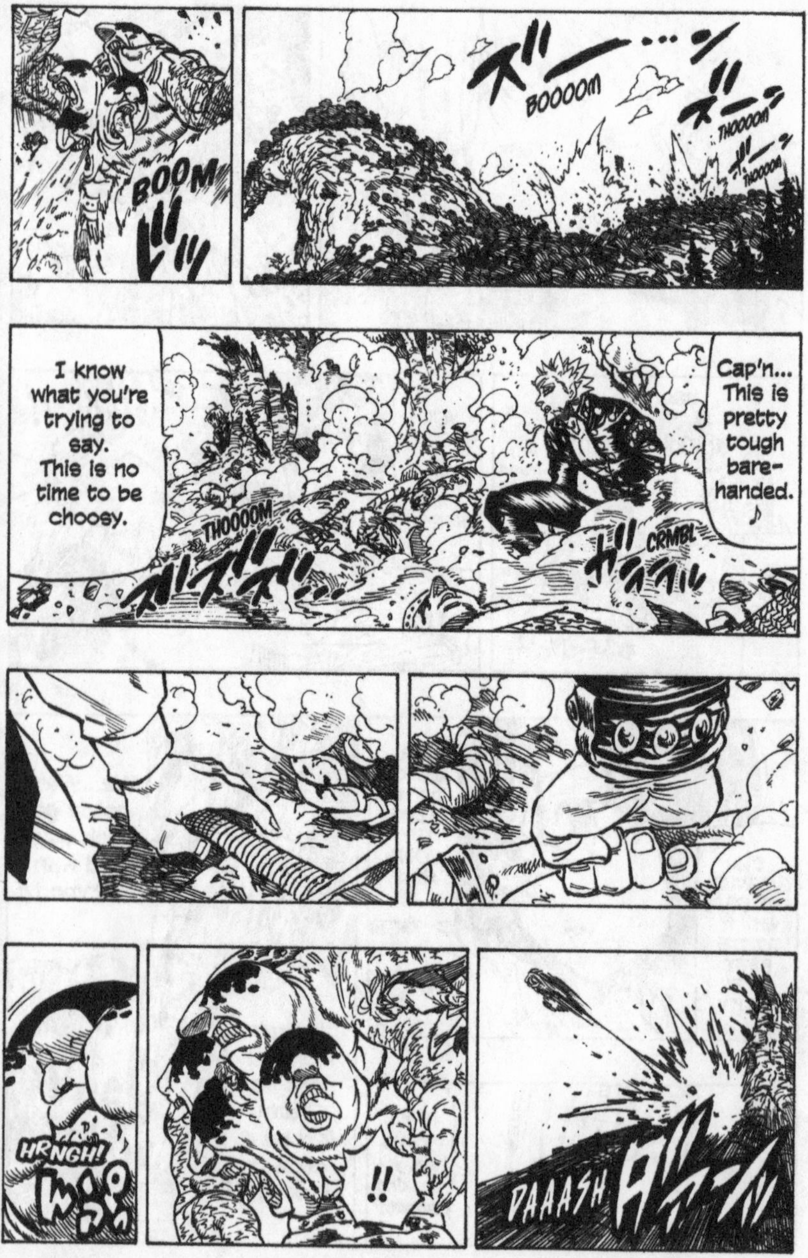
BOOOOM
THOOOOM
THOOOOM
BOOM
Cap'n... This is pretty tough bare-handed. ♪
CRMBL
THOOOOM
I know what you're trying to say. This is no time to be choosy.
DAAASH
!!
HRNGH!

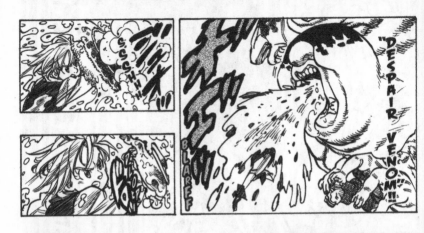

"DESPAIR VENOM!!"

GSSCHHH

BLARFF

WHIP

Will ordinary weapons work against a monster like this?!

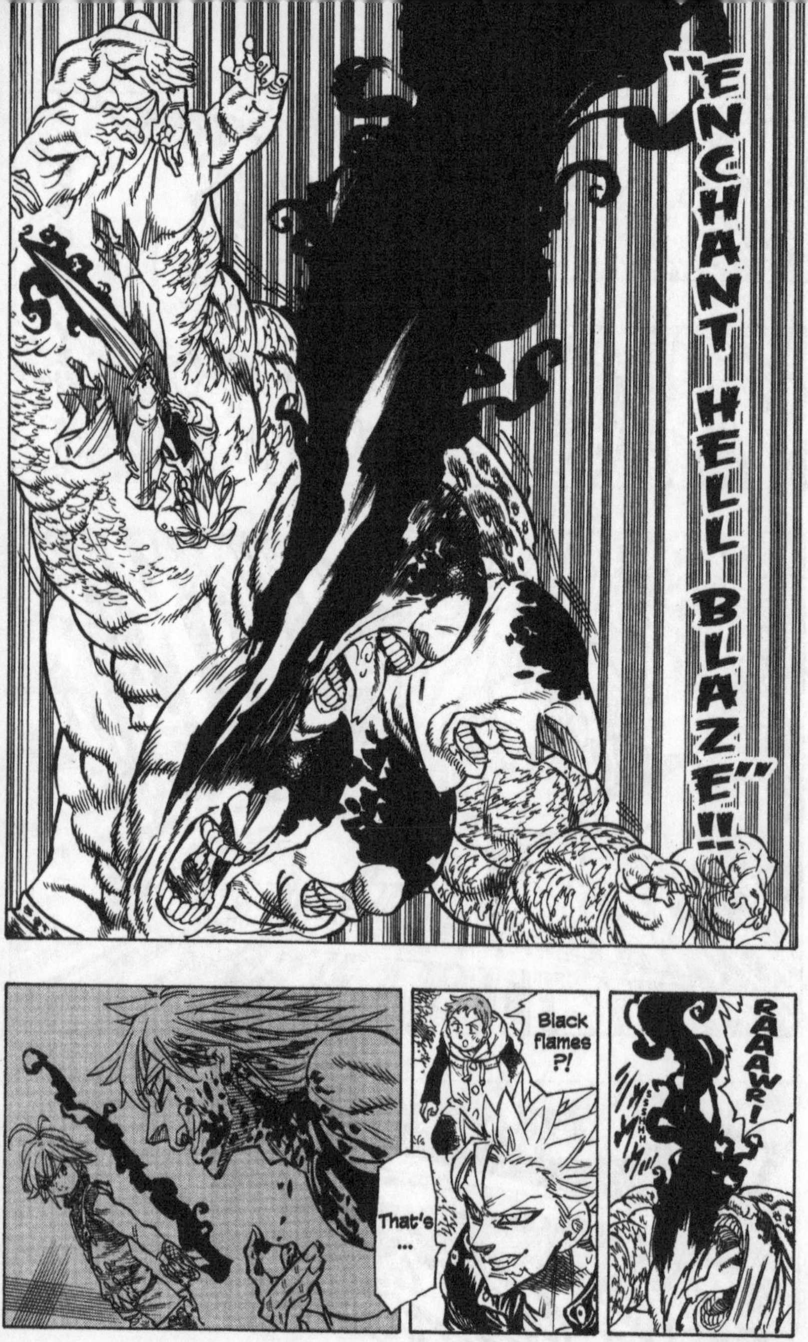
"ENCHANT HELL BLAZE"!!
RAAAWR!
SSSHHH
Black flames ?!
That's ...

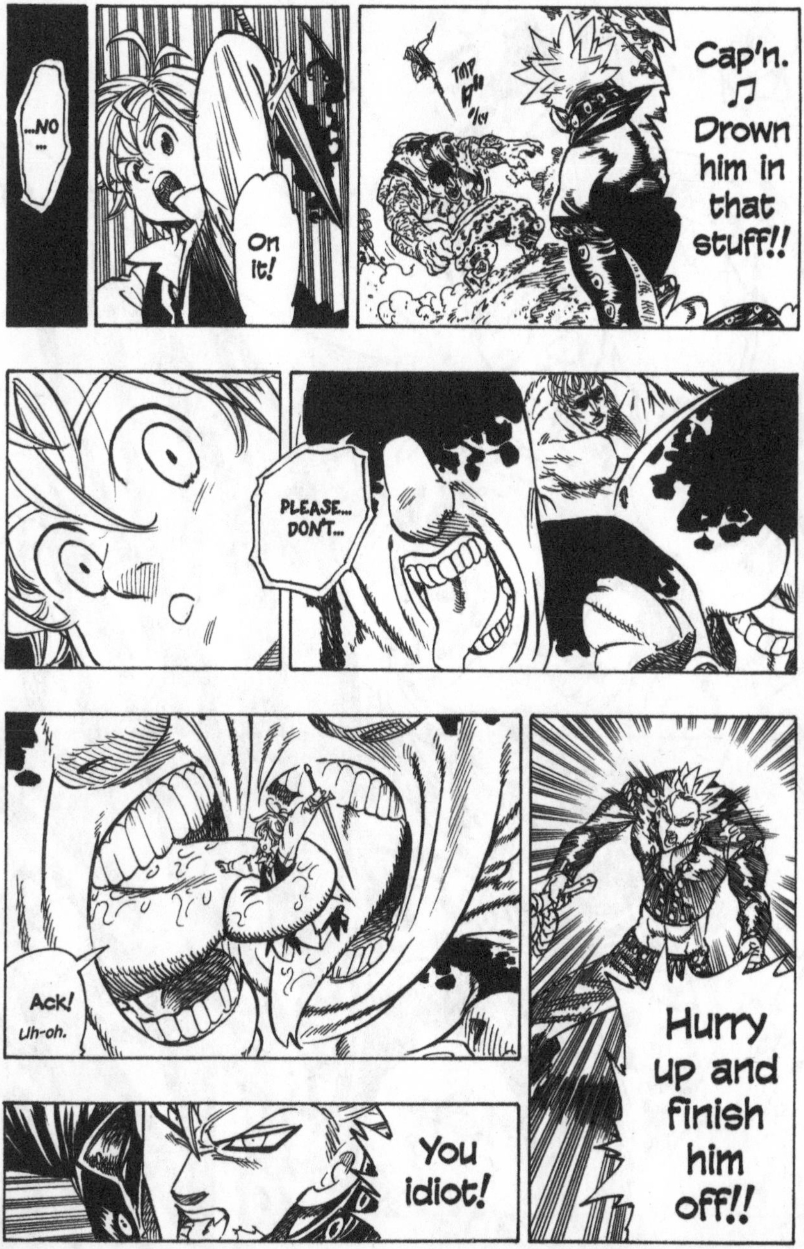
Cap'n. ♫ Drown him in that stuff!!
On it!
...NO ...
PLEASE... DON'T...
Hurry up and finish him off!!
Ack!
Uh-oh.
You idiot!

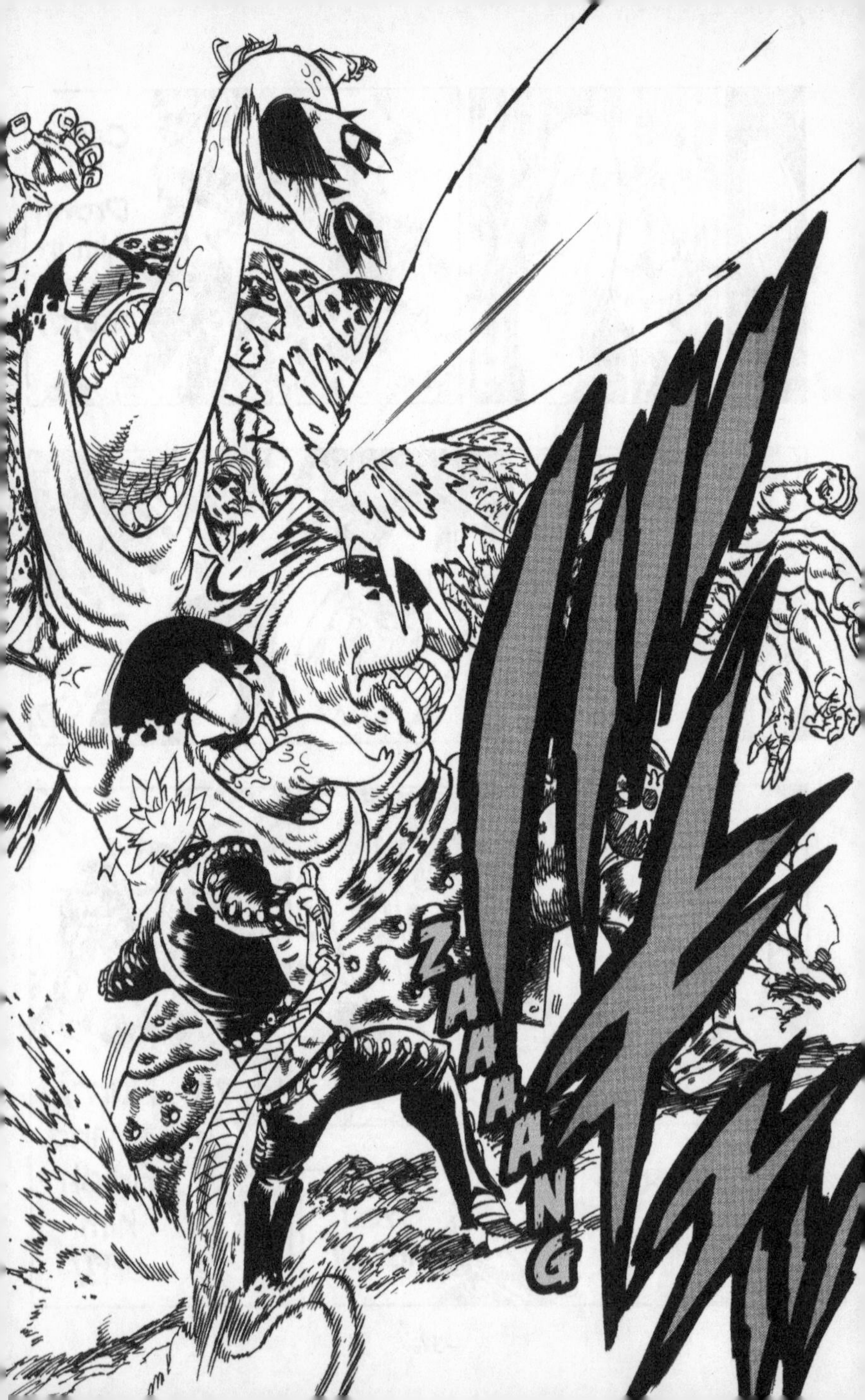
ZAAAAANG

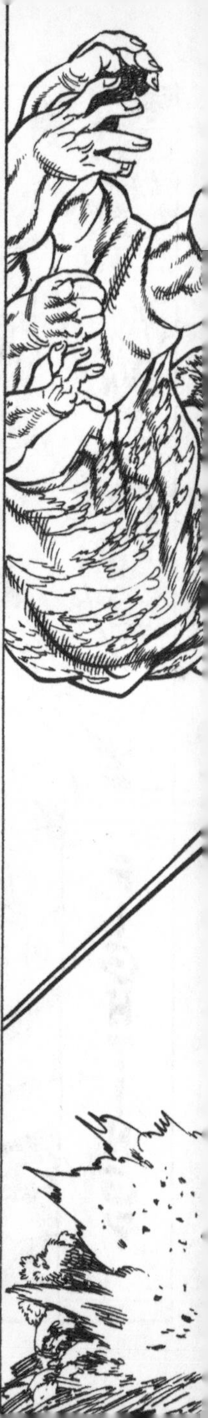

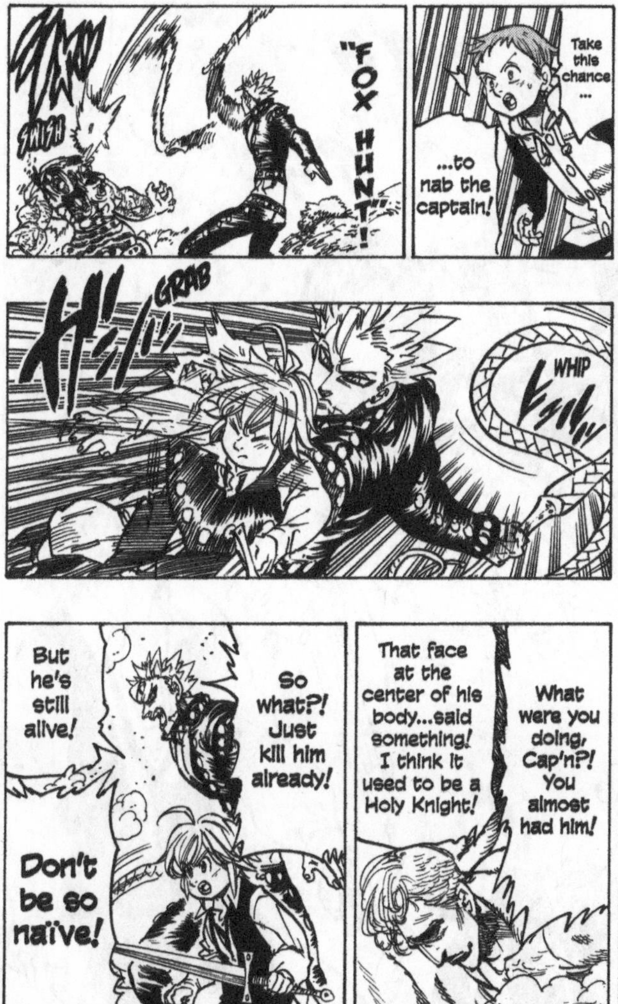
Take this chance...
...to nab the captain!
"FOX HUNT"!
SWISH
GRAB
WHIP
What were you doing, Cap'n?! You almost had him!
That face at the center of his body...said something! I think it used to be a Holy Knight!
So what?! Just kill him already!
But he's still alive!
Don't be so naïve!
...

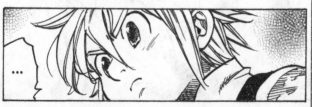

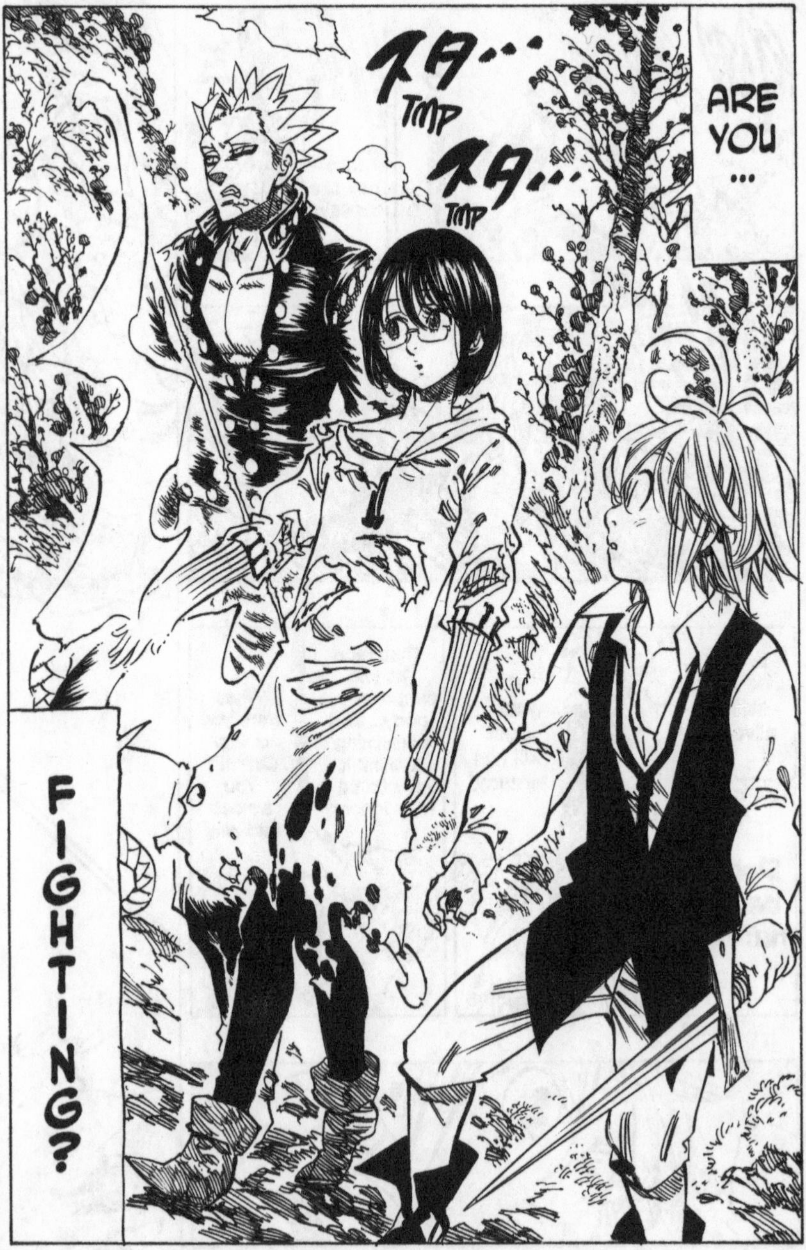
ARE YOU ...
スタ…
TMP
スタ…
TMP
FIGHTING?

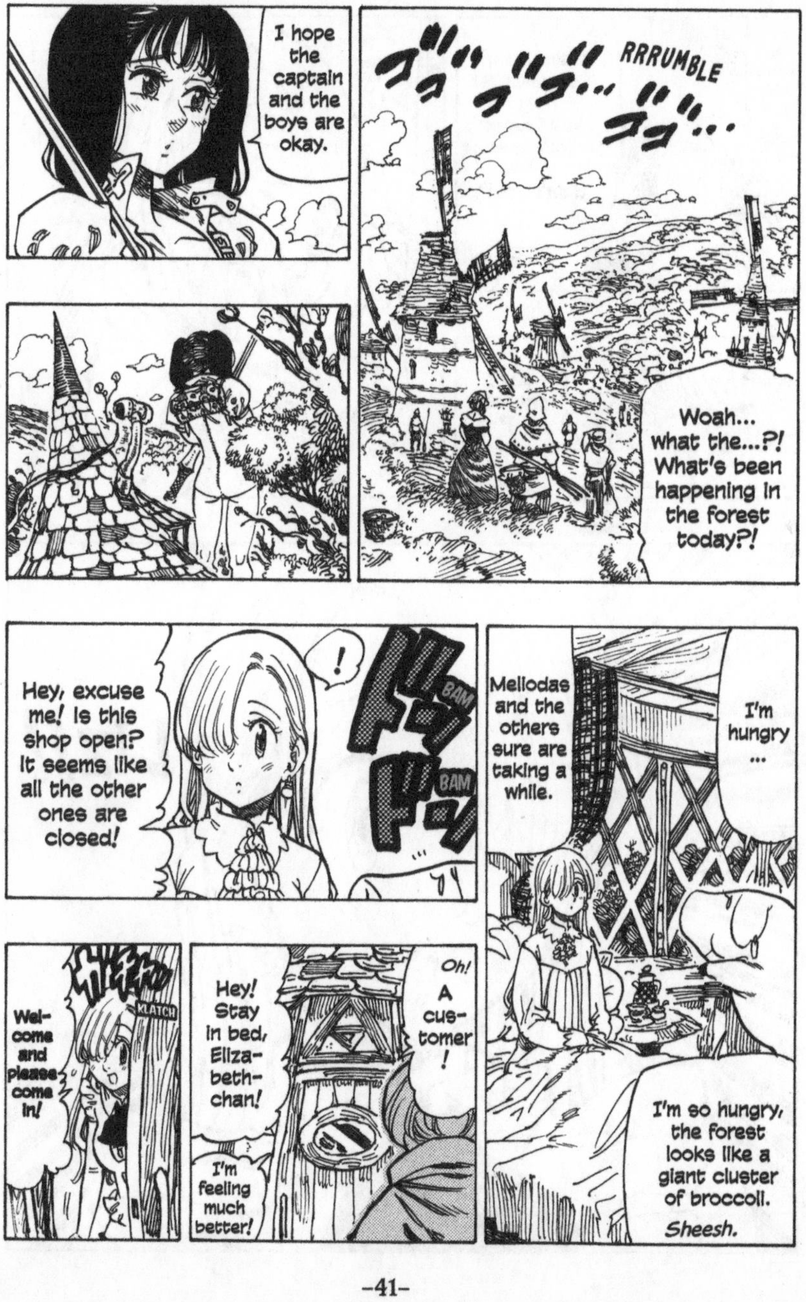
RRRUMBLE
Woah... what the...?! What's been happening in the forest today?!
I hope the captain and the boys are okay.
I'm hungry...
Meliodas and the others sure are taking a while.
I'm so hungry, the forest looks like a giant cluster of broccoli.
Sheesh.
BAM
BAM
!
Hey, excuse me! Is this shop open? It seems like all the other ones are closed!
...
Oh! A customer!
Hey! Stay in bed, Eliza-beth-chan!
I'm feeling much better!
KLATCH
Wel-come and please come in!

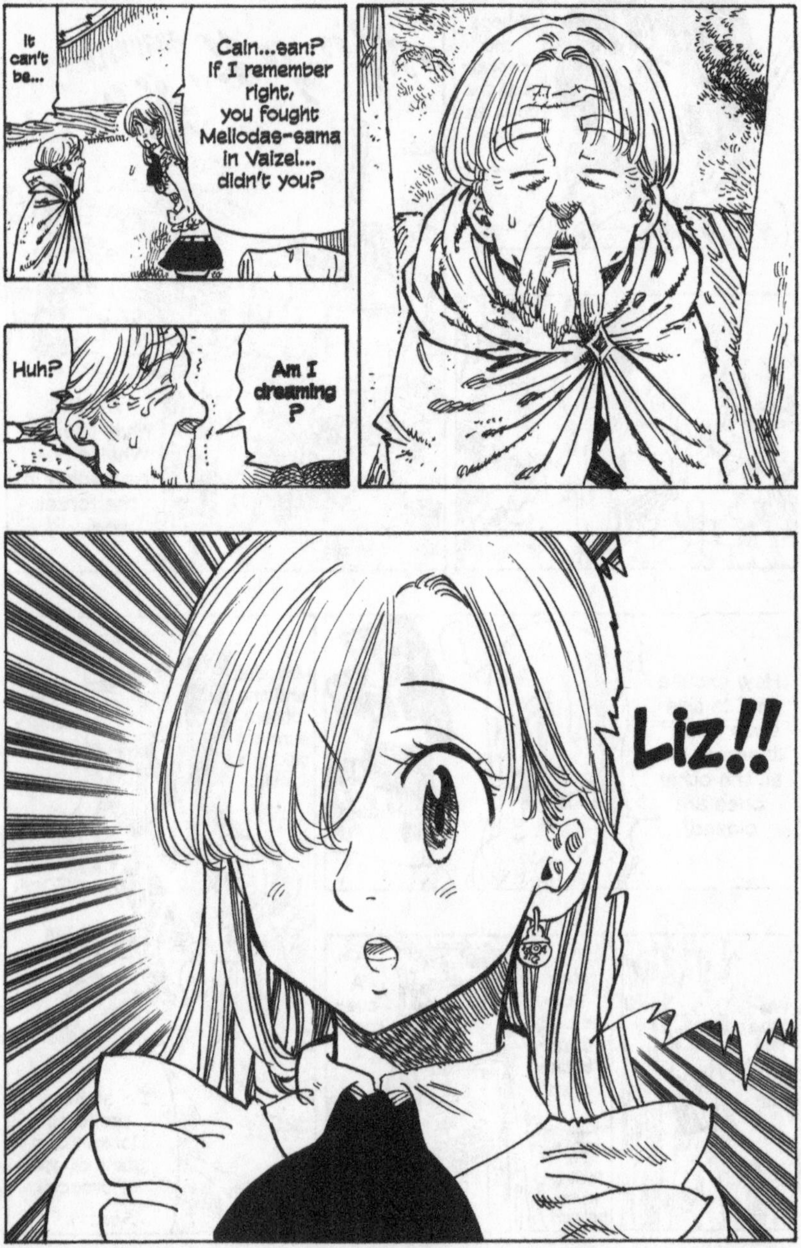
Cain...san? If I remember right, you fought Meliodas-sama in Vaizel... didn't you?
It can't be...
Am I dreaming?
Huh?
Liz!!

THE SEVEN DEADLY SINS

Chapter 57 - The Scene of a Far-off Day

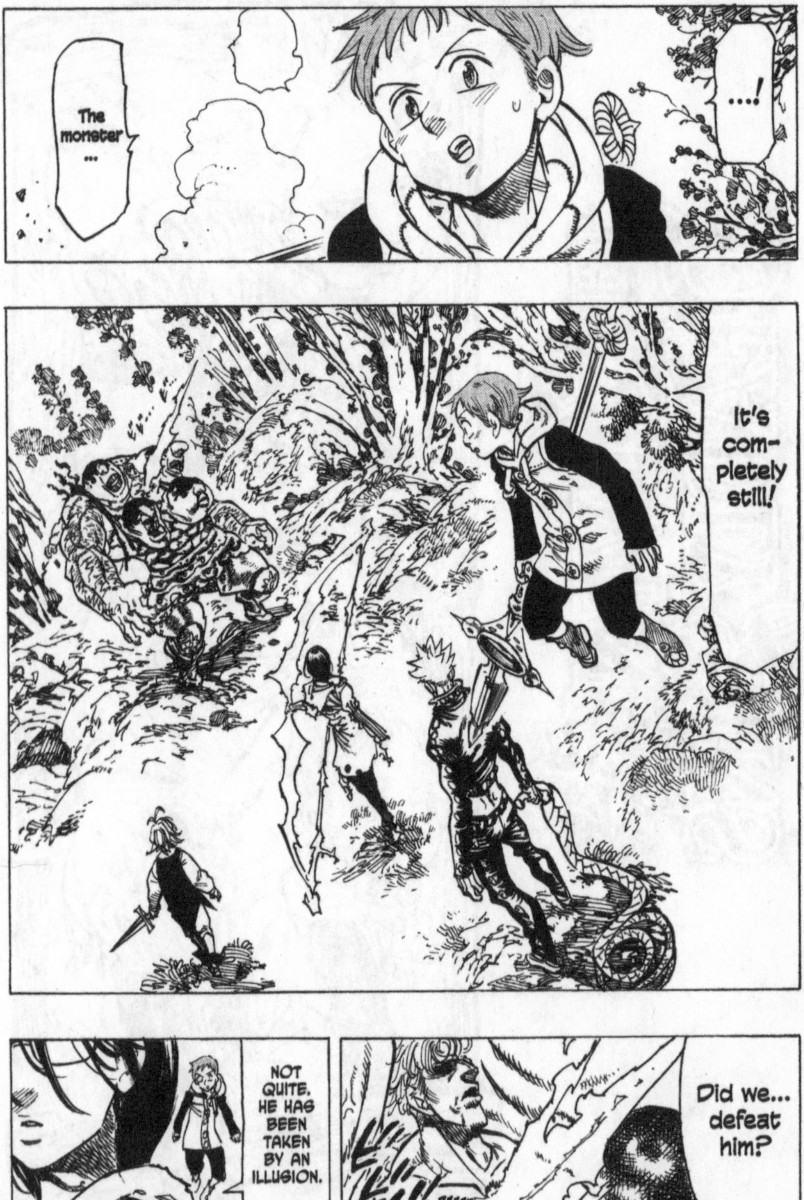
...!
The monster ...
It's com-pletely still!
Did we... defeat him?
NOT QUITE. HE HAS BEEN TAKEN BY AN ILLUSION.

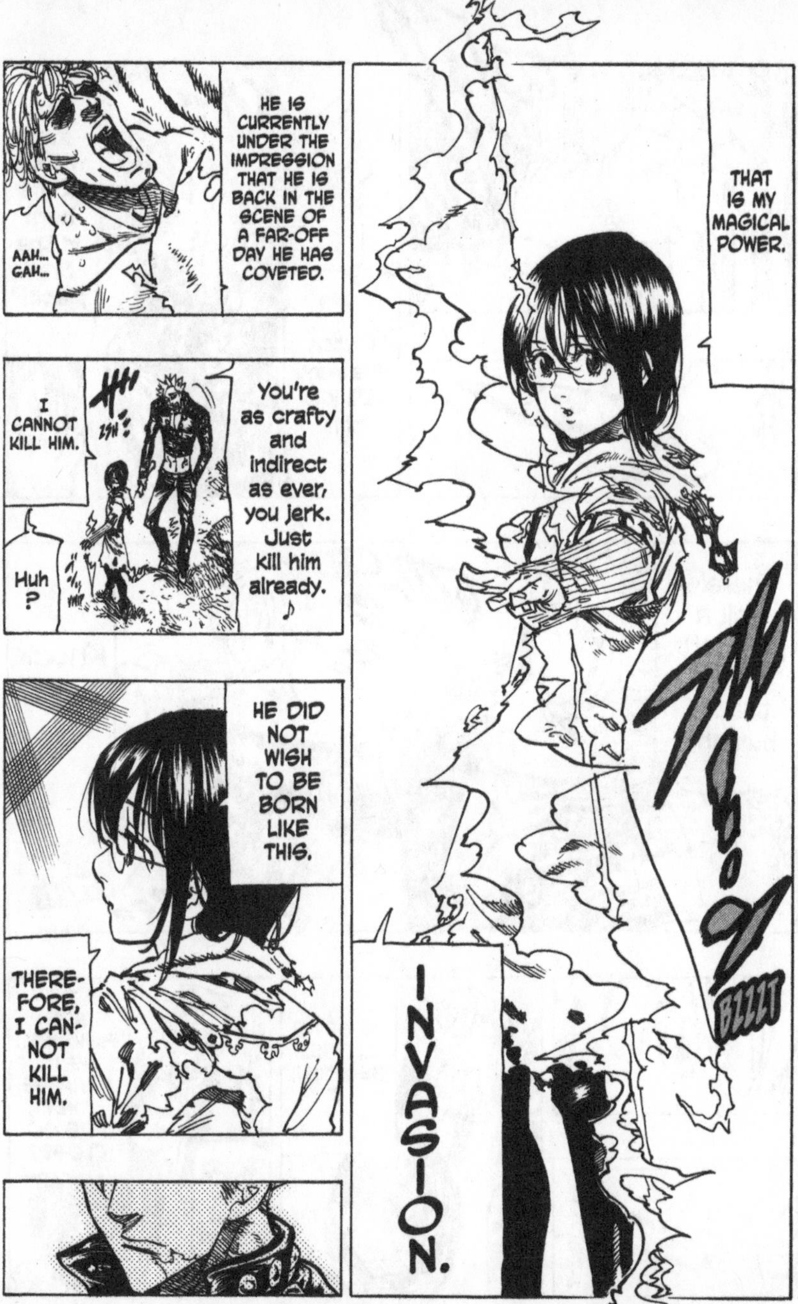
THAT IS MY MAGICAL POWER.
BZZZT
INVASION.
HE IS CURRENTLY UNDER THE IMPRESSION THAT HE IS BACK IN THE SCENE OF A FAR-OFF DAY HE HAS COVETED.
AAH... GAH...
You're as crafty and indirect as ever, you jerk. Just kill him already. ♪
I CANNOT KILL HIM.
Huh?
HE DID NOT WISH TO BE BORN LIKE THIS.
THEREFORE, I CANNOT KILL HIM.

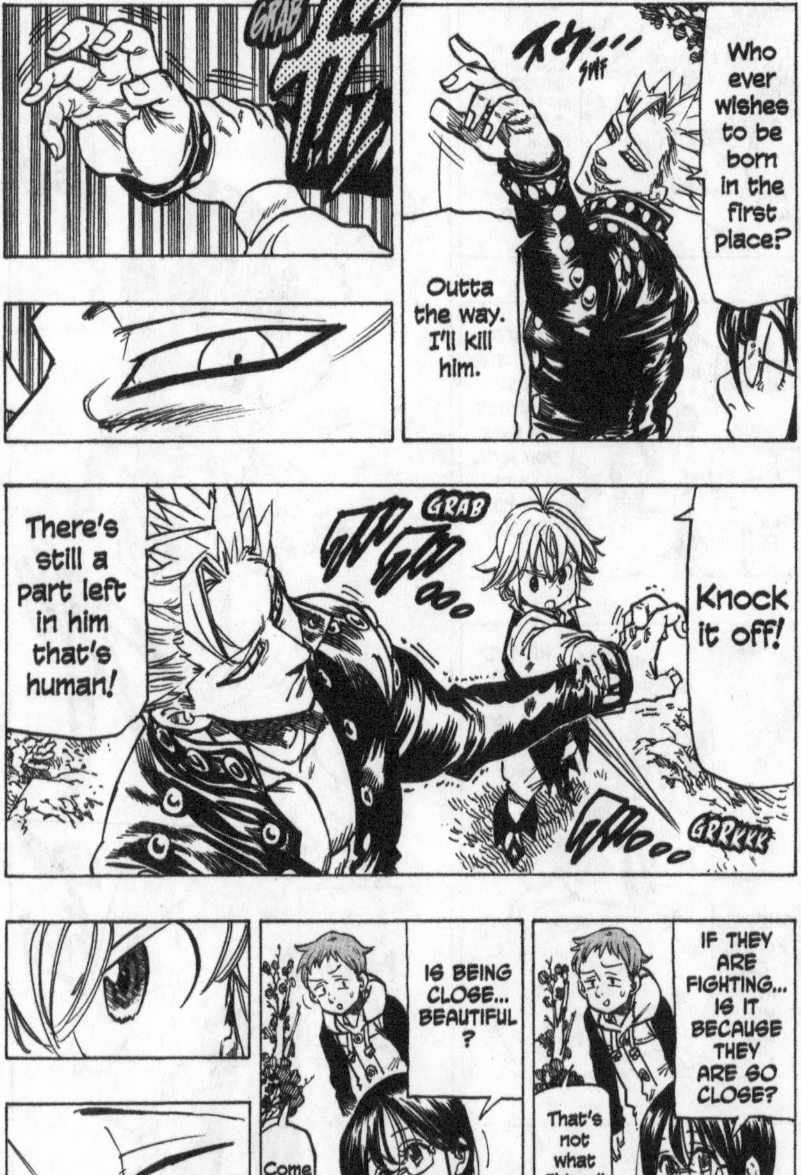
Who ever wishes to be born in the first place?
SNIF
Outta the way. I'll kill him.
GRAB
Knock it off!
GRAB
There's still a part left in him that's human!
GRRKKK
IF THEY ARE FIGHTING... IS IT BECAUSE THEY ARE SO CLOSE?
That's not what I'd call fighting.
IS BEING CLOSE... BEAUTIFUL?
Come again?
GRIN

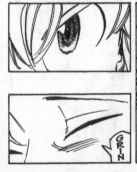

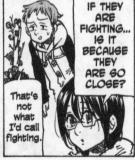

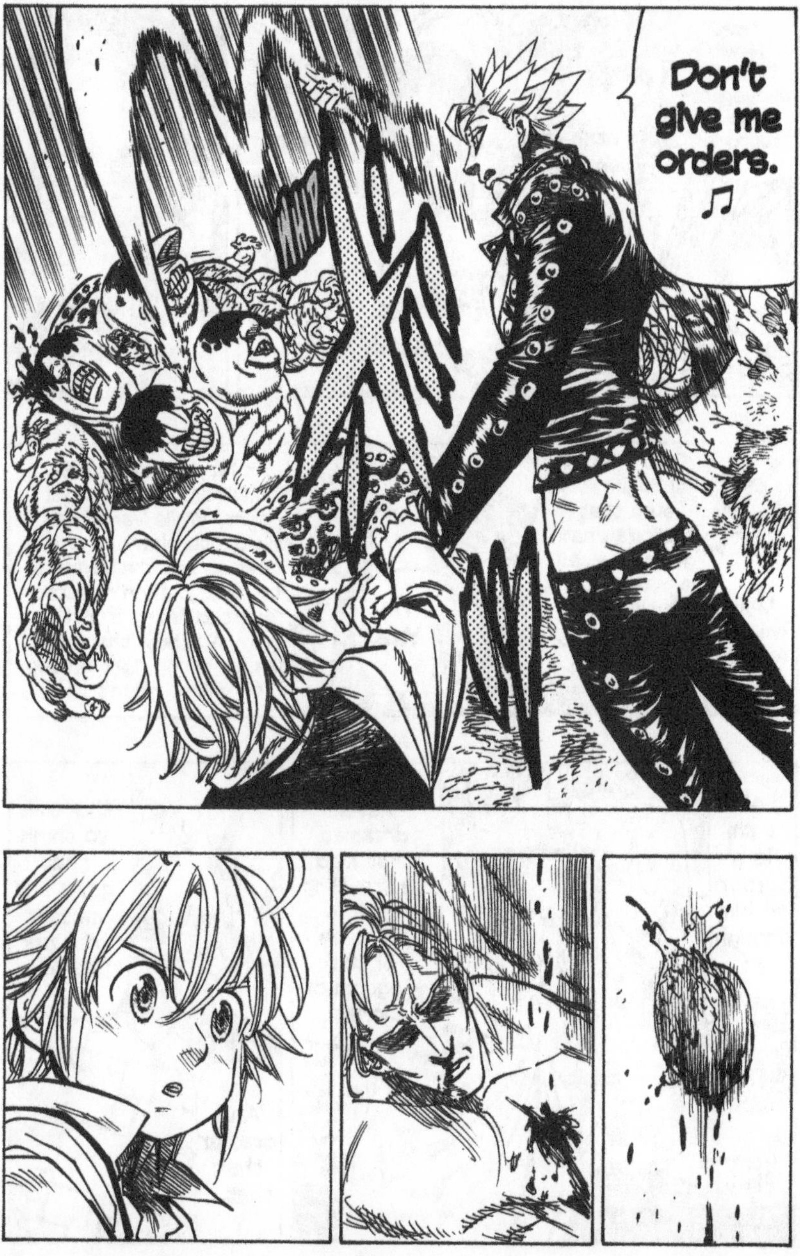
Don't give me orders. ♫

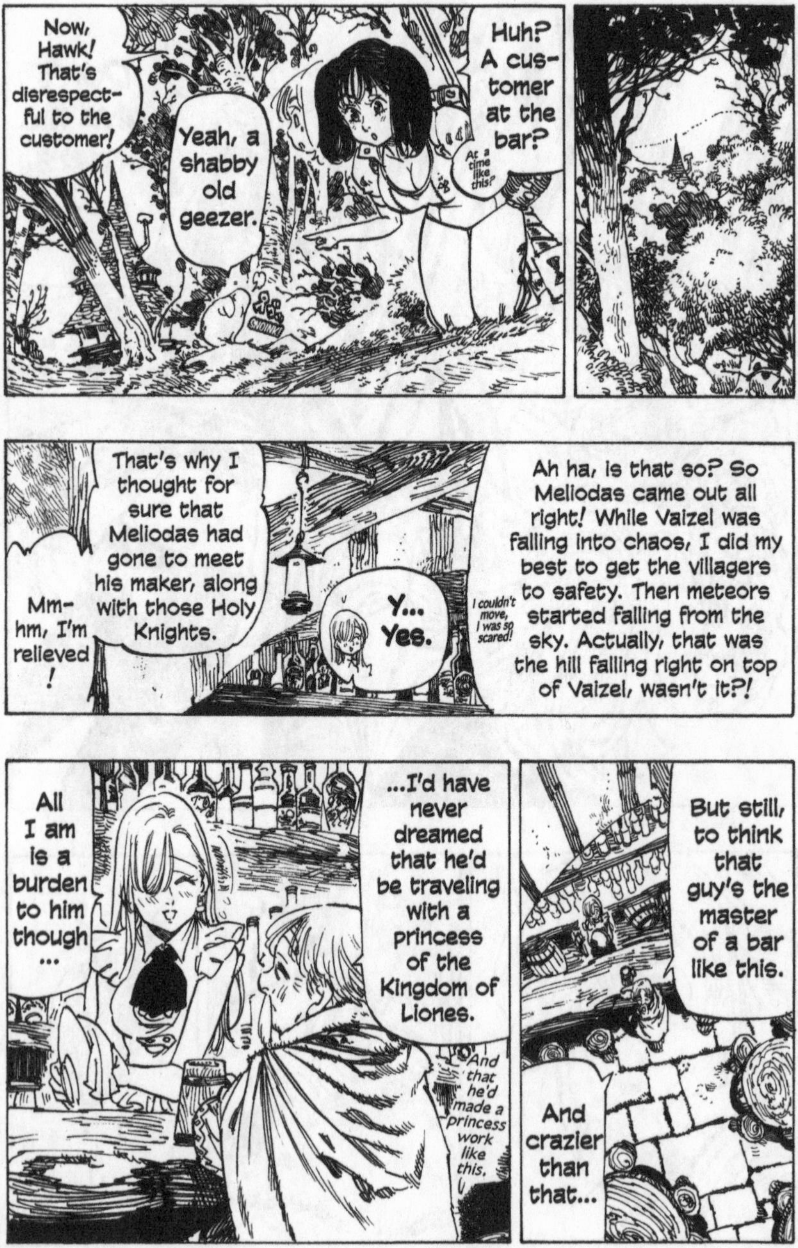
Huh? A customer at the bar?
At a time like this?
Yeah, a shabby old geezer.
SNOINK!
Now, Hawk! That's disrespectful to the customer!
Ah ha, is that so? So Meliodas came out all right! While Vaizel was falling into chaos, I did my best to get the villagers to safety. Then meteors started falling from the sky. Actually, that was the hill falling right on top of Vaizel, wasn't it?!
I couldn't move, I was so scared!
Y... Yes.
That's why I thought for sure that Meliodas had gone to meet his maker, along with those Holy Knights.
Mm-hm, I'm relieved!
But still, to think that guy's the master of a bar like this.
And crazier than that...
...I'd have never dreamed that he'd be traveling with a princess of the Kingdom of Liones.
And that he'd made a princess work like this.
All I am is a burden to him though...

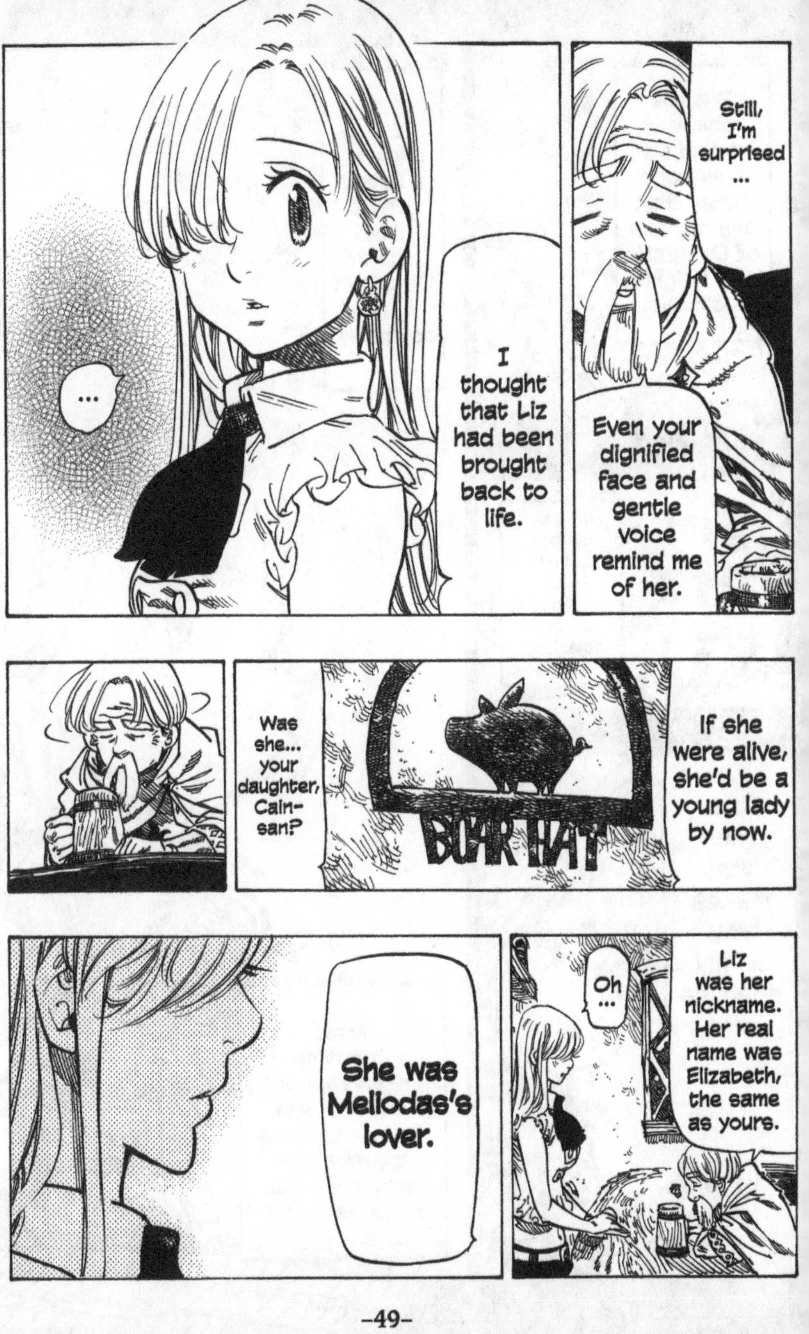
Still, I'm surprised ...
Even your dignified face and gentle voice remind me of her.
I thought that Liz had been brought back to life.
...
If she were alive, she'd be a young lady by now.
BOAR HAT
Was she... your daughter, Cain-san?
Liz was her nickname. Her real name was Elizabeth, the same as yours.
Oh ...
She was Meliodas's lover.

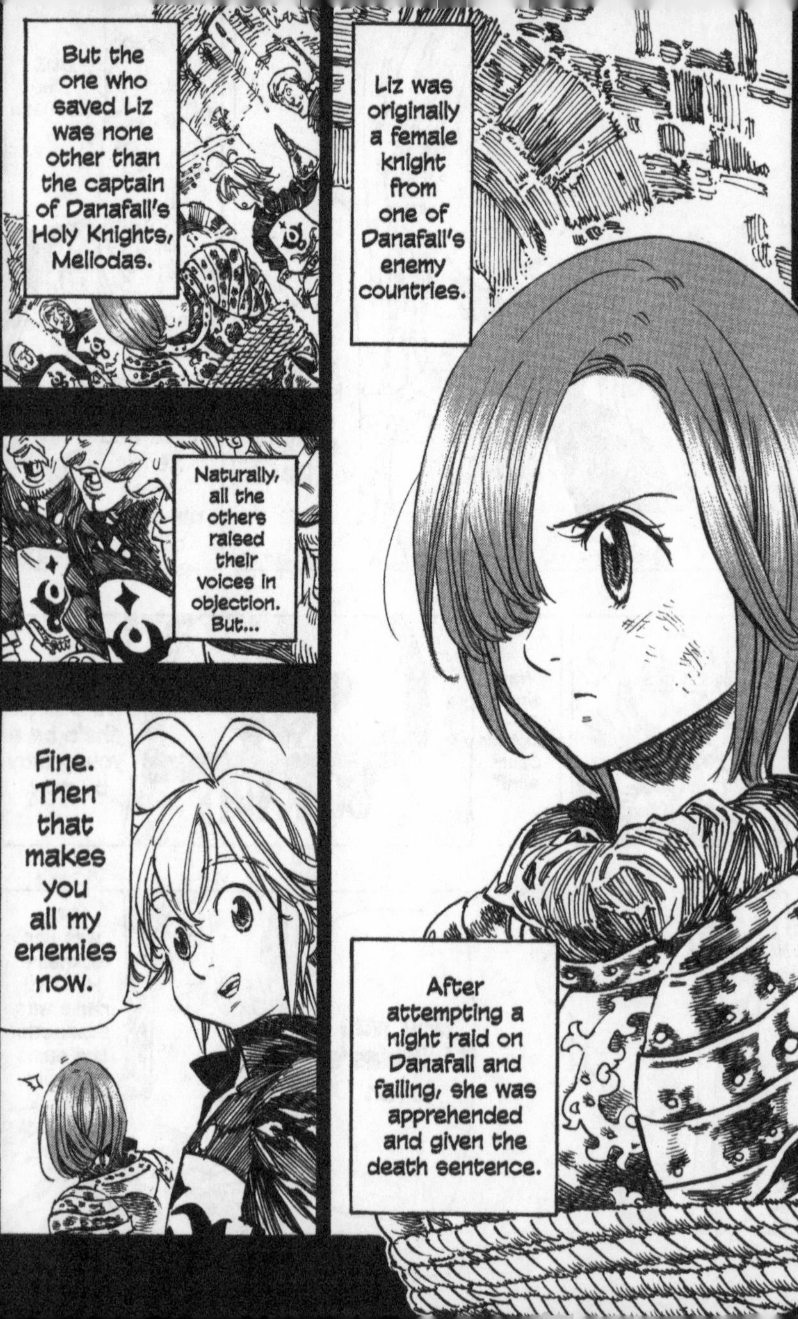
Liz was originally a female knight from one of Danafall's enemy countries.
After attempting a night raid on Danafall and failing, she was apprehended and given the death sentence.
But the one who saved Liz was none other than the captain of Danafall's Holy Knights, Meliodas.
Naturally, all the others raised their voices in objection. But...
Fine. Then that makes you all my enemies now.

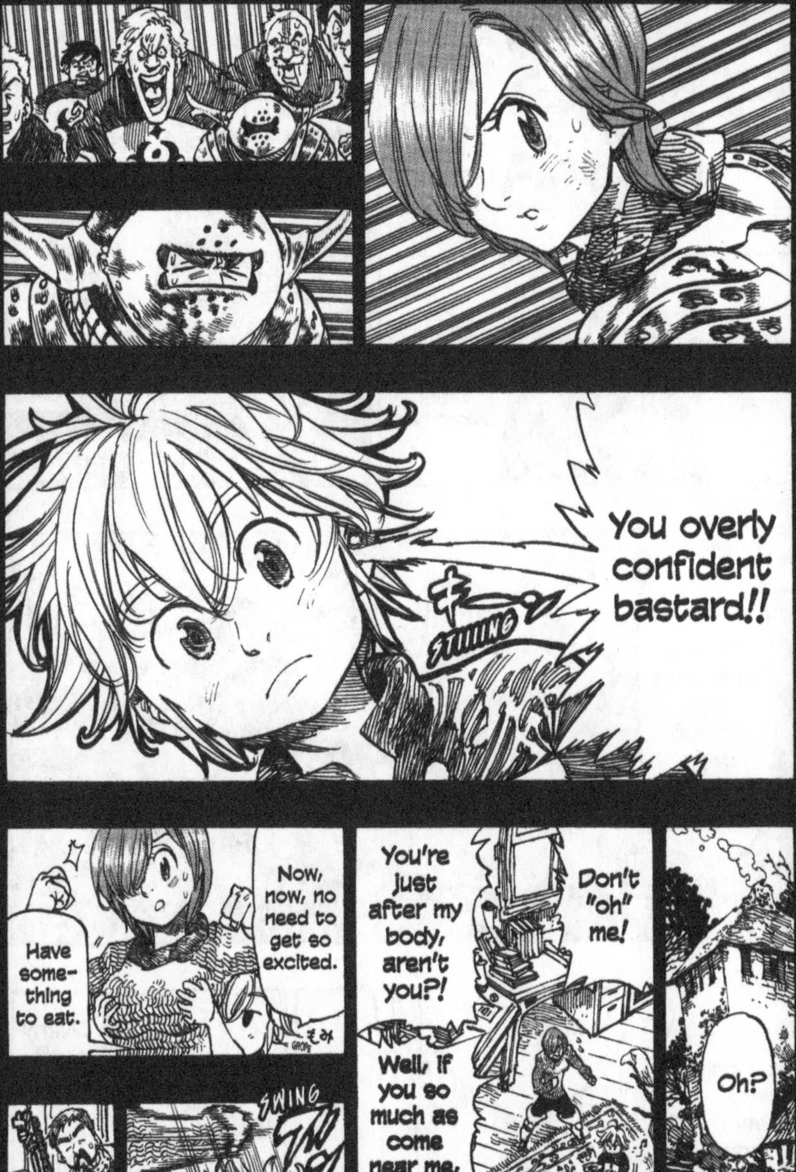
You overly confident bastard!!
キーン
STIIIING
Oh?
Don't "oh" me!
You're just after my body, aren't you?!
Well, if you so much as come near me, I'll kill you!
Now, now, no need to get so excited.
Have something to eat.
もみ
GROPE
SWING
...

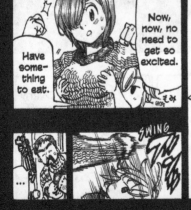

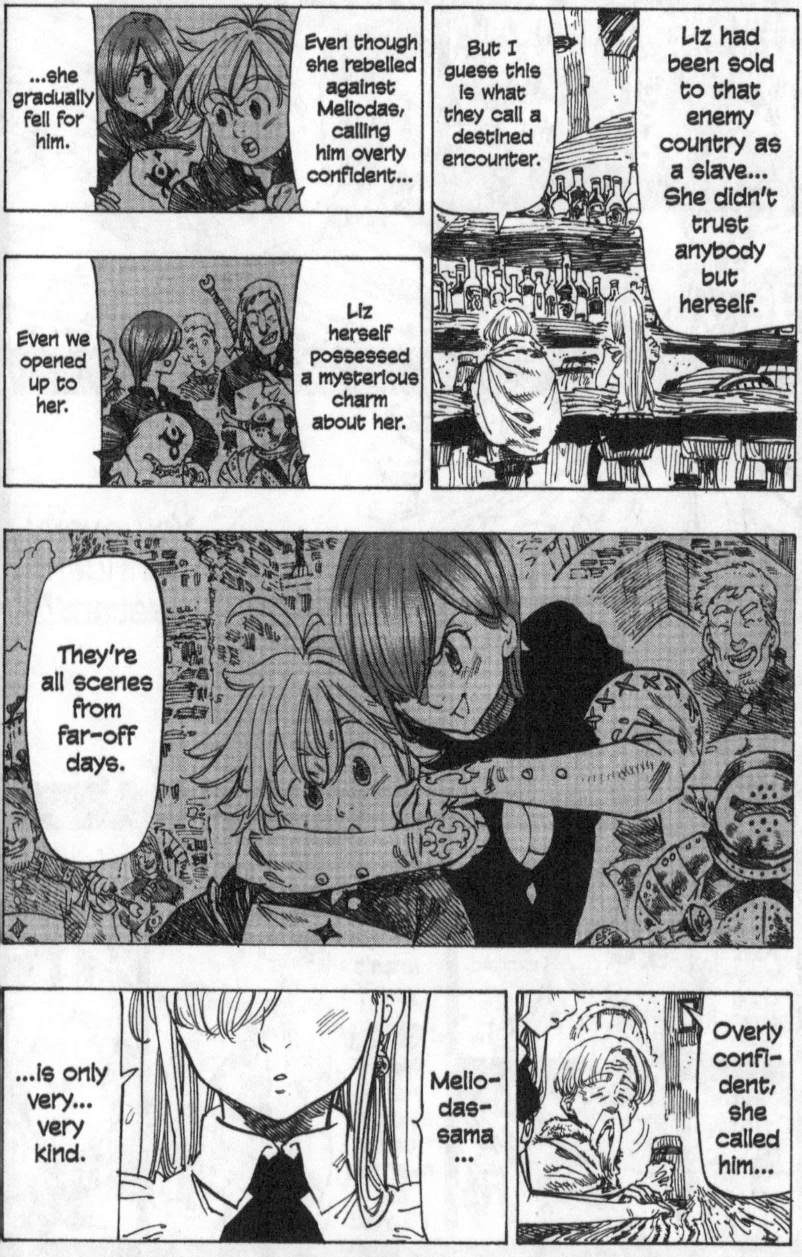
Liz had been sold to that enemy country as a slave... She didn't trust anybody but herself.
But I guess this is what they call a destined encounter.
Even though she rebelled against Meliodas, calling him overly confident...
...she gradually fell for him.
Liz herself possessed a mysterious charm about her.
Even we opened up to her.
They're all scenes from far-off days.
Overly confi-dent, she called him...
Melio-das-sama...
...is only very... very kind.

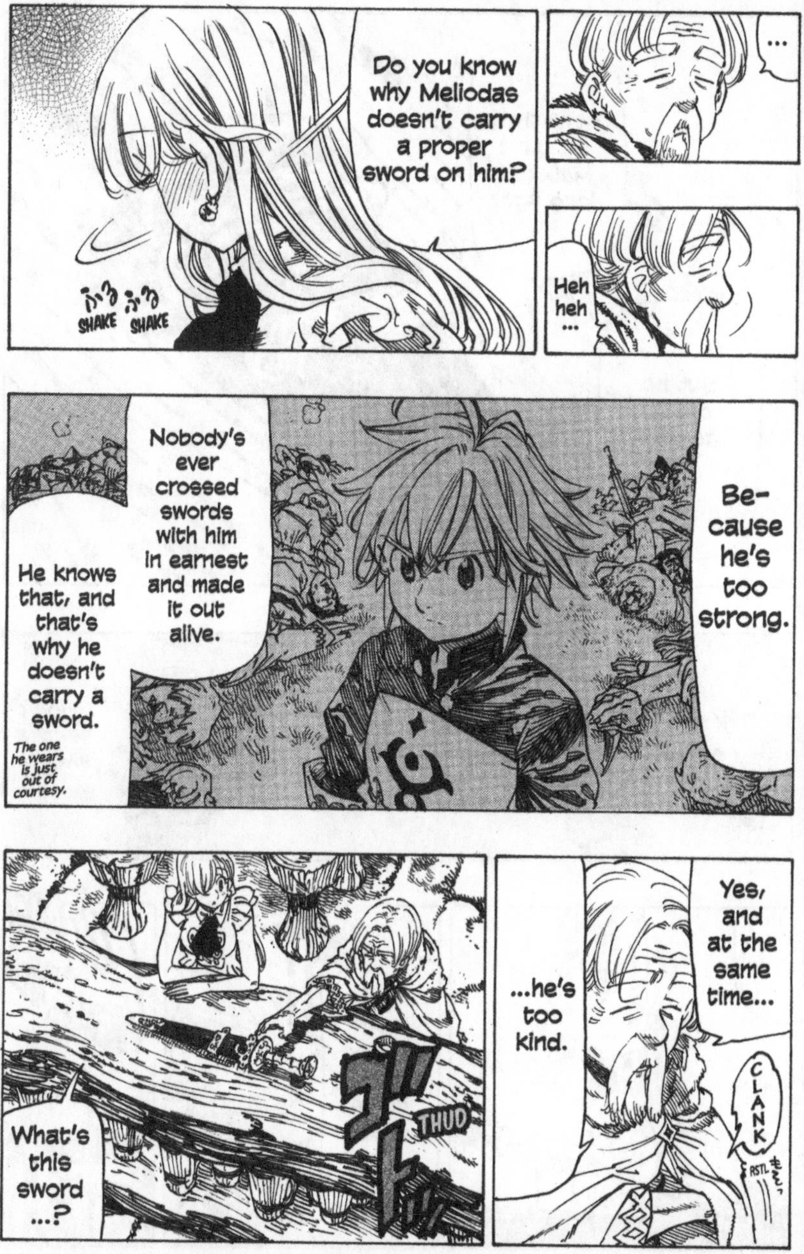
...
Heh heh...
Do you know why Meliodas doesn't carry a proper sword on him?
SHAKE SHAKE
Be-cause he's too strong.
Nobody's ever crossed swords with him in earnest and made it out alive.
He knows that, and that's why he doesn't carry a sword.
The one he wears is just out of courtesy.
Yes, and at the same time...
...he's too kind.
CLANK
RSTL
THUD
What's this sword...?

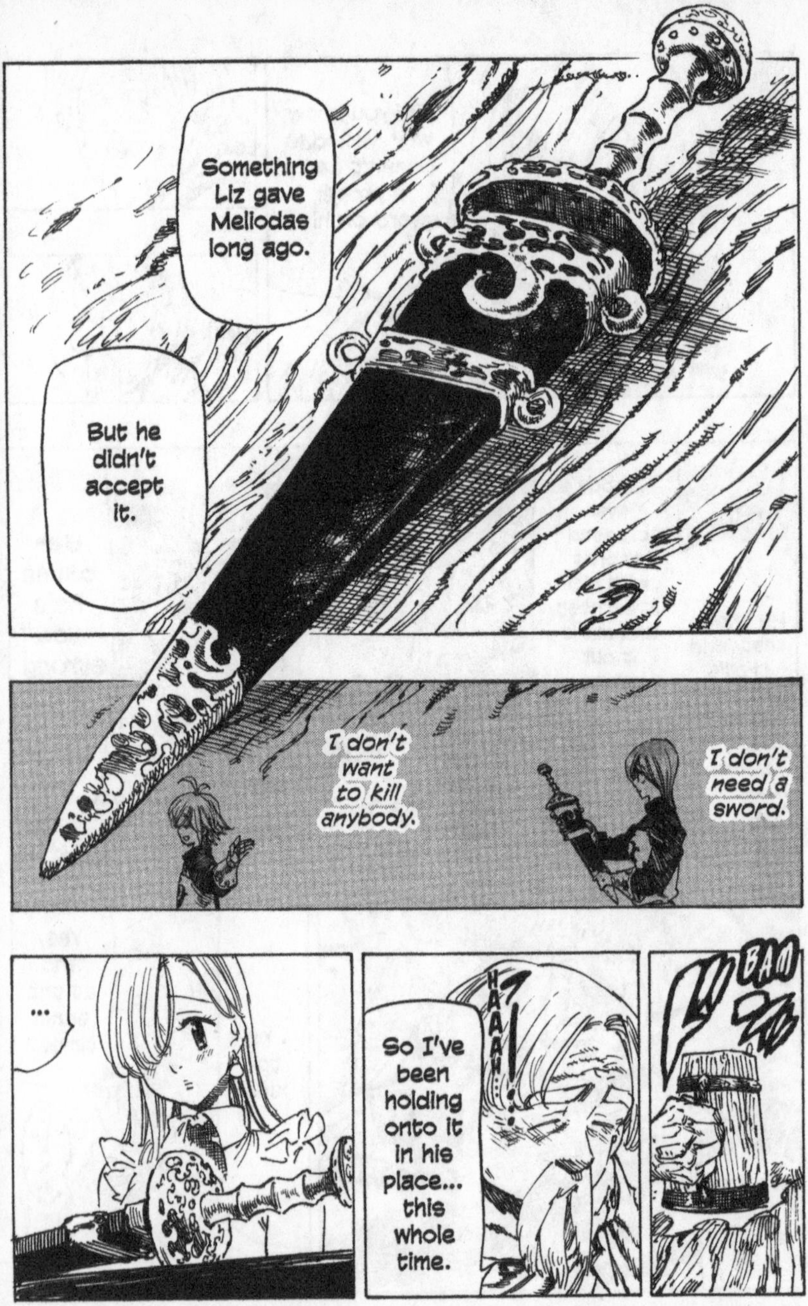
Something Liz gave Meliodas long ago.
But he didn't accept it.
I don't need a sword.
I don't want to kill anybody.
BAM
HAAAH...!!
So I've been holding onto it in his place... this whole time.
...

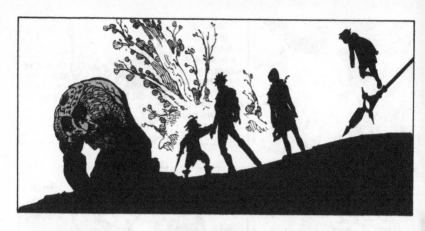

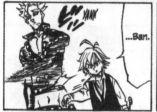

SPLUT
SPLUT
YANK
...Ban.
Why... did you kill him?!
The bastard had become a monster. I just drew the curtain to a close on his miserable existence.
You ought to be thanking me. ♪

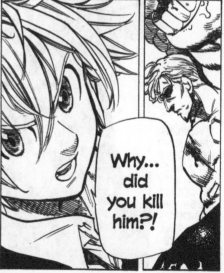

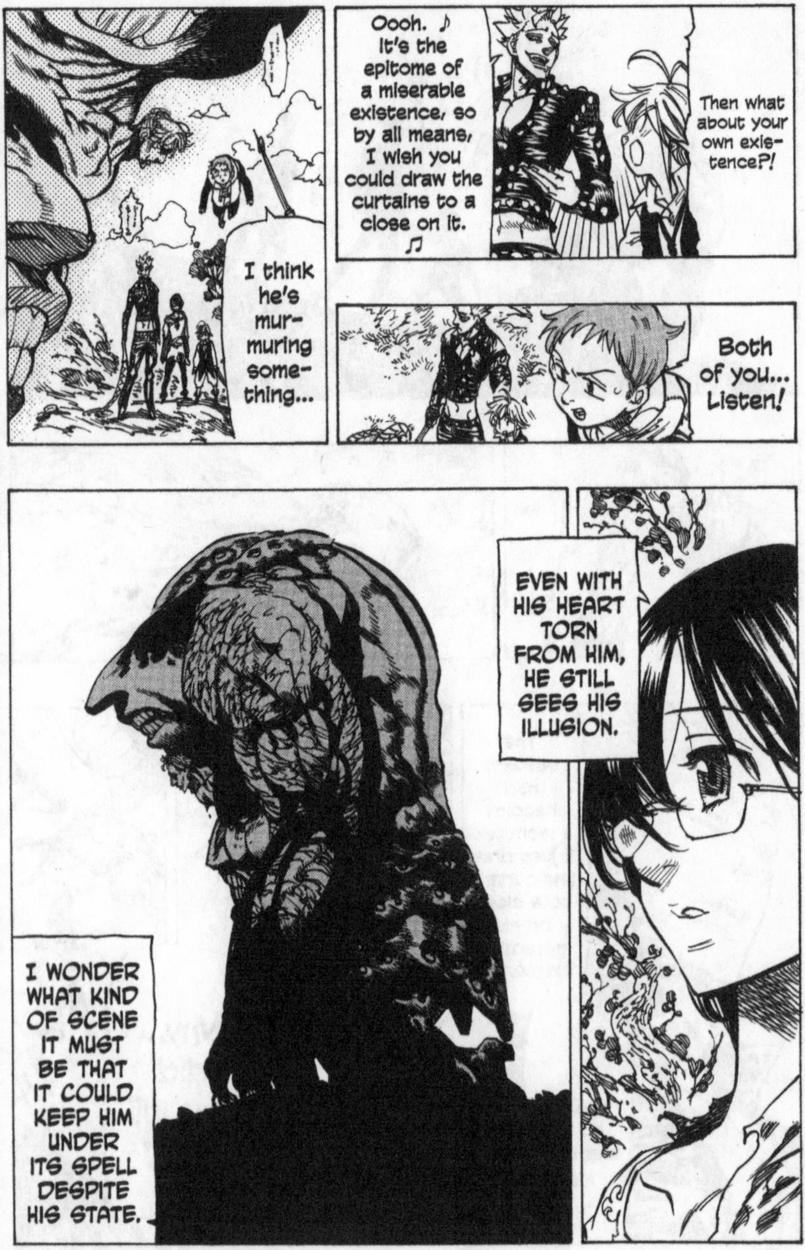

Oooh. ♪ It's the epitome of a miserable existence, so by all means, I wish you could draw the curtains to a close on it. ♫
Then what about your own existence?!
Both of you... Listen!
I think he's murmuring something...
EVEN WITH HIS HEART TORN FROM HIM, HE STILL SEES HIS ILLUSION.
I WONDER WHAT KIND OF SCENE IT MUST BE THAT IT COULD KEEP HIM UNDER ITS SPELL DESPITE HIS STATE.

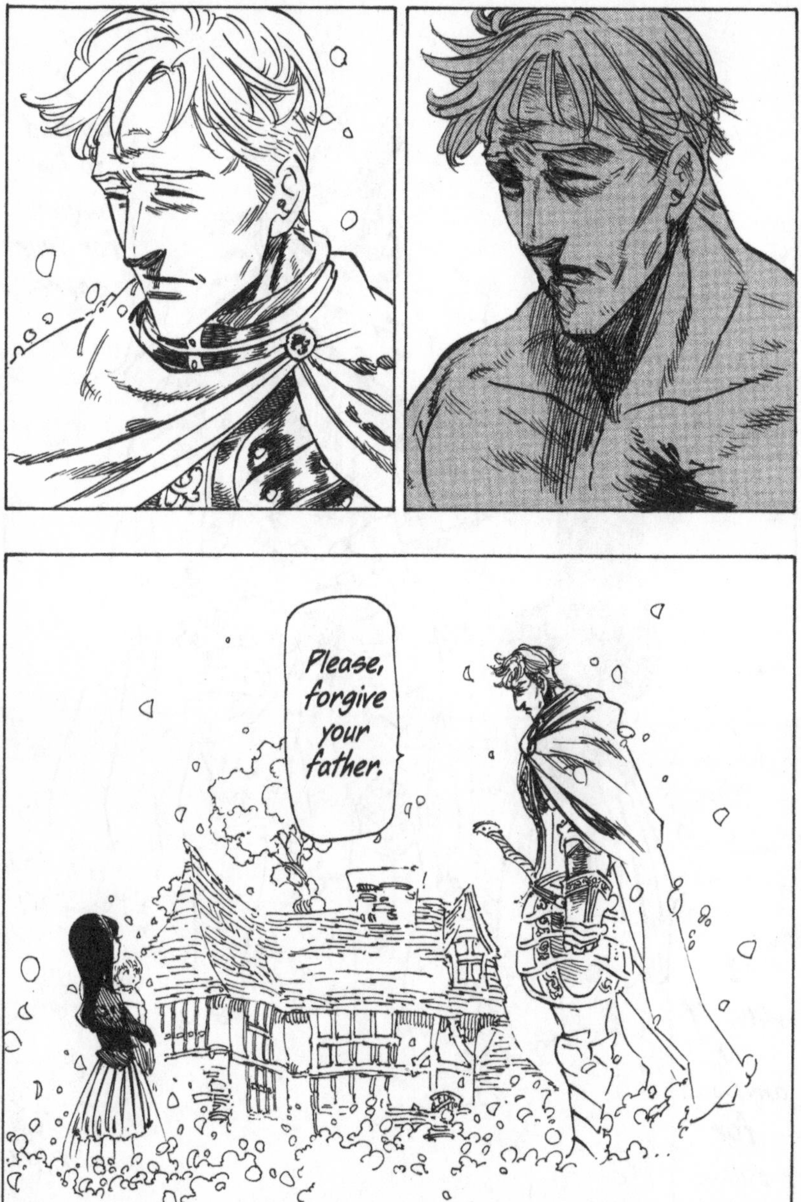
Please, forgive your father.

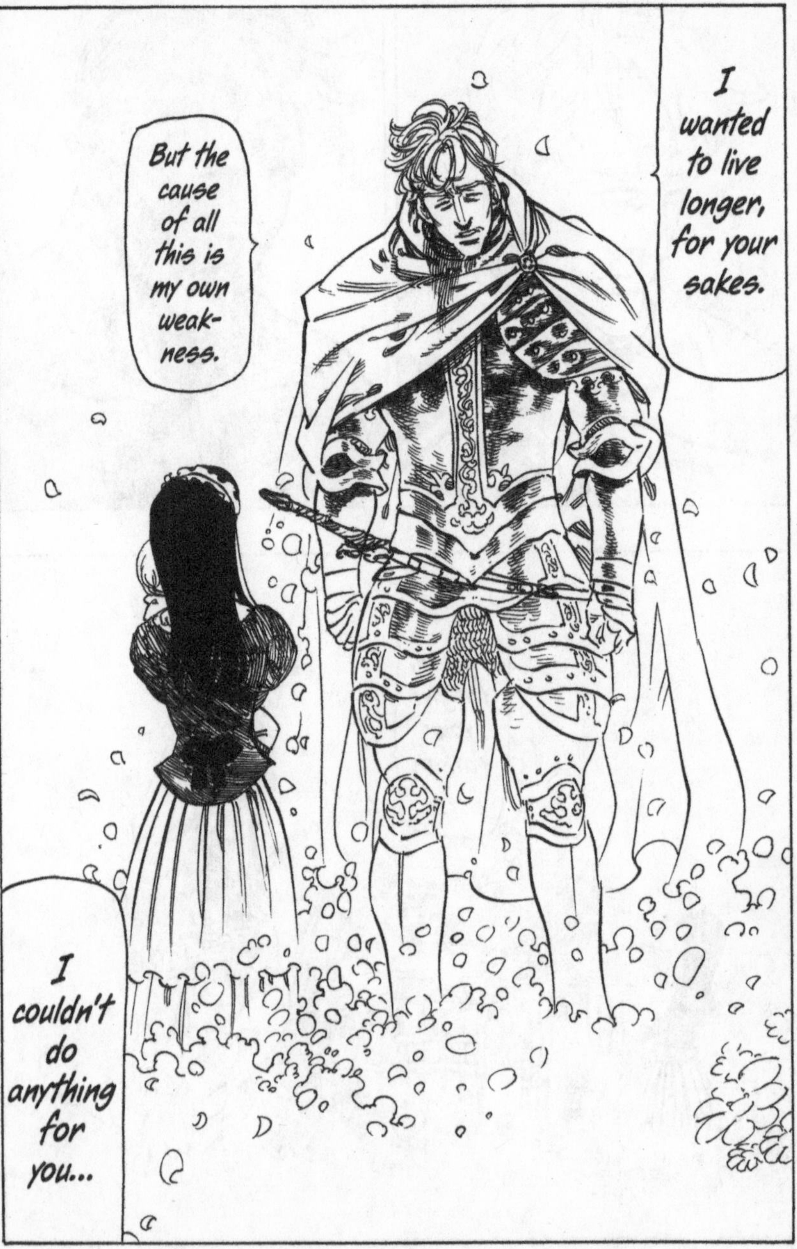
I wanted to live longer, for your sakes.
But the cause of all this is my own weak-ness.
I couldn't do anything for you...

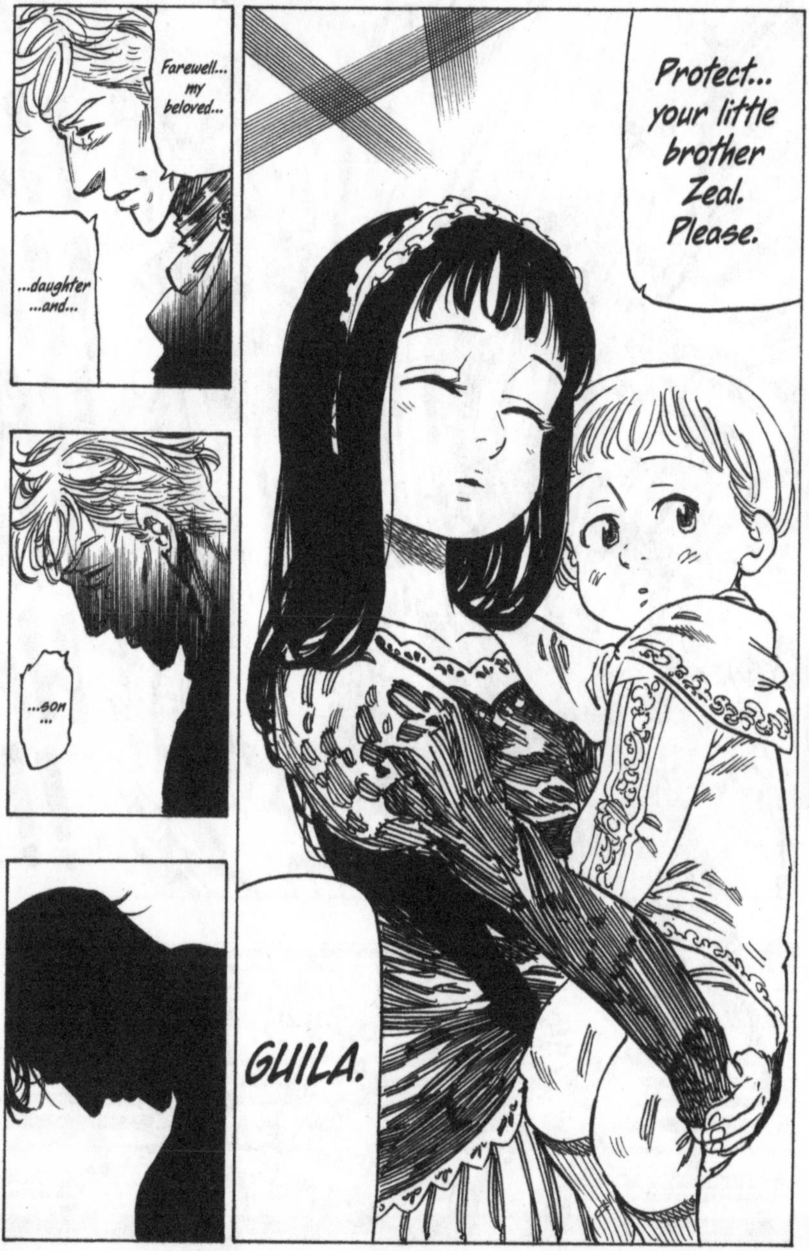
Protect... your little brother Zeal. Please.
GUILA.
Farewell... my beloved...
...daughter ...and...
...son ...

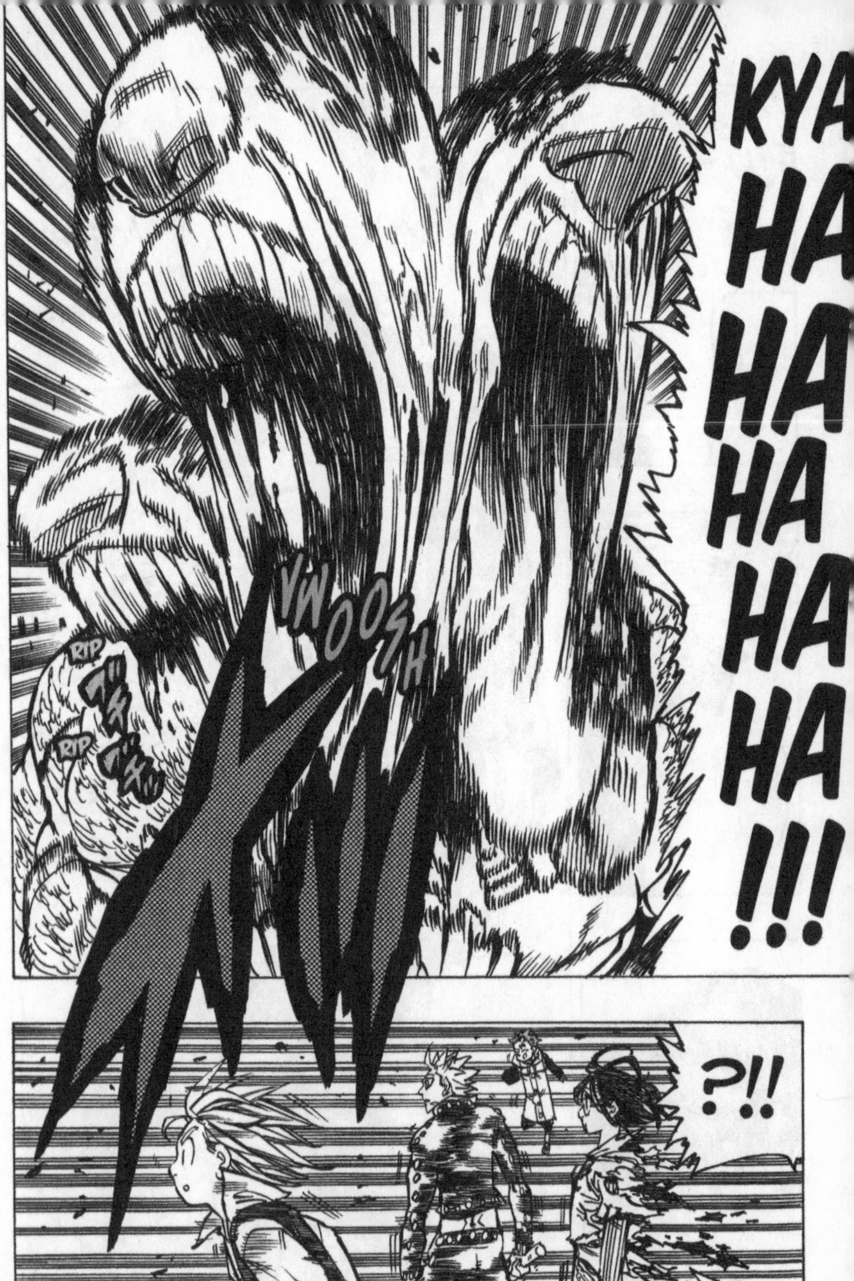
KYAHAHAHAHAHAHAHA!!!
VWOOSH
RIP
RIP
?!!

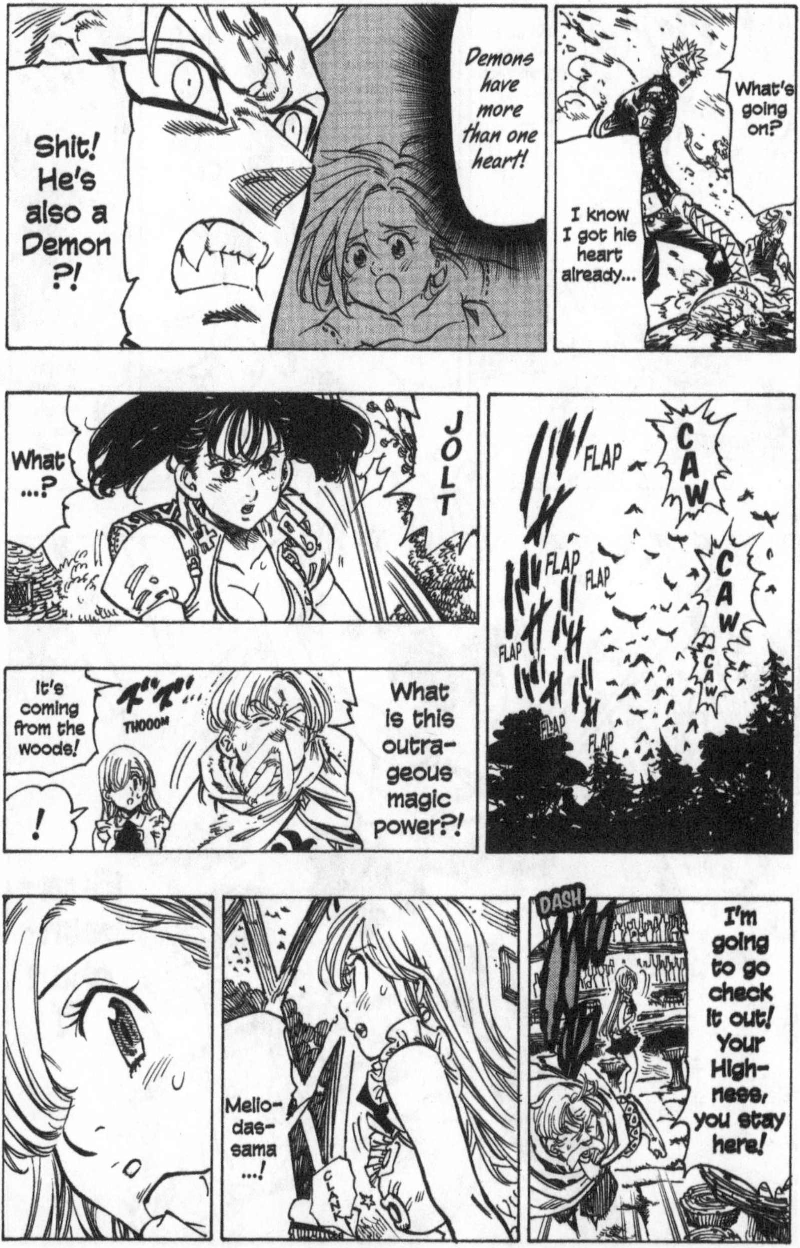
What's going on?
I know I got his heart already...
Demons have more than one heart!
Shit! He's also a Demon?!
CAW
FLAP
CAW
CAW
FLAP
FLAP
FLAP
FLAP
FLAP
JOLT
What ...?
What is this outrageous magic power?!
THOOOM
It's coming from the woods!
!
DASH
I'm going to go check it out! Your Highness, you stay here!
Melio-das-sama ...!
CLANK

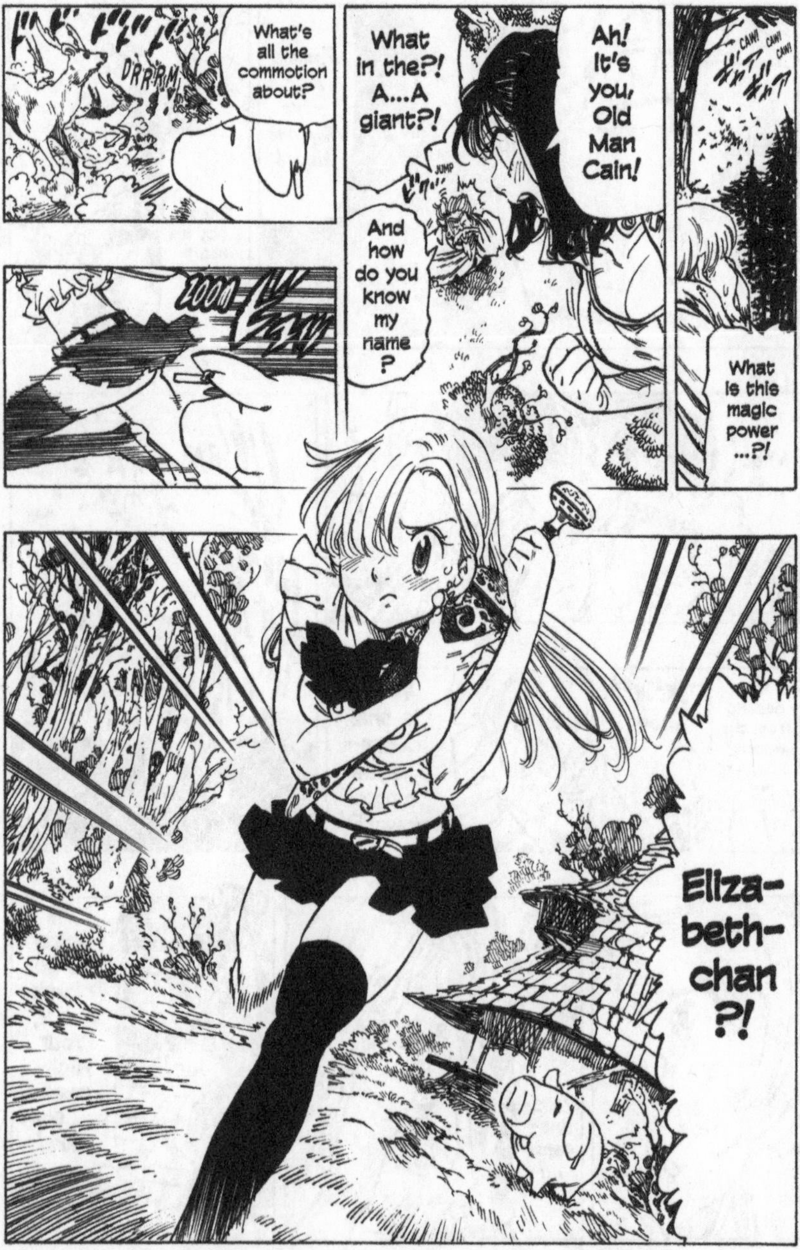
CAW! CAW! CAW!
What is this magic power ...?!
Ah! It's you, Old Man Cain!
What in the?! A...A giant?!
JUMP
And how do you know my name?
D'R'R'R'M
What's all the commotion about?
ZOOM
Eliza-beth-chan?!

Chapter 58 - Assumed Readiness

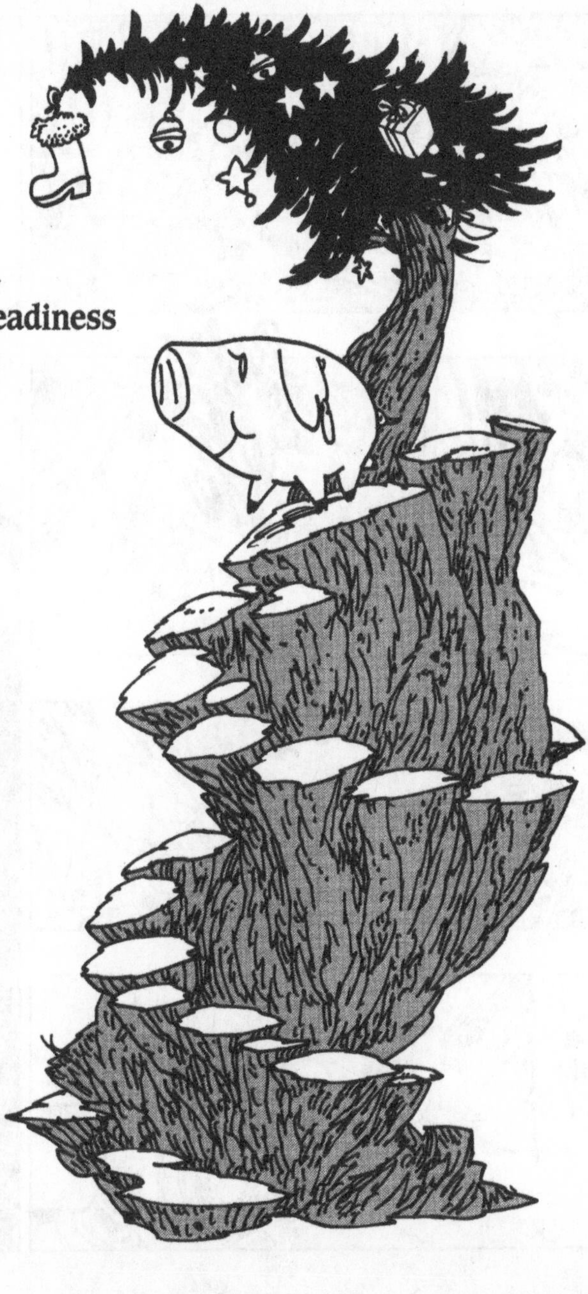

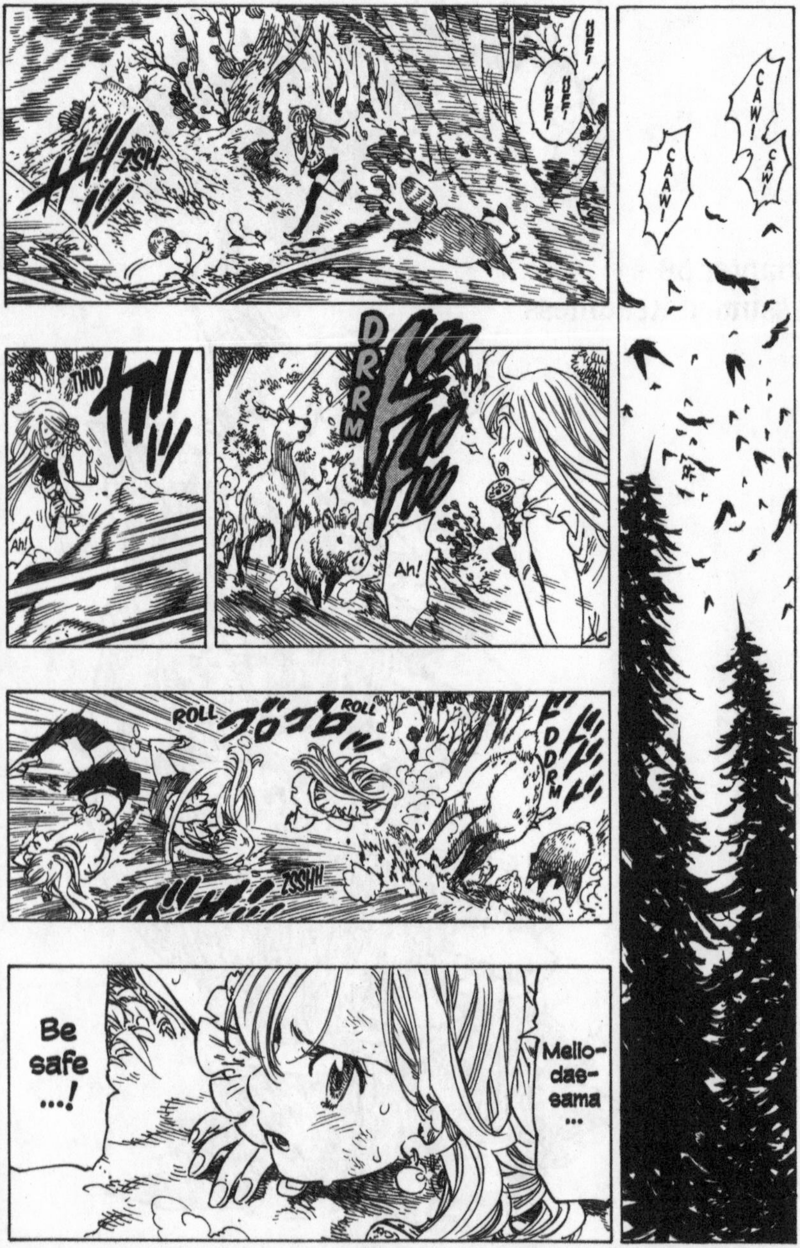

CAW!
CAW!
CAAW!
HUF!
HUF!
HUF!
ZSH
DRRM
Ah!
THUD
Ah!
DDRM
ROLL
ROLL
ZSSHH
Mello-
das-
sama
...
Be
safe
...!

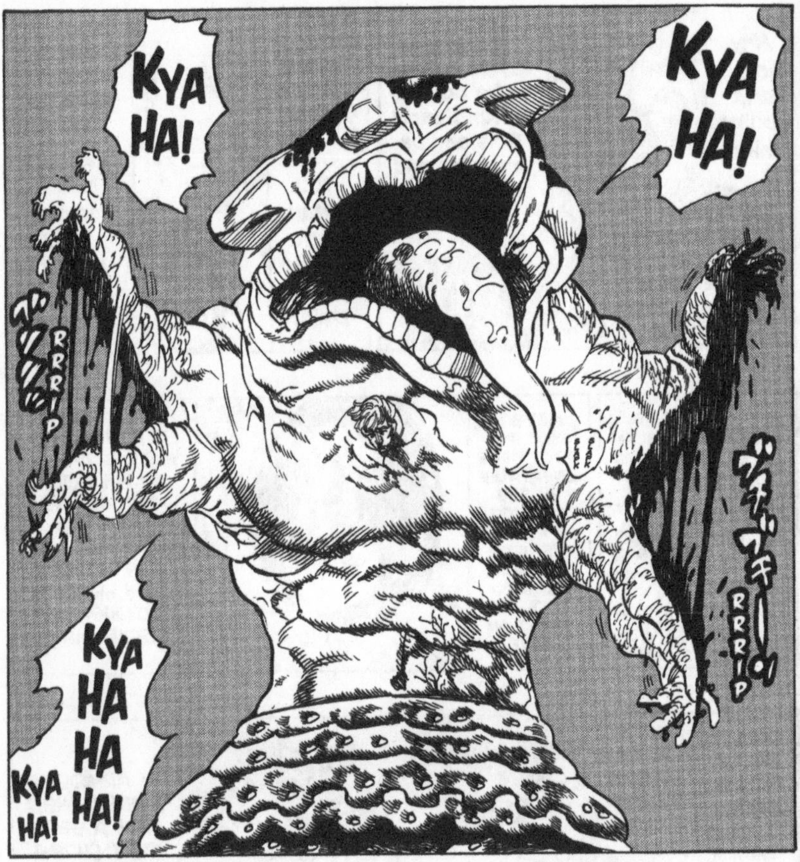
KYA HA!
KYA HA!
RRRIP
RRRIP
KYA HA HA HA!
KYA HA!
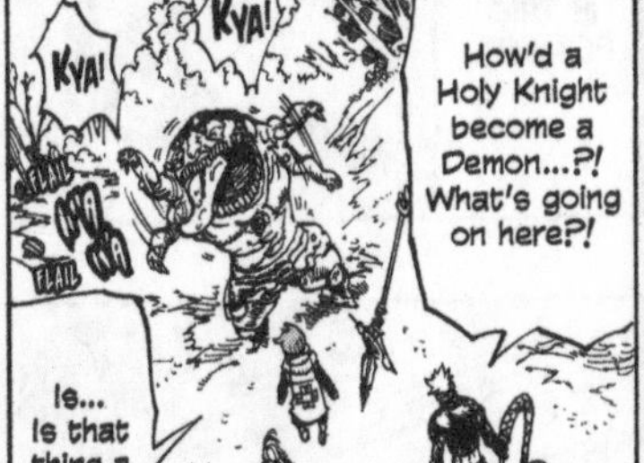
How'd a Holy Knight become a Demon...?! What's going on here?!
KYA!
KYA!
FLAIL
FLAIL
Is... Is that thing a Demon?
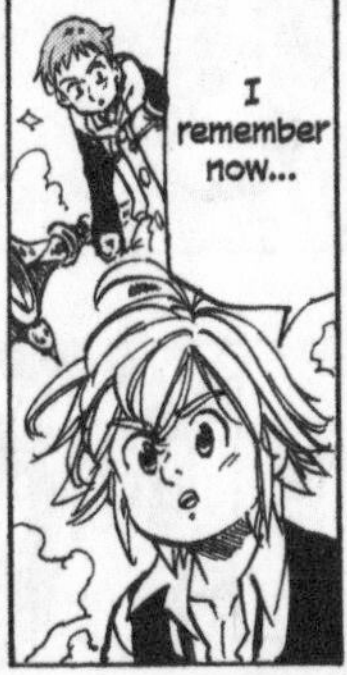
I remember now...
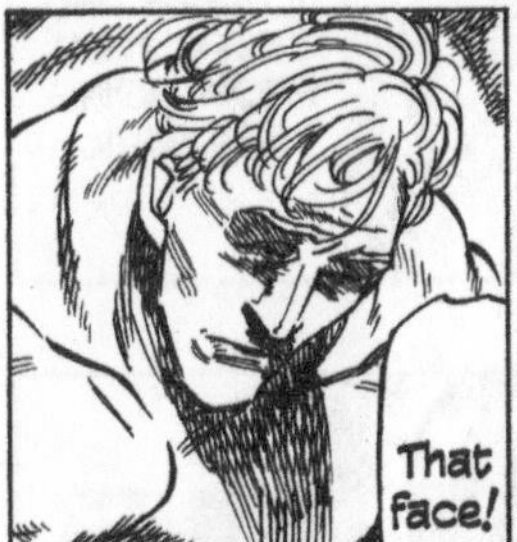
That face!

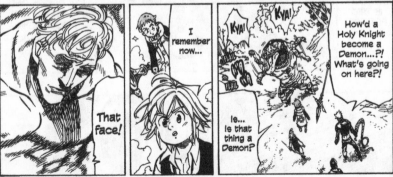

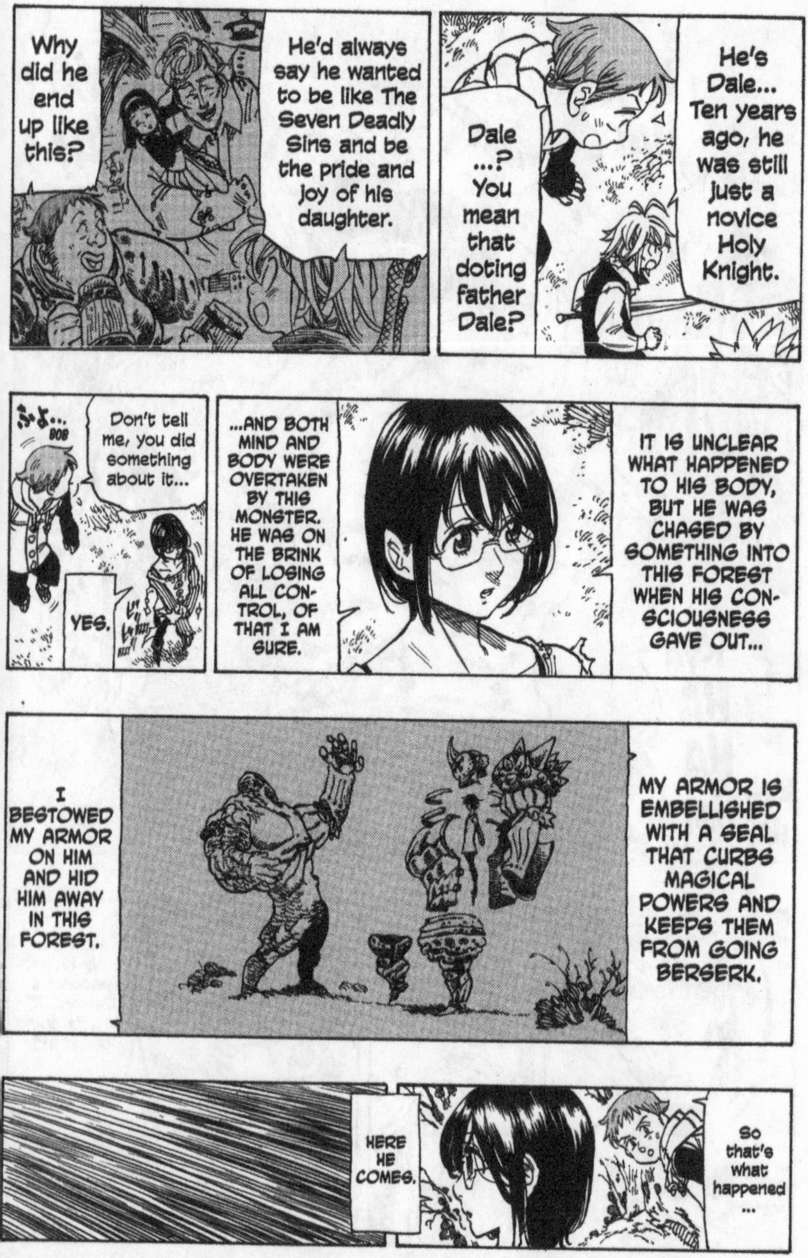
He's Dale... Ten years ago, he was still just a novice Holy Knight.
Dale ...? You mean that doting father Dale?
He'd always say he wanted to be like The Seven Deadly Sins and be the pride and joy of his daughter.
Why did he end up like this?
IT IS UNCLEAR WHAT HAPPENED TO HIS BODY, BUT HE WAS CHASED BY SOMETHING INTO THIS FOREST WHEN HIS CON-SCIOUSNESS GAVE OUT...
...AND BOTH MIND AND BODY WERE OVERTAKEN BY THIS MONSTER. HE WAS ON THE BRINK OF LOSING ALL CON-TROL, OF THAT I AM SURE.
ふよ... BOB
Don't tell me, you did something about it...
YES.
MY ARMOR IS EMBELLISHED WITH A SEAL THAT CURBS MAGICAL POWERS AND KEEPS THEM FROM GOING BERSERK.
I BESTOWED MY ARMOR ON HIM AND HID HIM AWAY IN THIS FOREST.
So that's what happened ...
HERE HE COMES.

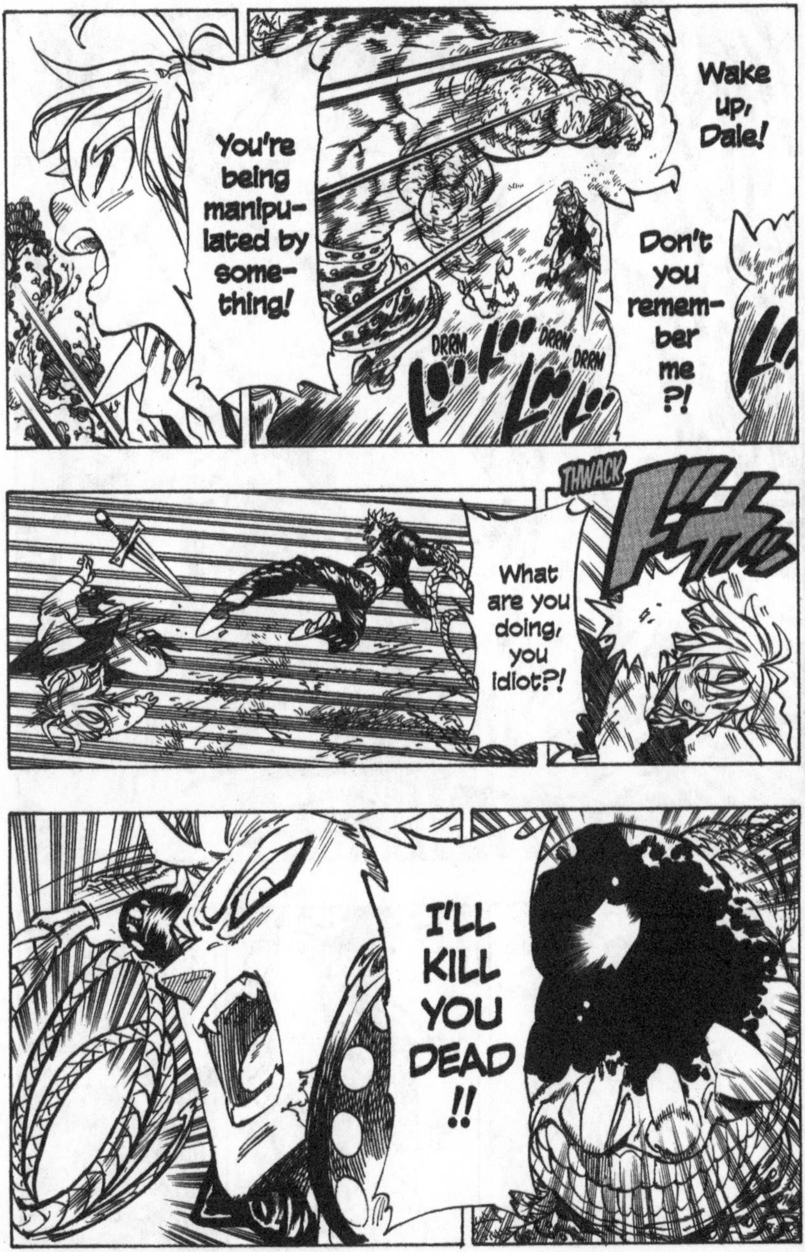

Wake up, Dale!
Don't you remember me?!
DRRM
DRRM
DRRM
You're being manipulated by something!
THWACK
What are you doing, you idiot?!
I'LL KILL YOU DEAD!!

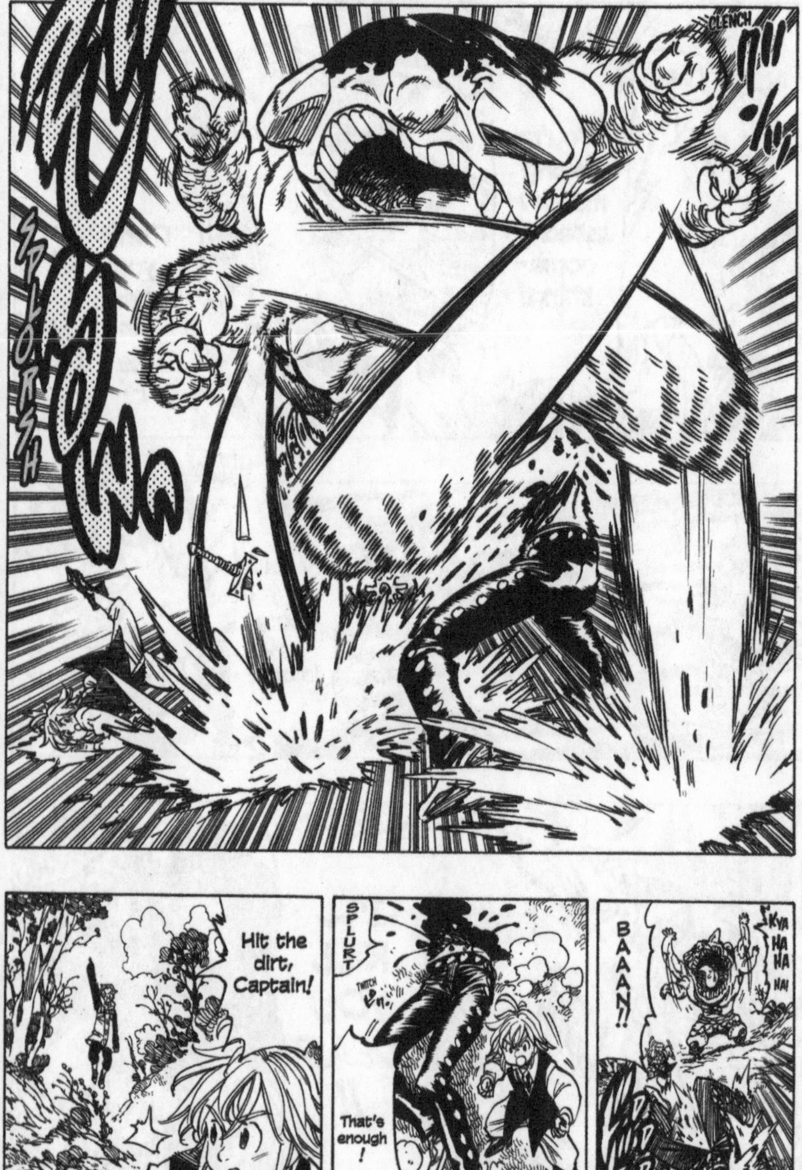
SPLORSH
CLENCH
BAAAN!!
KYA HA HA HA!
SPLURT
TWITCH
That's enough!
Hit the dirt, Captain!

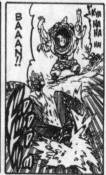

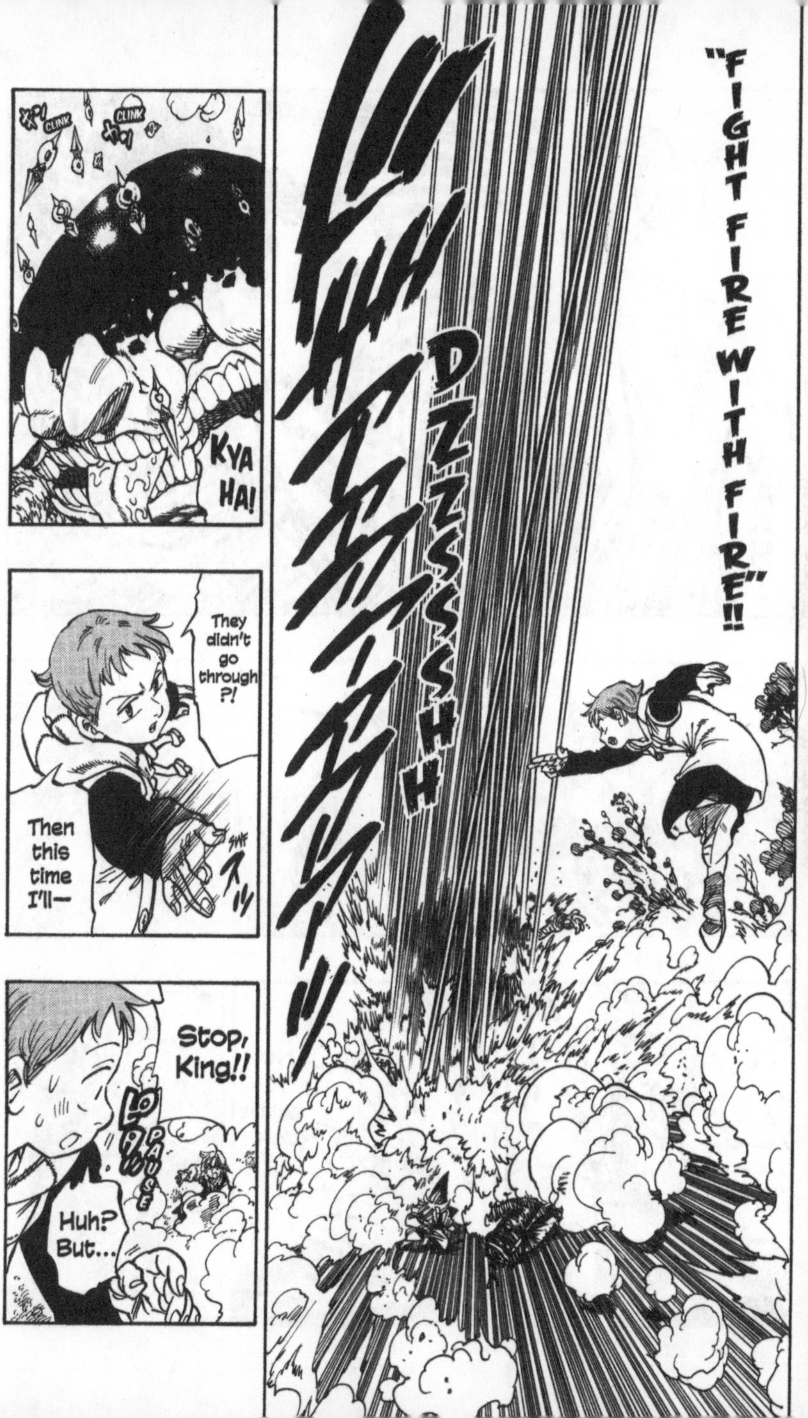
"FIGHT FIRE WITH FIRE"!!
DZZSSSHH
CLINK
CLINK
KYA HA!
They didn't go through?!
Then this time I'll—
SWF
Stop, King!!
PAUSE
Huh? But...

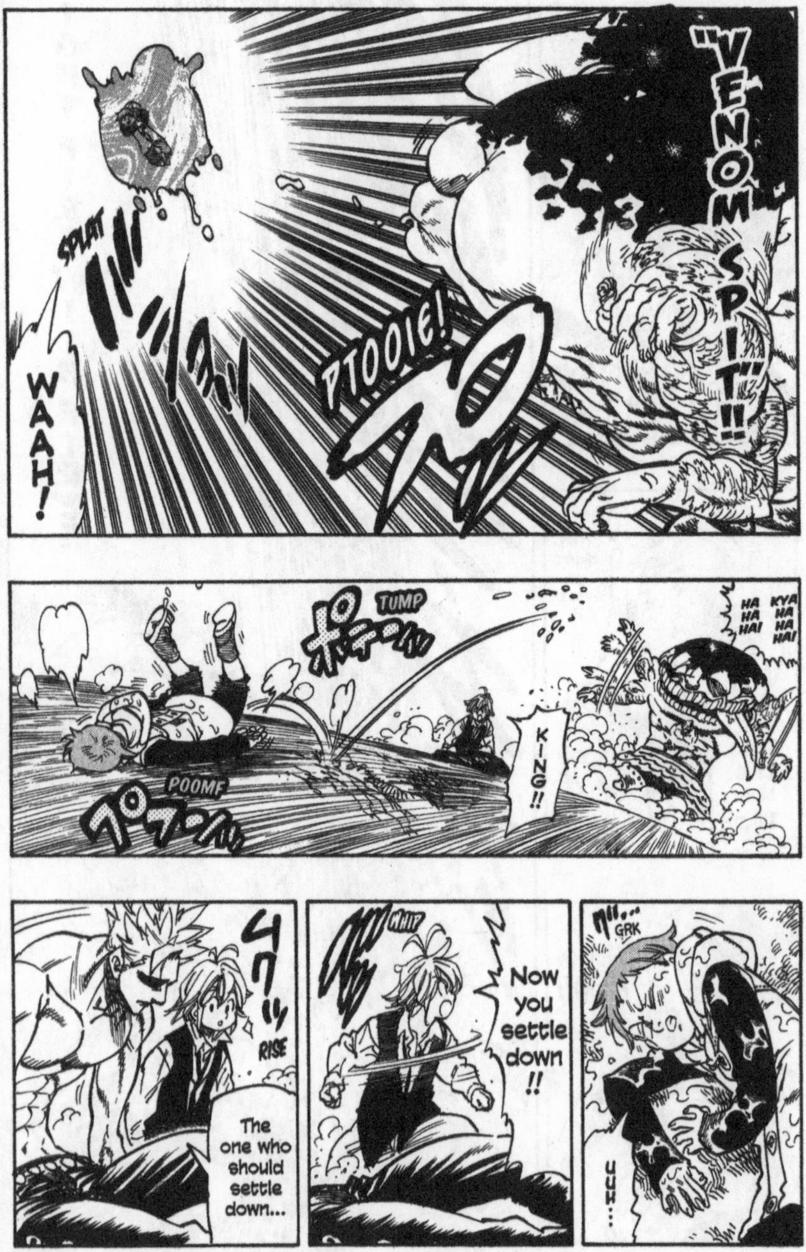
"VENOM SPIT"!!
PTOOIE!
SPLAT
WAAH!
HA HA HA! KYA HA HA HA!
KING!!
TUMP
POOMF
GRK
UUH...
Now you settle down!!
WHIP
RISE
The one who should settle down...

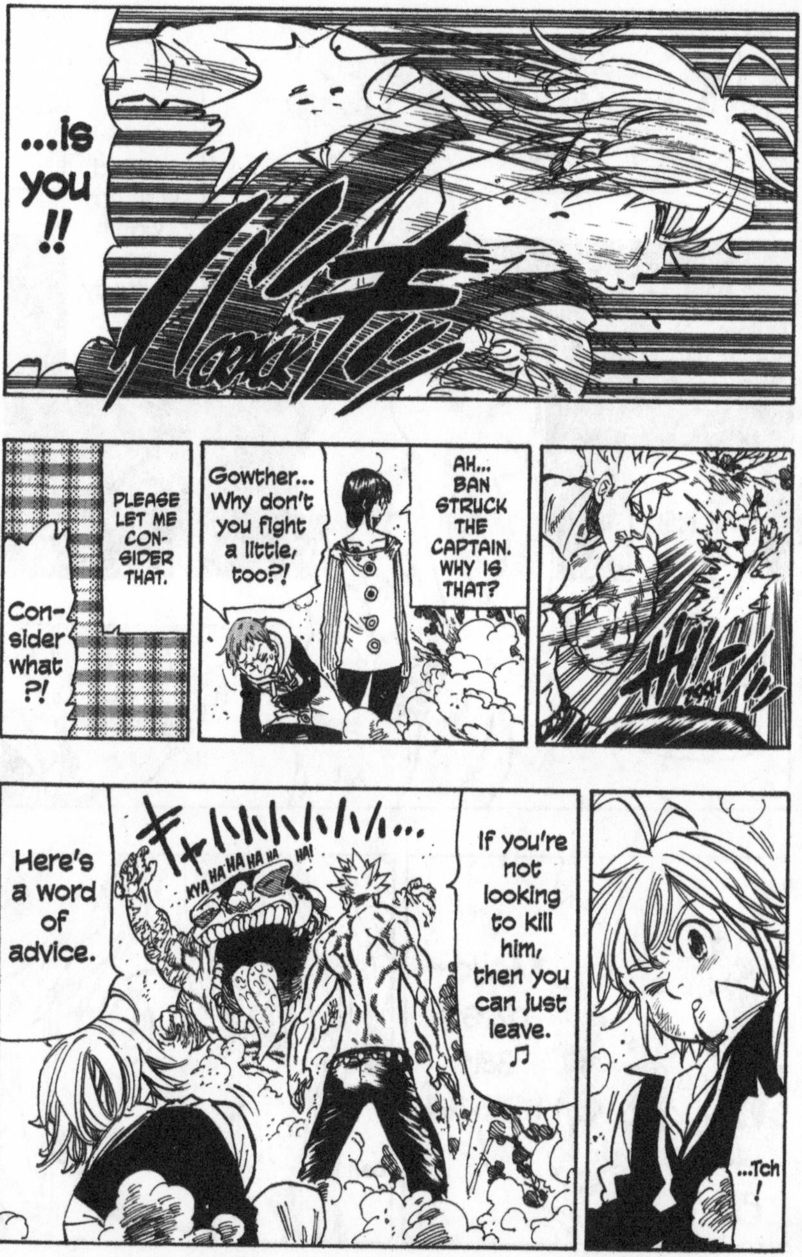
...is you!!
CRACK
AH... BAN STRUCK THE CAPTAIN. WHY IS THAT?
Gowther... Why don't you fight a little, too?!
PLEASE LET ME CONSIDER THAT.
Consider what?!
...Tch!
KYA HA HA HA HA HA!
If you're not looking to kill him, then you can just leave. ♫
Here's a word of advice.

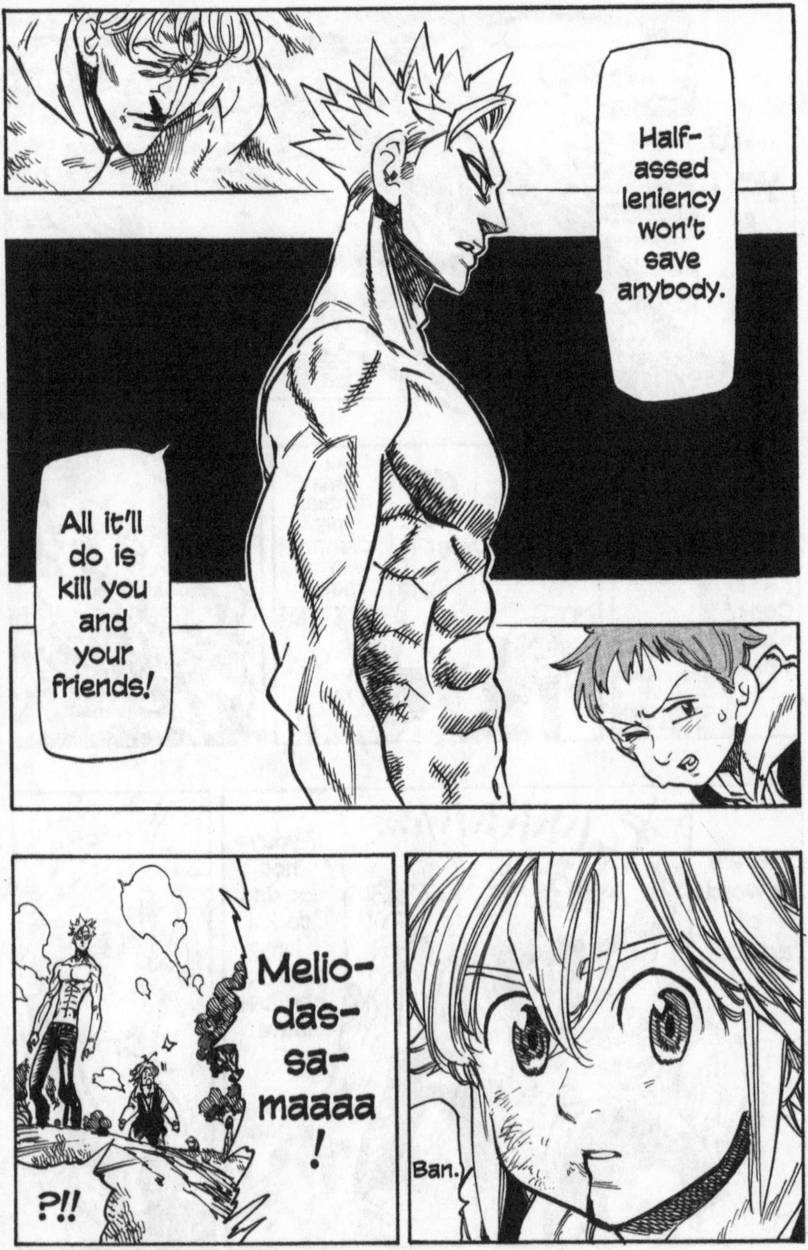
Half-assed leniency won't save anybody.
All it'll do is kill you and your friends!
Ban.
Melio-das-sa-maaaa!
?!!

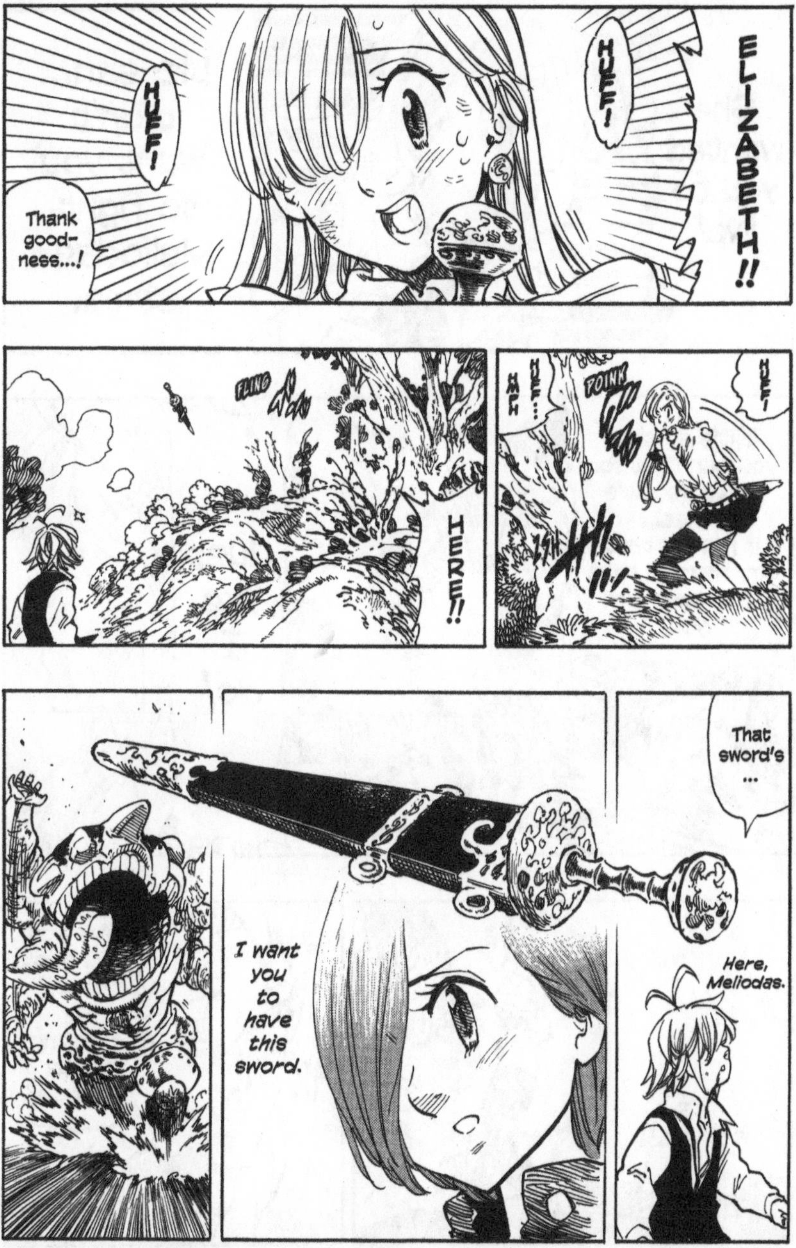
ELIZABETH!!
HUFF!
HUFF!
Thank goodness...!
HUFF!
HUFF... HMPH
POINK
ZSH
HERE!!
FLING
That sword's...
Here, Meliodas.
I want you to have this sword.

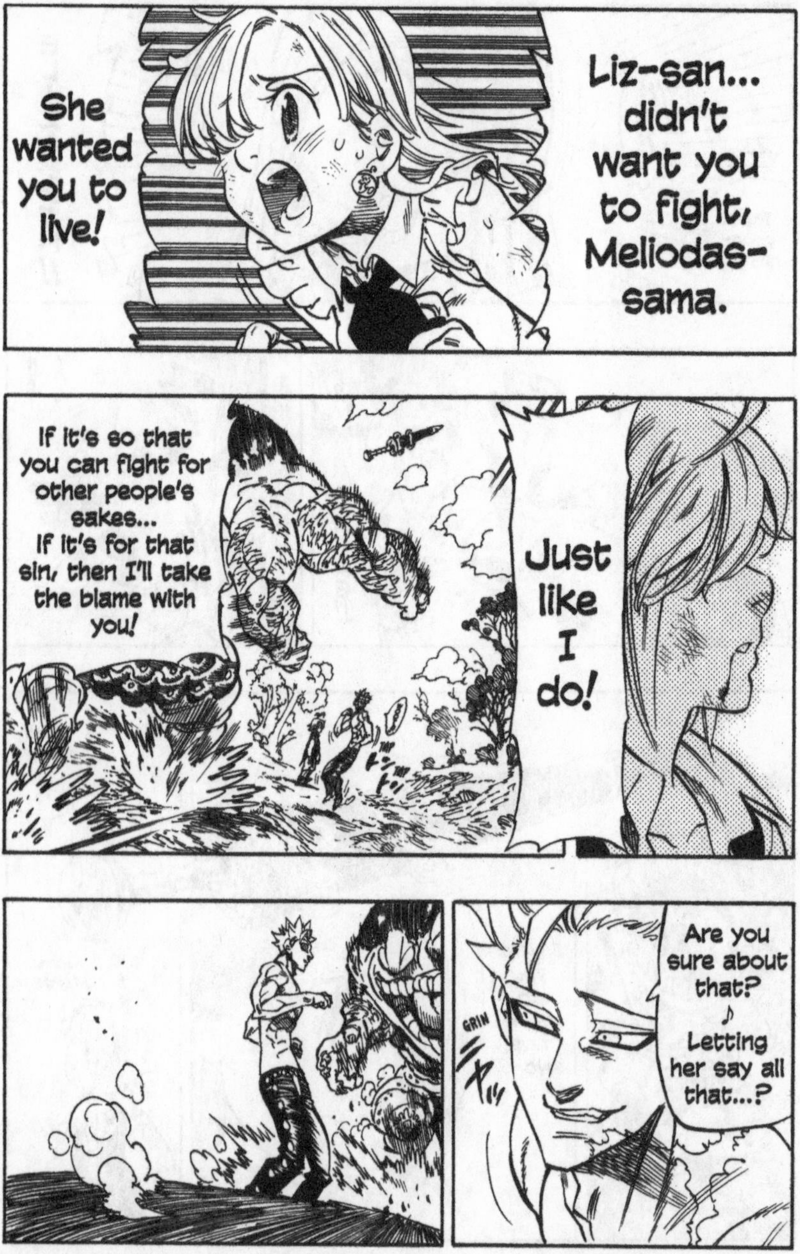
Liz-san... didn't want you to fight, Meliodas-sama.
She wanted you to live!
Just like I do!
If it's so that you can fight for other people's sakes... If it's for that sin, then I'll take the blame with you!
GRIN
Are you sure about that? ♪ Letting her say all that...?

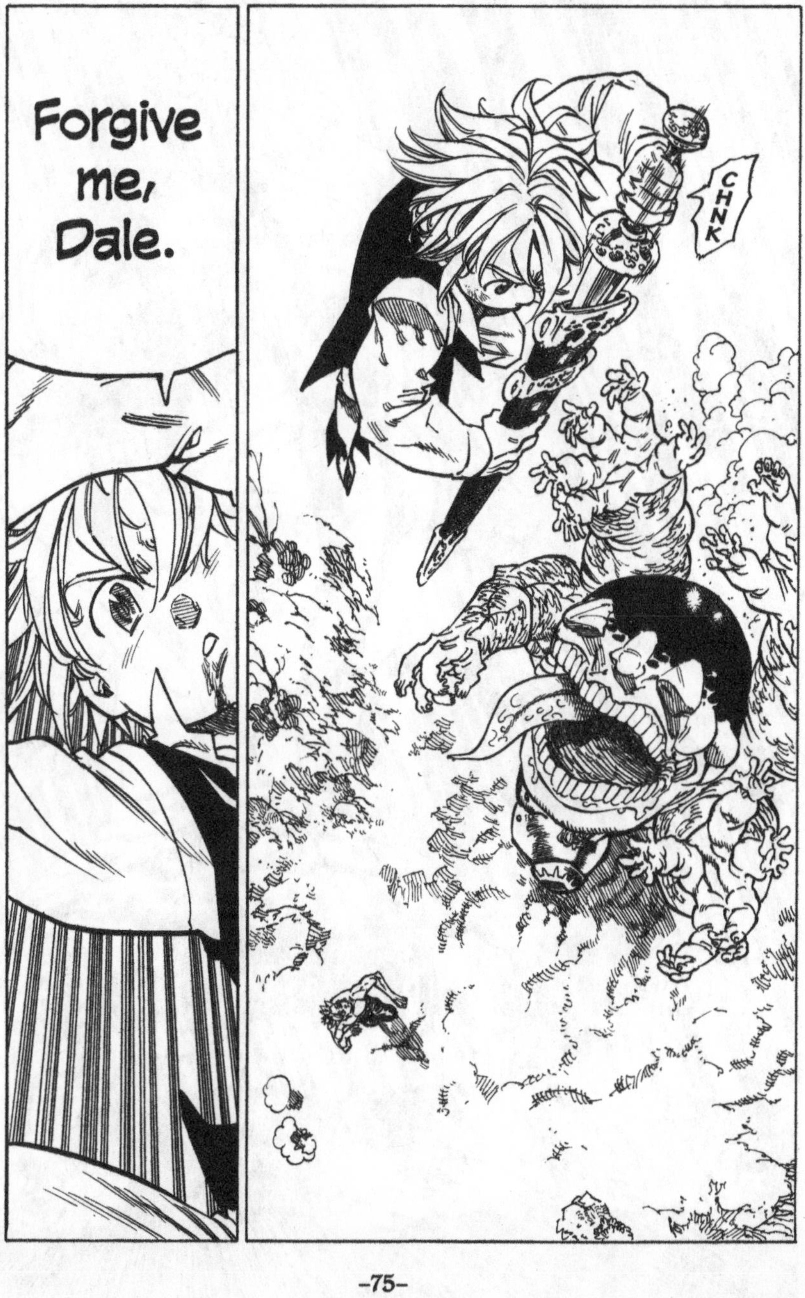
CHNK
Forgive me, Dale.

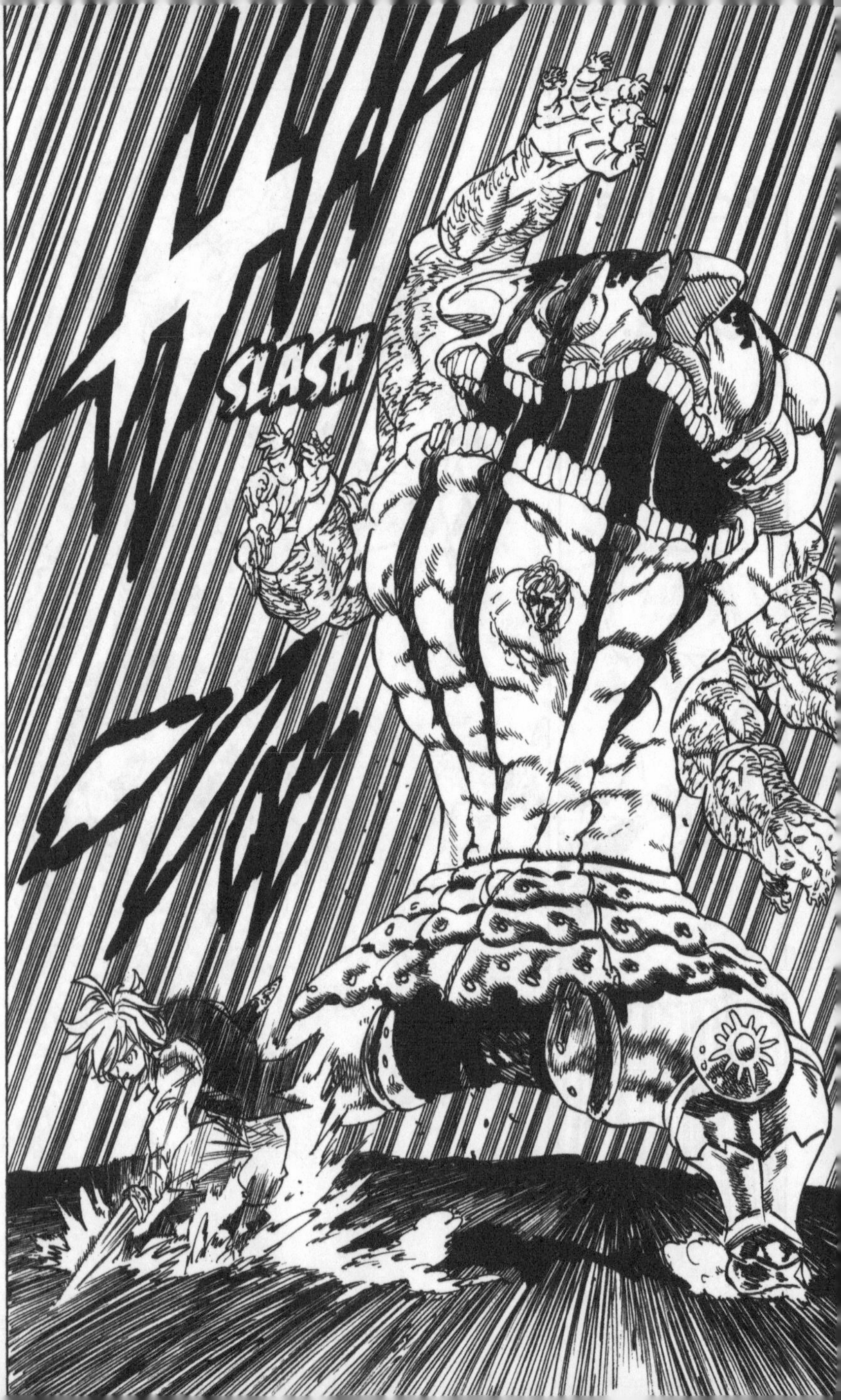
SLASH

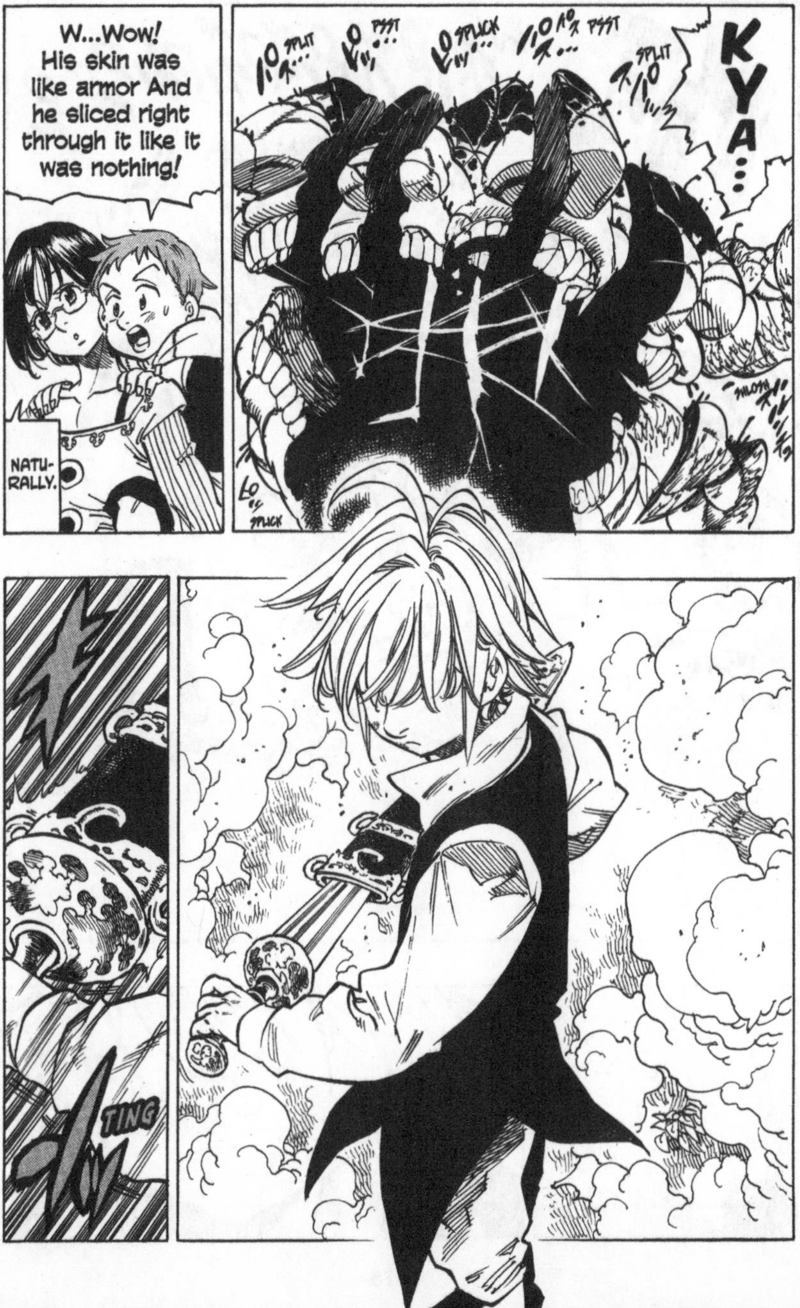
KYA...
SPLIT
PSST
SPLUCK
PSST
SPLIT
SPLUCK
W...Wow! His skin was like armor And he sliced right through it like it was nothing!
NATU-RALLY.
TING

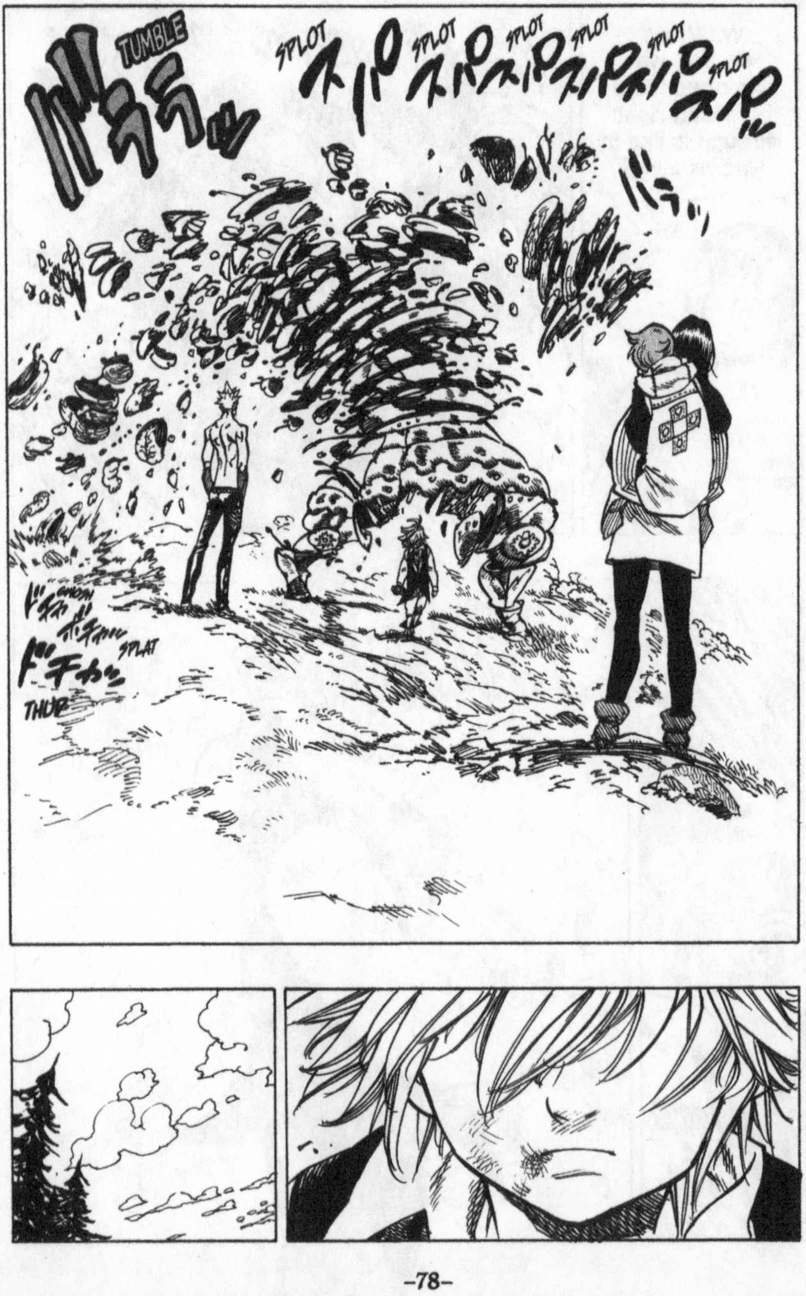
SPLOT
SPLOT
SPLOT
SPLOT
SPLOT
SPLOT
TUMBLE
GNOSH
SPLAT
THUD

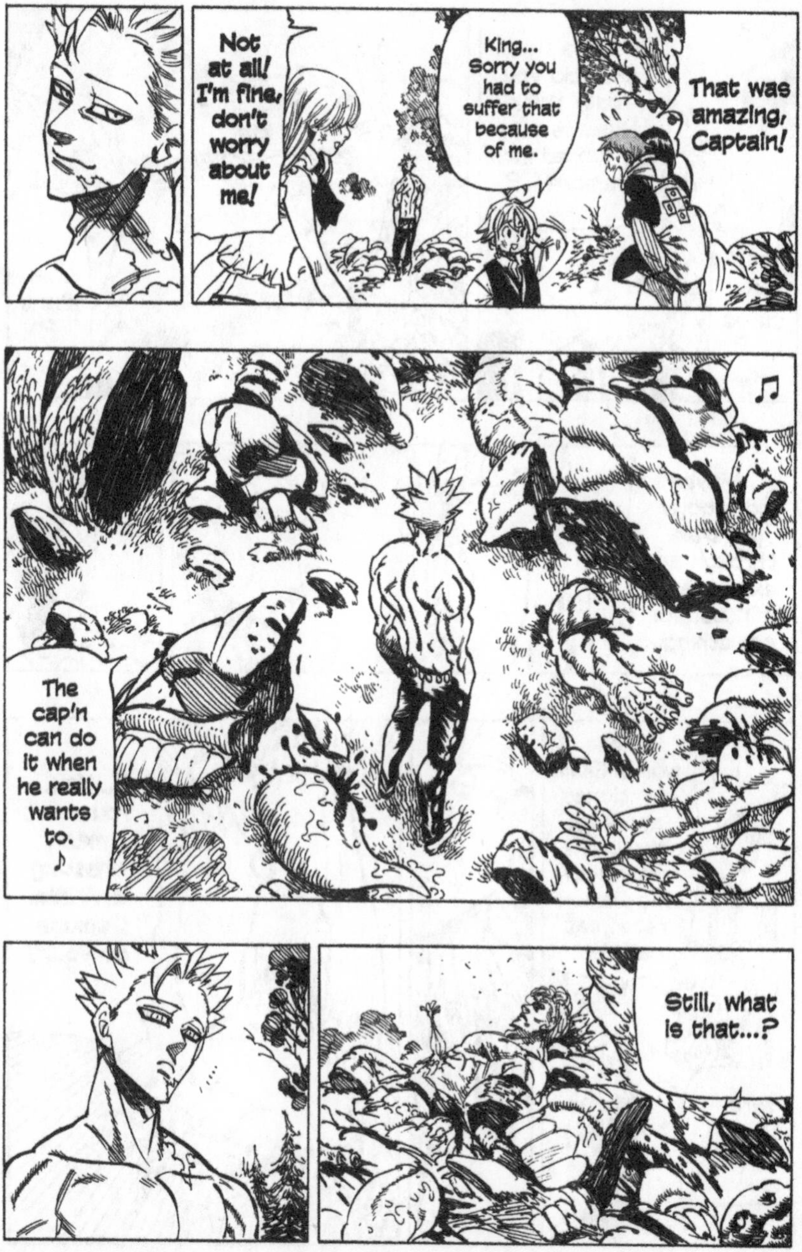
That was amazing, Captain!
King... Sorry you had to suffer that because of me.
Not at all! I'm fine, don't worry about me!
♫
The cap'n can do it when he really wants to. ♪
Still, what is that...?

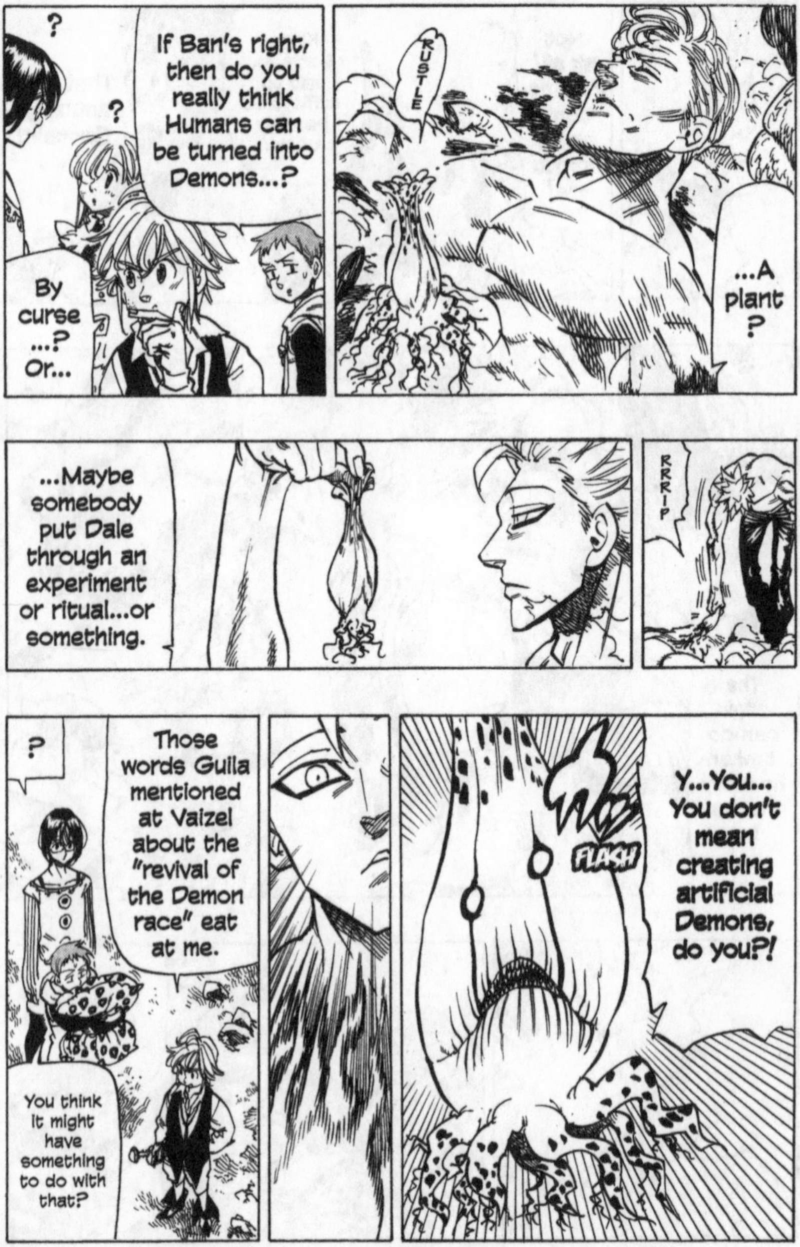
RUSTLE
...A plant?
?
?
If Ban's right, then do you really think Humans can be turned into Demons...?
By curse...? Or...
RRRIP
...Maybe somebody put Dale through an experiment or ritual...or something.
FLASH
Y...You... You don't mean creating artificial Demons, do you?!
?
Those words Guila mentioned at Vaizel about the "revival of the Demon race" eat at me.
You think it might have something to do with that?

...it means our opponents aren't only the Holy Knights anymore.

If it does...

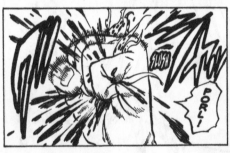

PORI!

PORI! PORI! PORI! PORI!

ISH

TOSS

Th... ank... y... ou...

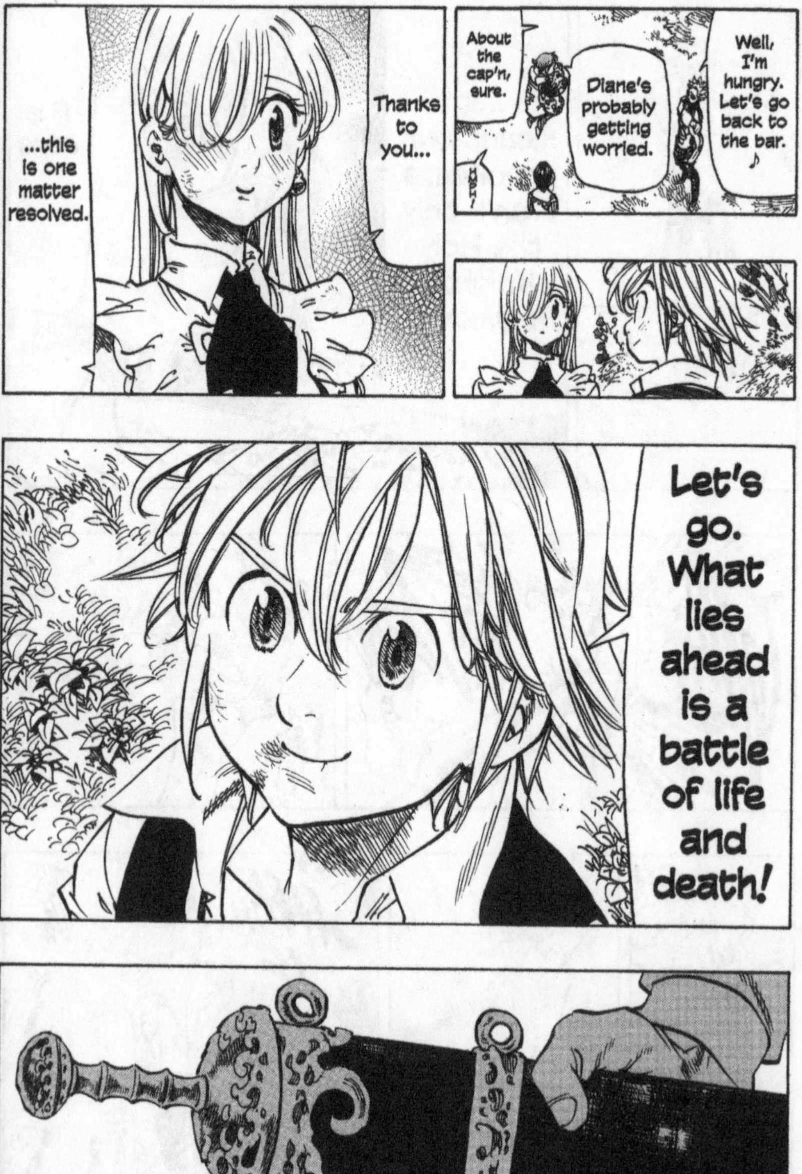
Well, I'm hungry. Let's go back to the bar. ♪
Diane's probably getting worried.
About the cap'n, sure.
Thanks to you...
...this is one matter resolved.
Let's go. What lies ahead is a battle of life and death!

Chapter 59 - The Unreadable Man

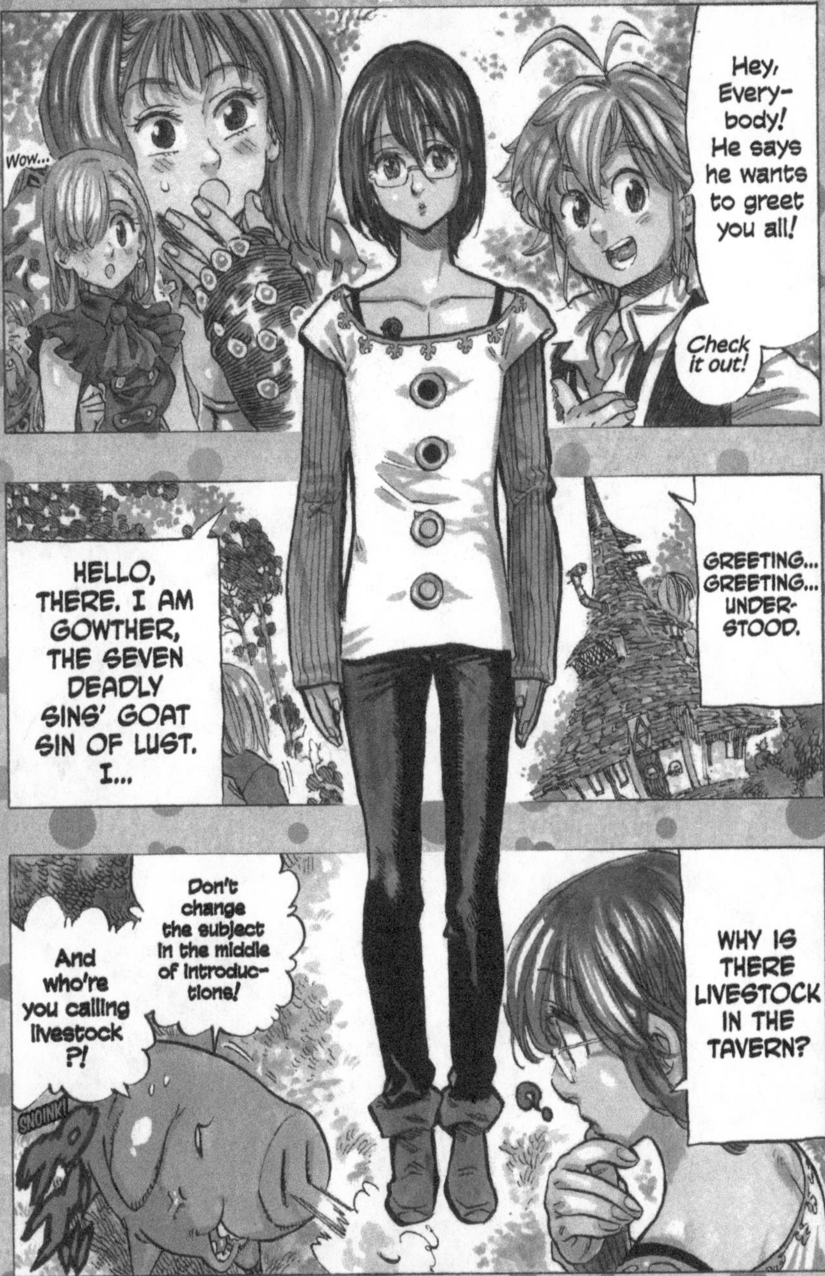
Hey, Everybody! He says he wants to greet you all!
Check it out!
Wow...
GREETING... GREETING... UNDERSTOOD.
HELLO, THERE. I AM GOWTHER, THE SEVEN DEADLY SINS' GOAT SIN OF LUST. I...
WHY IS THERE LIVESTOCK IN THE TAVERN?
Don't change the subject in the middle of introductions!
And who're you calling livestock ?!
SNOINK!

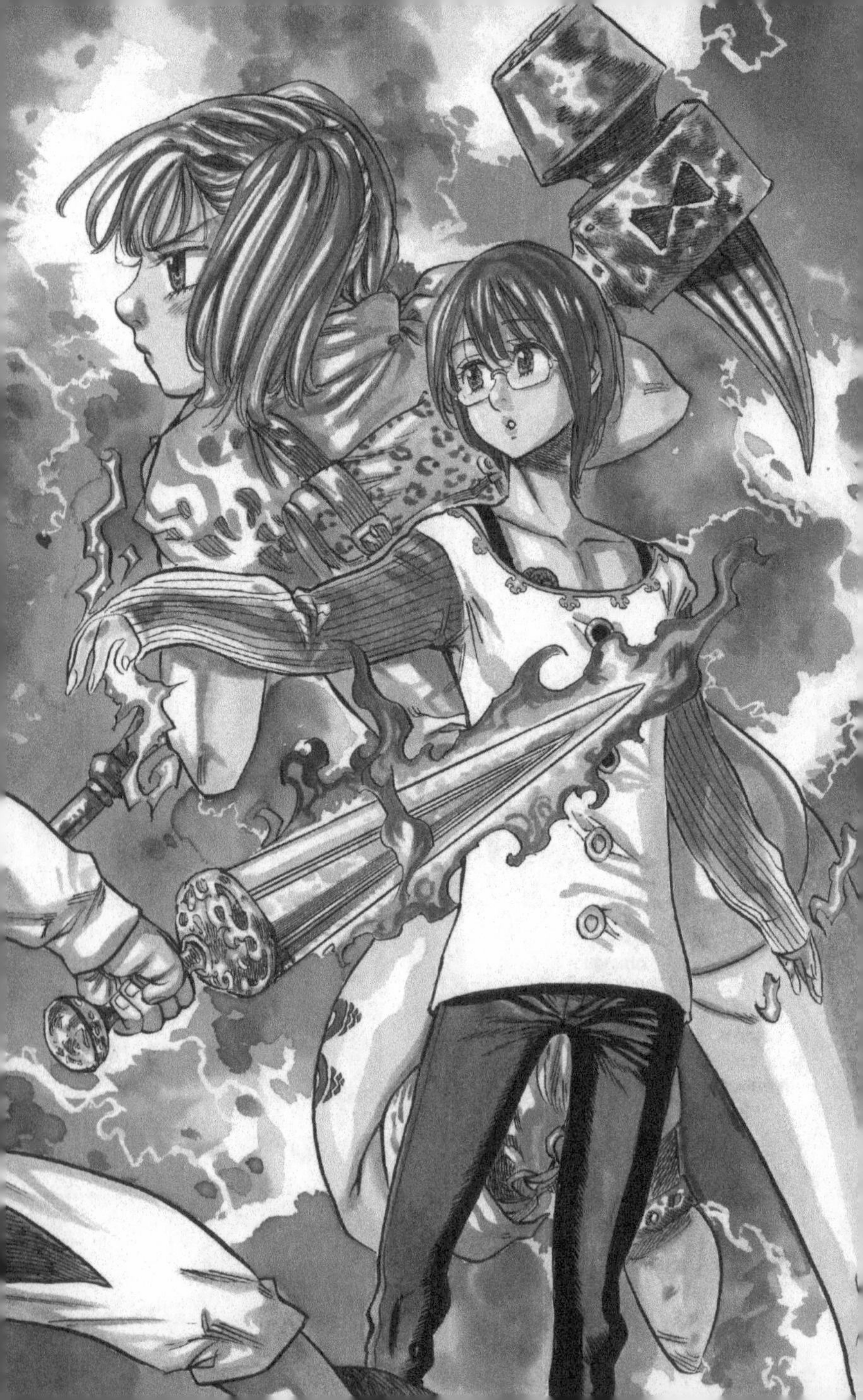

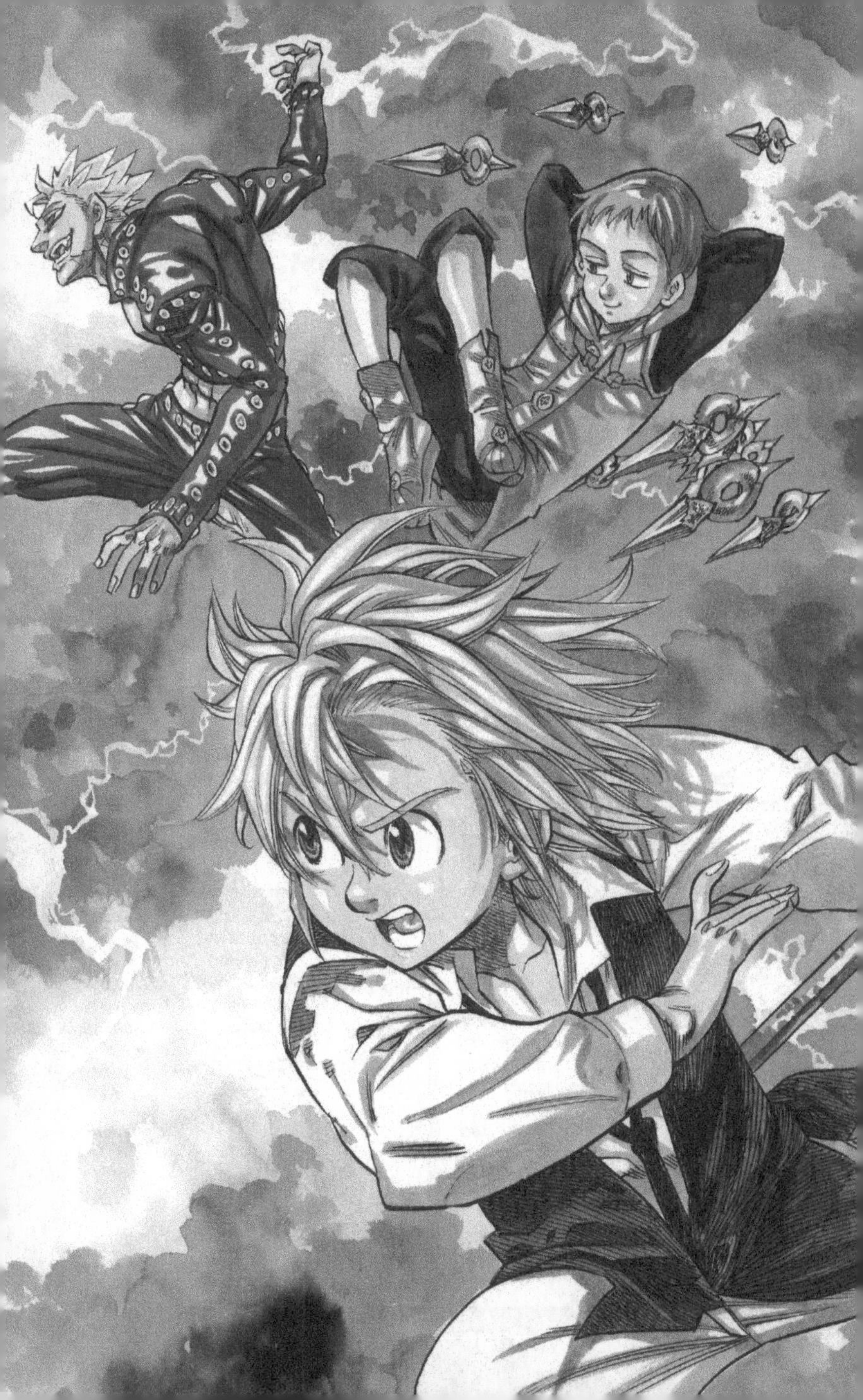

The Seven Deadly Sins Q&A Corner

Please include your name and location in your postcards!

"CHATTING KNIGHTHOOD" I

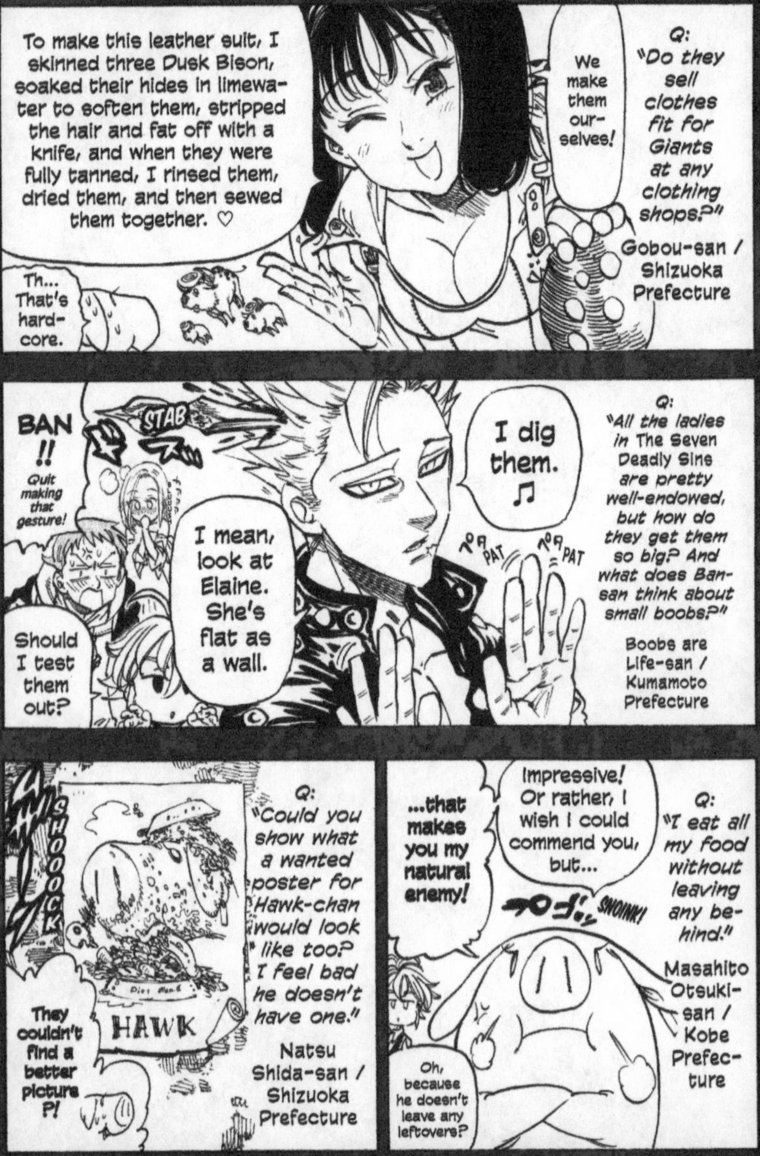

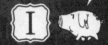

Q: "Do they sell clothes fit for Giants at any clothing shops?"
Gobou-san / Shizuoka Prefecture
We make them our-selves!
To make this leather suit, I skinned three Dusk Bison, soaked their hides in limewa-ter to soften them, stripped the hair and fat off with a knife, and when they were fully tanned, I rinsed them, dried them, and then sewed them together. ♡
Th... That's hard-core.
Q: "All the ladies in The Seven Deadly Sins are pretty well-endowed, but how do they get them so big? And what does Ban-san think about small boobs?"
Boobs are Life-san / Kumamoto Prefecture
I dig them. ♫
PAT PAT
STAB
BAN!! Quit making that gesture!
I mean, look at Elaine. She's flat as a wall.
Should I test them out?
Q: "I eat all my food without leaving any be-hind!"
Masahito Otsuki-san / Kobe Prefecture
Impressive! Or rather, I wish I could commend you, but...
...that makes you my natural enemy!
SNOINK!
Oh, because he doesn't leave any leftovers?
Q: "Could you show what a wanted poster for Hawk-chan would look like too? I feel bad he doesn't have one."
Natsu Shida-san / Shizuoka Prefecture
SHOOOCK
HAWK
They couldn't find a better picture?!

To Be Continued on Page 114

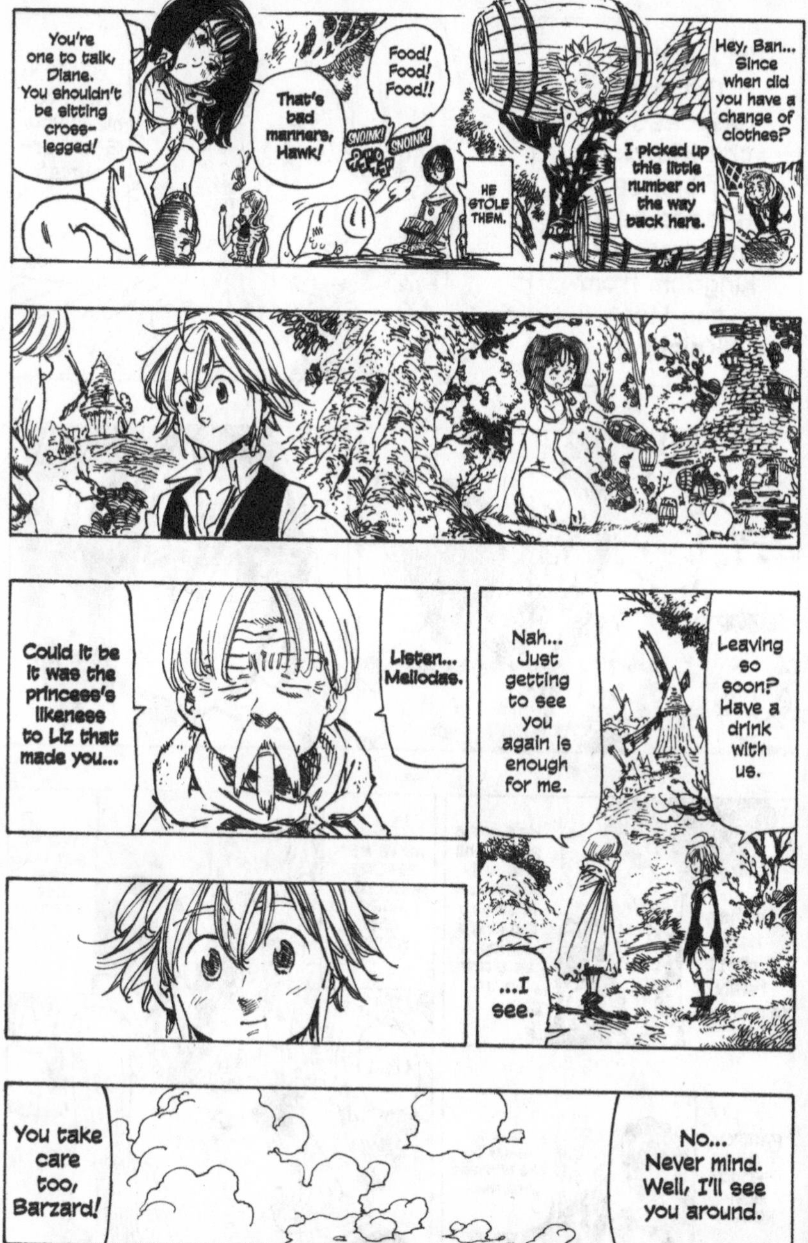
Hey, Ban... Since when did you have a change of clothes?
I picked up this little number on the way back here.
HE STOLE THEM.
Food! Food! Food!!
SNOINK!
SNOINK!
That's bad manners, Hawk!
You're one to talk, Diane. You shouldn't be sitting cross-legged!
Leaving so soon? Have a drink with us.
Nah... Just getting to see you again is enough for me.
...I see.
Listen... Meliodas.
Could it be it was the princess's likeness to Liz that made you...
No... Never mind. Well, I'll see you around.
You take care too, Barzard!

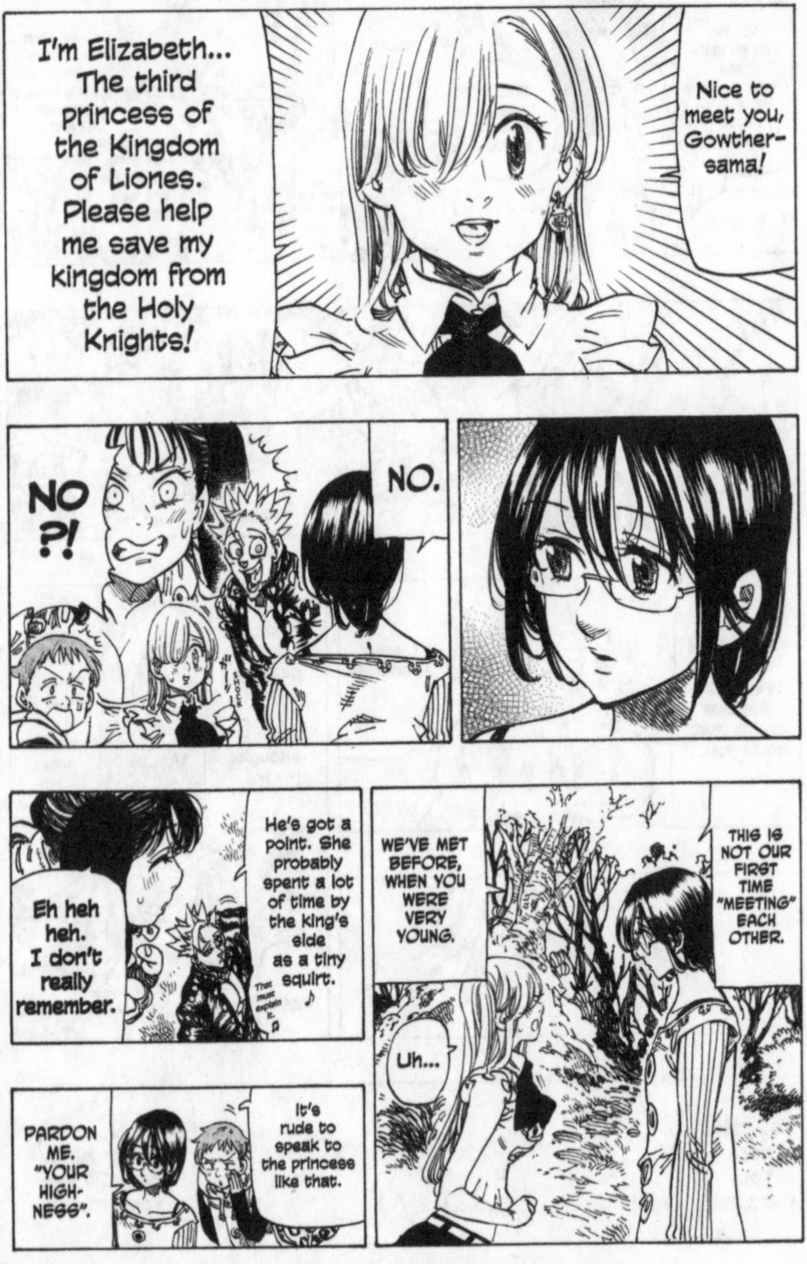
Nice to meet you, Gowther-sama!
I'm Elizabeth... The third princess of the Kingdom of Liones. Please help me save my kingdom from the Holy Knights!
NO.
NO ?!
SHOCK
THIS IS NOT OUR FIRST TIME "MEETING" EACH OTHER.
WE'VE MET BEFORE, WHEN YOU WERE VERY YOUNG.
Uh...
He's got a point. She probably spent a lot of time by the king's side as a tiny squirt. ♪
That must explain it. ♫
Eh heh heh. I don't really remember.
It's rude to speak to the princess like that.
PARDON ME. "YOUR HIGHNESS".

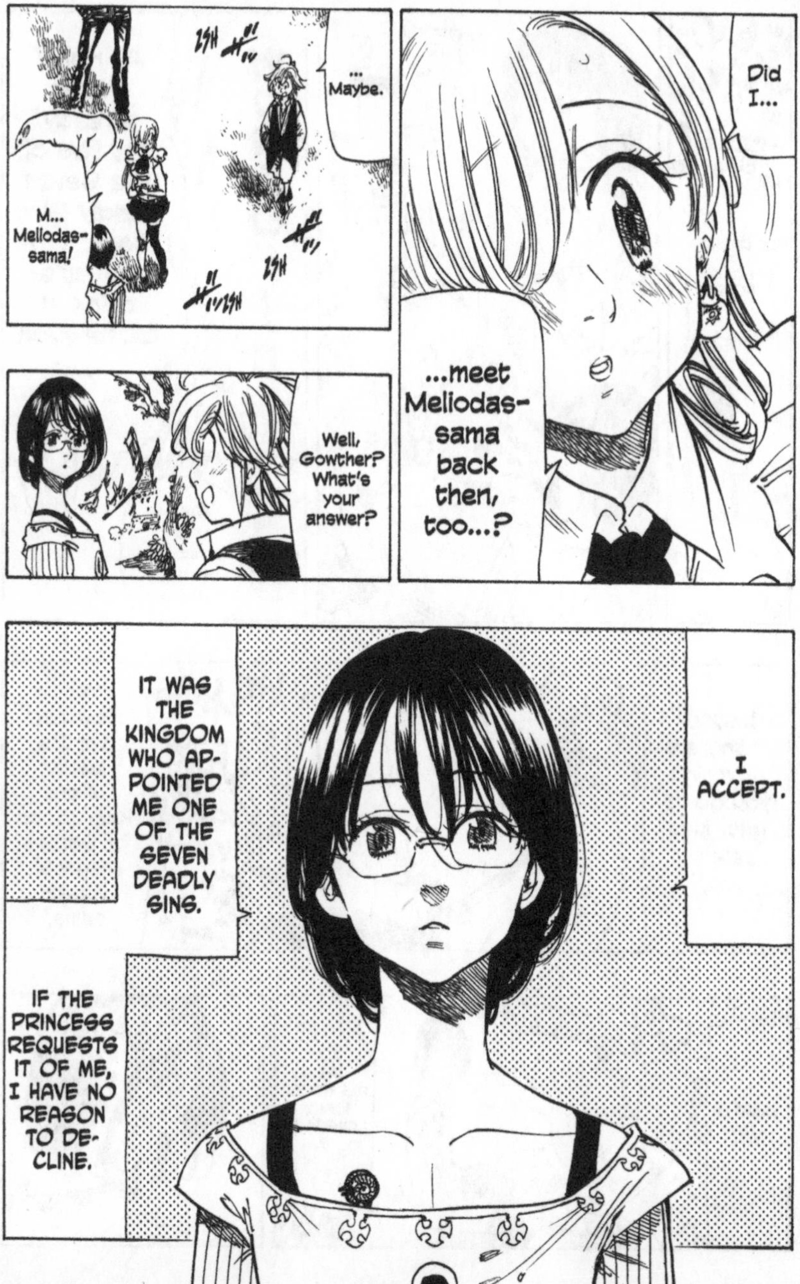
Did I...
...meet Meliodas-sama back then, too...?
...Maybe.
ZSH
ZSH
ZSH
M... Meliodas-sama!
Well, Gowther? What's your answer?
I ACCEPT.
IT WAS THE KINGDOM WHO APPOINTED ME ONE OF THE SEVEN DEADLY SINS.
IF THE PRINCESS REQUESTS IT OF ME, I HAVE NO REASON TO DECLINE.

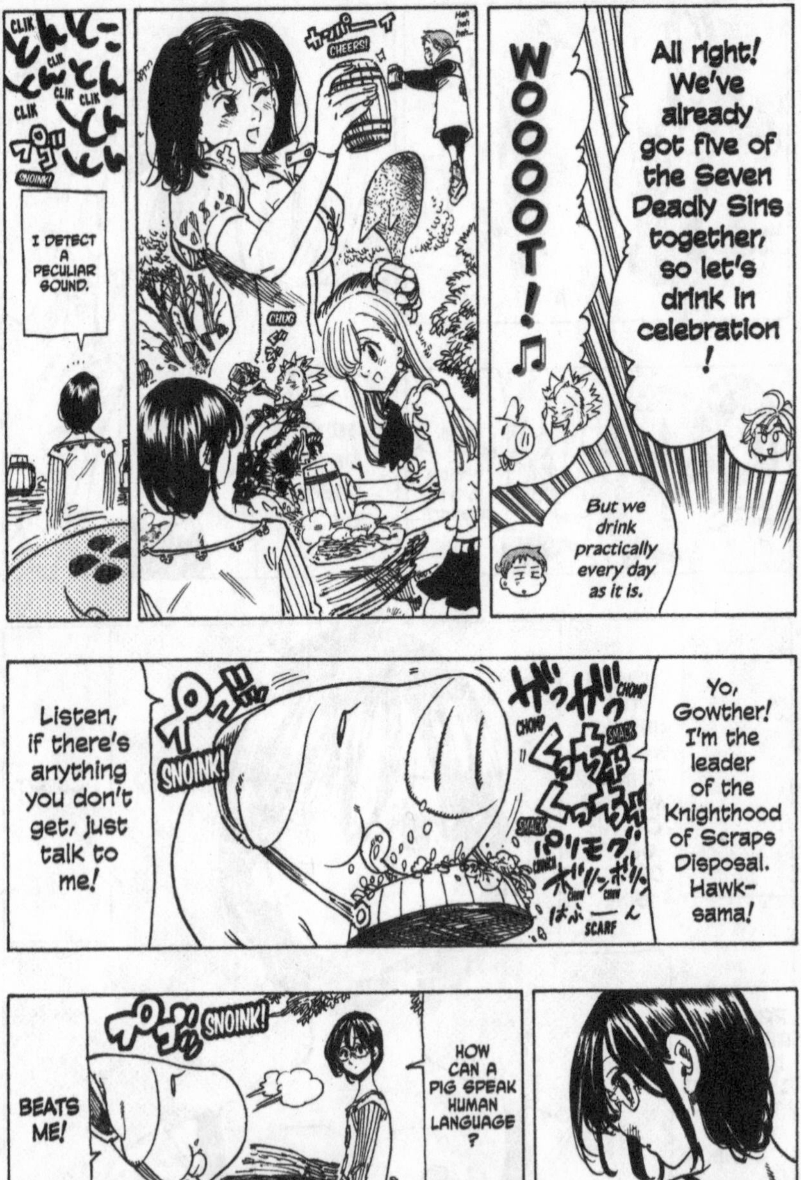
All right! We've already got five of the Seven Deadly Sins together, so let's drink in celebration!
WOOOOOT! ♫
But we drink practically every day as it is.
CHEERS!
Heh heh heh...
CHUG
CLIK
CLIK
CLIK
CLIK
CLIK
SNOINK!
I DETECT A PECULIAR SOUND.
Yo, Gowther! I'm the leader of the Knighthood of Scraps Disposal. Hawk-sama!
CHOMP
CHOMP
SMACK
SMACK
CRUNCH
CHEW
CHEW
SCARF
SNOINK!
Listen, if there's anything you don't get, just talk to me!
HOW CAN A PIG SPEAK HUMAN LANGUAGE?
SNOINK!
BEATS ME!

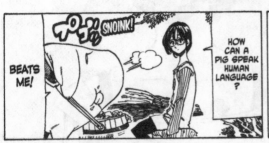

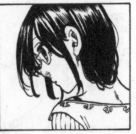

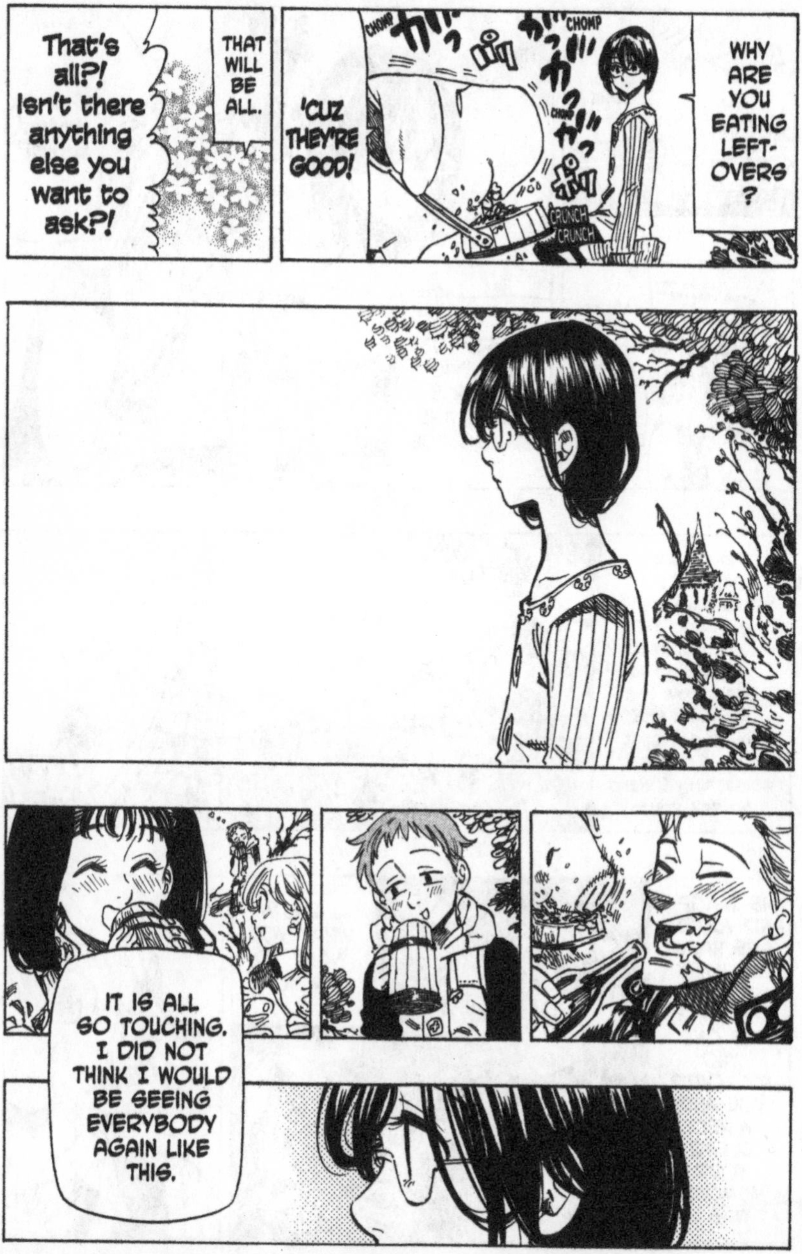
WHY ARE YOU EATING LEFT-OVERS?
CHOMP
CHOMP
CHOMP
CRUNCH CRUNCH
'CUZ THEY'RE GOOD!
THAT WILL BE ALL.
That's all?! Isn't there anything else you want to ask?!
IT IS ALL SO TOUCHING. I DID NOT THINK I WOULD BE SEEING EVERYBODY AGAIN LIKE THIS.

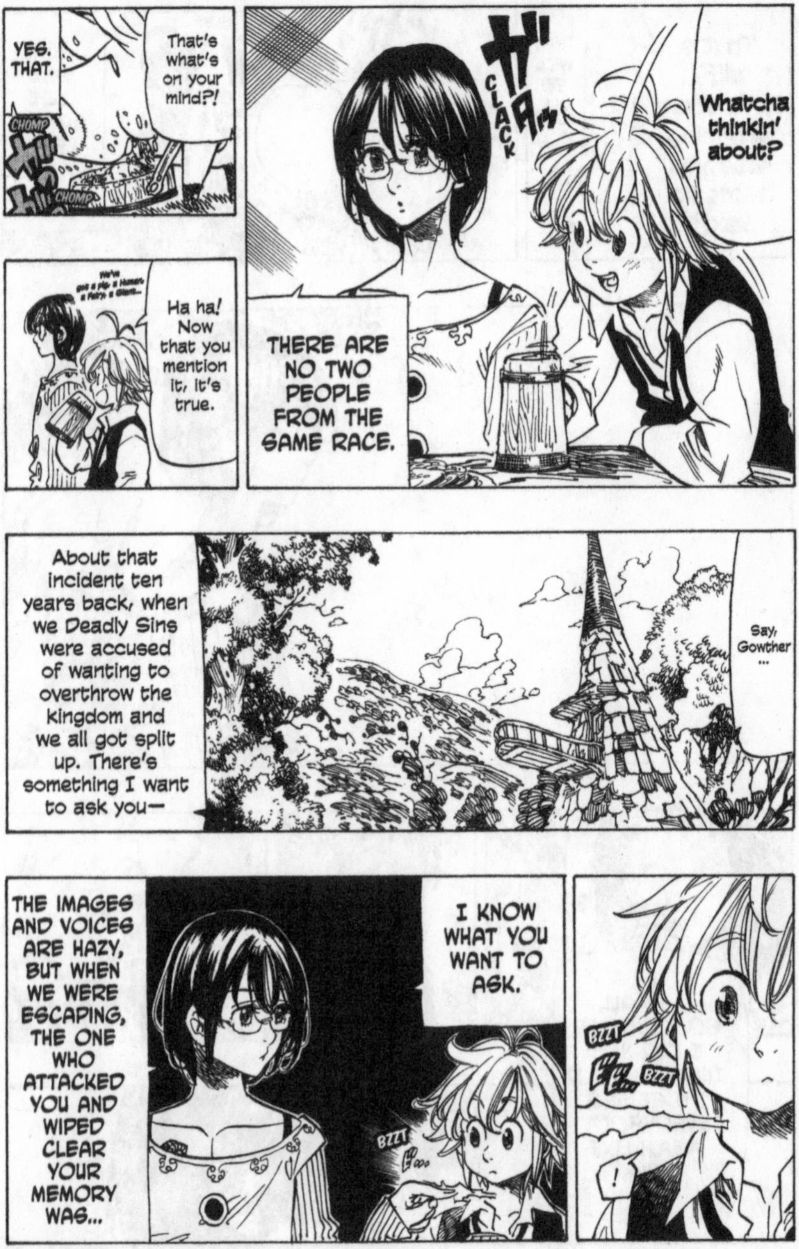
Whatcha thinkin' about?
CLACK
THERE ARE NO TWO PEOPLE FROM THE SAME RACE.
That's what's on your mind?!
YES. THAT.
CHOMP
CHOMP
We've got a pig, a Human, a Fairy, a Giant...
Ha ha! Now that you mention it, it's true.
Say, Gowther...
About that incident ten years back, when we Deadly Sins were accused of wanting to overthrow the kingdom and we all got split up. There's something I want to ask you—
BZZT
BZZT
!
I KNOW WHAT YOU WANT TO ASK.
THE IMAGES AND VOICES ARE HAZY, BUT WHEN WE WERE ESCAPING, THE ONE WHO ATTACKED YOU AND WIPED CLEAR YOUR MEMORY WAS...
BZZT

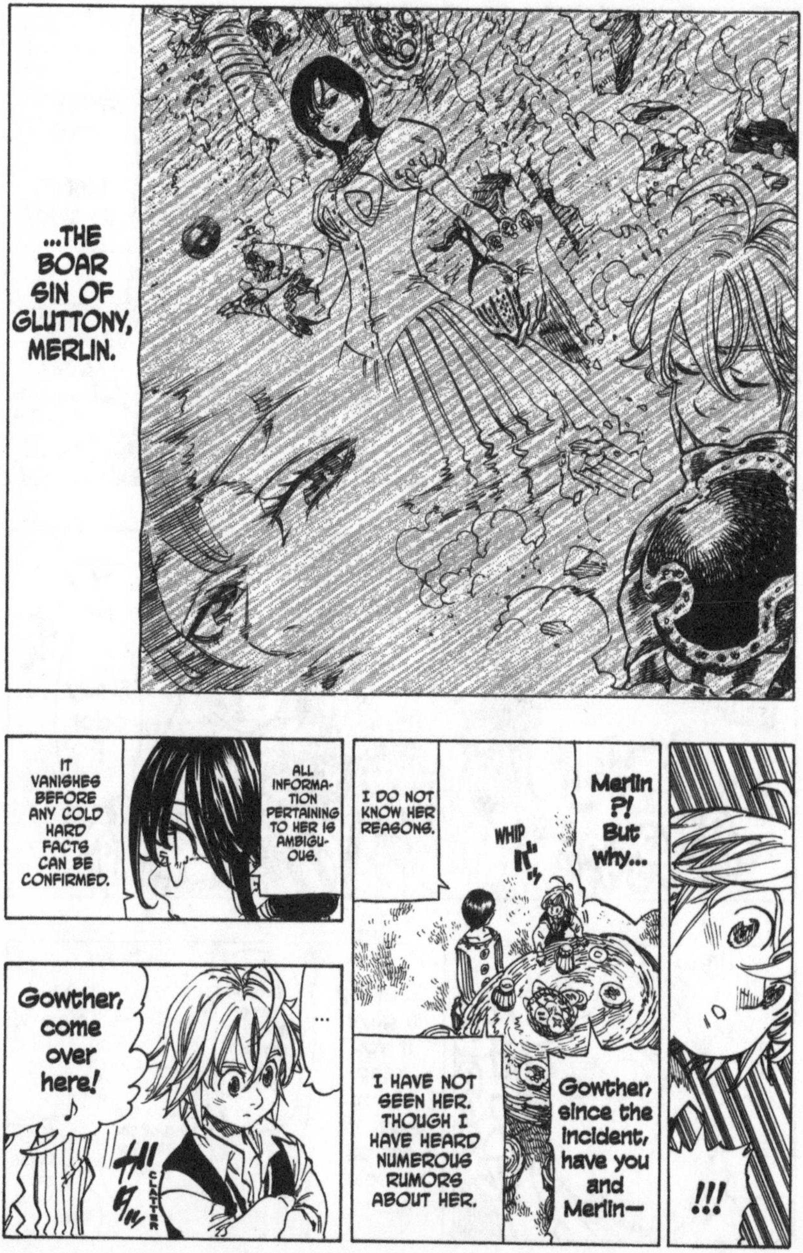
...THE BOAR SIN OF GLUTTONY, MERLIN.
!!!
Merlin?! But why...
I DO NOT KNOW HER REASONS.
WHIP
Gowther, since the incident, have you and Merlin—
I HAVE NOT SEEN HER. THOUGH I HAVE HEARD NUMEROUS RUMORS ABOUT HER.
ALL INFORMATION PERTAINING TO HER IS AMBIGUOUS.
IT VANISHES BEFORE ANY COLD HARD FACTS CAN BE CONFIRMED.
...
Gowther, come over here! ♪
CLATTER

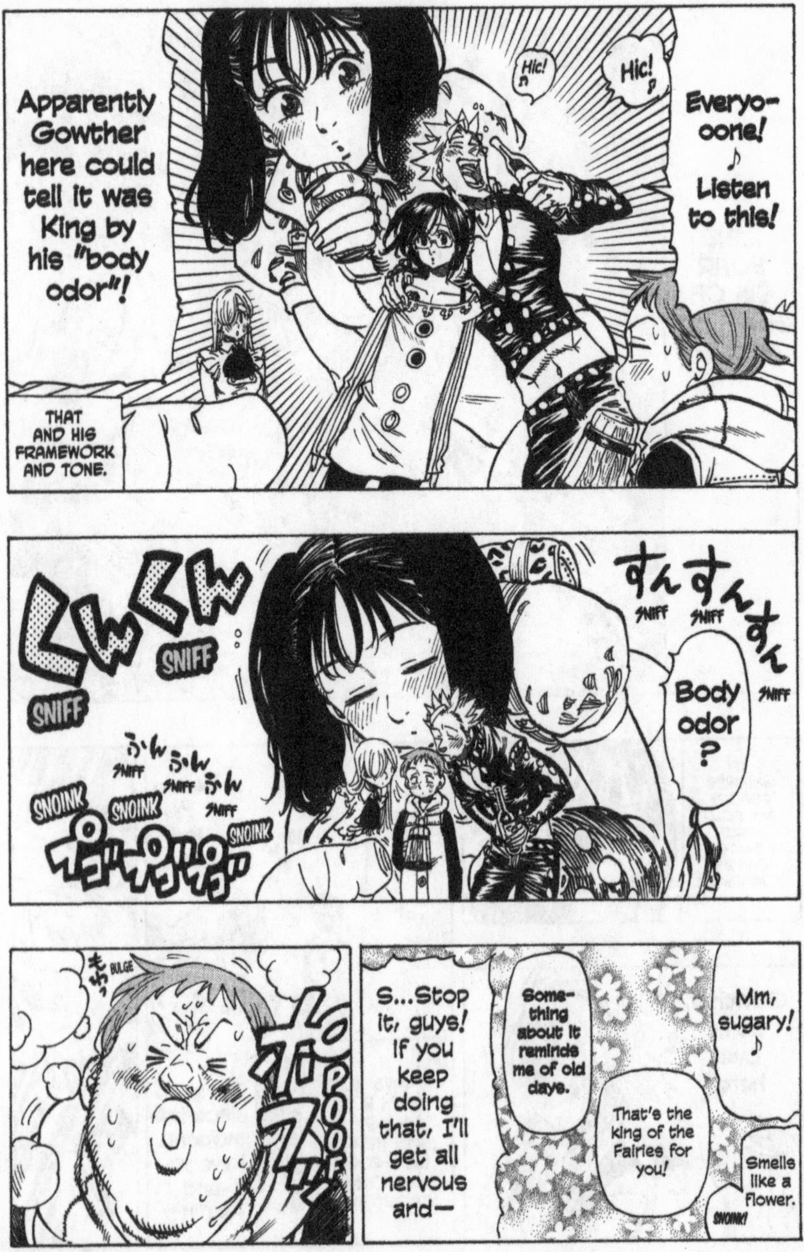
Hic! ♪
Hic! ♪
Everyo-oone! ♪ Listen to this!
Apparently Gowther here could tell it was King by his "body odor"!
THAT AND HIS FRAMEWORK AND TONE.
すんすんすん
SNIFF SNIFF SNIFF
Body odor?
くんくん
SNIFF
SNIFF
ふんふんふん
SNIFF SNIFF SNIFF
SNOINK SNOINK SNOINK
プゴプゴプゴ
Mm, sugary! ♪
Something about it reminds me of old days.
That's the king of the Fairies for you!
Smells like a flower.
SNOINK!
S...Stop it, guys! If you keep doing that, I'll get all nervous and—
ポフッ
POOOF
もわっ
BULGE

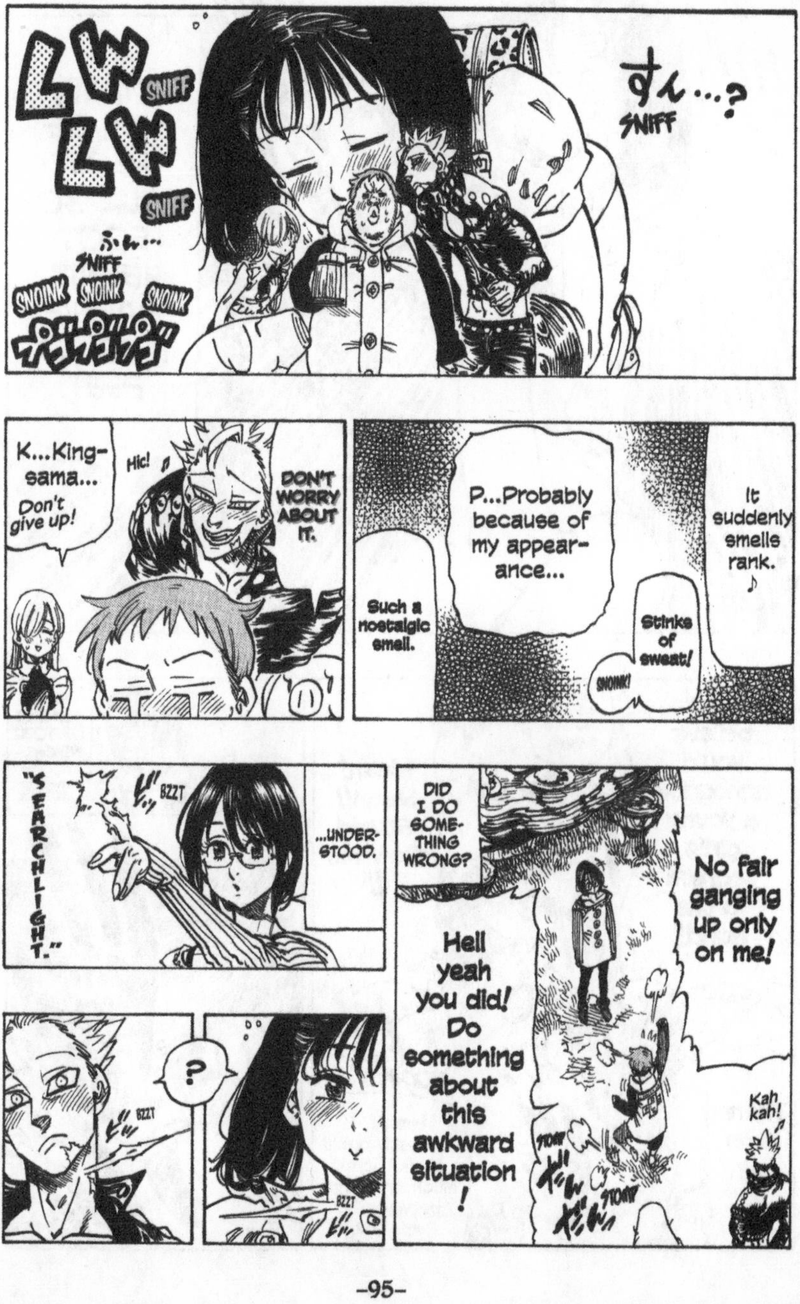
すん…?
SNIFF
SNIFF
SNIFF
ふん…
SNIFF
SNOINK SNOINK SNOINK
It suddenly smells rank. ♪
P...Probably because of my appearance...
Stinks of sweat!
SNOINK!
Such a nostalgic smell.
DON'T WORRY ABOUT IT.
Hic! ♪
K...King-sama... Don't give up!
DID I DO SOMETHING WRONG?
No fair ganging up only on me!
Hell yeah you did! Do something about this awkward situation!
STOMP
STOMP
Kah kah! ♪
...UNDERSTOOD.
BZZT
"SEARCHLIGHT."
?
BZZT
BZZT

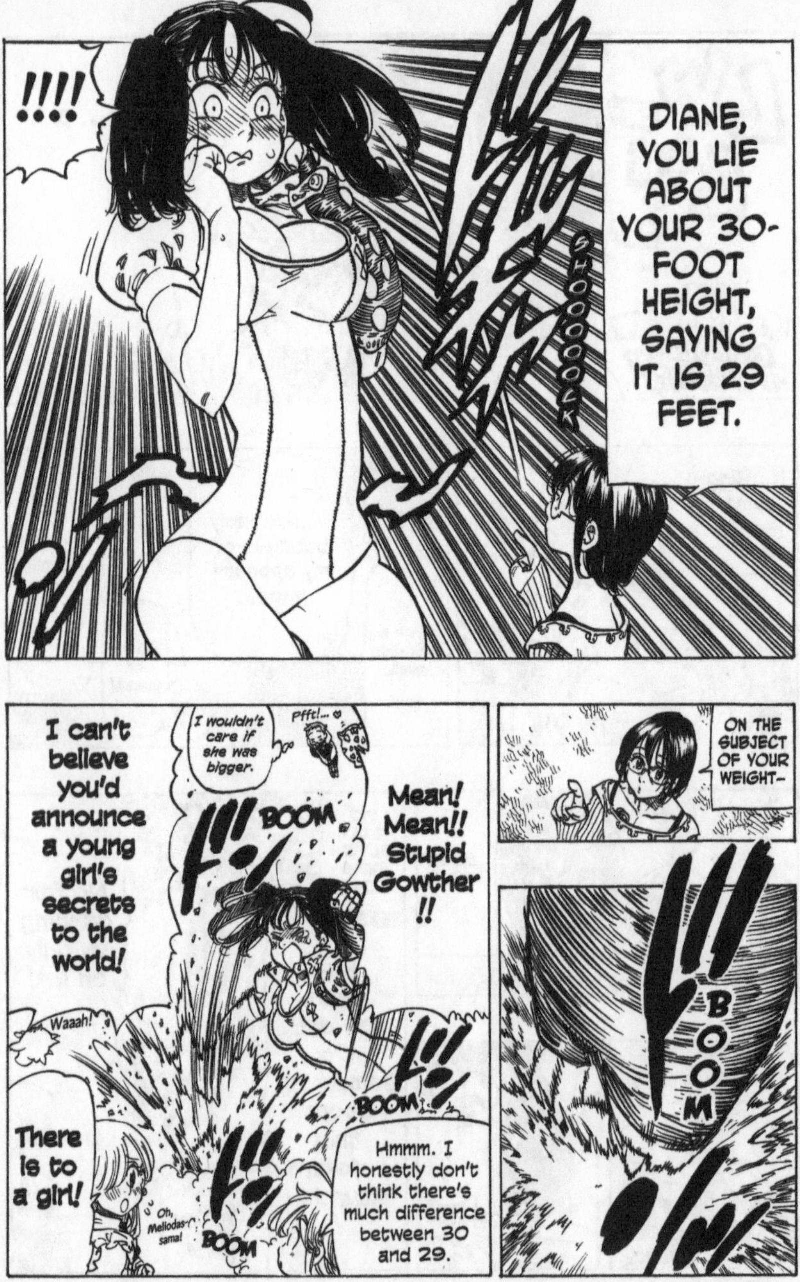
DIANE, YOU LIE ABOUT YOUR 30-FOOT HEIGHT, SAYING IT IS 29 FEET.
SHOOOOOOCK
!!!!
ON THE SUBJECT OF YOUR WEIGHT-
BOOM
Mean! Mean!! Stupid Gowther!!
Pfft!...
I wouldn't care if she was bigger.
BOOM
I can't believe you'd announce a young girl's secrets to the world!
BOOM
Waaah!
Hmmm. I honestly don't think there's much difference between 30 and 29.
BOOM
Oh, Meliodas-sama!
There is to a girl!

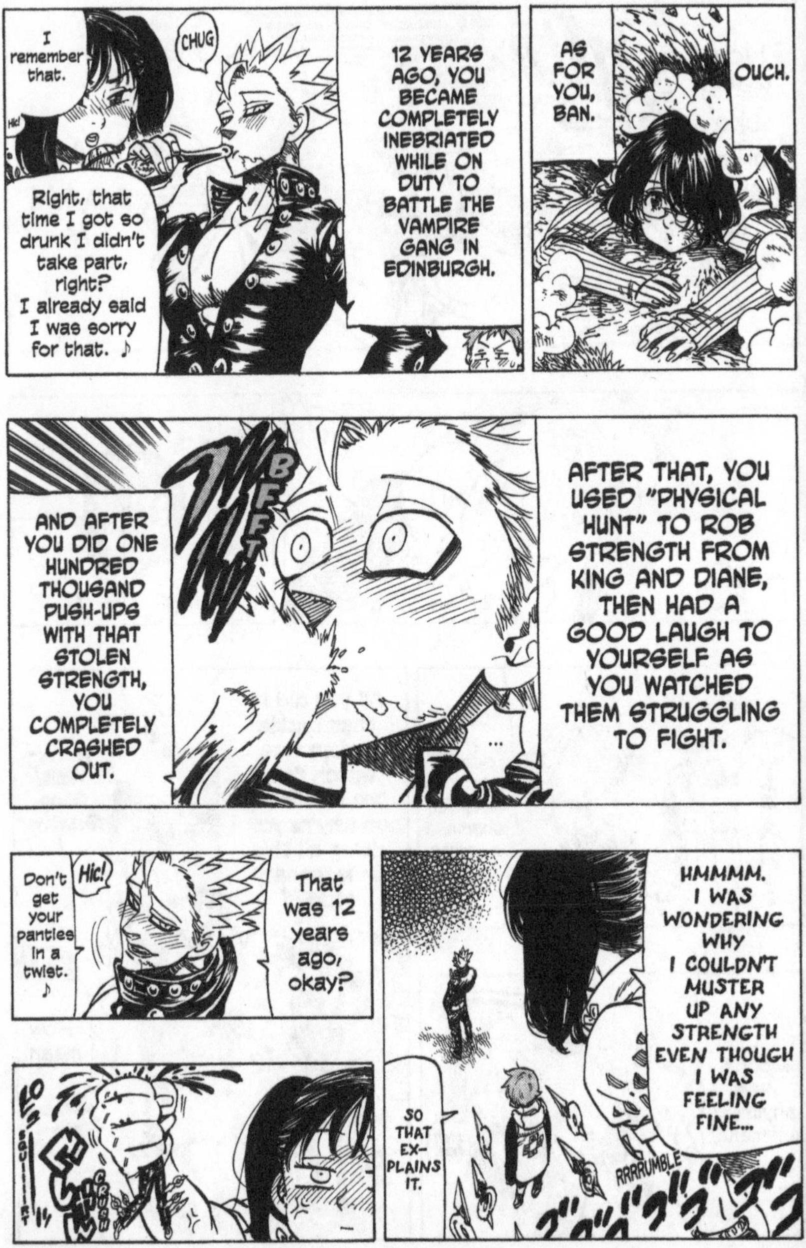
AS FOR YOU, BAN.
OUCH.
12 YEARS AGO, YOU BECAME COMPLETELY INEBRIATED WHILE ON DUTY TO BATTLE THE VAMPIRE GANG IN EDINBURGH.
CHUG
I remember that.
Hic!
Right, that time I got so drunk I didn't take part, right? I already said I was sorry for that. ♪
AFTER THAT, YOU USED "PHYSICAL HUNT" TO ROB STRENGTH FROM KING AND DIANE, THEN HAD A GOOD LAUGH TO YOURSELF AS YOU WATCHED THEM STRUGGLING TO FIGHT.
BFFFT
...
AND AFTER YOU DID ONE HUNDRED THOUSAND PUSH-UPS WITH THAT STOLEN STRENGTH, YOU COMPLETELY CRASHED OUT.
HMMMM. I WAS WONDERING WHY I COULDN'T MUSTER UP ANY STRENGTH EVEN THOUGH I WAS FEELING FINE...
SO THAT EX-PLAINS IT.
RRRRUMBLE
That was 12 years ago, okay?
Hic!
Don't get your panties in a twist. ♪
SQUIIIRT

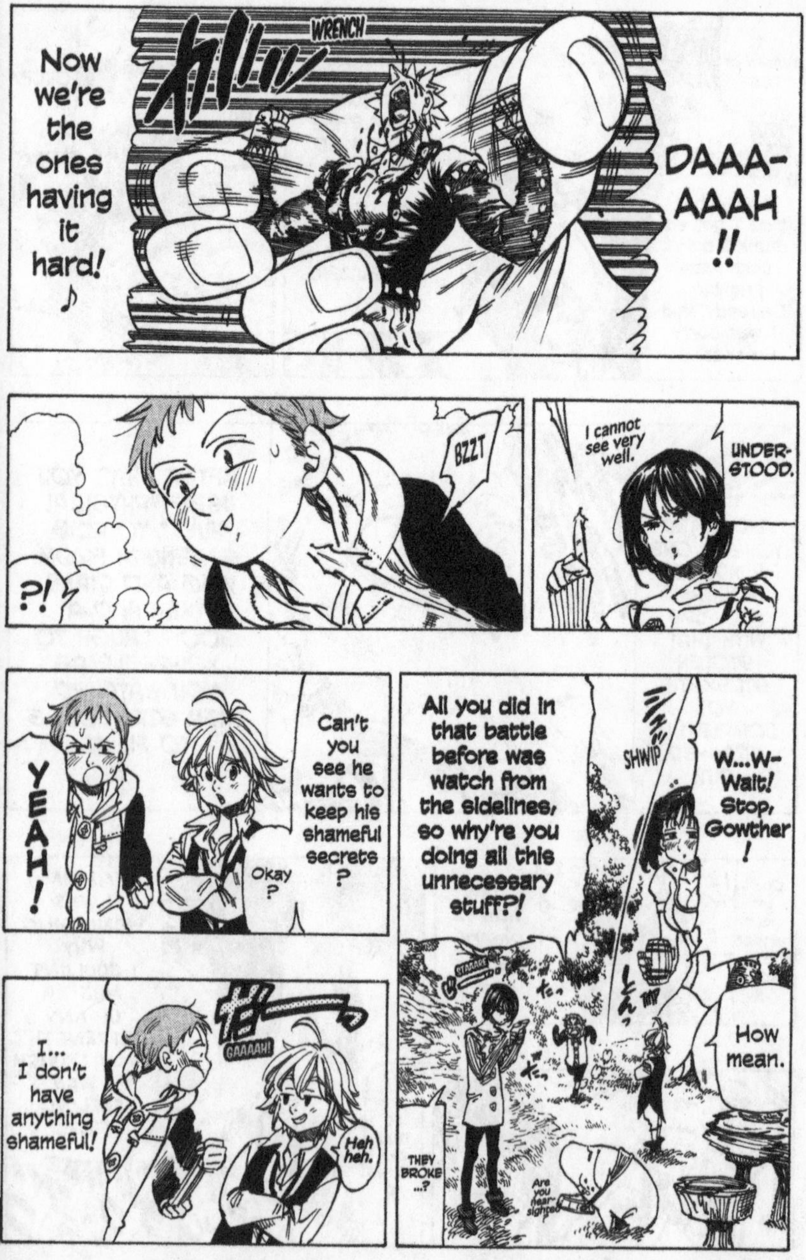
WRENCH
DAAAAAAH!!
Now we're the ones having it hard! ♪
UNDERSTOOD.
I cannot see very well.
BZZT
?!
SHWIP
W...W-Wait! Stop, Gowther!
All you did in that battle before was watch from the sidelines, so why're you doing all this unnecessary stuff?!
STAAARE
How mean.
THEY BROKE ...?
Are you near-sighted?
Can't you see he wants to keep his shameful secrets?
Okay?
YEAH!
GAAAAH!
Heh heh.
I... I don't have anything shameful!

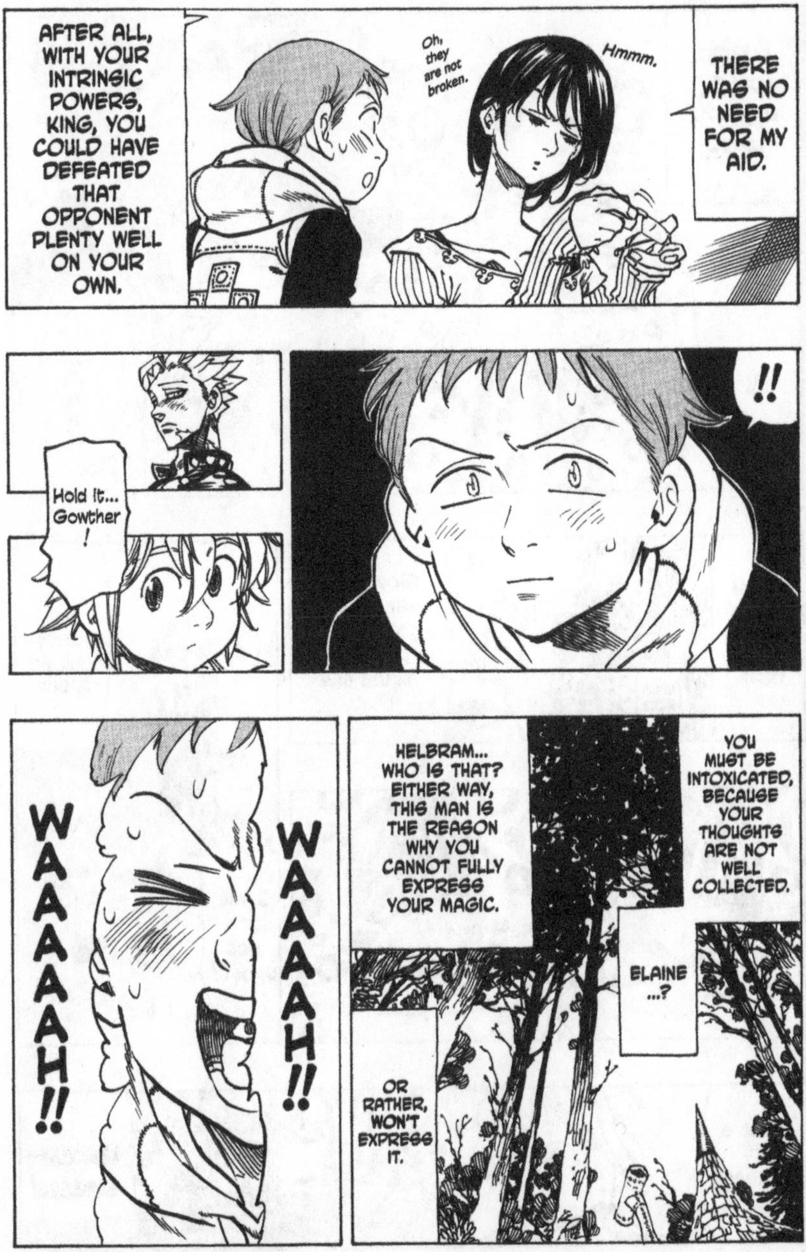
THERE WAS NO NEED FOR MY AID.
Hmmm.
Oh, they are not broken.
AFTER ALL, WITH YOUR INTRINSIC POWERS, KING, YOU COULD HAVE DEFEATED THAT OPPONENT PLENTY WELL ON YOUR OWN.
!!
Hold it... Gowther!
YOU MUST BE INTOXICATED, BECAUSE YOUR THOUGHTS ARE NOT WELL COLLECTED.
HELBRAM... WHO IS THAT? EITHER WAY, THIS MAN IS THE REASON WHY YOU CANNOT FULLY EXPRESS YOUR MAGIC.
ELAINE ...?
OR RATHER, WON'T EXPRESS IT.
WAAAAAH!!
WAAAAAH!!

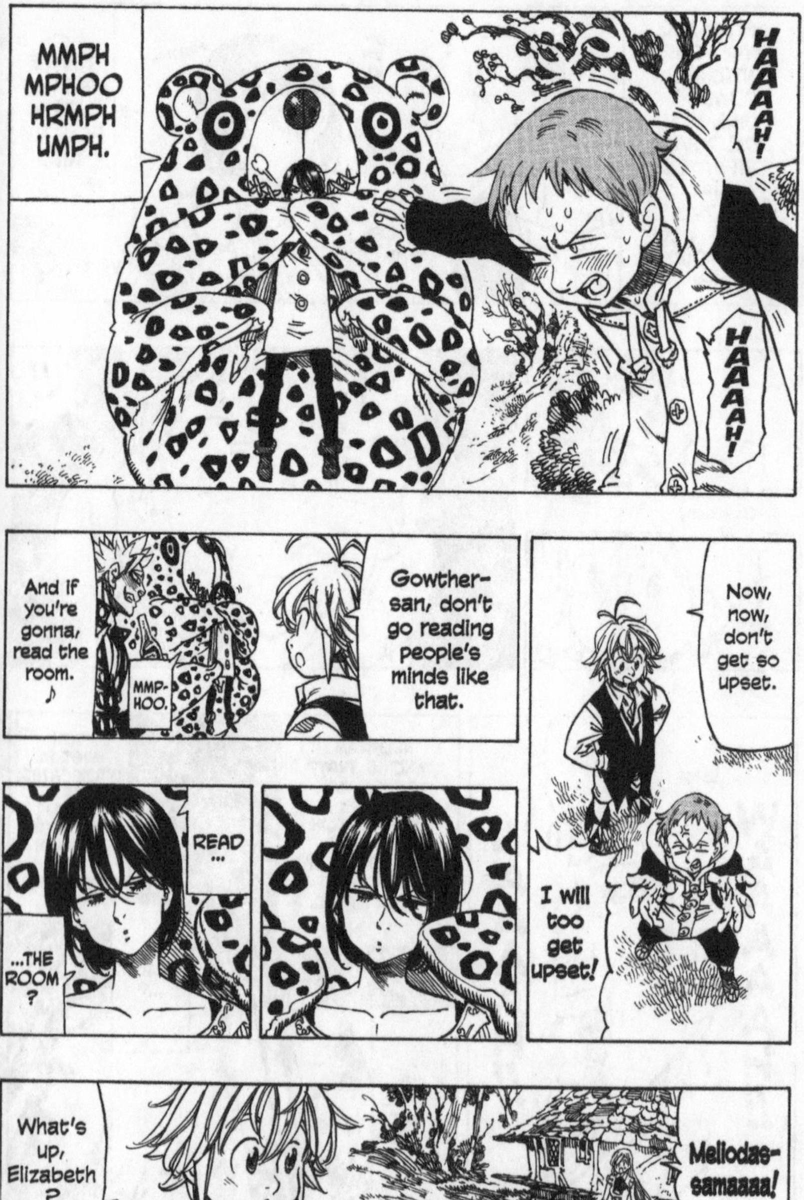
HAAAAH!
HAAAAH!
MMPH MPHOO HRMPH UMPH.
Now, now, don't get so upset.
I will too get upset!
Gowther-san, don't go reading people's minds like that.
And if you're gonna, read the room. ♪
MMP-HOO.
READ ...
...THE ROOM ?
Meliodas-samaaaa!
What's up, Elizabeth ?

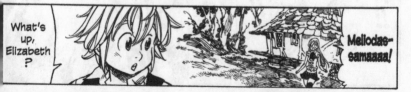

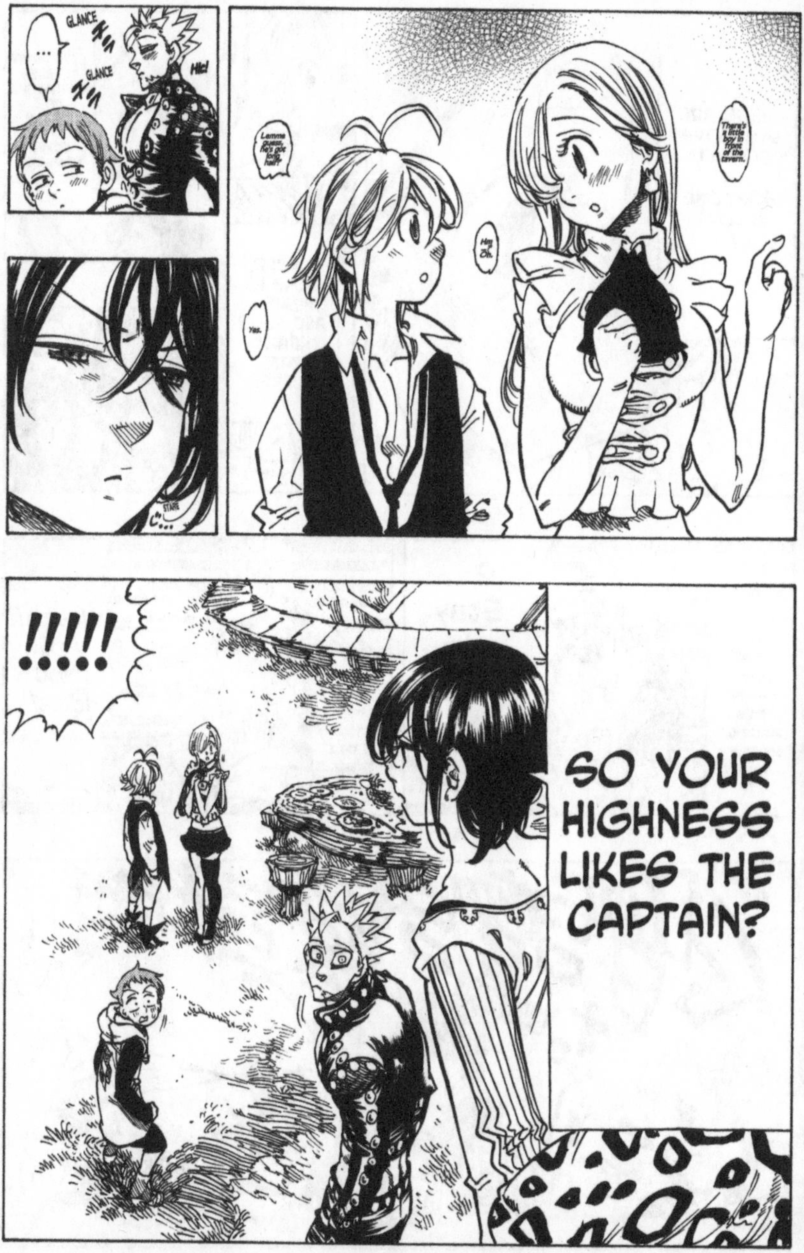
There's a little boy in front of the tavern.
Hm? Oh.
Lemme guess, he's got long hair?
Yes.
...
GLANCE
GLANCE
Hic!
STARE
!!!!!
SO YOUR HIGHNESS LIKES THE CAPTAIN?

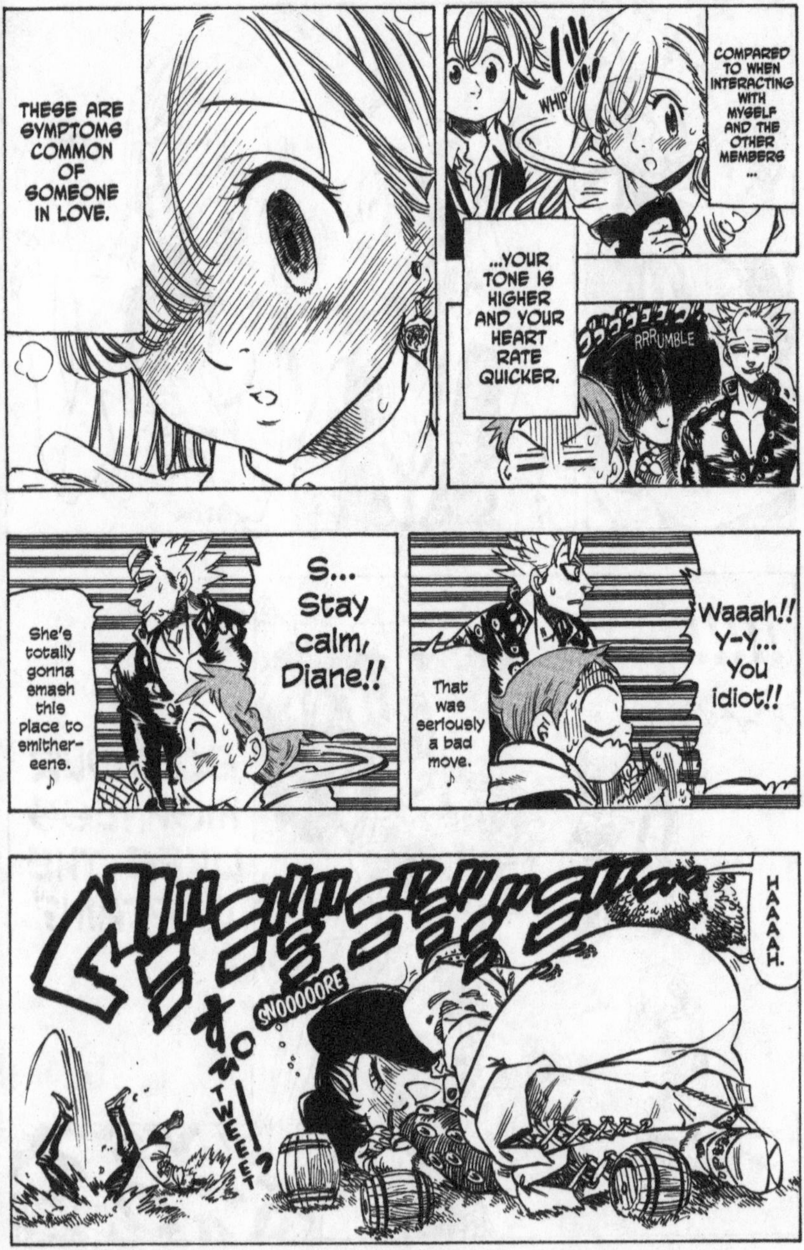
COMPARED TO WHEN INTERACTING WITH MYSELF AND THE OTHER MEMBERS ...
WHIP
...YOUR TONE IS HIGHER AND YOUR HEART RATE QUICKER.
RRRUMBLE
THESE ARE SYMPTOMS COMMON OF SOMEONE IN LOVE.
Waaah!! Y-Y... You idiot!!
That was seriously a bad move. ♪
S... Stay calm, Diane!!
She's totally gonna smash this place to smithereens. ♪
HAAAAH.
SNOOOOORE
TWEEEET

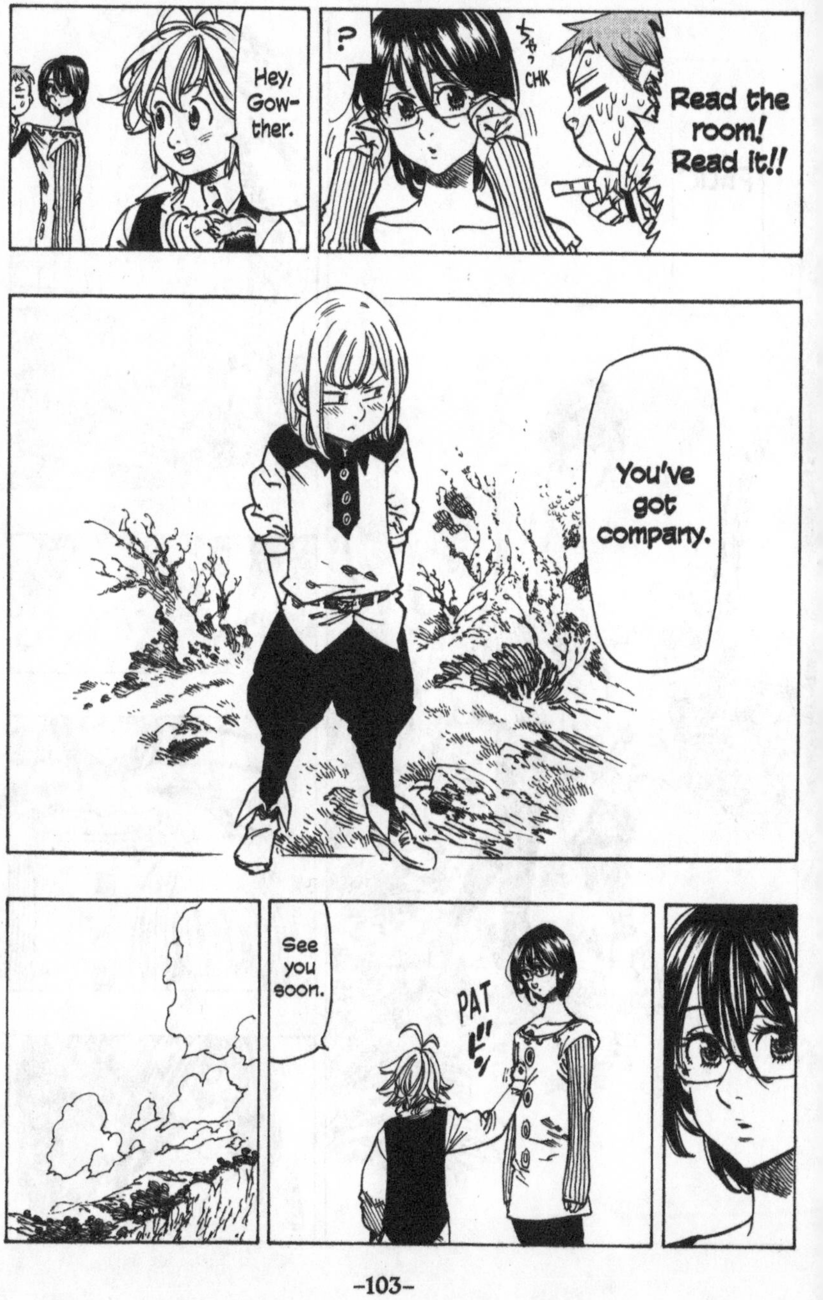
?
CHK
Read the room! Read it!!
Hey, Gowther.
You've got company.
See you soon.
PAT

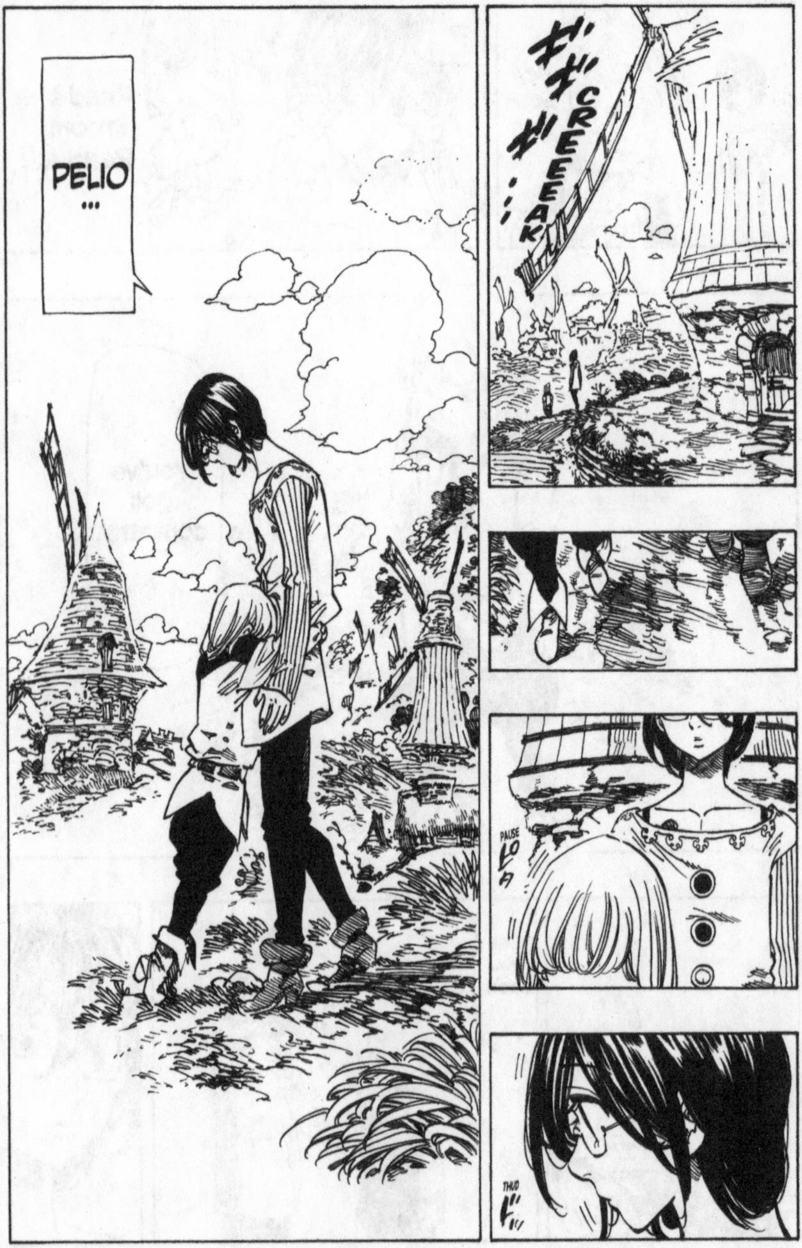
CREEEEAK
PAUSE
THUD
PELIO...

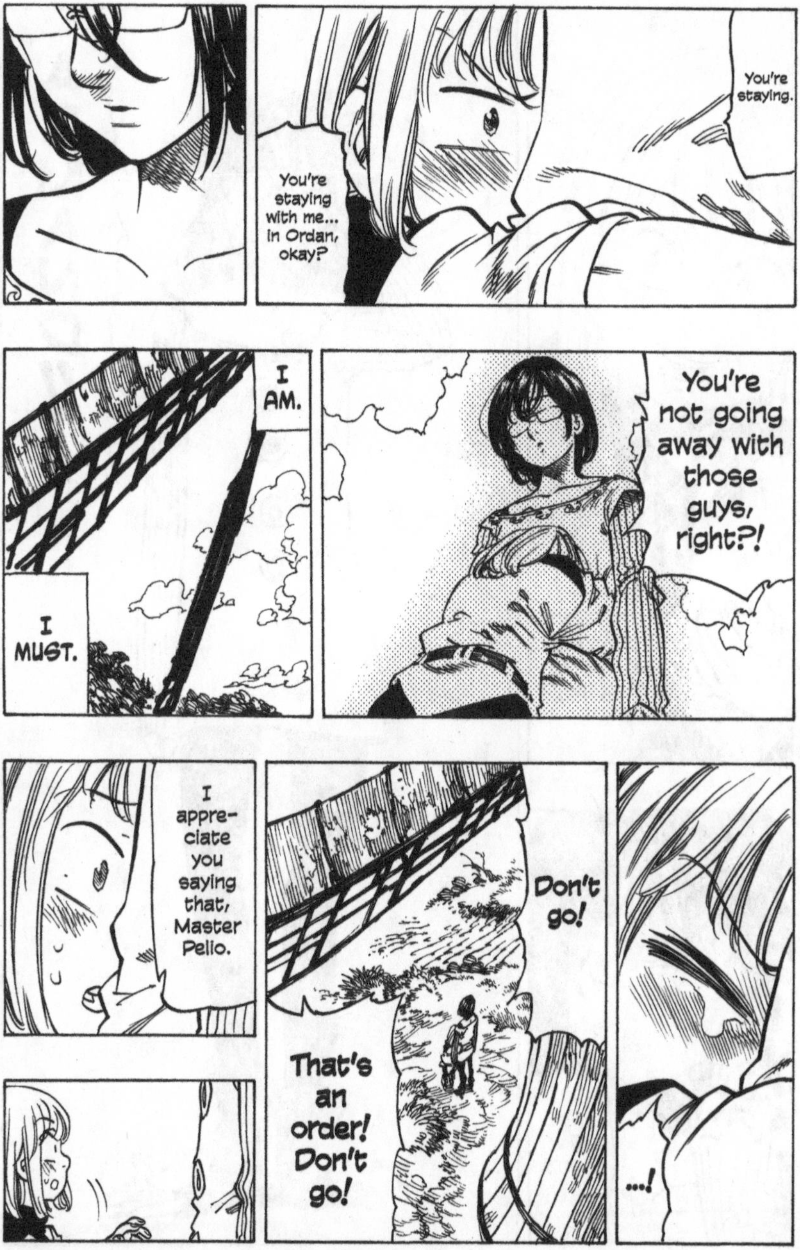
You're staying.
You're staying with me... in Ordan, okay?
You're not going away with those guys, right?!
I AM.
I MUST.
...!
Don't go!
That's an order! Don't go!
I appreciate you saying that, Master Pelio.

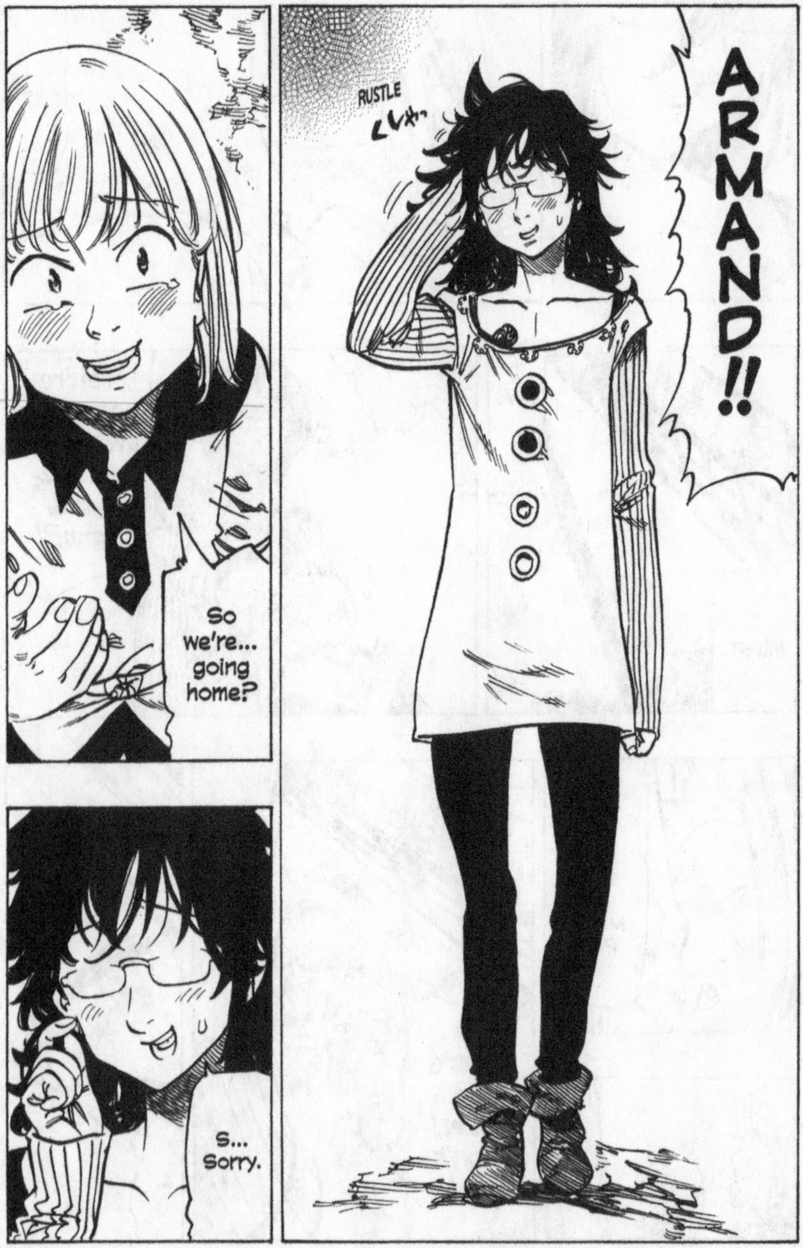
ARMAND!!
RUSTLE
So we're... going home?
S... Sorry.

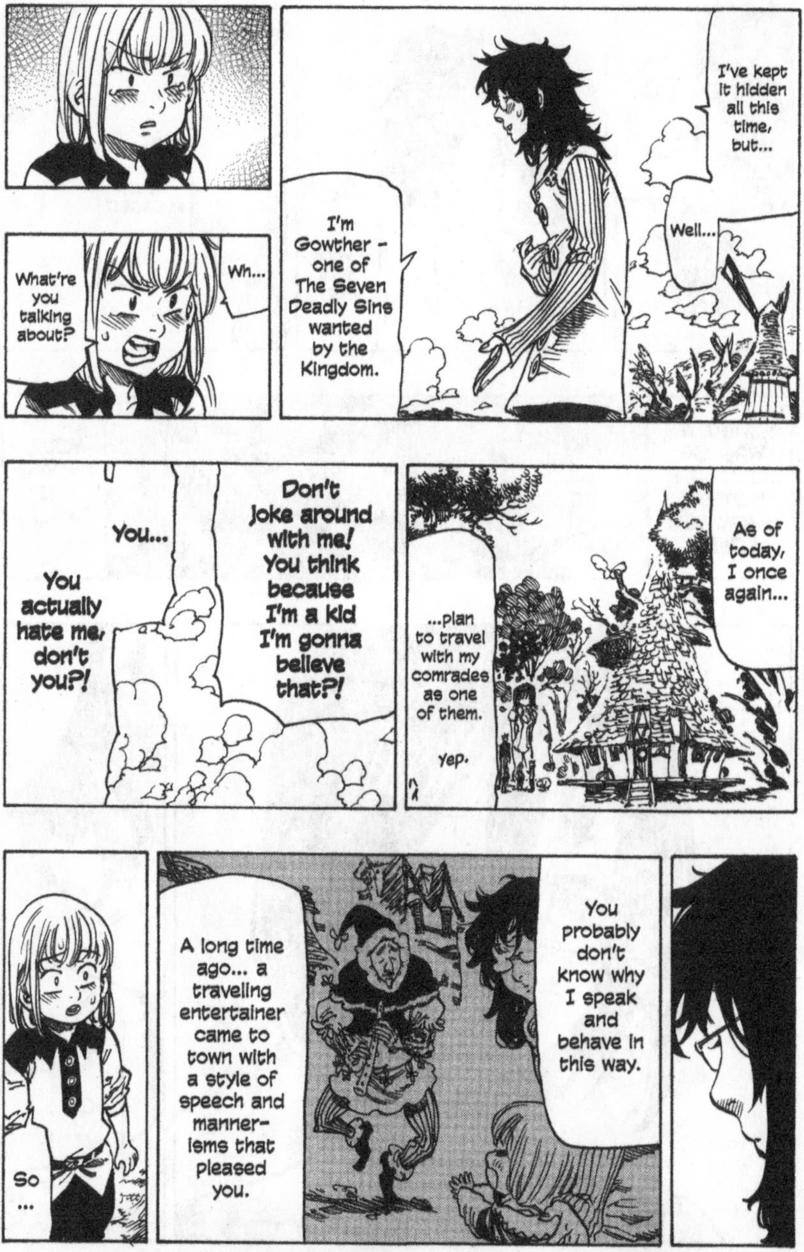

I've kept it hidden all this time, but...
Well...
I'm Gowther - one of The Seven Deadly Sins wanted by the Kingdom.
Wh...
What're you talking about?
As of today, I once again...
...plan to travel with my comrades as one of them.
Yep.
Don't joke around with me! You think because I'm a kid I'm gonna believe that?!
You...
You actually hate me, don't you?!
You probably don't know why I speak and behave in this way.
A long time ago... a traveling entertainer came to town with a style of speech and mannerisms that pleased you.
So ...

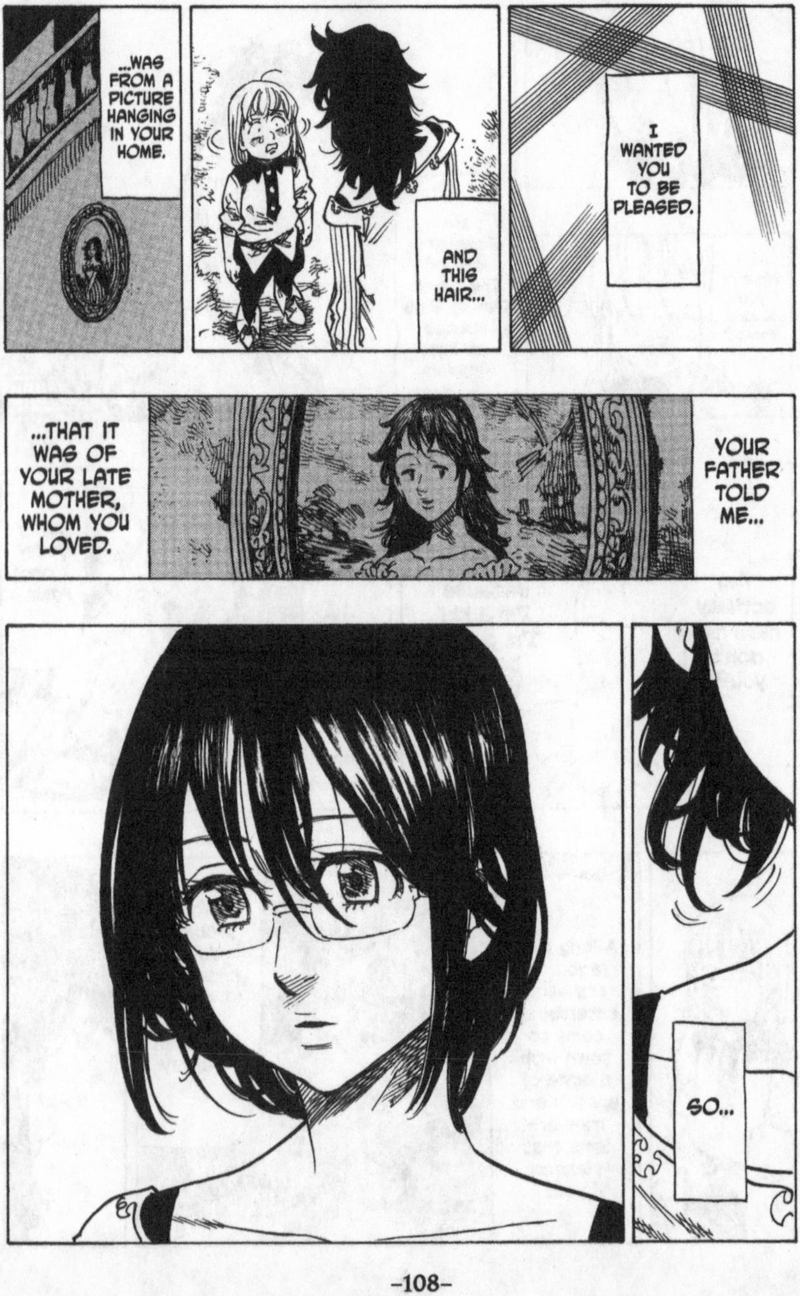
I WANTED YOU TO BE PLEASED.
AND THIS HAIR...
...WAS FROM A PICTURE HANGING IN YOUR HOME.
YOUR FATHER TOLD ME...
...THAT IT WAS OF YOUR LATE MOTHER, WHOM YOU LOVED.
SO...

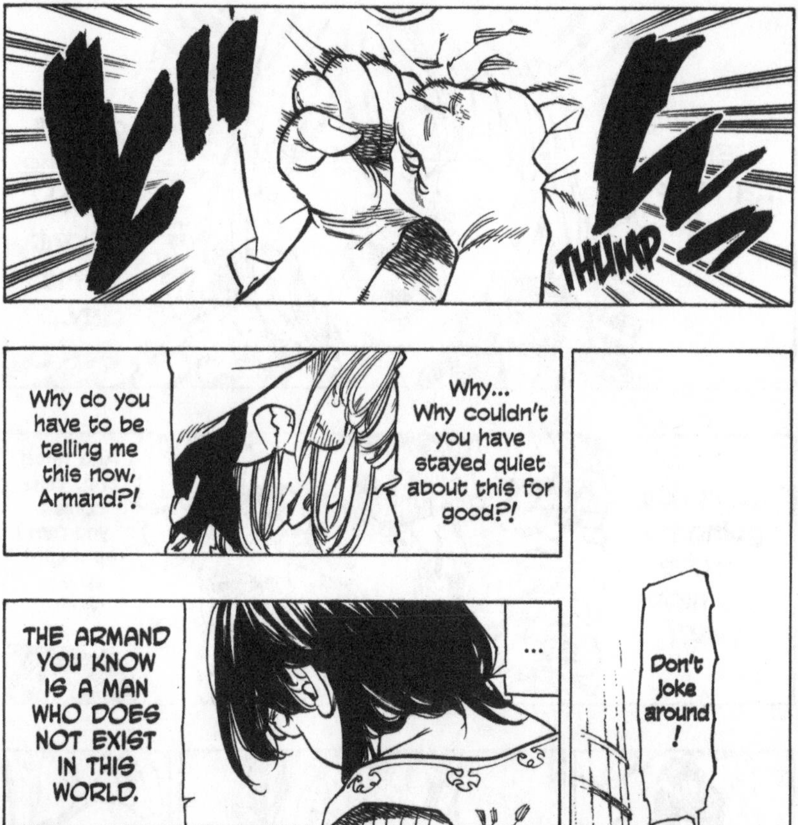
THUMP
Don't joke around!
Why... Why couldn't you have stayed quiet about this for good?!
Why do you have to be telling me this now, Armand?!
...
THE ARMAND YOU KNOW IS A MAN WHO DOES NOT EXIST IN THIS WORLD.
SHOVE
... Fine.
Go.
If you ...
...really are one of The Seven Deadly Sins you say you are...

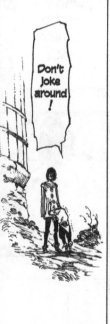

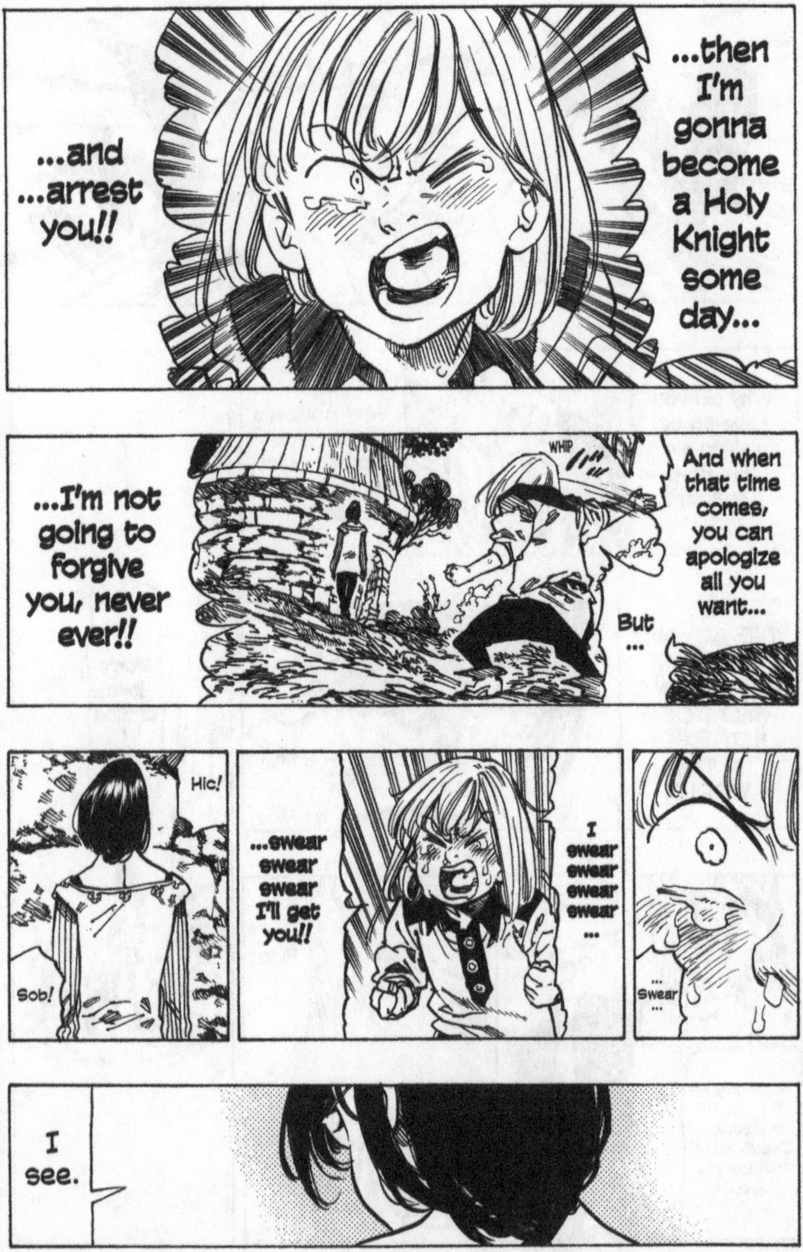
...then I'm gonna become a Holy Knight some day...
...and ...arrest you!!
And when that time comes, you can apologize all you want...
WHIP
But ...
...I'm not going to forgive you, never ever!!
... Swear ...
I swear swear swear swear ...
...swear swear swear I'll get you!!
Hic!
Sob!
I see.

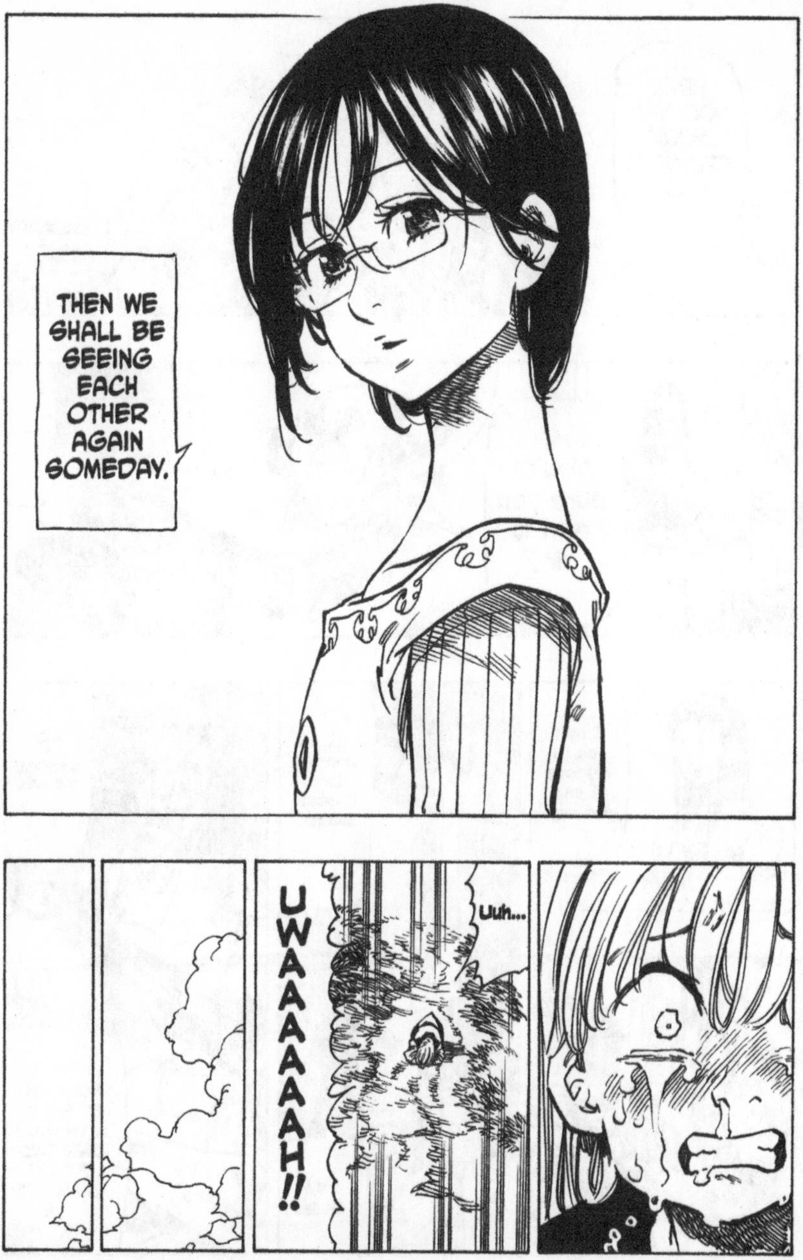
THEN WE SHALL BE SEEING EACH OTHER AGAIN SOMEDAY.
Uuh...
UWAAAAAAAH!!

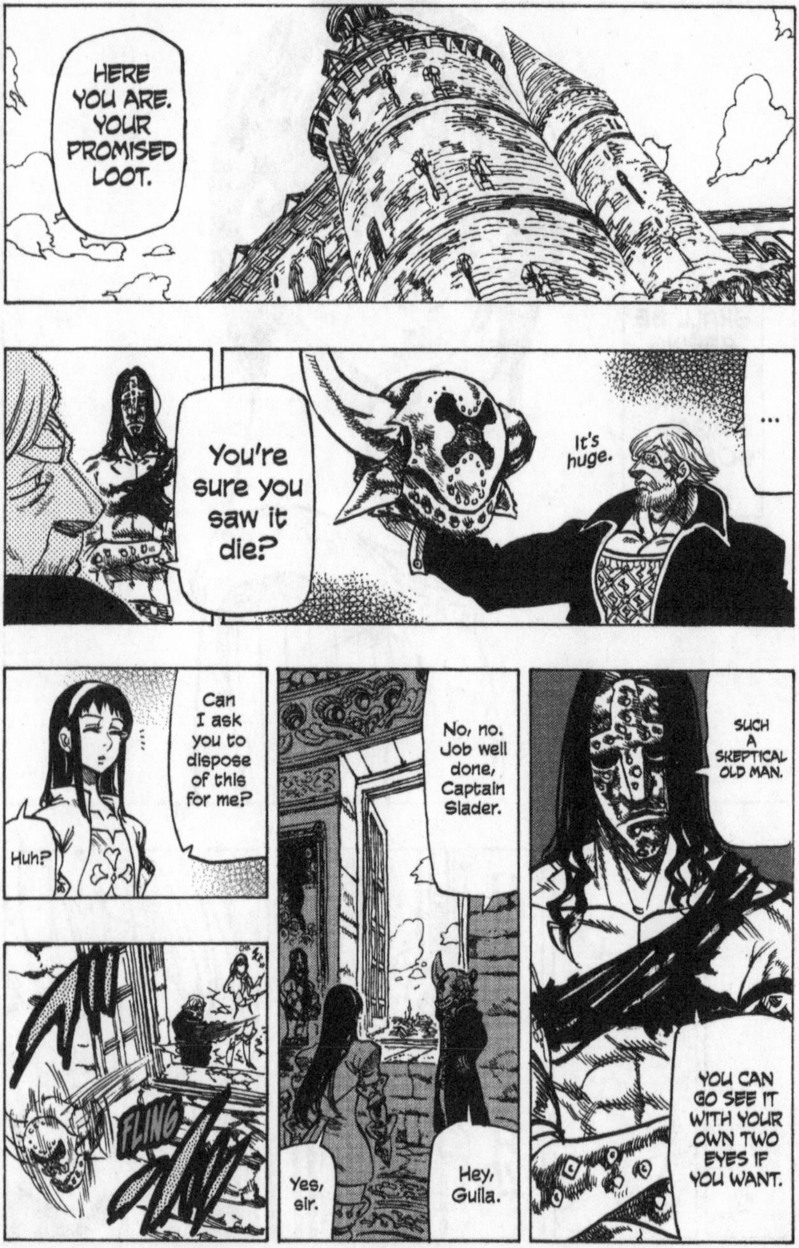
HERE YOU ARE. YOUR PROMISED LOOT.
...
It's huge.
You're sure you saw it die?
SUCH A SKEPTICAL OLD MAN.
YOU CAN GO SEE IT WITH YOUR OWN TWO EYES IF YOU WANT.
No, no. Job well done, Captain Slader.
Hey, Guila.
Yes, sir.
Can I ask you to dispose of this for me?
Huh?
FLING

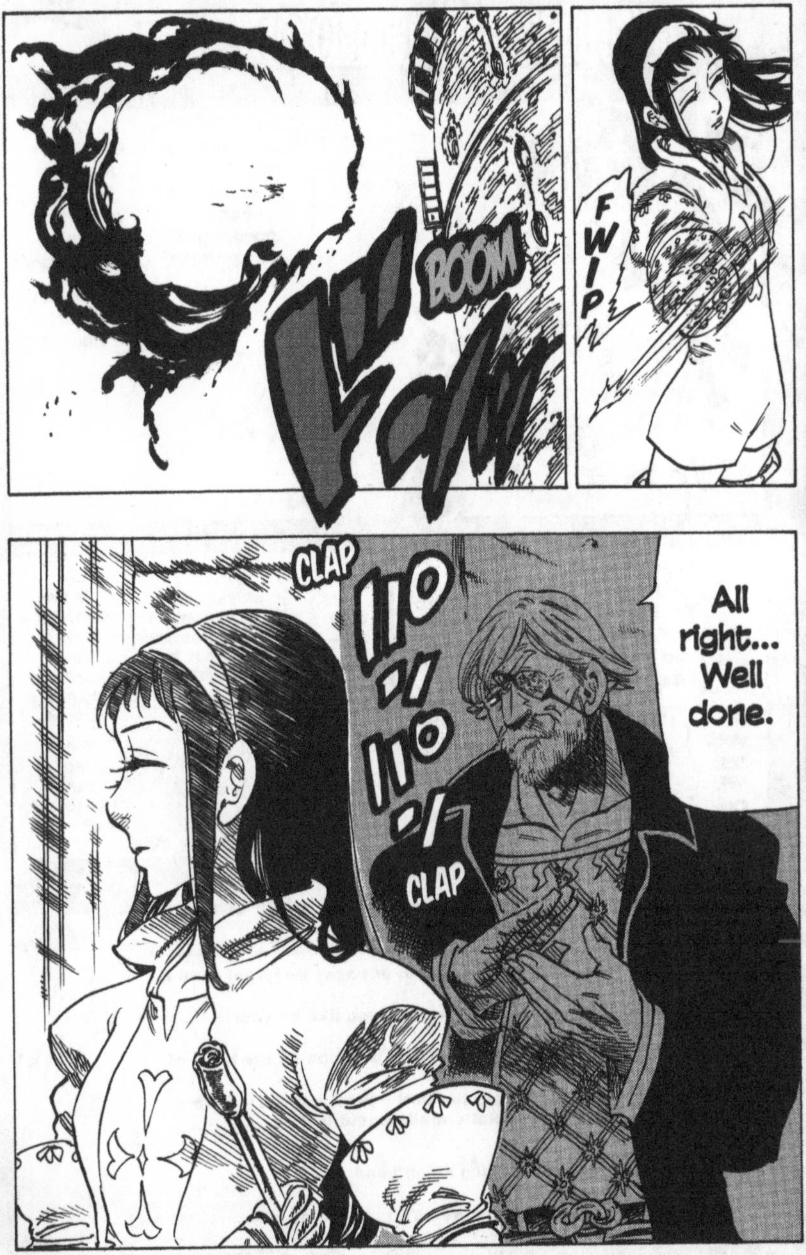
FWIP
BOOM
All right... Well done.
CLAP
CLAP

The Seven Deadly Sins Q&A Corner

"CHATTING KNIGHTHOOD" II

Please include your name and location in your postcards!

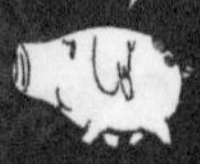

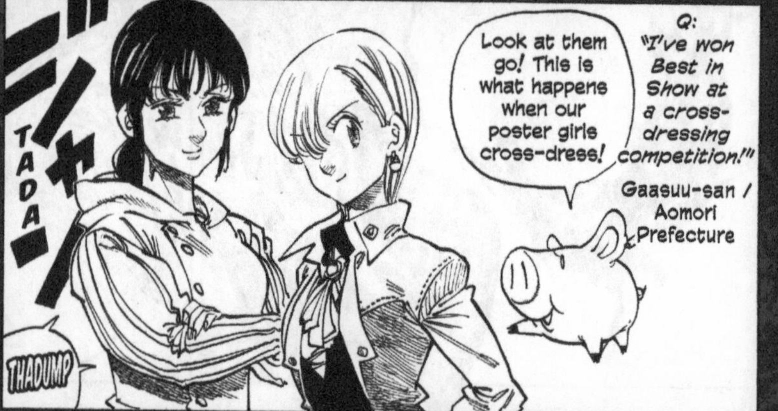
Q: "I've won Best in Show at a cross-dressing competition!"
Gaasuu-san / Aomori Prefecture
Look at them go! This is what happens when our poster girls cross-dress!
TADA
THADUMP

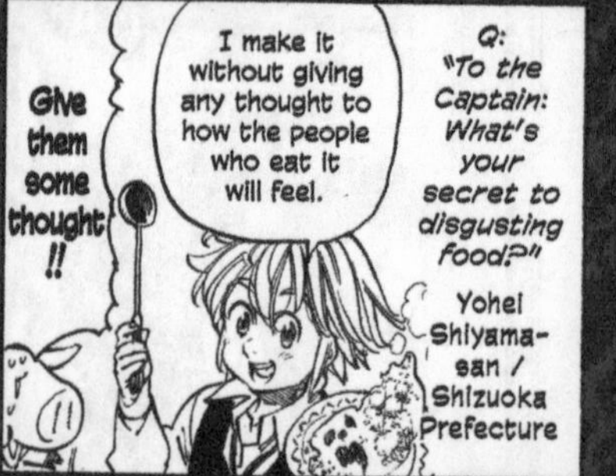
Q: "To the Captain: What's your secret to disgusting food?"
Yohei Shiyama-san / Shizuoka Prefecture
I make it without giving any thought to how the people who eat it will feel.
Give them some thought!!

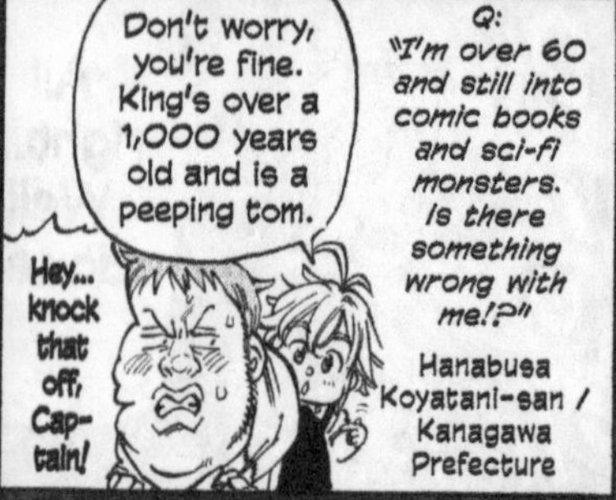
Q: "I'm over 60 and still into comic books and sci-fi monsters. Is there something wrong with me!?"
Hanabusa Koyatani-san / Kanagawa Prefecture
Don't worry, you're fine. King's over a 1,000 years old and is a peeping tom.
Hey... knock that off, Captain!

Now Accepting Applicants for the "Chatting Knighthood"!

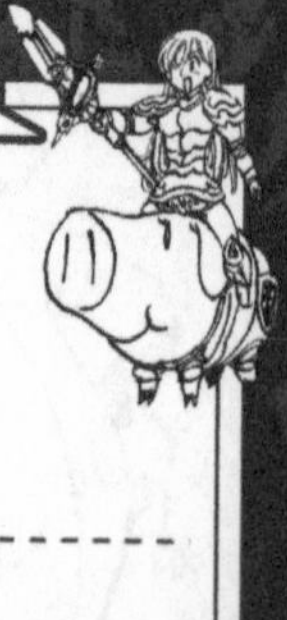

- **Write your question on a postcard, or paper no larger than a postcard, and send it in!**
- **You can write as many questions as you like on your postcard!**
- **Don't forget to write your name and location on the back of your postcard!**
- **Chosen questions that are run in the print edition will be gifted with a signed, specially-made postcard!**

Send to:
The Seven Deadly Sins Chatting Knighthood
c/o Kodansha Comics
451 Park Ave. South, 7th Floor, New York, NY 10016

Chapter 60 - A Creeping Chaos

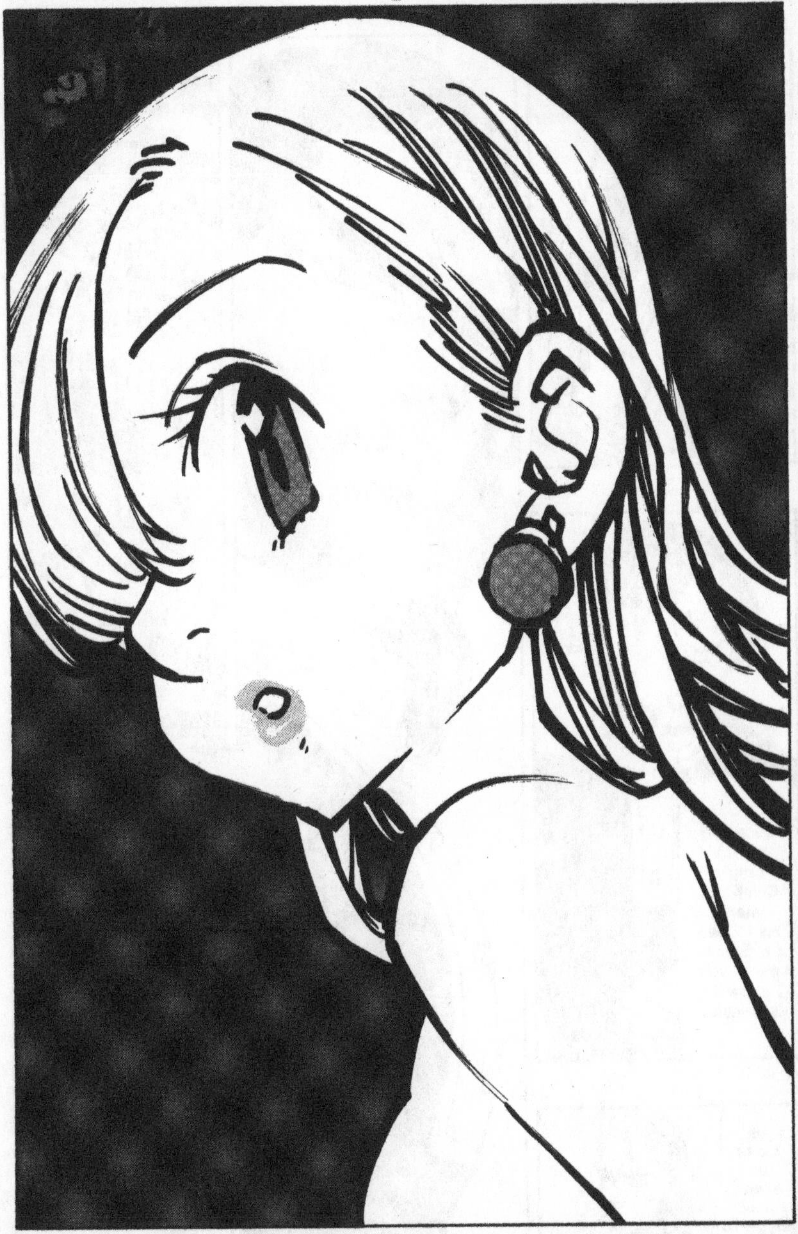

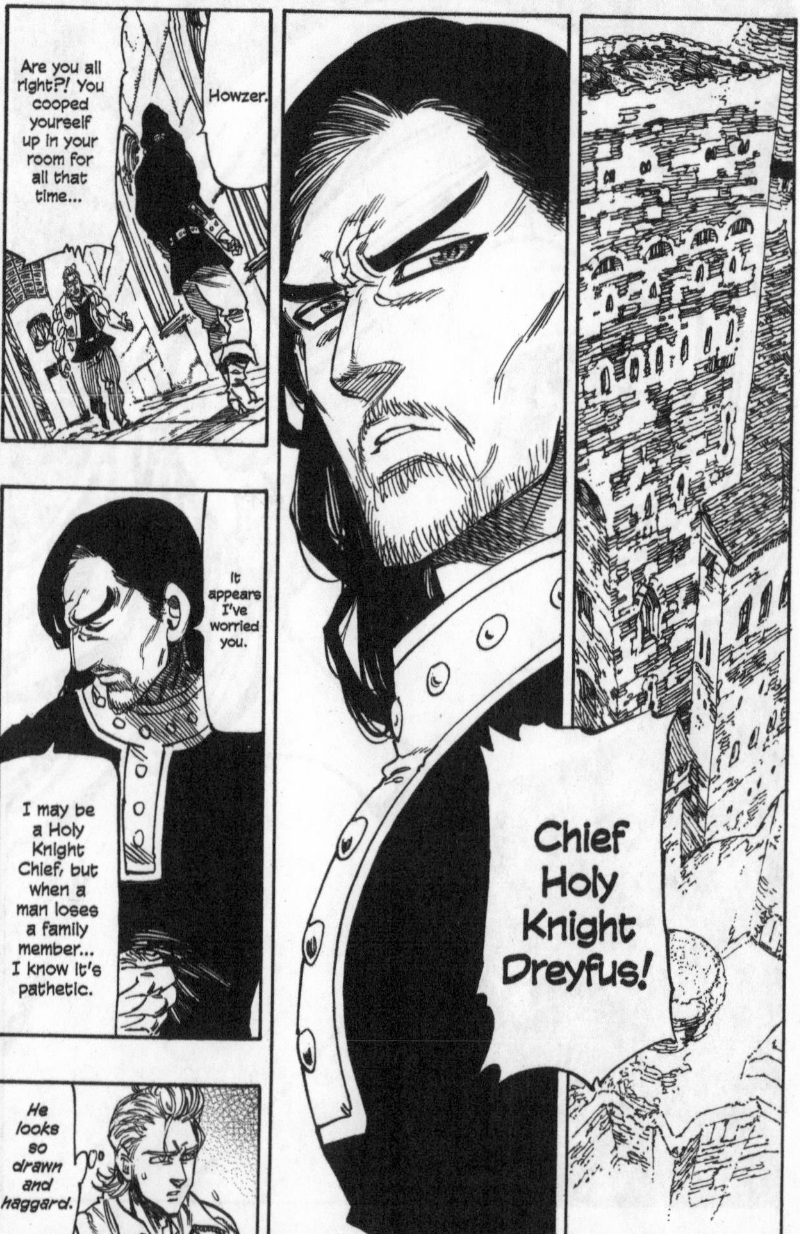
Chief Holy Knight Dreyfus!
Howzer.
Are you all right?! You cooped yourself up in your room for all that time...
It appears I've worried you.
I may be a Holy Knight Chief, but when a man loses a family member... I know it's pathetic.
He looks so drawn and haggard.

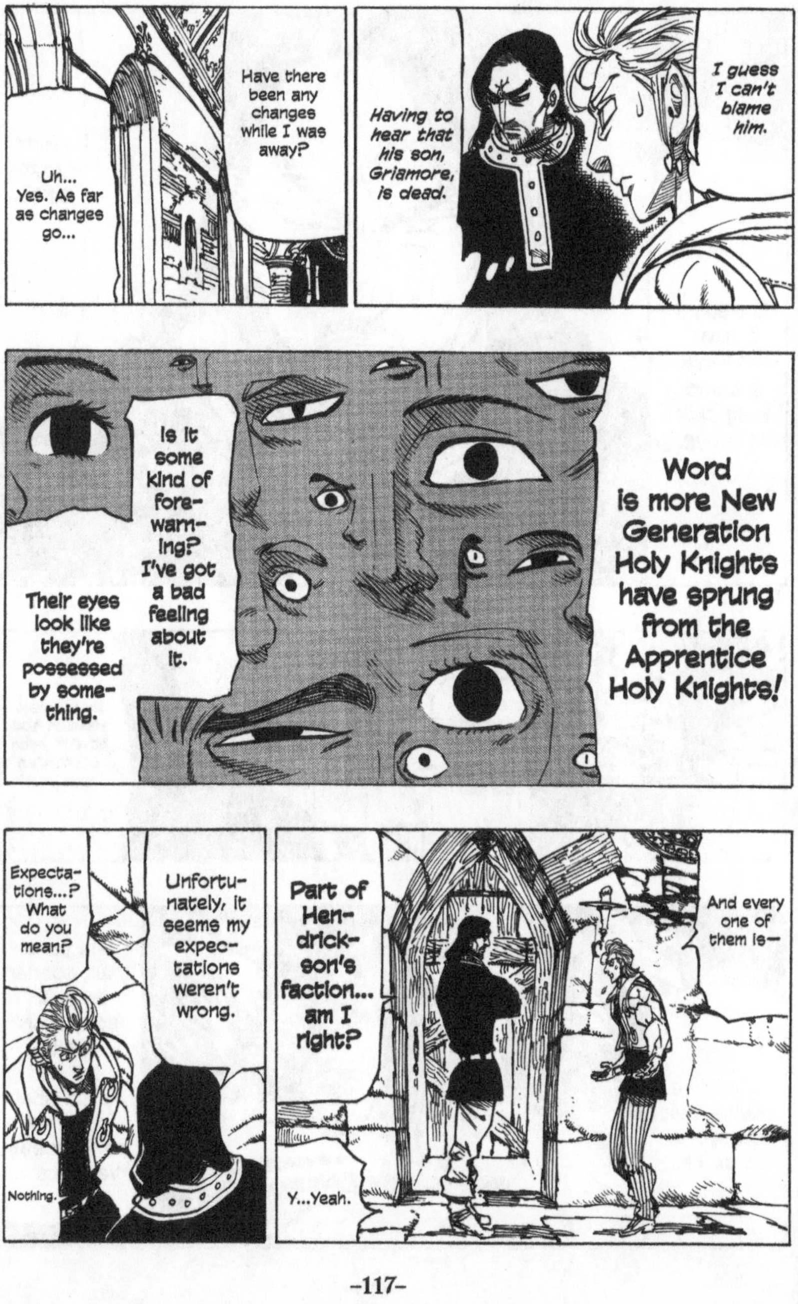
I guess I can't blame him.
Having to hear that his son, Griamore, is dead.
Have there been any changes while I was away?
Uh... Yes. As far as changes go...
Word is more New Generation Holy Knights have sprung from the Apprentice Holy Knights!
Is it some kind of fore-warning? I've got a bad feeling about it.
Their eyes look like they're possessed by some-thing.
And every one of them is—
Part of Hen-drickson's faction... am I right?
Y...Yeah.
Unfortu-nately, it seems my expec-tations weren't wrong.
Expecta-tions...? What do you mean?
Nothing.

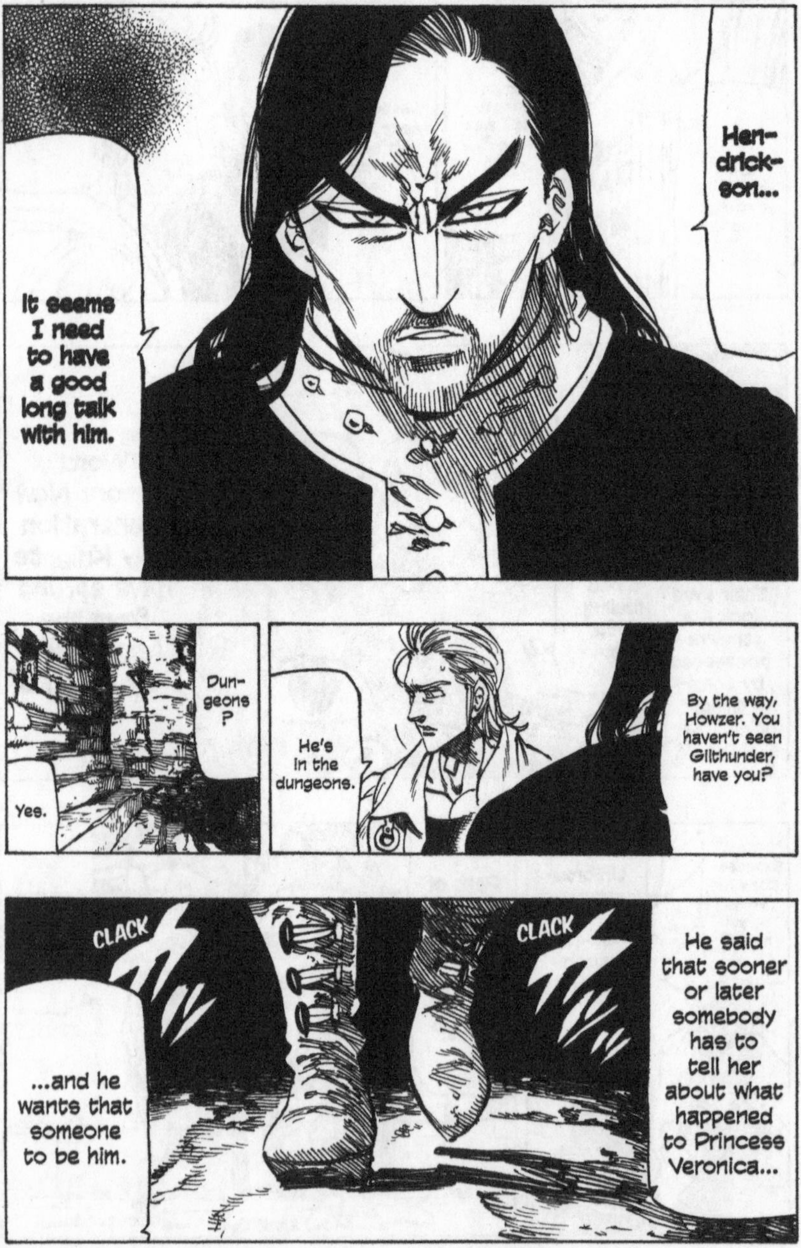
Hen-drick-son...
It seems I need to have a good long talk with him.
By the way, Howzer. You haven't seen Gilthunder, have you?
He's in the dungeons.
Dungeons?
Yes.
He said that sooner or later somebody has to tell her about what happened to Princess Veronica...
CLACK
CLACK
...and he wants that someone to be him.

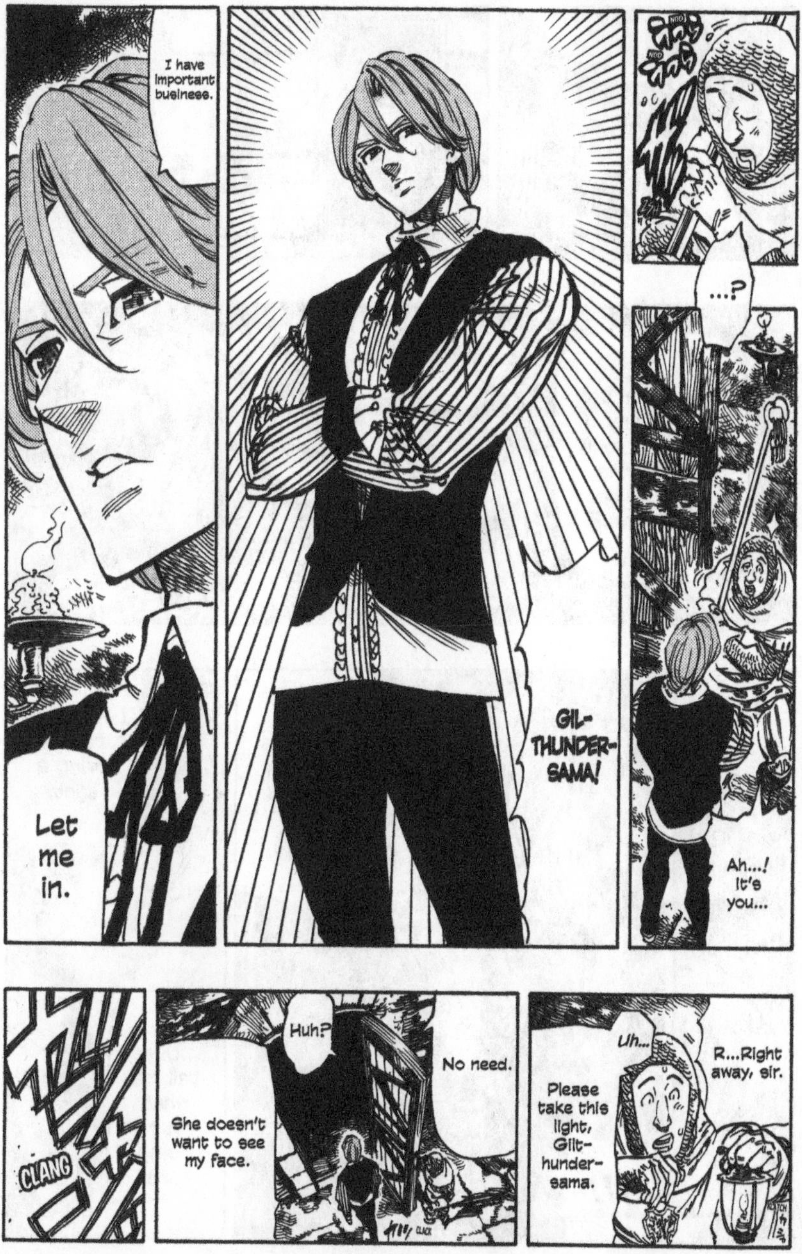
NOD NOD
...?
Ah...! It's you...
GIL-THUNDER-SAMA!
I have important business.
Let me in.
R...Right away, sir.
Uh...
Please take this light, Gilthunder-sama.
No need.
Huh?
She doesn't want to see my face.
CLICK
CLANG

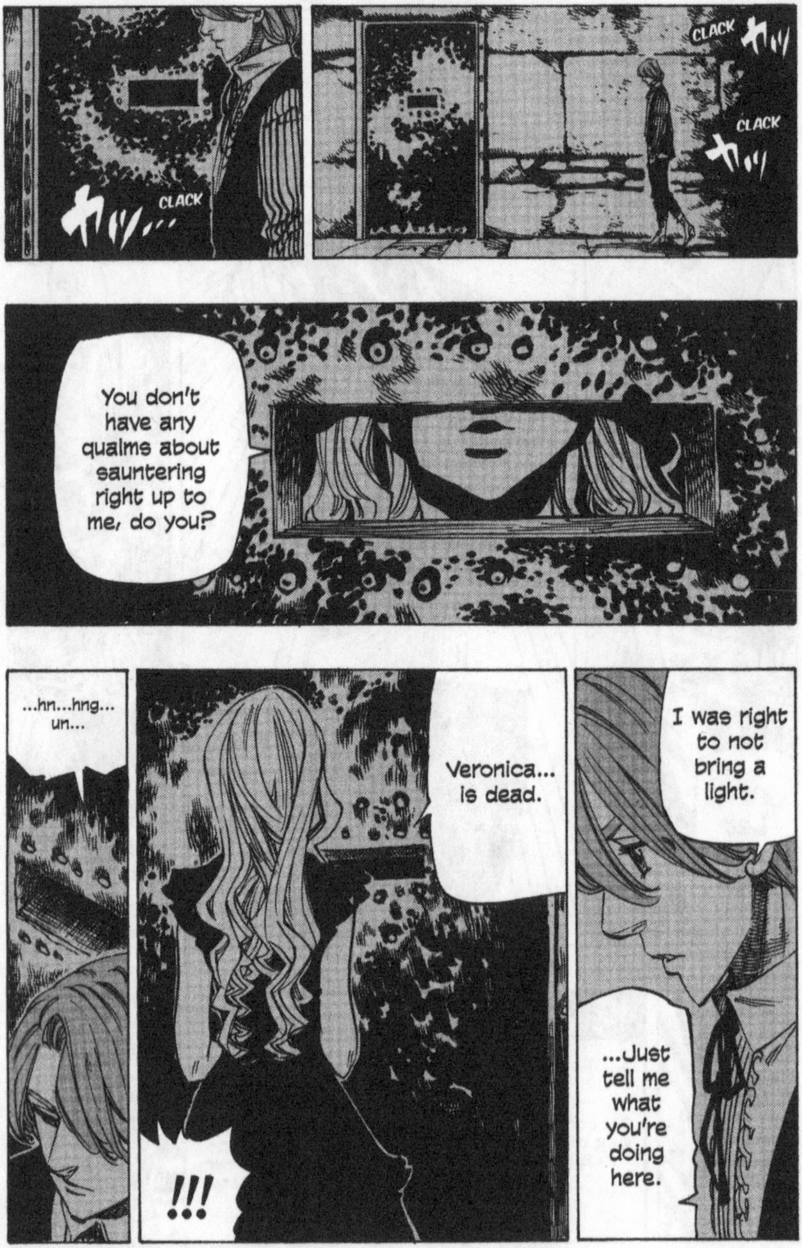
CLACK
カッ
CLACK
カッ
CLACK
カッ…
You don't have any qualms about sauntering right up to me, do you?
I was right to not bring a light.
...Just tell me what you're doing here.
Veronica... is dead.
!!!
...hn...hng... un...

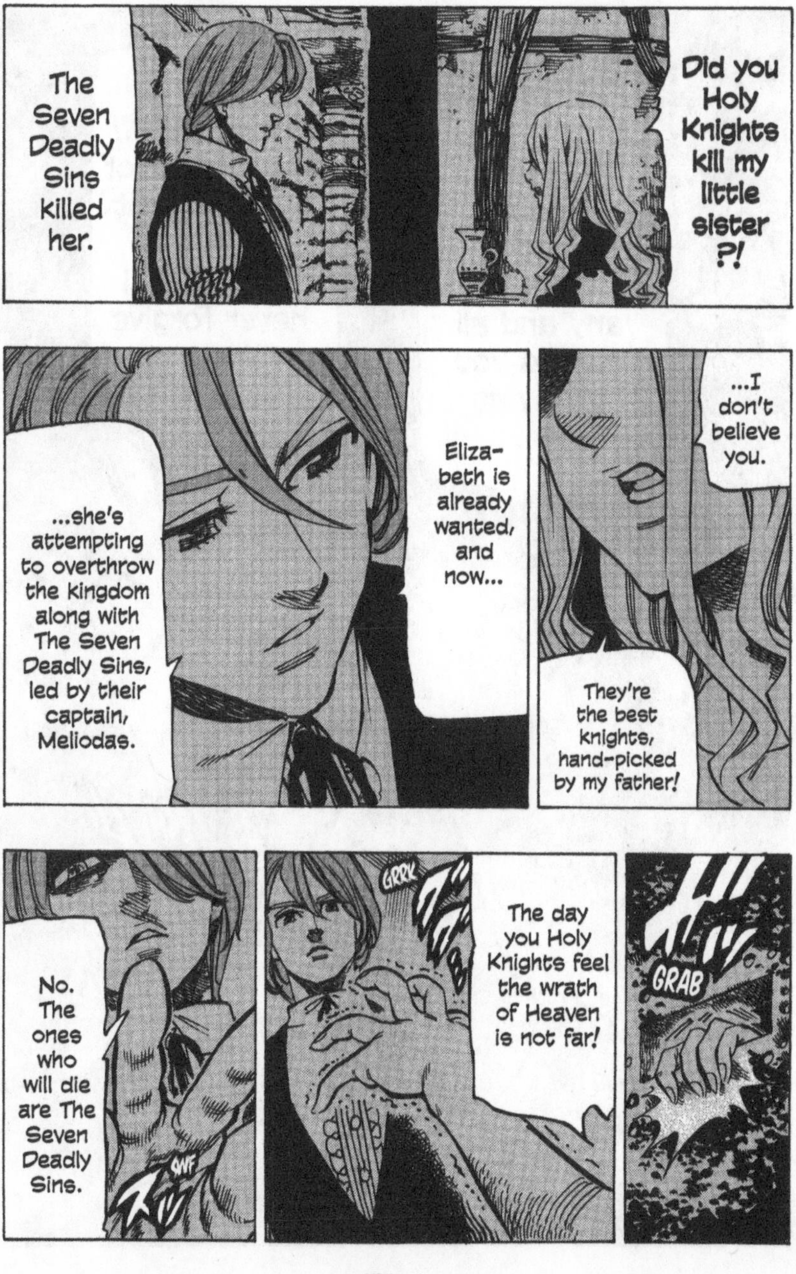
Did you Holy Knights kill my little sister?!
The Seven Deadly Sins killed her.
...I don't believe you.
They're the best knights, hand-picked by my father!
Eliza-beth is already wanted, and now...
...she's attempting to overthrow the kingdom along with The Seven Deadly Sins, led by their captain, Meliodas.
GRAB
GRRK
The day you Holy Knights feel the wrath of Heaven is not far!
No. The ones who will die are The Seven Deadly Sins.
GNF

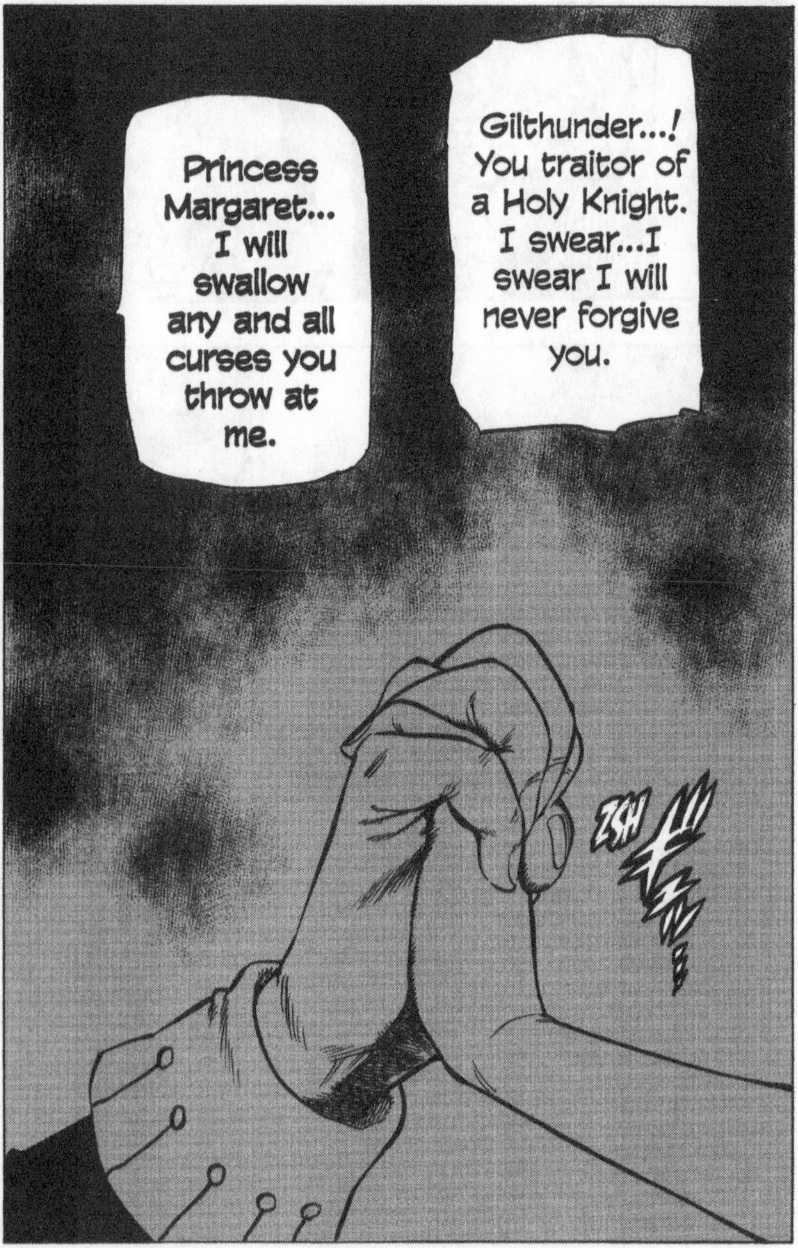
Gilthunder...! You traitor of a Holy Knight. I swear...I swear I will never forgive you.
Princess Margaret... I will swallow any and all curses you throw at me.
ZSH

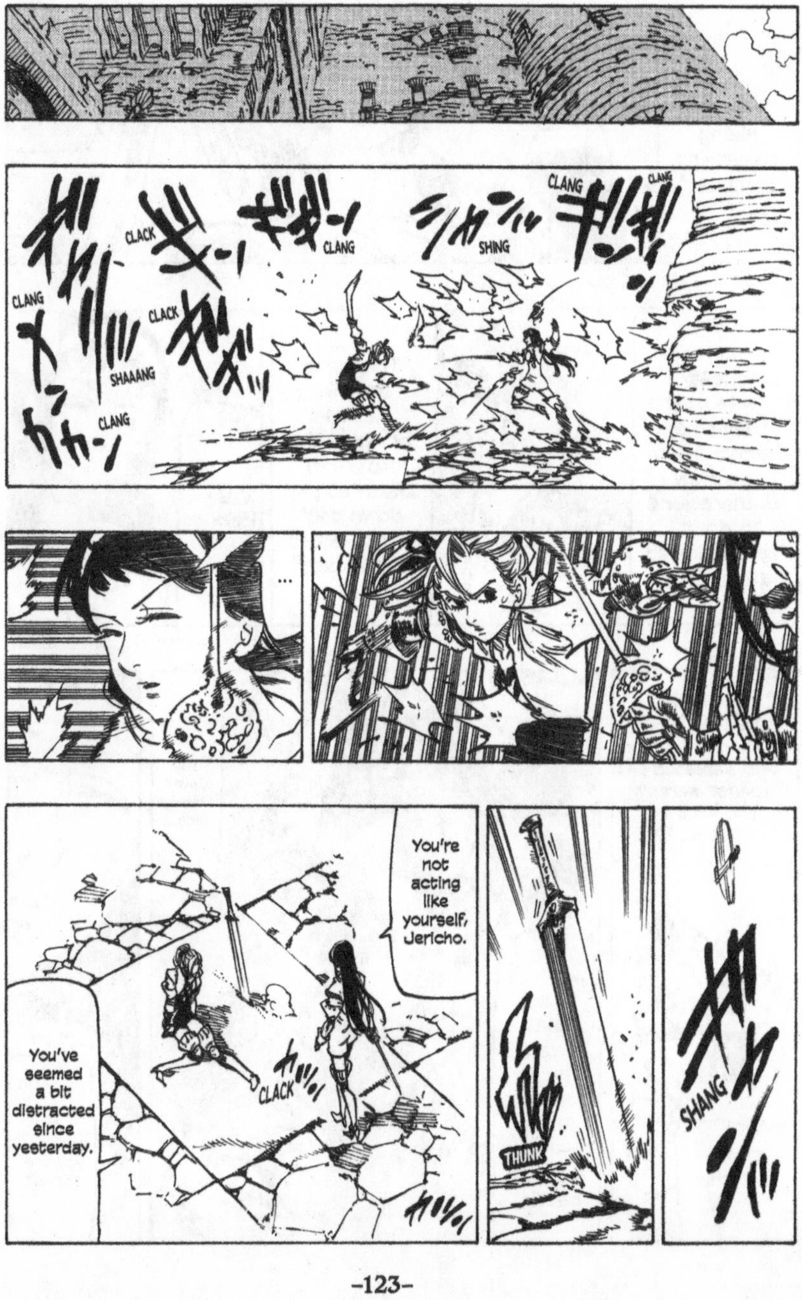
CLANG
CLANG
SHING
CLANG
CLACK
CLANG
CLACK
SHAAANG
CLANG
...
SHANG
THUNK
You're not acting like yourself, Jericho.
CLACK
You've seemed a bit distracted since yesterday.

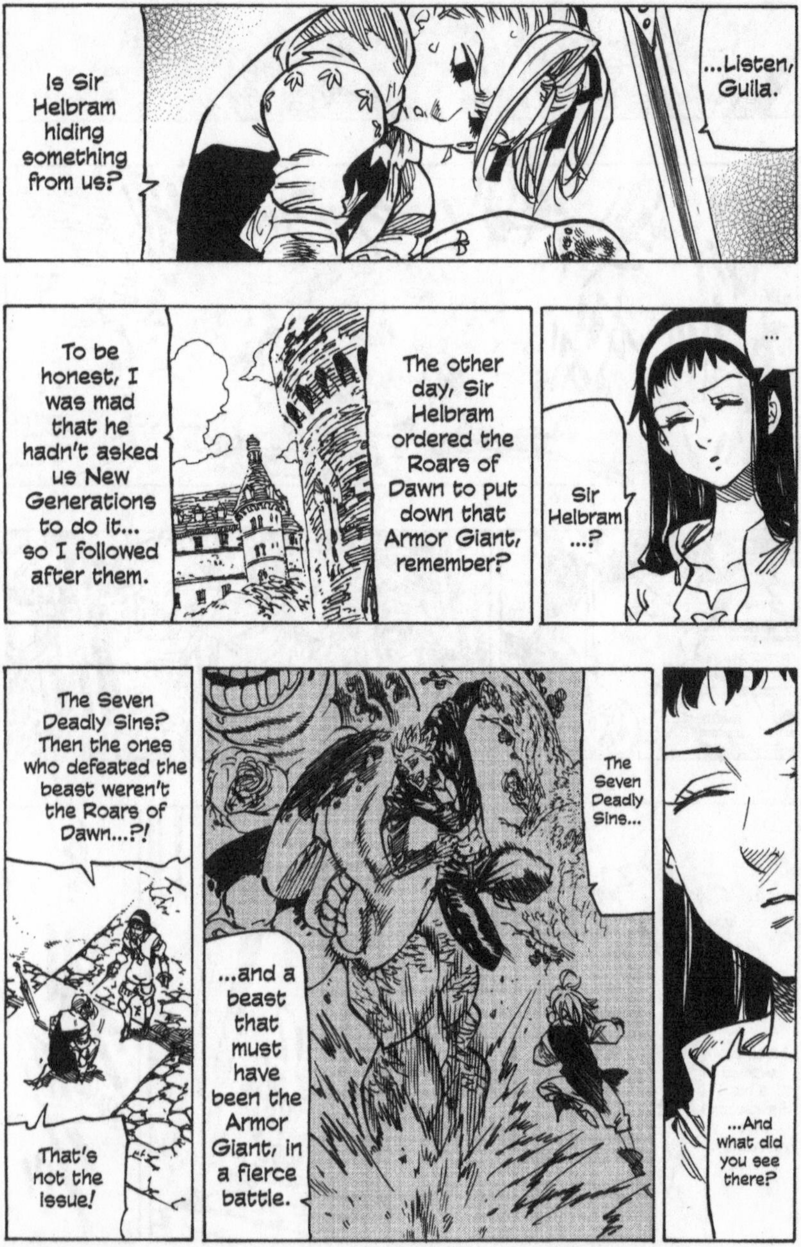
...Listen, Guila.
Is Sir Helbram hiding something from us?
...
Sir Helbram ...?
The other day, Sir Helbram ordered the Roars of Dawn to put down that Armor Giant, remember?
To be honest, I was mad that he hadn't asked us New Generations to do it... so I followed after them.
...And what did you see there?
The Seven Deadly Sins...
...and a beast that must have been the Armor Giant, in a fierce battle.
The Seven Deadly Sins? Then the ones who defeated the beast weren't the Roars of Dawn...?!
That's not the issue!

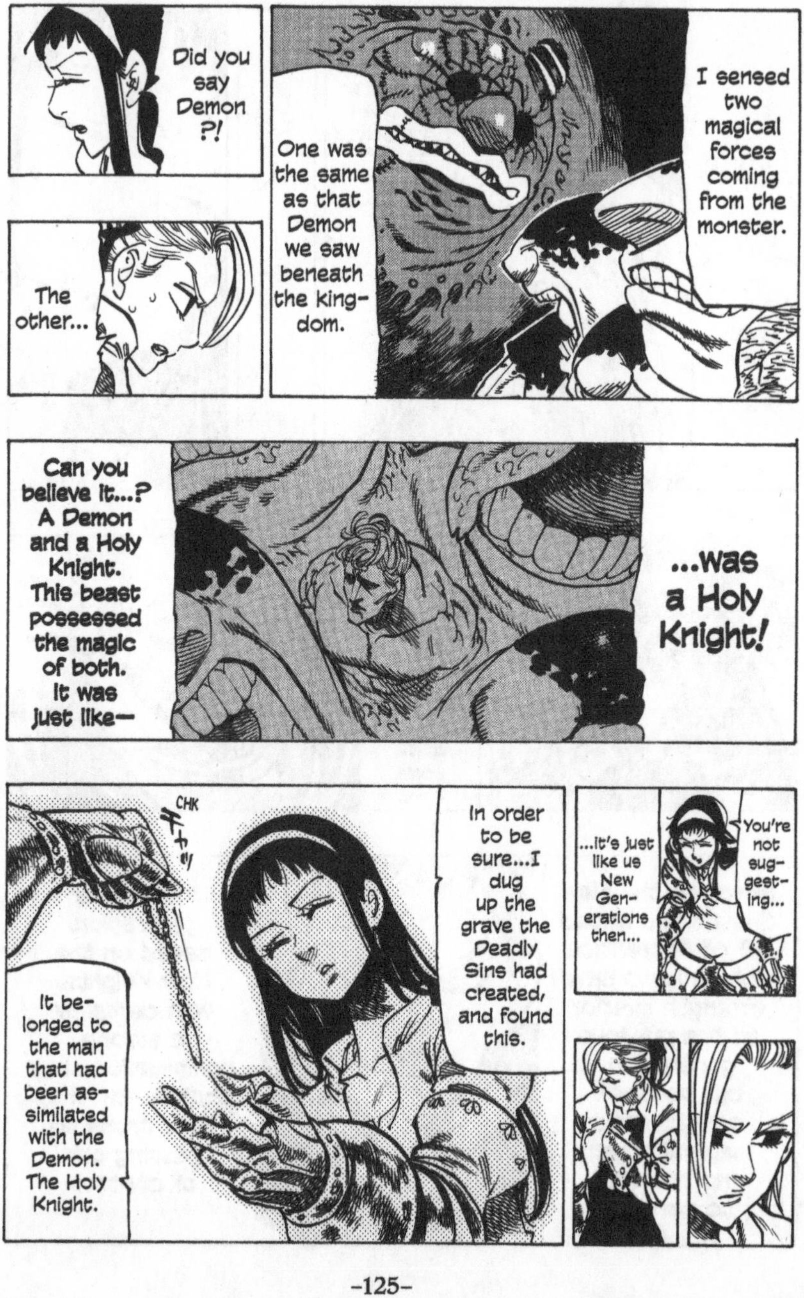

I sensed two magical forces coming from the monster.
One was the same as that Demon we saw beneath the kingdom.
Did you say Demon ?!
The other...
...was a Holy Knight!
Can you believe it...? A Demon and a Holy Knight. This beast possessed the magic of both. It was just like—
You're not sug-gest-ing...
...it's just like us New Gen-erations then...
CHK
In order to be sure...I dug up the grave the Deadly Sins had created, and found this.
It be-longed to the man that had been as-similated with the Demon. The Holy Knight.

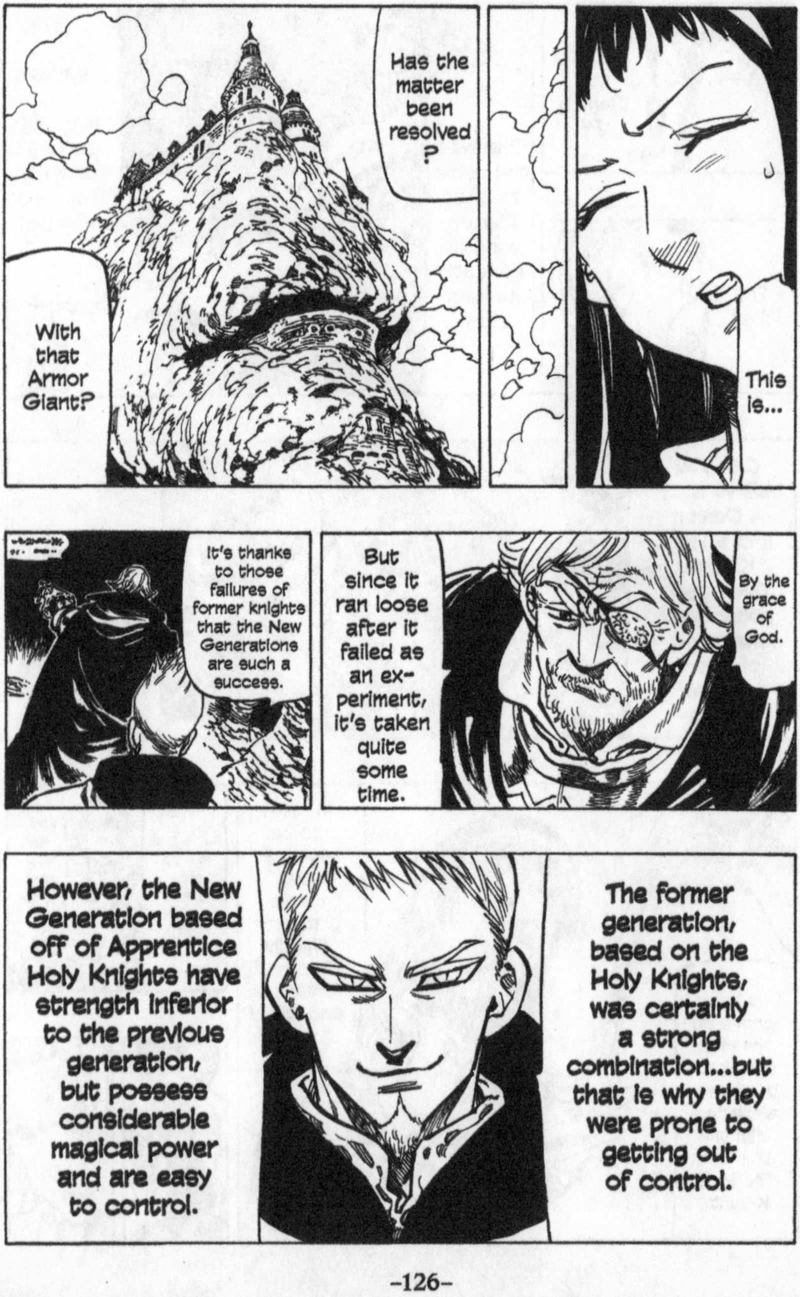
This is...
Has the matter been resolved?
With that Armor Giant?
By the grace of God.
But since it ran loose after it failed as an experiment, it's taken quite some time.
It's thanks to those failures of former knights that the New Generations are such a success.
The former generation, based on the Holy Knights, was certainly a strong combination...but that is why they were prone to getting out of control.
However, the New Generation based off of Apprentice Holy Knights have strength inferior to the previous generation, but possess considerable magical power and are easy to control.

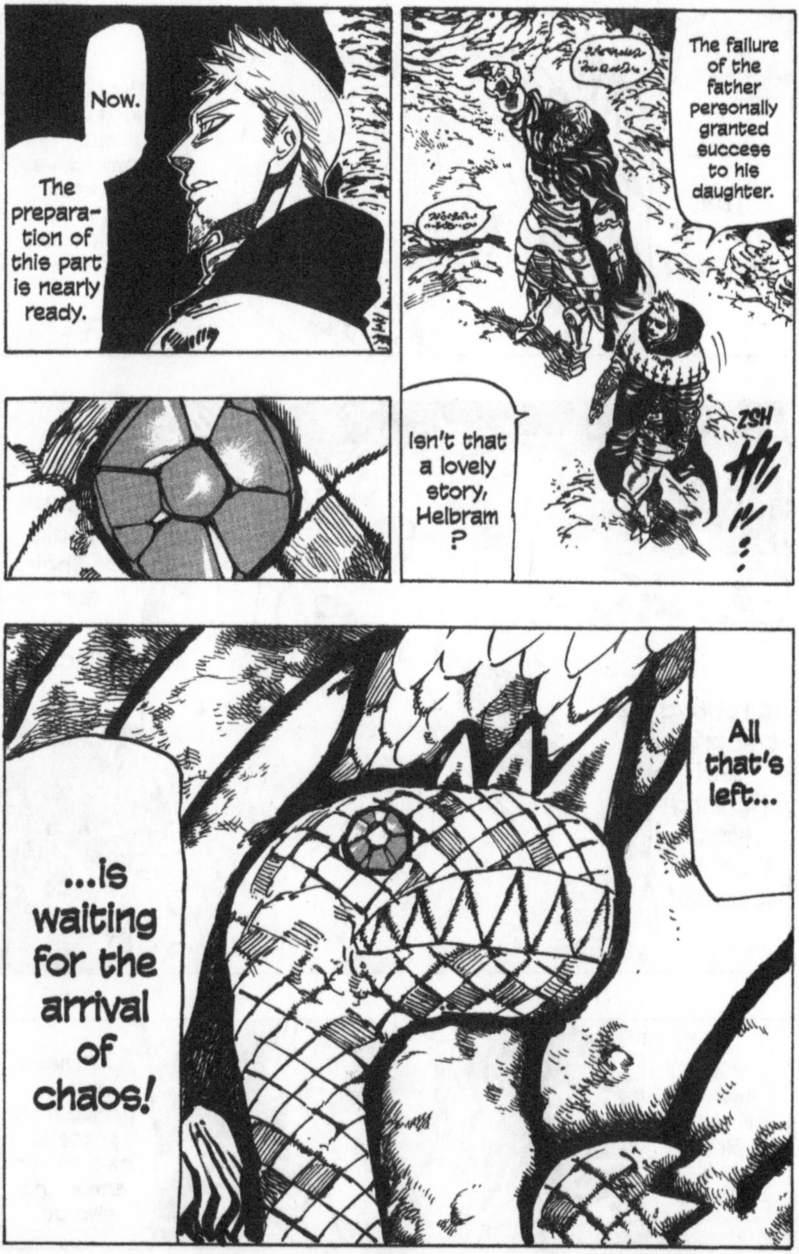
The failure of the father personally granted success to his daughter.
Isn't that a lovely story, Helbram?
ZSH
Now.
The preparation of this part is nearly ready.
All that's left...
...is waiting for the arrival of chaos!

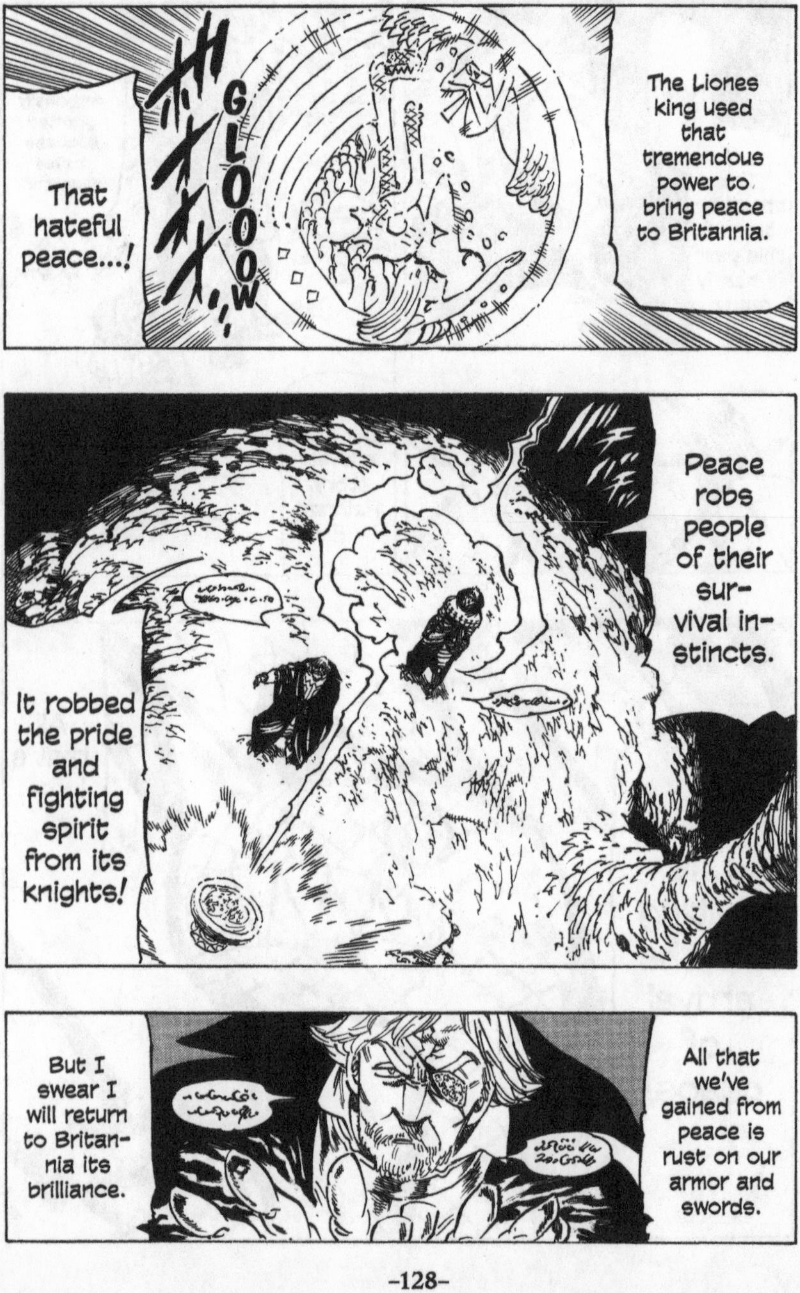
The Liones king used that tremendous power to bring peace to Britannia.
GLOOOW
That hateful peace...!
Peace robs people of their sur-vival in-stincts.
It robbed the pride and fighting spirit from its knights!
All that we've gained from peace is rust on our armor and swords.
But I swear I will return to Britan-nia its brilliance.

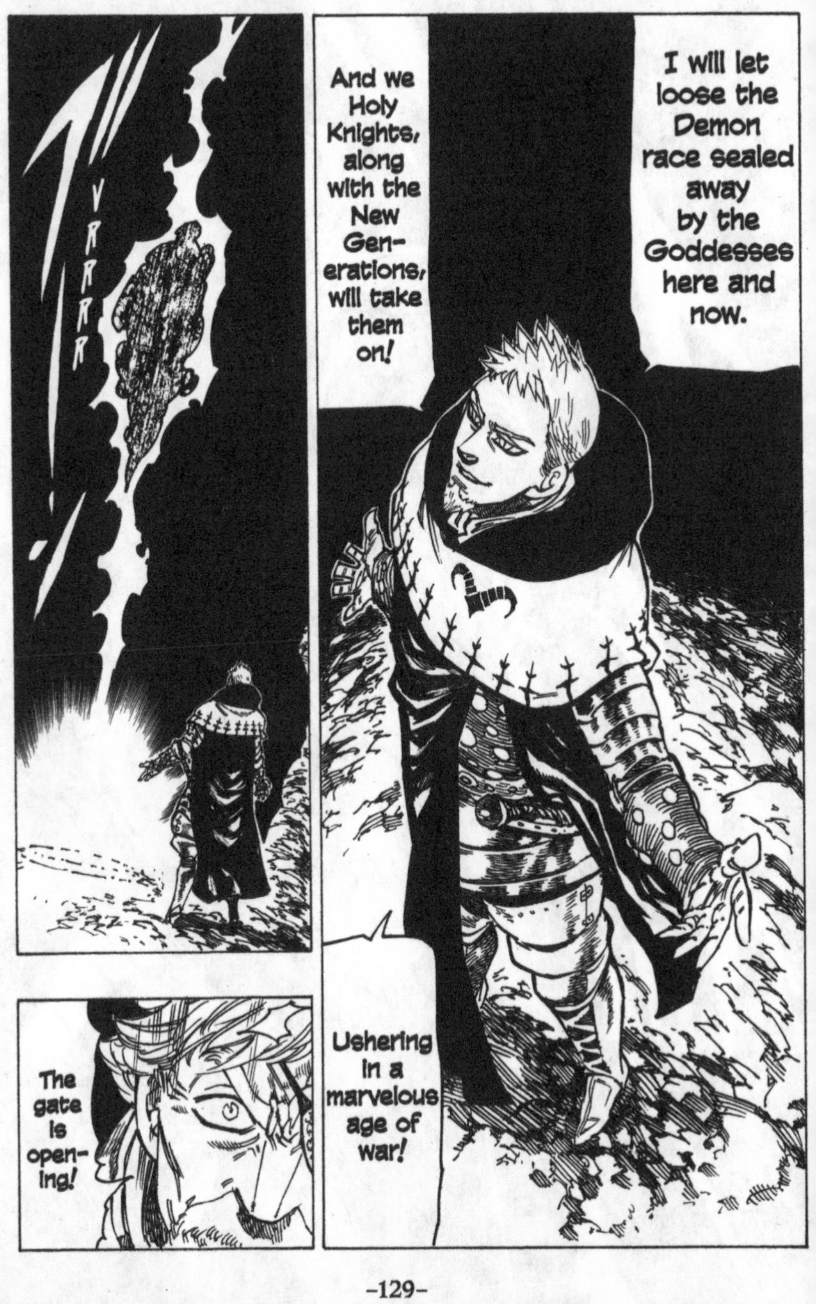
I will let loose the Demon race sealed away by the Goddesses here and now.
And we Holy Knights, along with the New Generations, will take them on!
Ushering in a marvelous age of war!
VRRRR
The gate is opening!

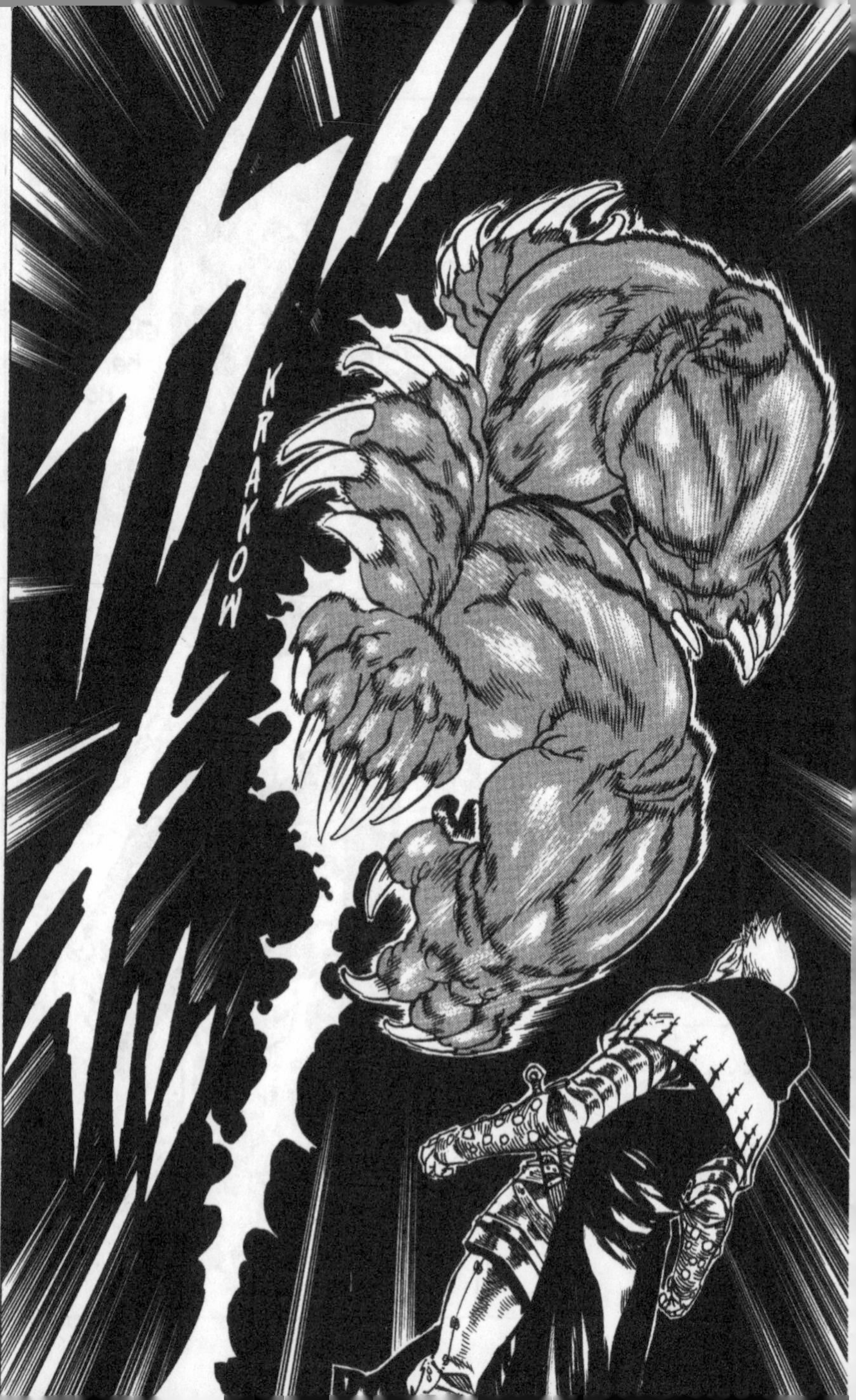
KRAKOW

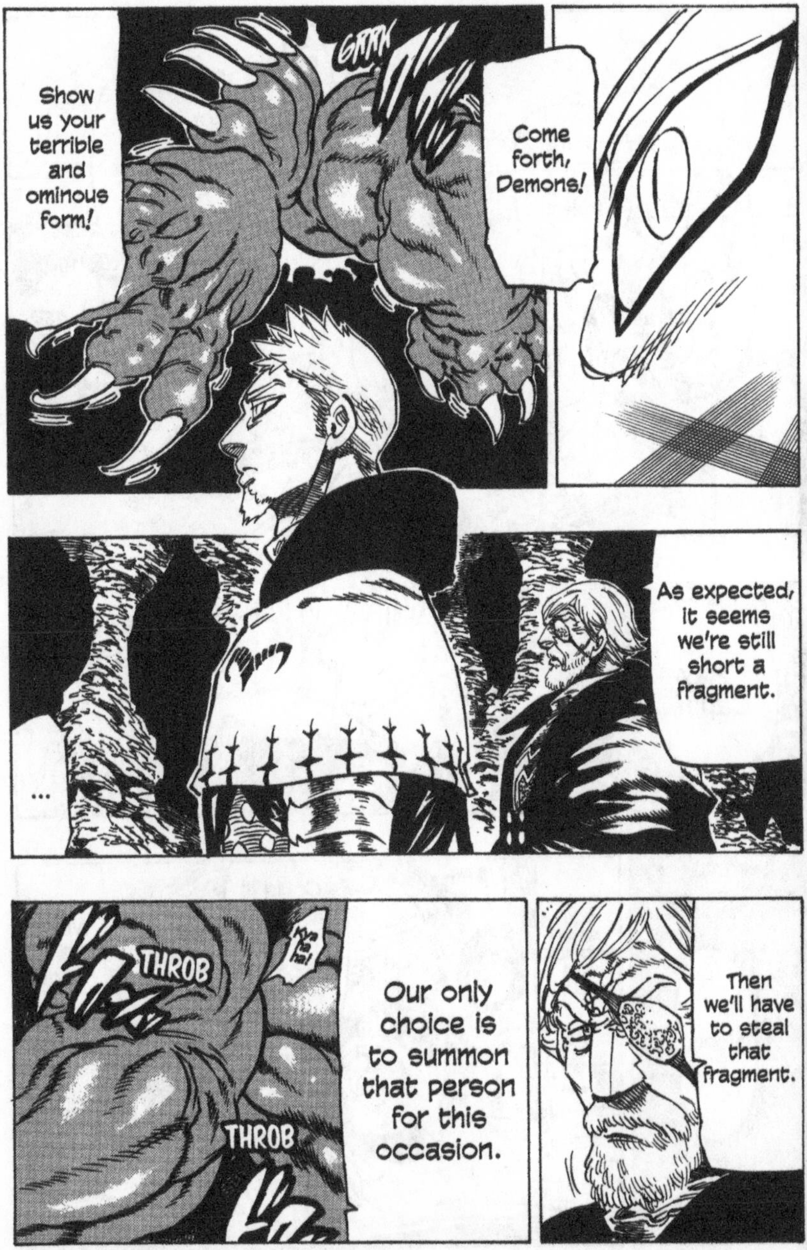
Come forth, Demons!
GRRK
Show us your terrible and ominous form!
As expected, it seems we're still short a fragment.
...
Then we'll have to steal that fragment.
Our only choice is to summon that person for this occasion.
Kya ha ha!
THROB
THROB

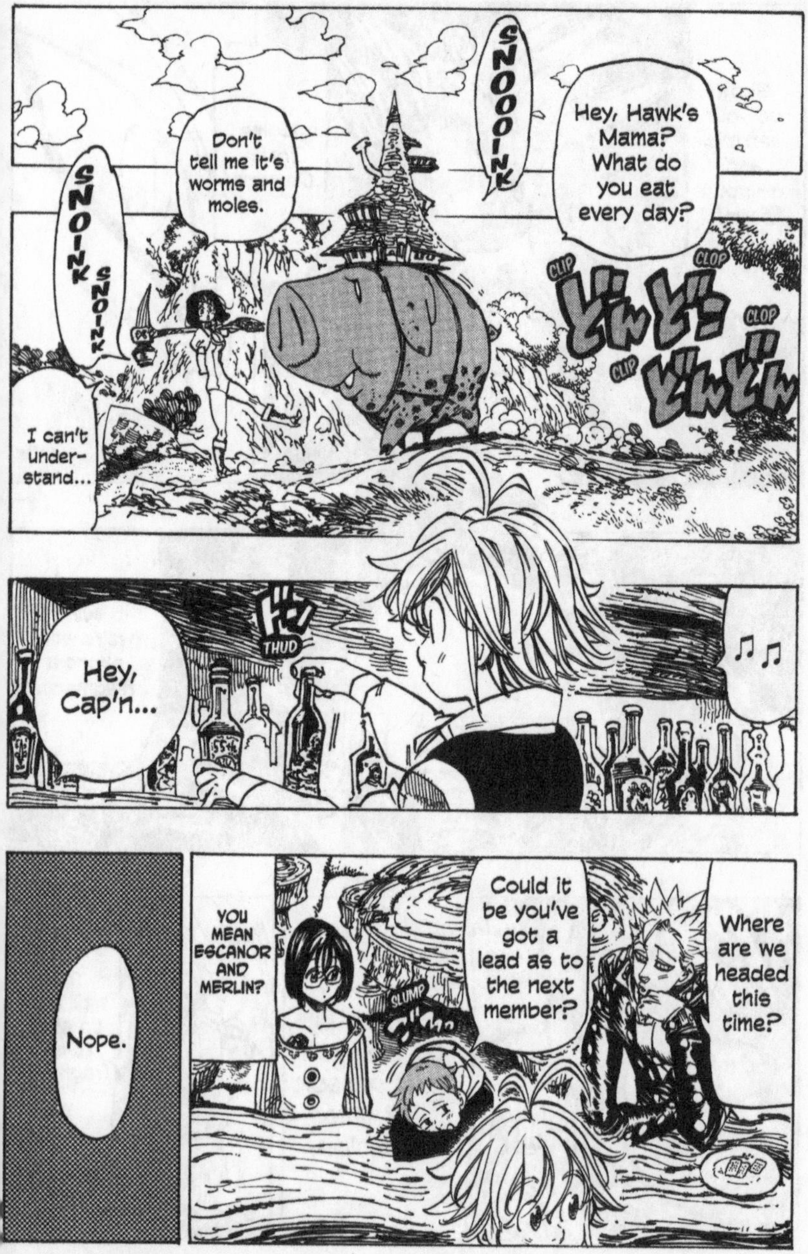
Hey, Hawk's Mama? What do you eat every day?
SNOOOOINK
Don't tell me it's worms and moles.
SNOINK SNOINK
CLOP
CLIP
CLOP
CLIP
I can't under-stand...
♫♫
THUD
Hey, Cap'n...
Where are we headed this time?
Could it be you've got a lead as to the next member?
SLUMP
YOU MEAN ESCANOR AND MERLIN?
Nope.

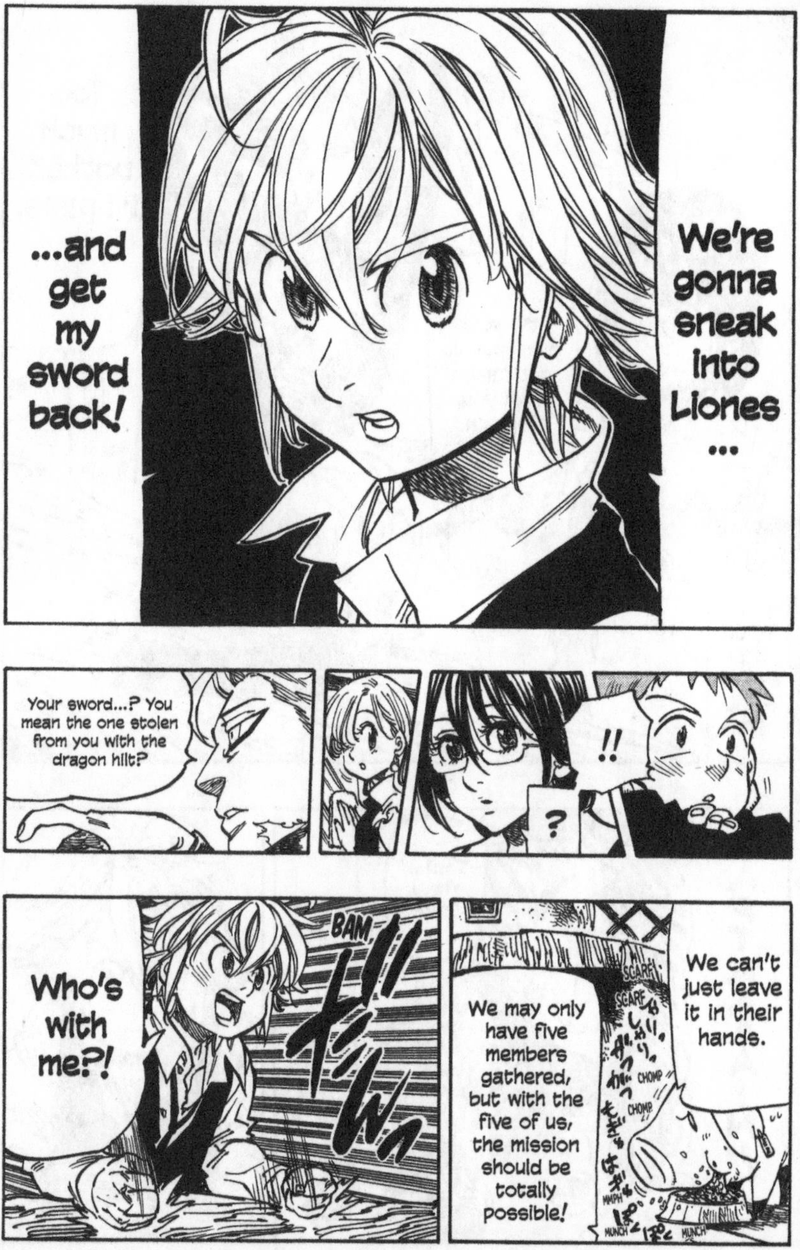
We're gonna sneak into Liones...
...and get my sword back!
!!
?
Your sword...? You mean the one stolen from you with the dragon hilt?
We can't just leave it in their hands.
SCARF
SCARF
CHOMP
CHOMP
MMPH
MUNCH
MUNCH
We may only have five members gathered, but with the five of us, the mission should be totally possible!
BAM
Who's with me?!

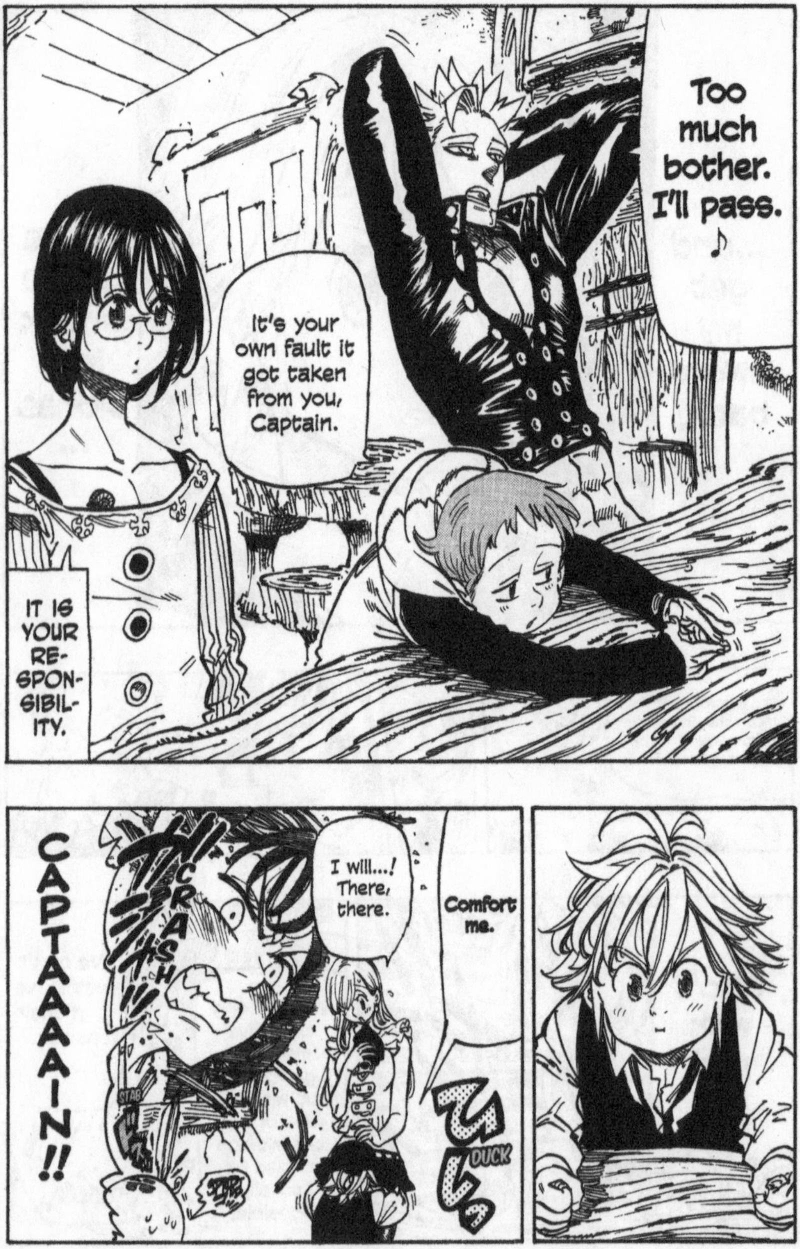
Too much bother. I'll pass. ♪
It's your own fault it got taken from you, Captain.
IT IS YOUR RE-SPON-SIBIL-ITY.
Comfort me.
I will...! There, there.
CRASH
CAPTAAAAAIN!!
DUCK
STAB

Chapter 61 - The Legends Get Stirred Up

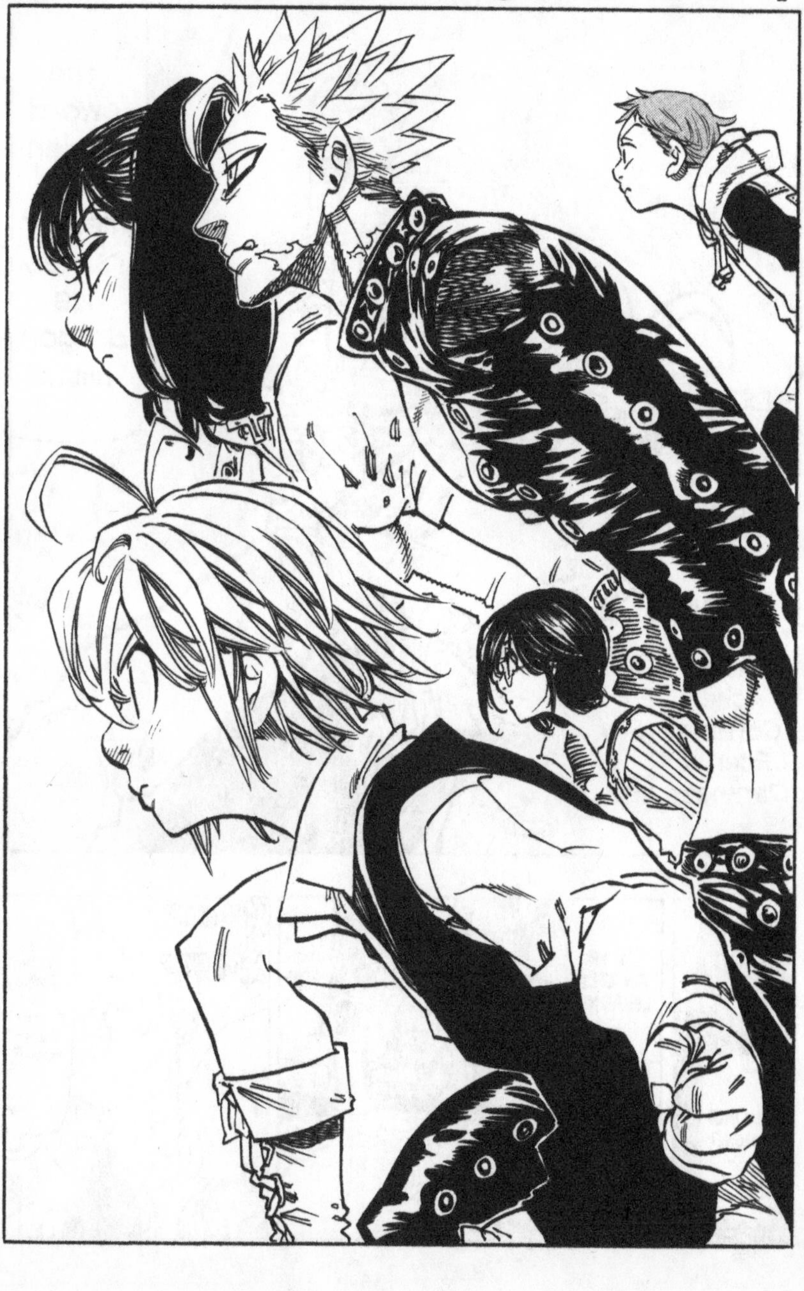

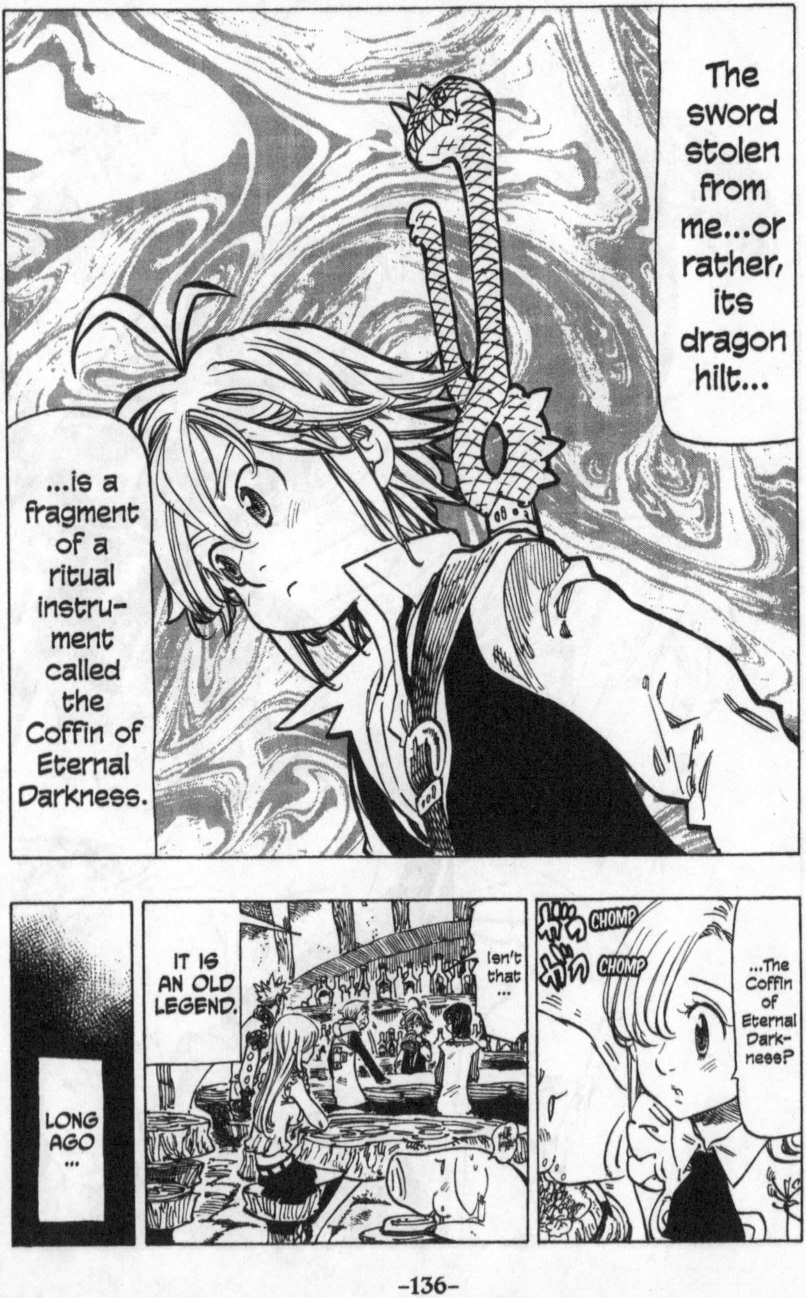
The sword stolen from me...or rather, its dragon hilt...
...is a fragment of a ritual instrument called the Coffin of Eternal Darkness.
CHOMP
CHOMP
...The Coffin of Eternal Dark-ness?
Isn't that ...
IT IS AN OLD LEGEND.
LONG AGO ...

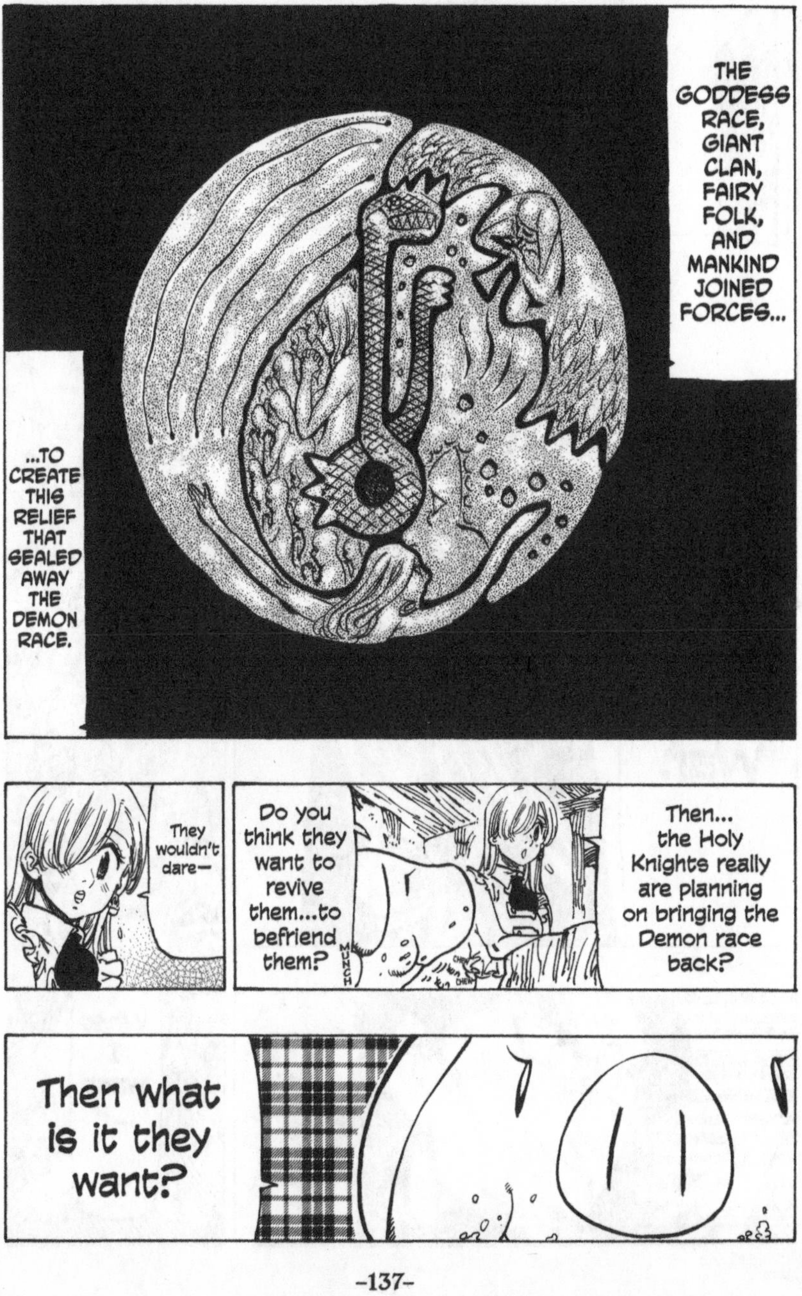
THE GODDESS RACE, GIANT CLAN, FAIRY FOLK, AND MANKIND JOINED FORCES...
...TO CREATE THIS RELIEF THAT SEALED AWAY THE DEMON RACE.
Then... the Holy Knights really are planning on bringing the Demon race back?
Do you think they want to revive them...to befriend them?
MUNCH
CHEW CHEW
They wouldn't dare—
Then what is it they want?

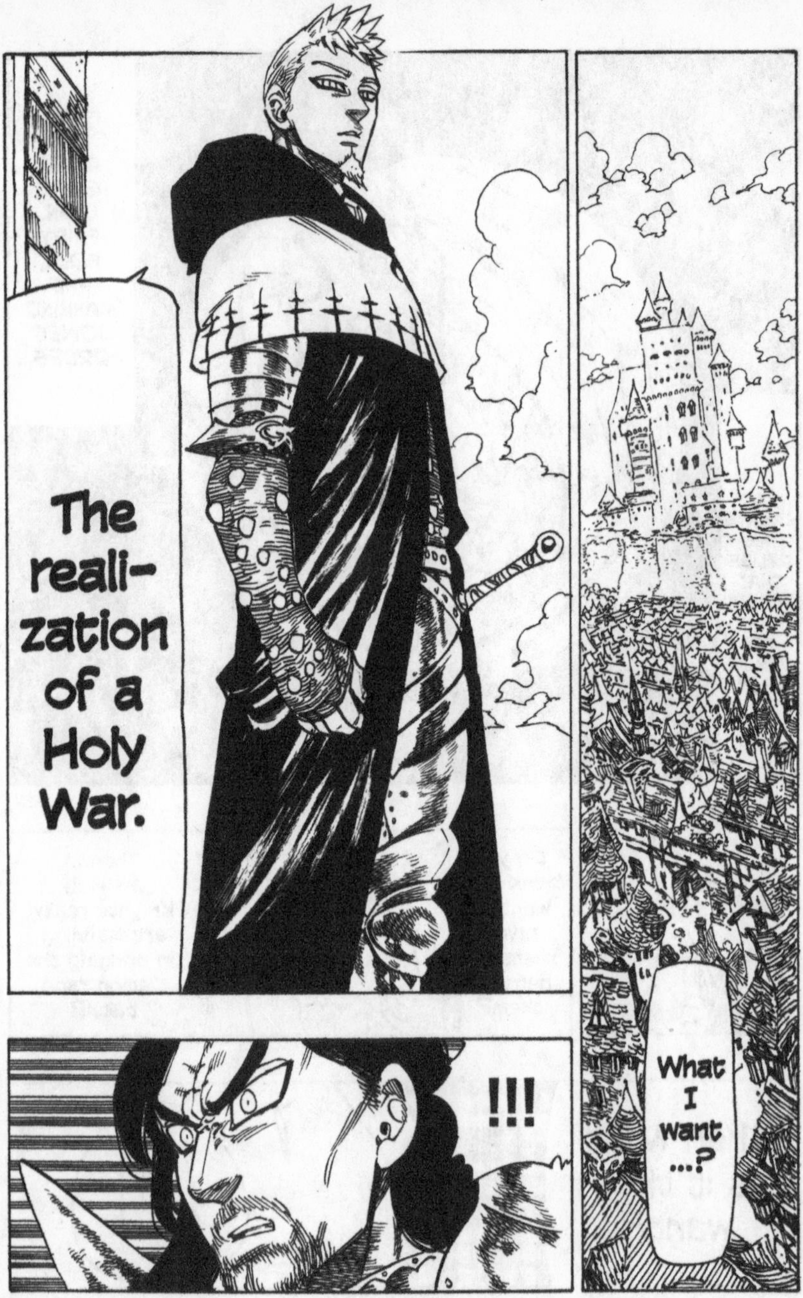
What I want ...?
The realization of a Holy War.
!!!

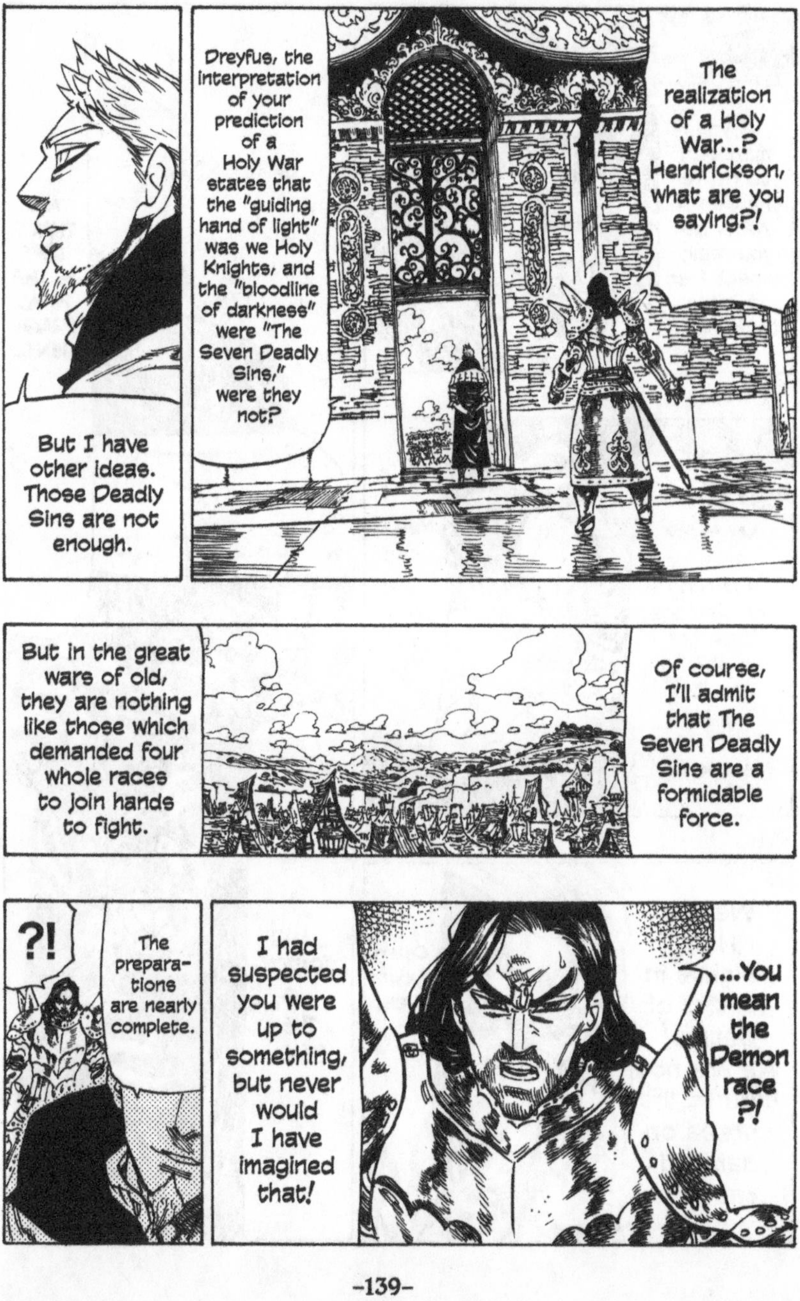
The realization of a Holy War...? Hendrickson, what are you saying?!
Dreyfus, the interpretation of your prediction of a Holy War states that the "guiding hand of light" was we Holy Knights, and the "bloodline of darkness" were "The Seven Deadly Sins," were they not?
But I have other ideas. Those Deadly Sins are not enough.
Of course, I'll admit that The Seven Deadly Sins are a formidable force.
But in the great wars of old, they are nothing like those which demanded four whole races to join hands to fight.
...You mean the Demon race?!
I had suspected you were up to something, but never would I have imagined that!
The prepara-tions are nearly complete.
?!

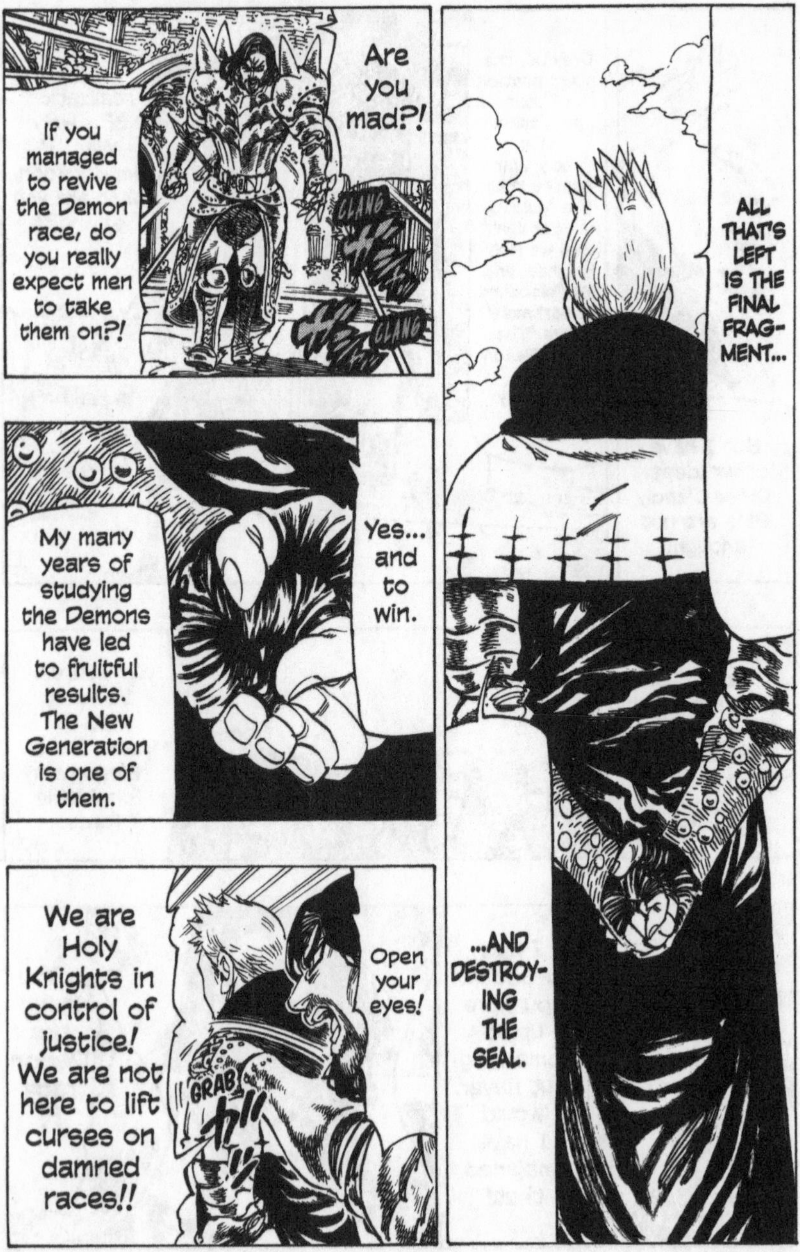
ALL THAT'S LEFT IS THE FINAL FRAGMENT...
...AND DESTROYING THE SEAL.
Are you mad?!
If you managed to revive the Demon race, do you really expect men to take them on?!
CLANG
CLANG
Yes... and to win.
My many years of studying the Demons have led to fruitful results. The New Generation is one of them.
Open your eyes!
We are Holy Knights in control of justice! We are not here to lift curses on damned races!!
GRAB

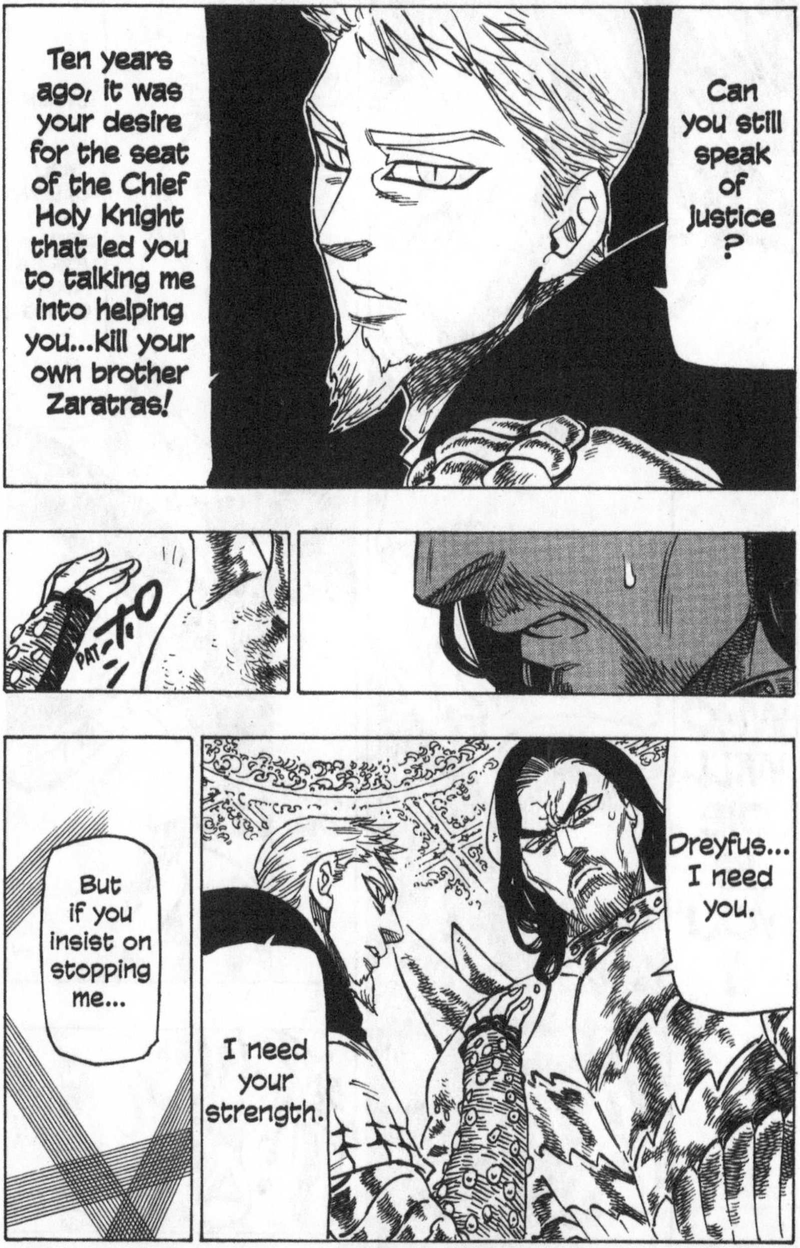
Can you still speak of justice?
Ten years ago, it was your desire for the seat of the Chief Holy Knight that led you to talking me into helping you...kill your own brother Zaratras!
PAT
Dreyfus... I need you.
I need your strength.
But if you insist on stopping me...

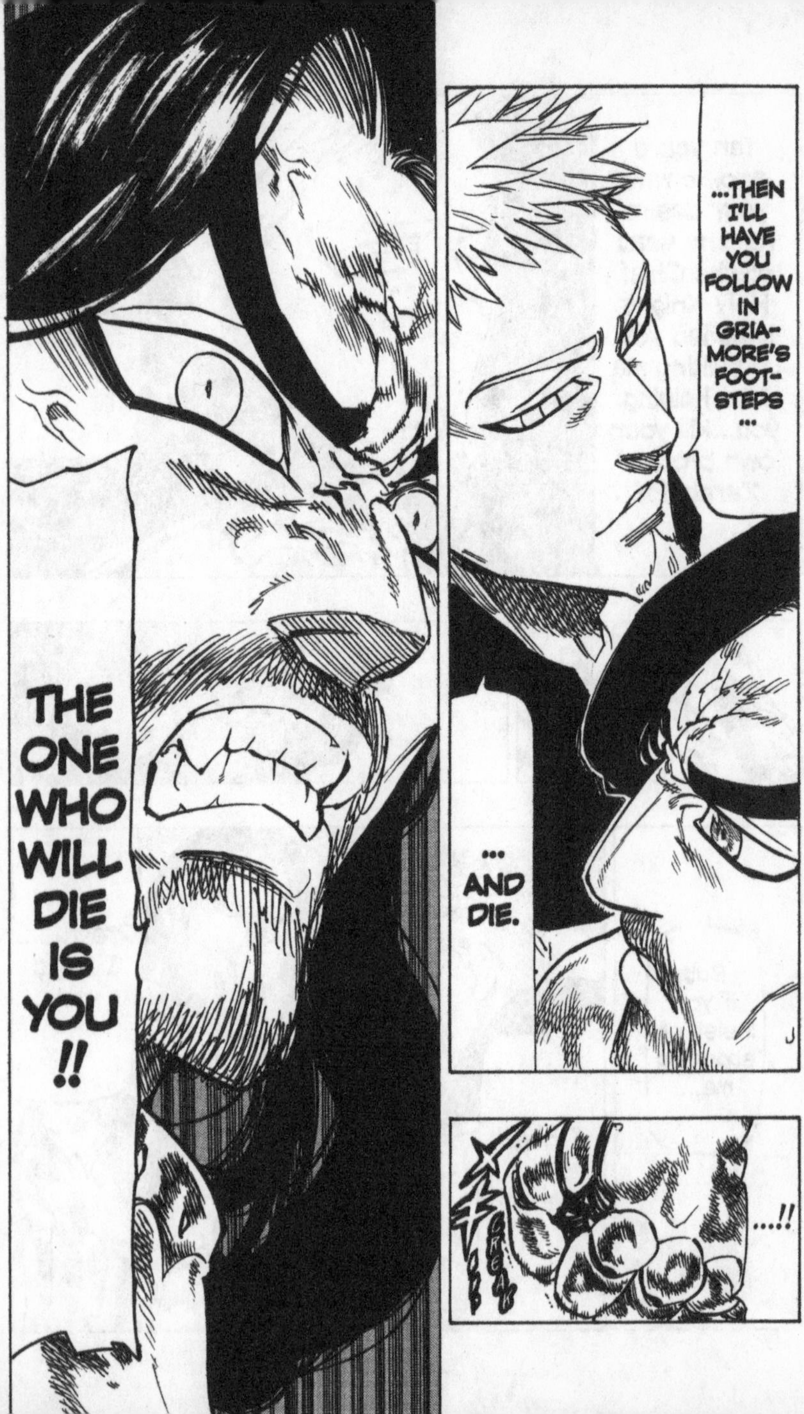

...THEN I'LL HAVE YOU FOLLOW IN GRIAMORE'S FOOTSTEPS...
...AND DIE.
CREAK
...!!
THE ONE WHO WILL DIE IS YOU!!

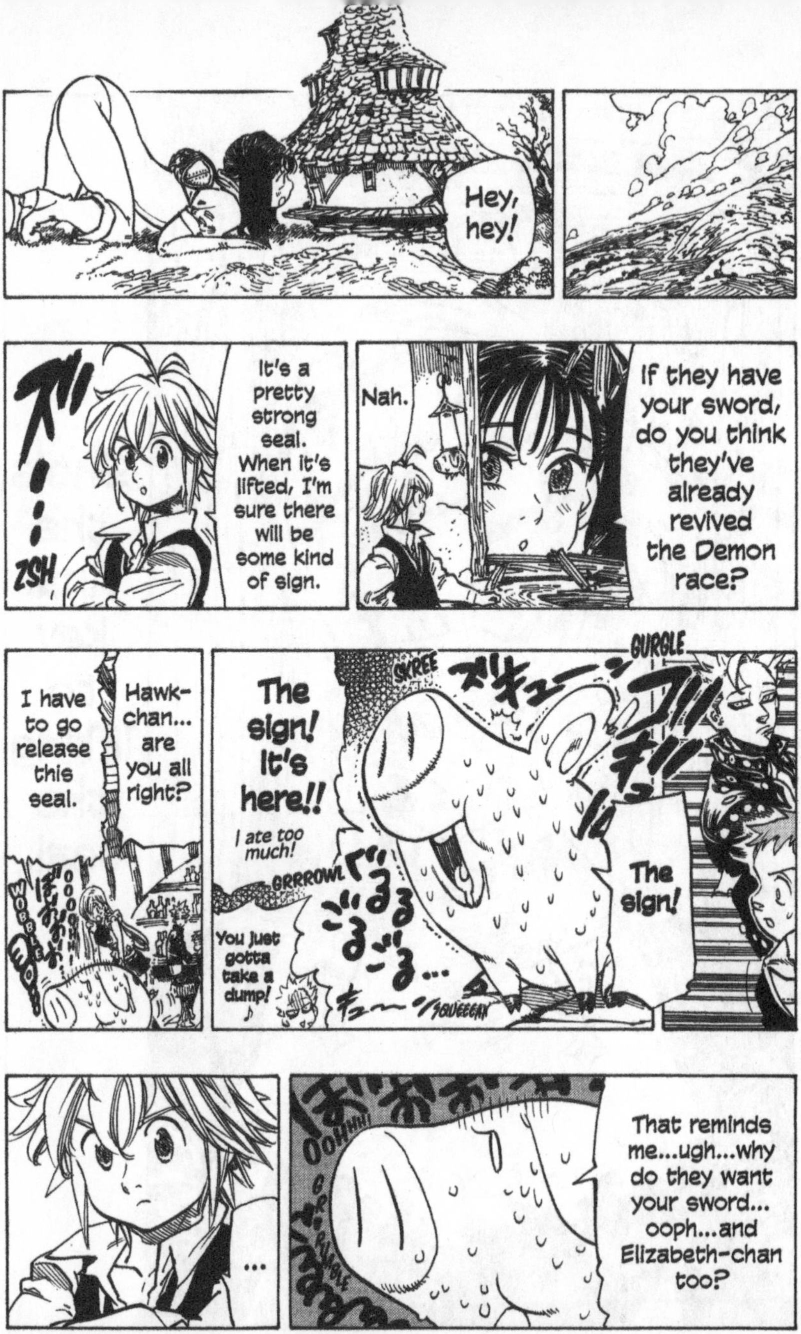
Hey, hey!
If they have your sword, do you think they've already revived the Demon race?
Nah.
It's a pretty strong seal. When it's lifted, I'm sure there will be some kind of sign.
ZSH
The sign!
GURGLE
SKREE
The sign! It's here!!
I ate too much!
GRRROWL
You just gotta take a dump! ♪
SQUEEEAK
Hawk-chan... are you all right?
I have to go release this seal.
OOOOHH!
WOBBLE
That reminds me...ugh...why do they want your sword... ooph...and Elizabeth-chan too?
OOHHH
...

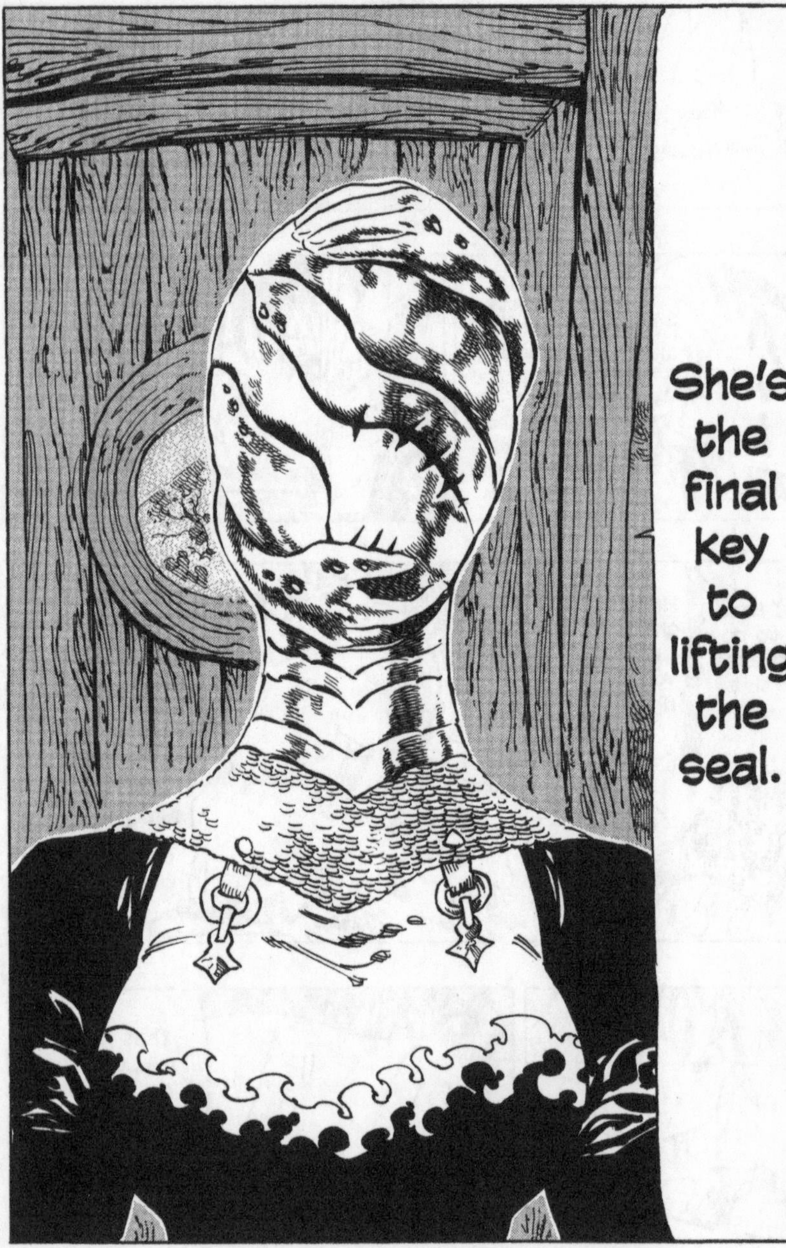
She's the final key to lifting the seal.

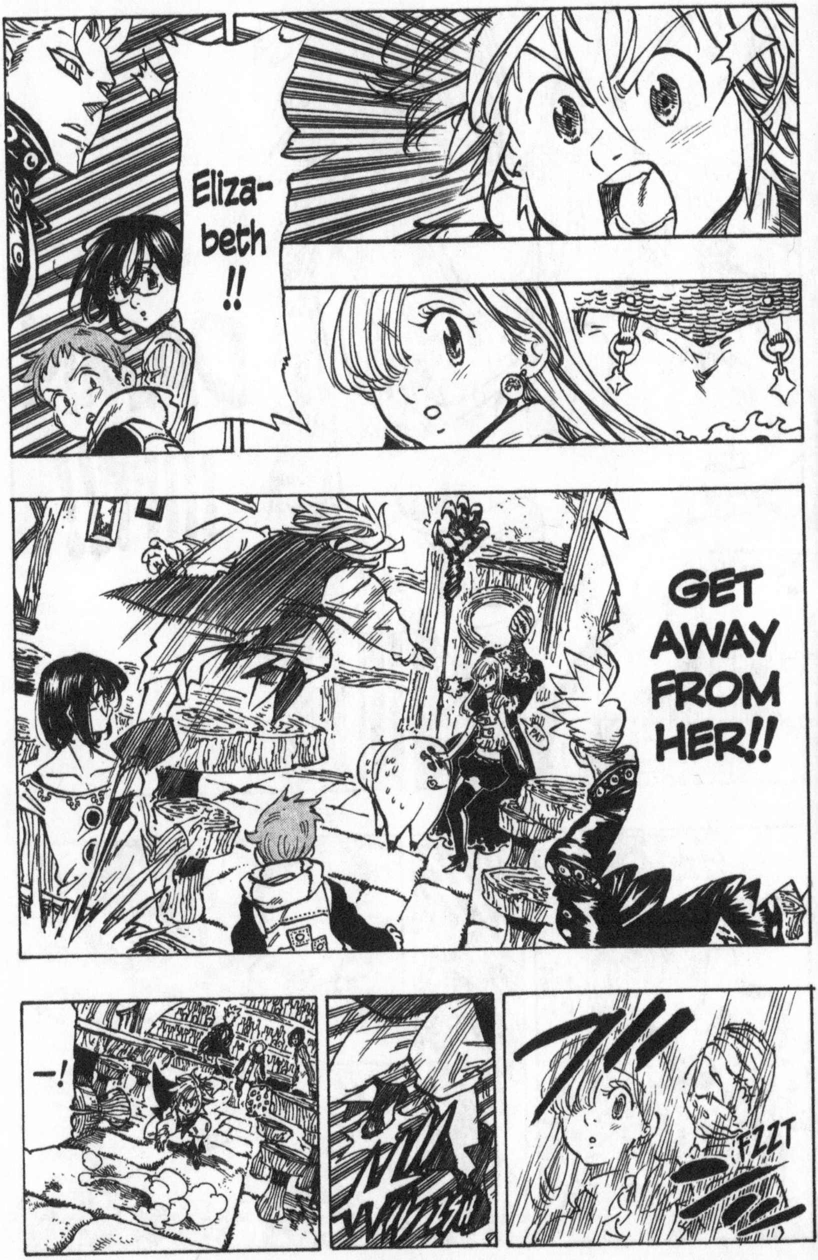
Eliza-
beth
!!
GET AWAY FROM HER!!
PAT
FZZT
—!

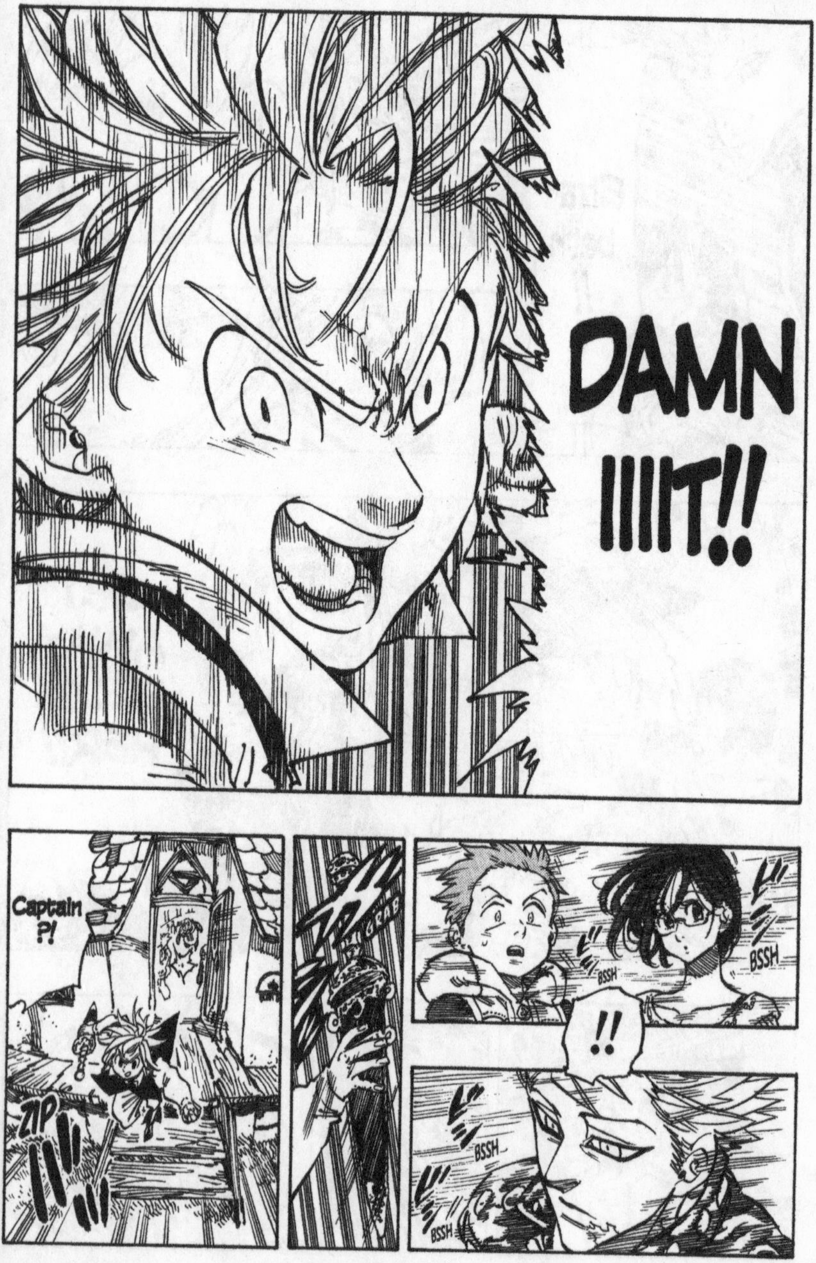
DAMN IIIIT!!
BSSH
BSSH
!!
BSSH
BSSH
GRAB
Captain ?!
ZIP

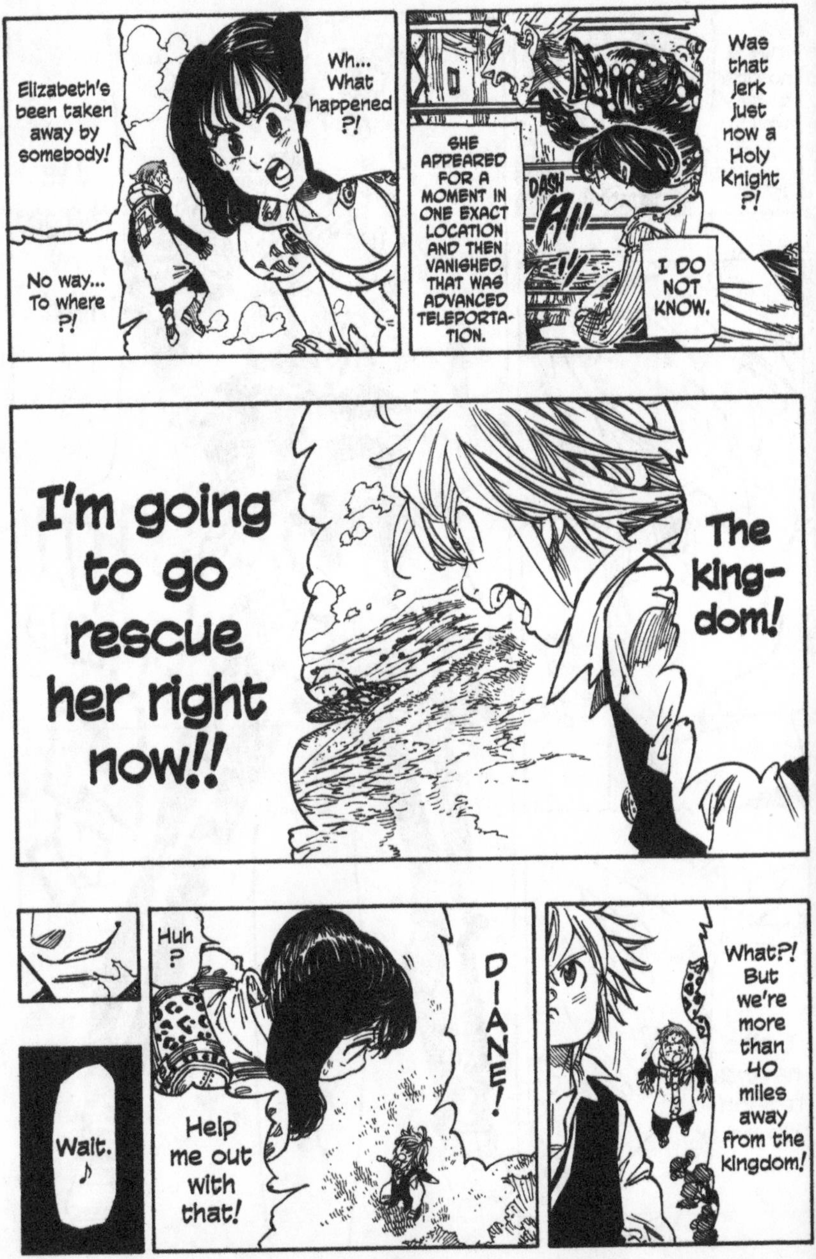

Was that jerk just now a Holy Knight?!
DASH
I DO NOT KNOW.
SHE APPEARED FOR A MOMENT IN ONE EXACT LOCATION AND THEN VANISHED. THAT WAS ADVANCED TELEPORTATION.
Wh... What happened?!
Elizabeth's been taken away by somebody!
No way... To where?!
The kingdom!
I'm going to go rescue her right now!!
What?! But we're more than 40 miles away from the kingdom!
DIANE!
Huh?
Help me out with that!
Wait. ♪

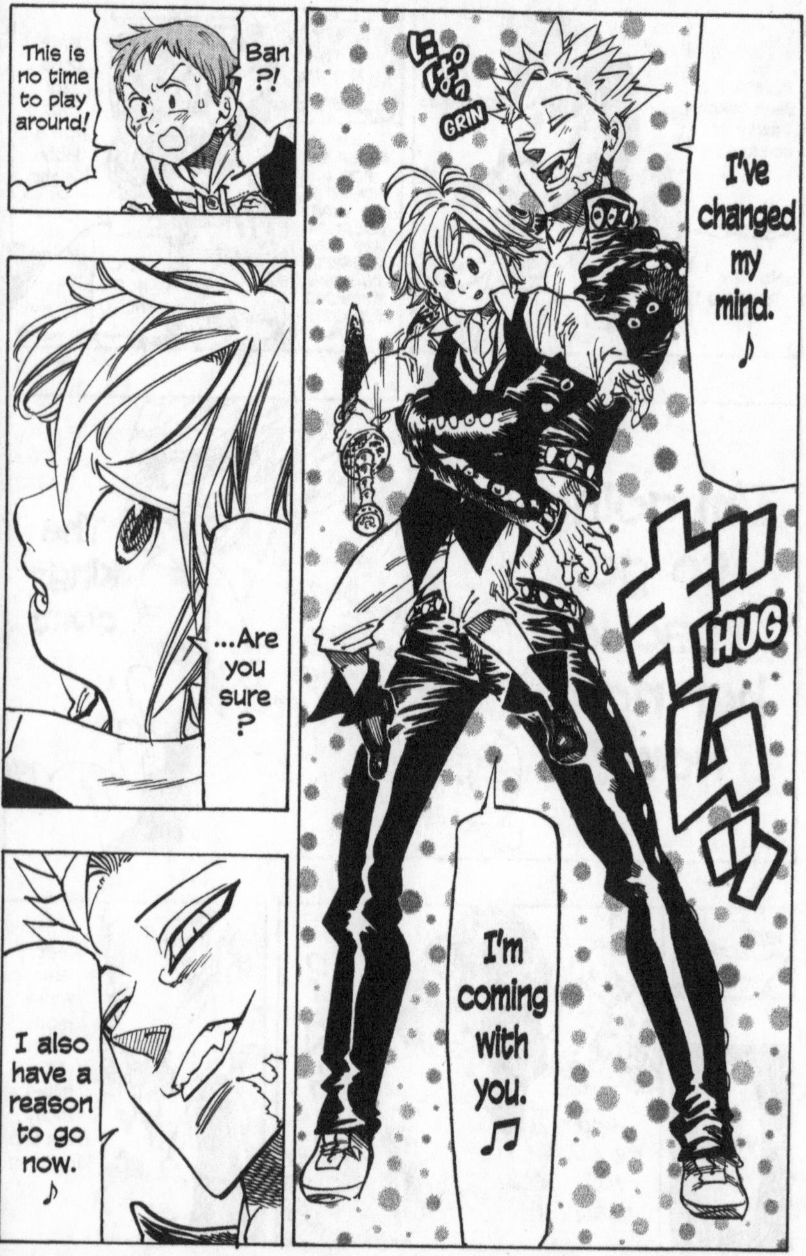
にぽっ
GRIN
I've changed my mind. ♪
ギュッ
HUG
I'm coming with you. ♫
Ban ?!
This is no time to play around!
...Are you sure ?
I also have a reason to go now. ♪

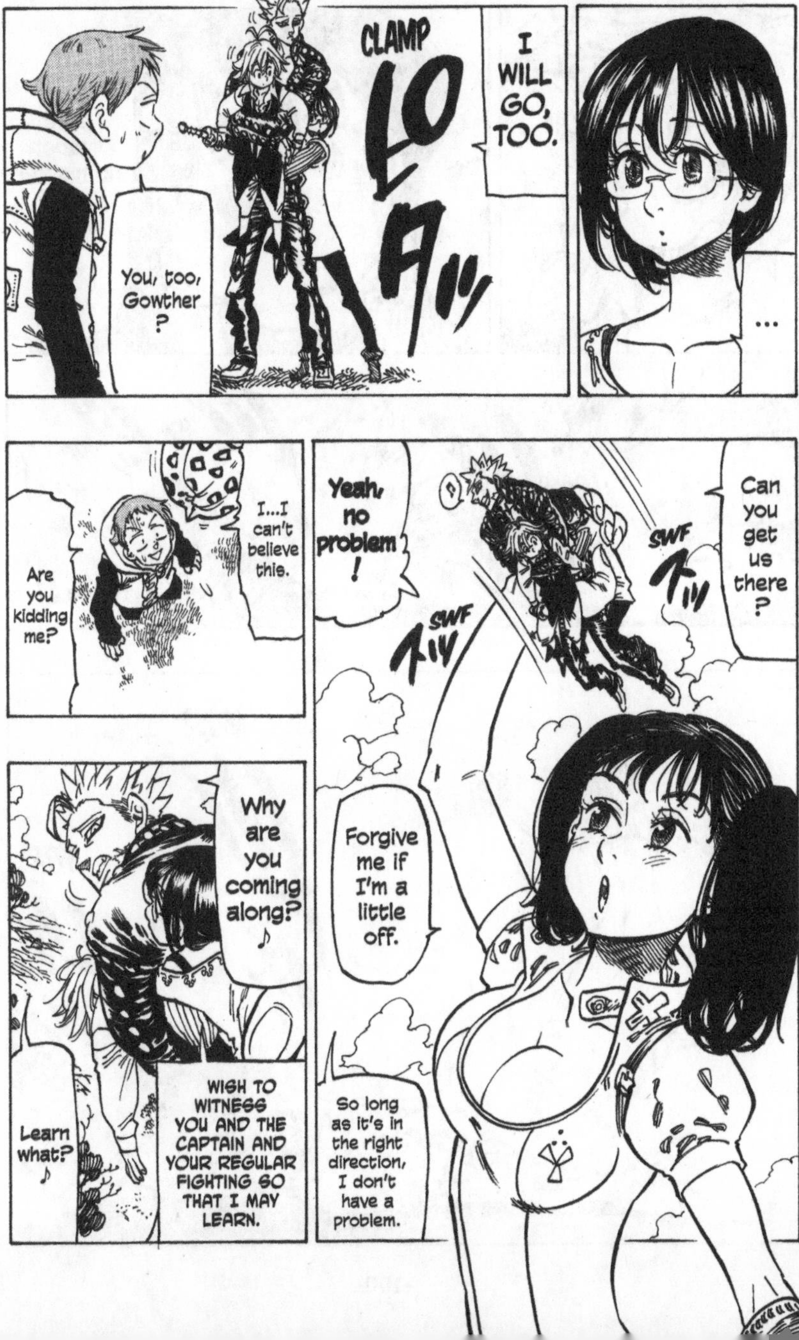
...
I WILL GO, TOO.
CLAMP
You, too, Gowther?
Can you get us there?
SWF
Yeah, no problem!
SWF
Forgive me if I'm a little off.
So long as it's in the right direction, I don't have a problem.
I...I can't believe this.
Are you kidding me?
Why are you coming along? ♪
WISH TO WITNESS YOU AND THE CAPTAIN AND YOUR REGULAR FIGHTING SO THAT I MAY LEARN.
Learn what? ♪

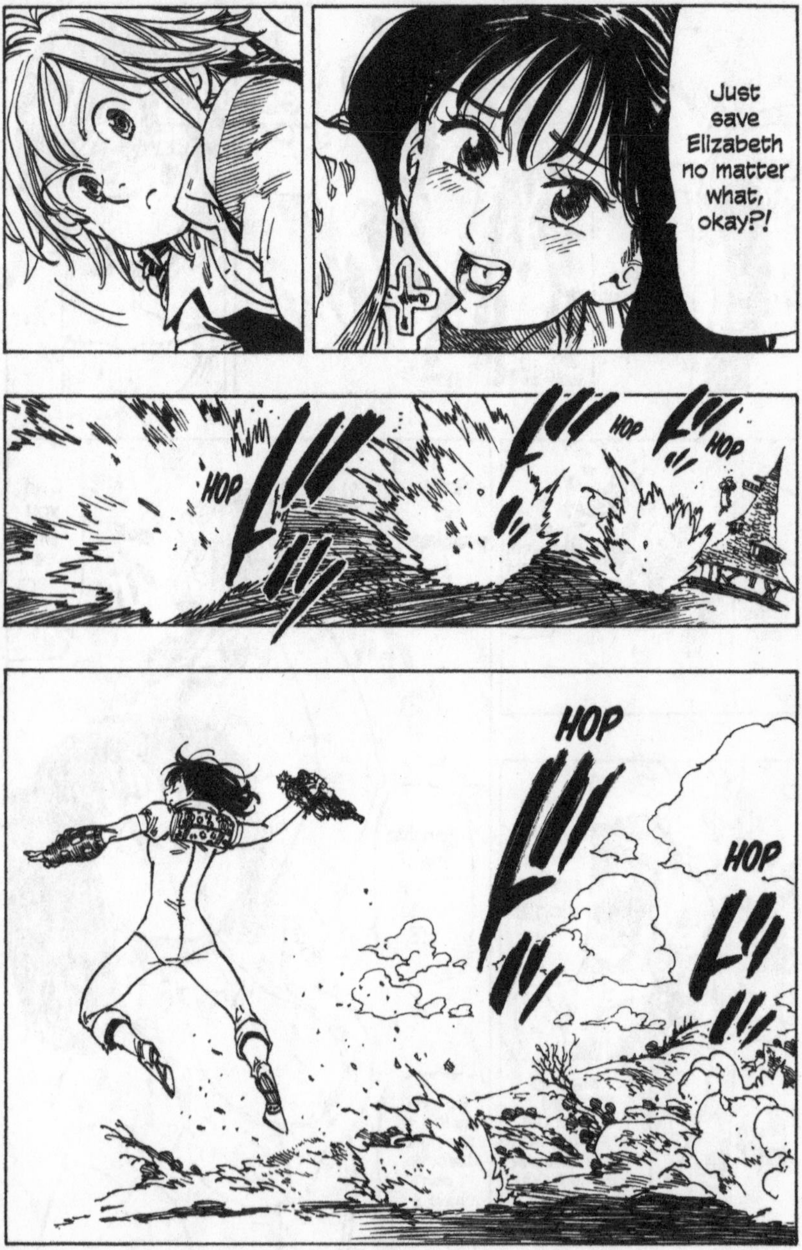
Just save Elizabeth no matter what, okay?!
HOP
HOP
HOP
HOP
HOP

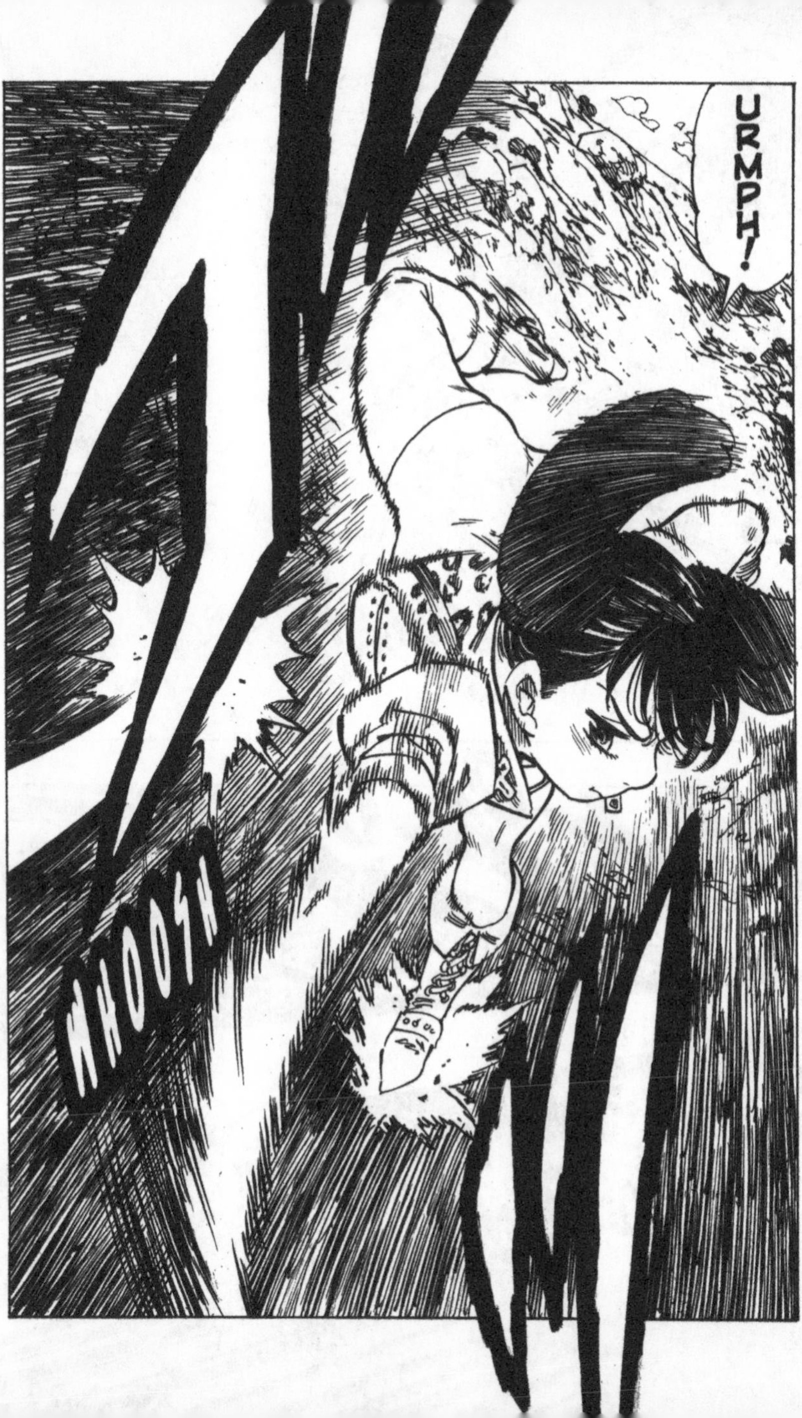
URMPH!
WHOOSH

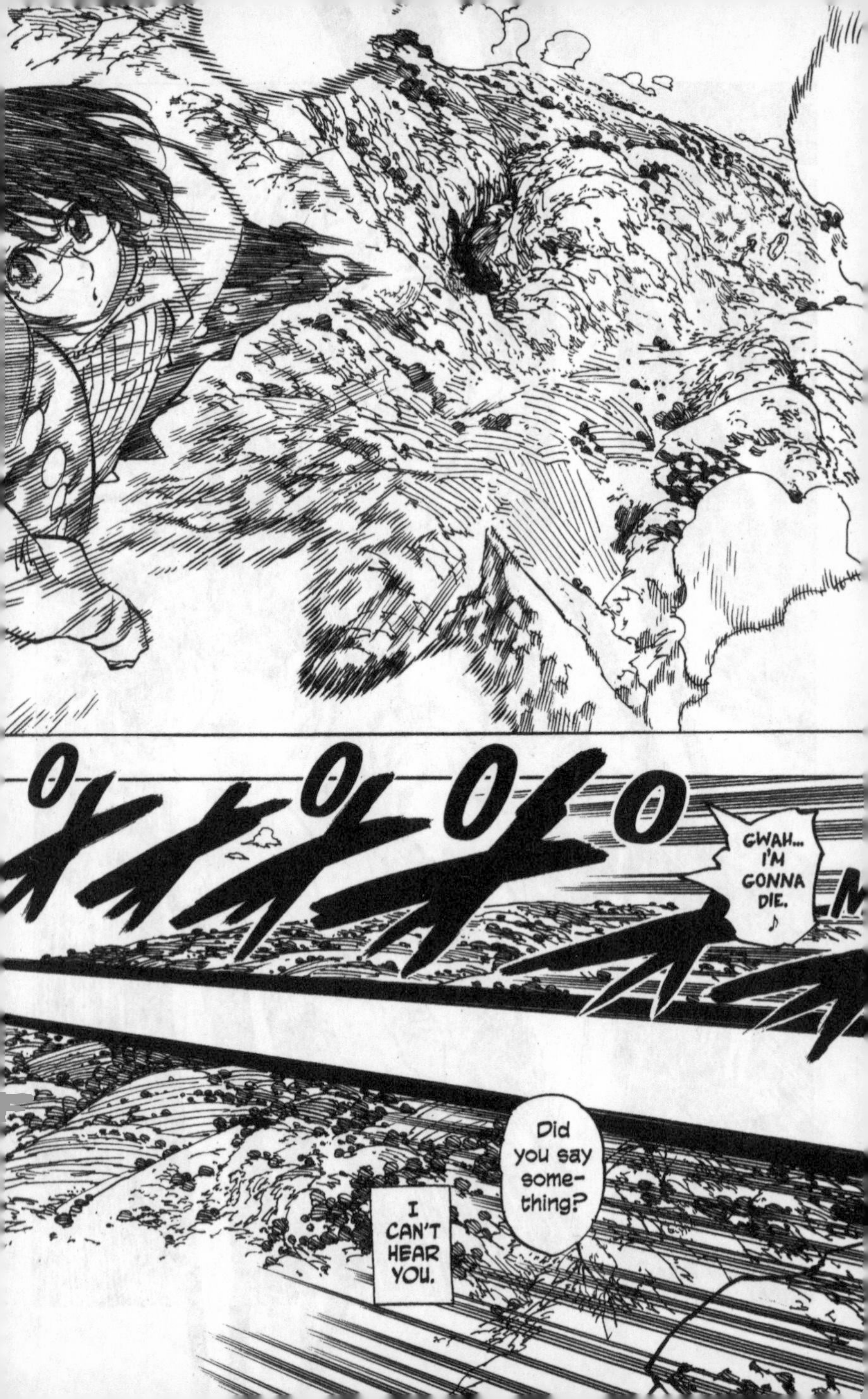
GWAH... I'M GONNA DIE. ♪
Did you say some-thing?
I CAN'T HEAR YOU.

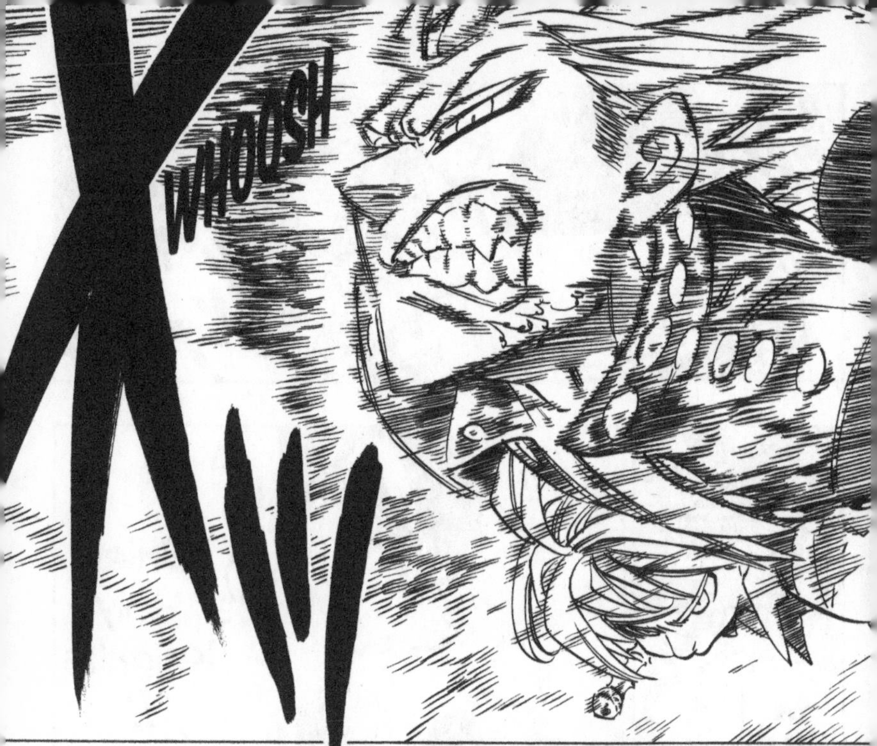
WHOOSH
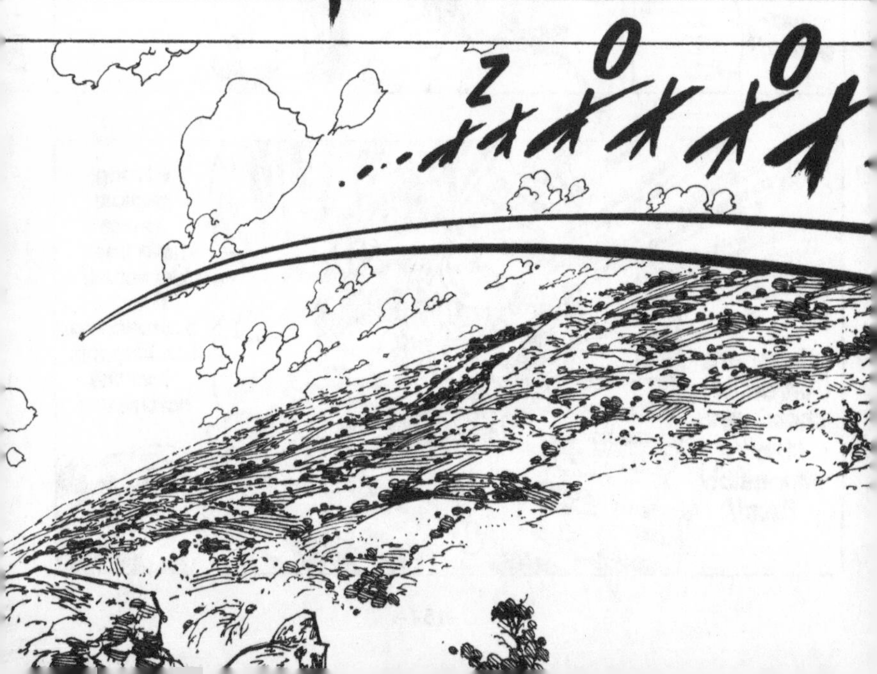

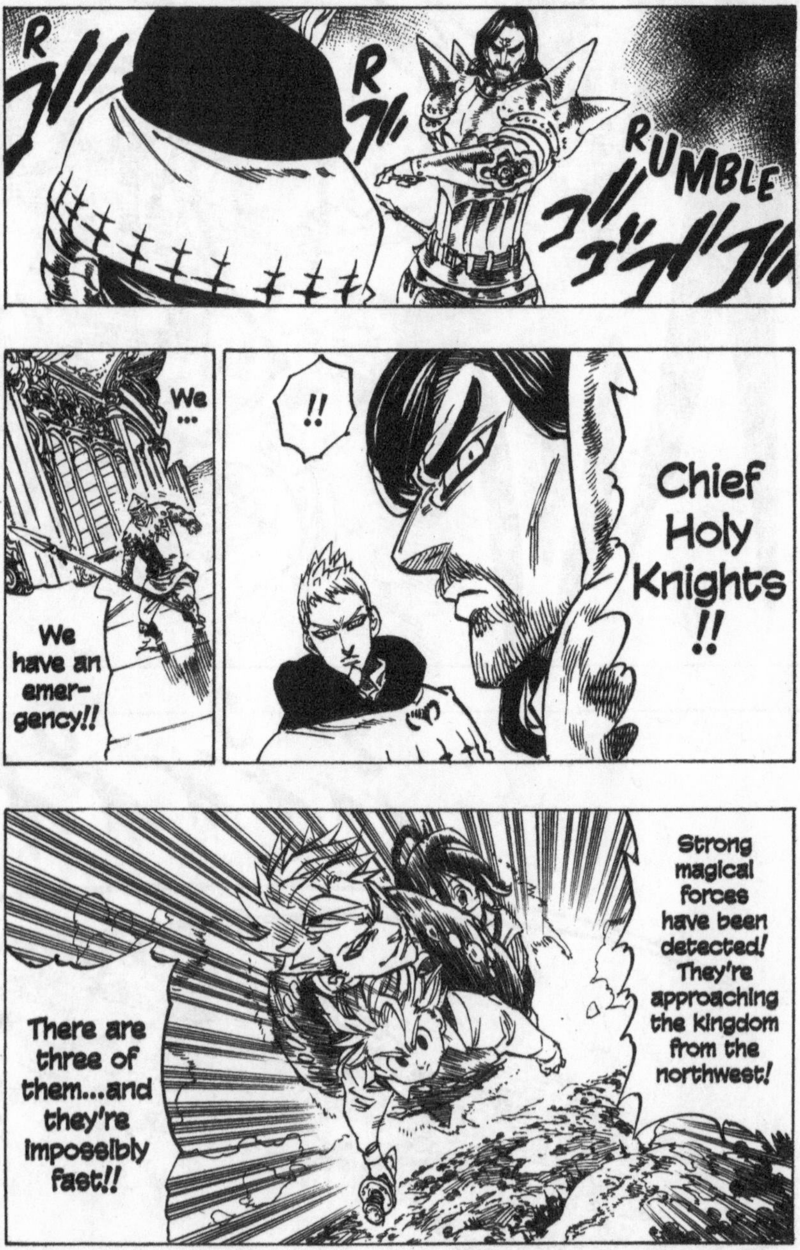
RUMBLE
R
R
Chief Holy Knights!!
!!
We...
We have an emergency!!
Strong magical forces have been detected! They're approaching the kingdom from the northwest!
There are three of them...and they're impossibly fast!!

Chapter 62 -The Devil Won't Stop

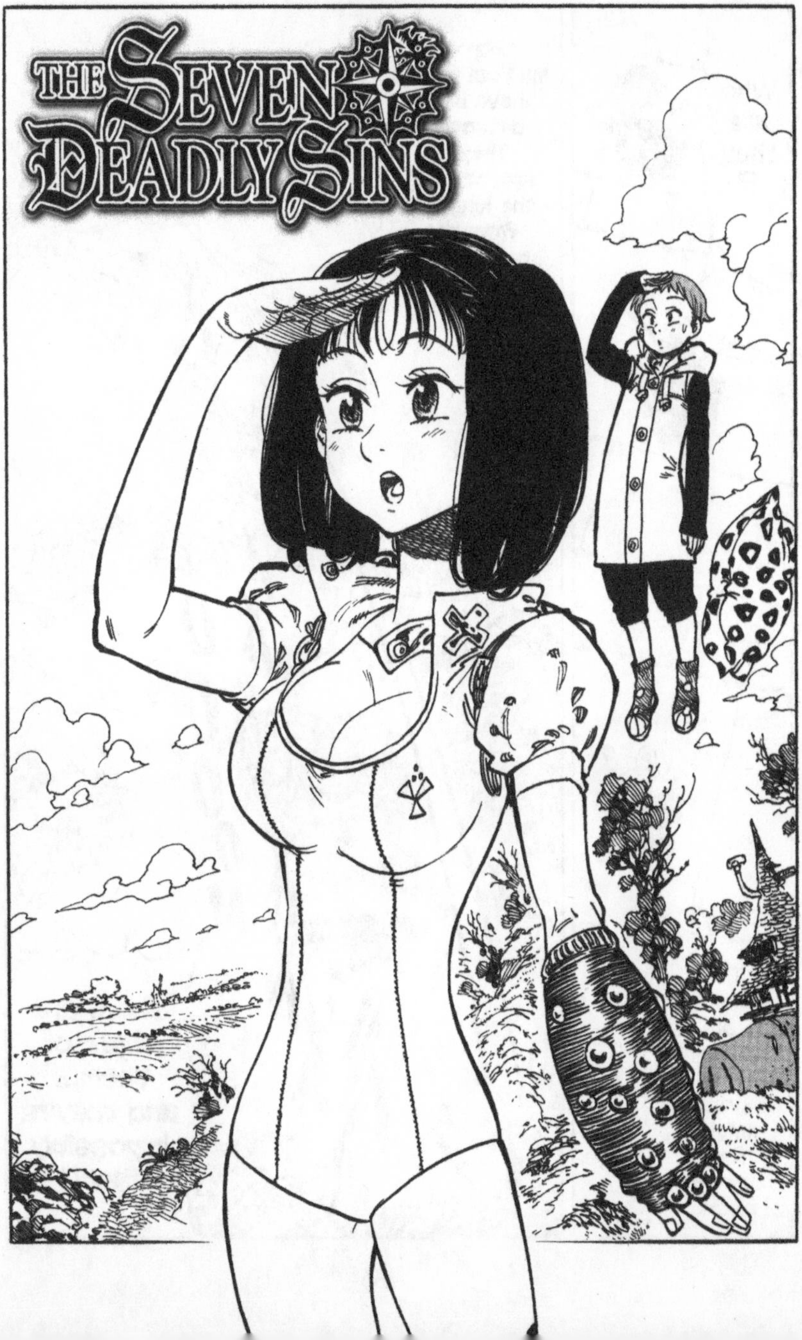
THE SEVEN DEADLY SINS

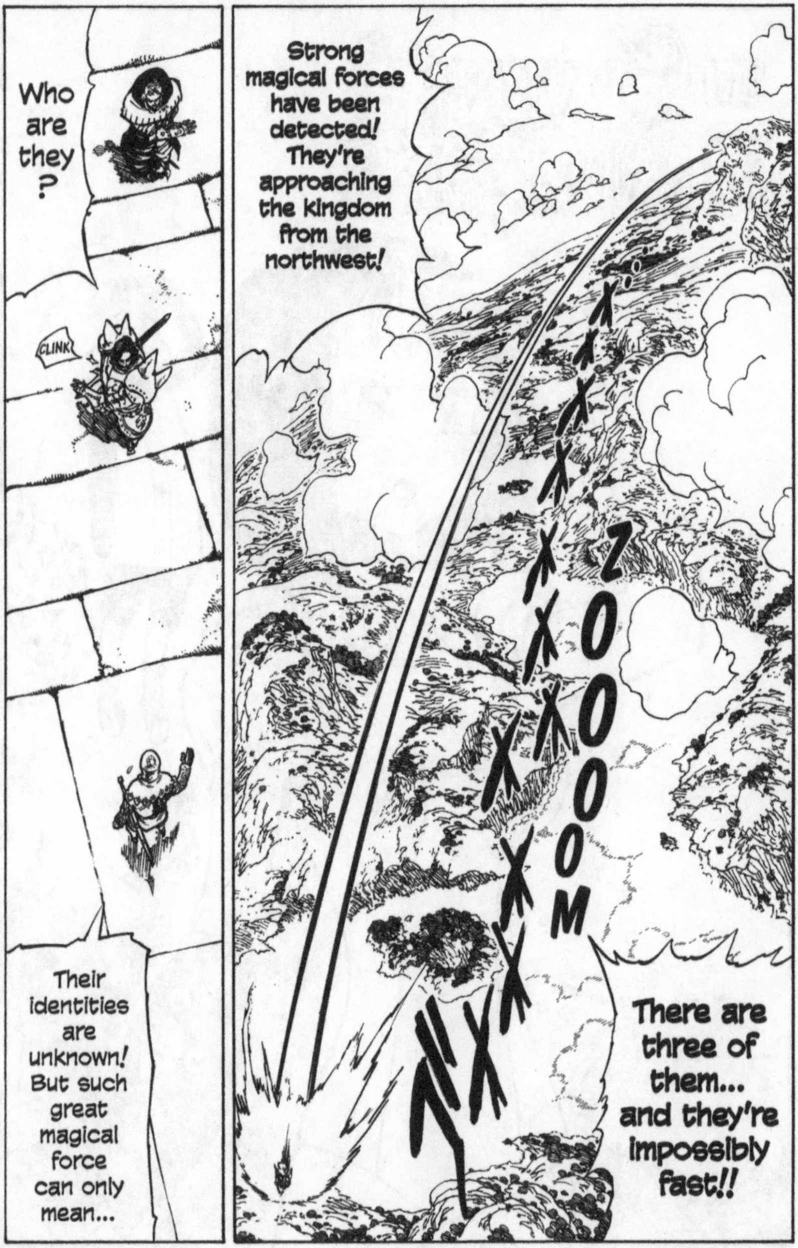
Strong magical forces have been detected! They're approaching the kingdom from the northwest!
ZOOOOOM
There are three of them... and they're impossibly fast!!
Who are they?
CLINK
Their identities are unknown! But such great magical force can only mean...

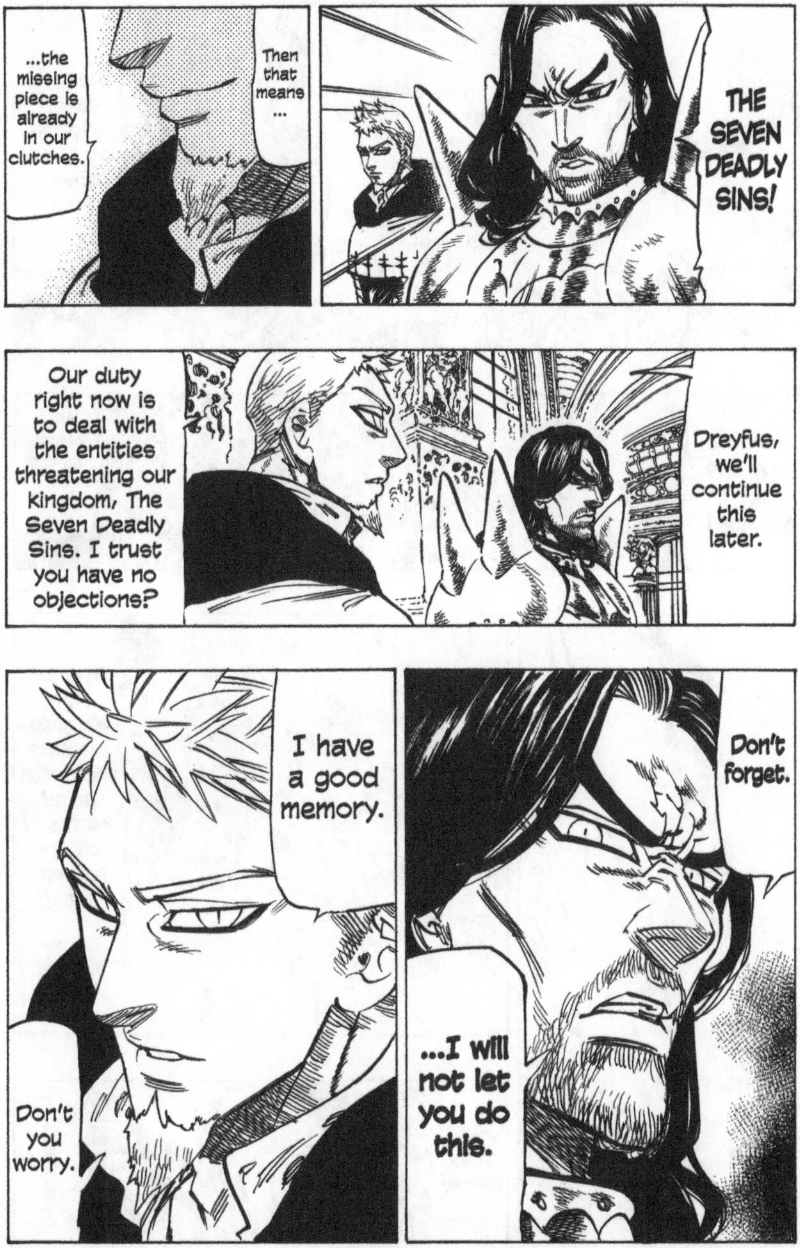

THE SEVEN DEADLY SINS!
Then that means ...
...the missing piece is already in our clutches.
Dreyfus, we'll continue this later.
Our duty right now is to deal with the entities threatening our kingdom, The Seven Deadly Sins. I trust you have no objections?
Don't forget.
...I will not let you do this.
I have a good memory.
Don't you worry.

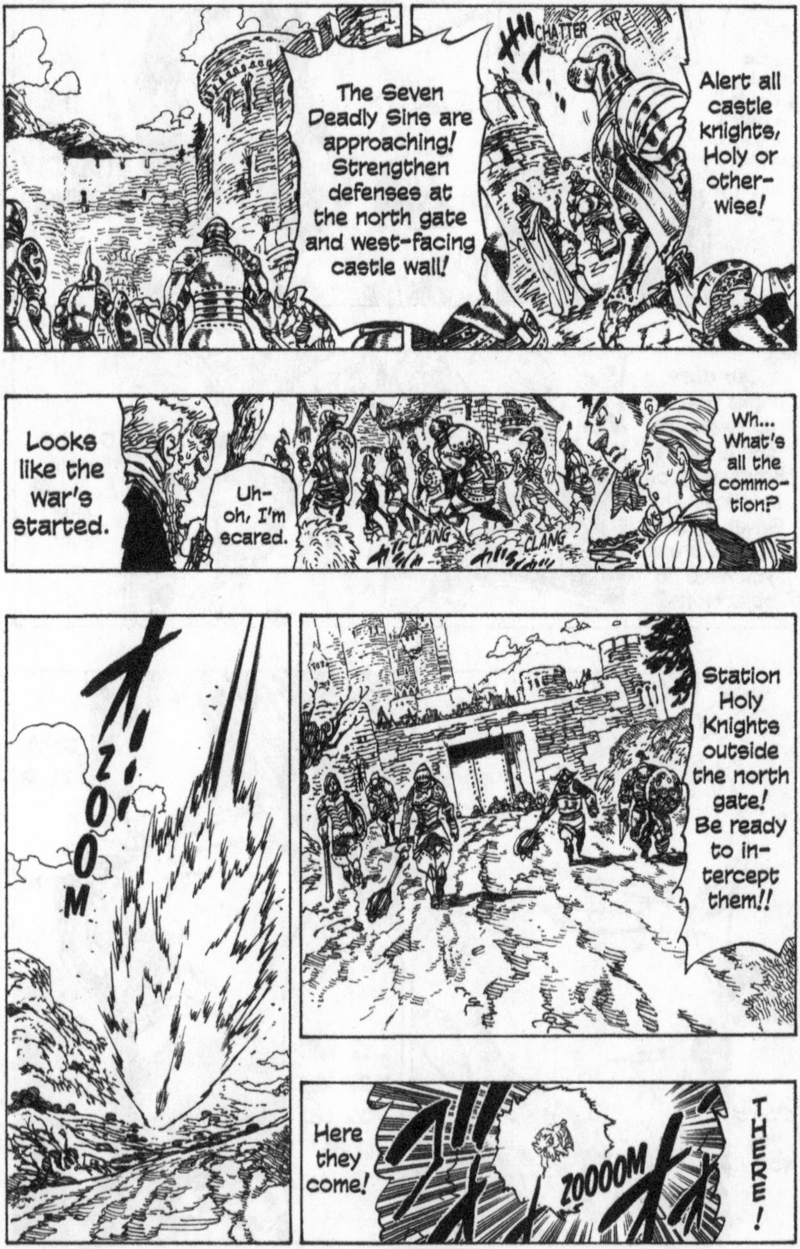
CHATTER
Alert all castle knights, Holy or other-wise!
The Seven Deadly Sins are approaching! Strengthen defenses at the north gate and west-facing castle wall!
Wh... What's all the commo-tion?
CLANG
CLANG
Uh-oh, I'm scared.
Looks like the war's started.
Station Holy Knights outside the north gate! Be ready to in-tercept them!!
THERE!
ZOOOOM
Here they come!
ZOOOM

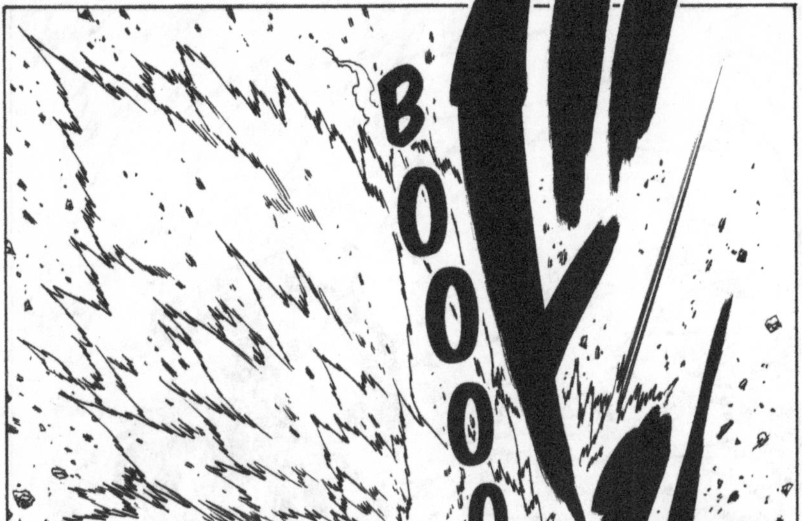
BOOOOOM

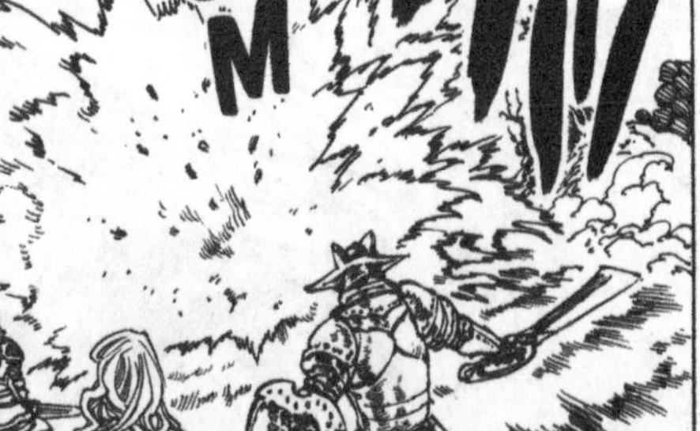
Impact con-firmed!
Get ready to engage!

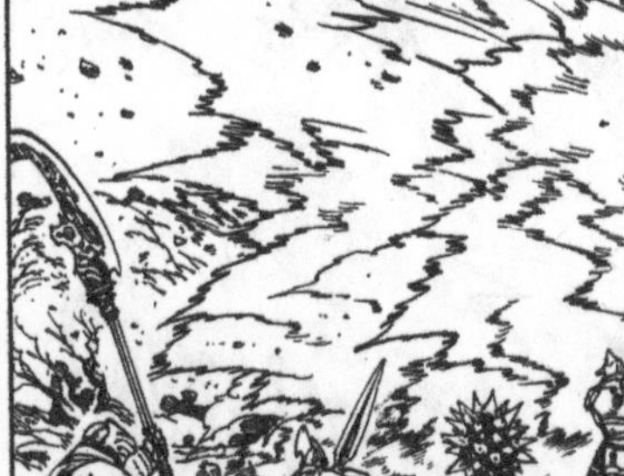
VOOM

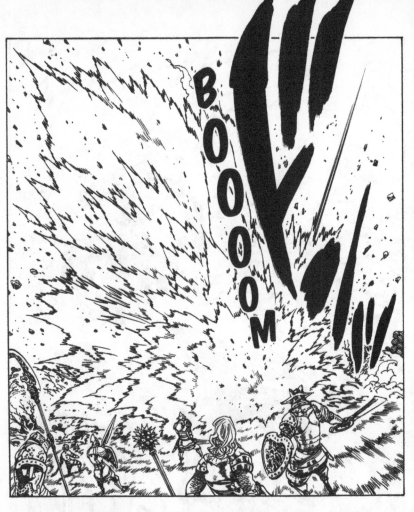

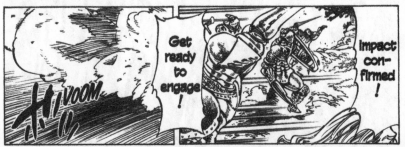

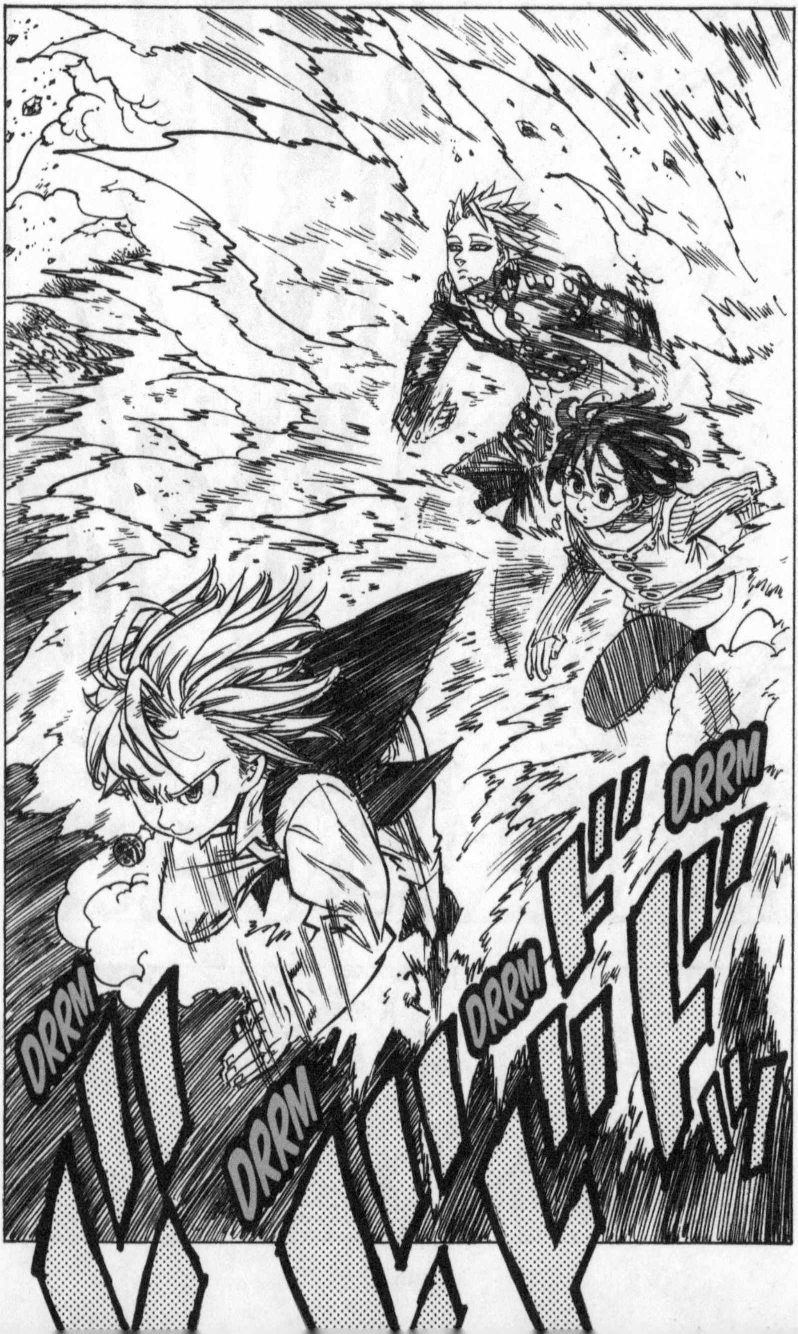
DRRM
DRRM
DRRM
DRRM

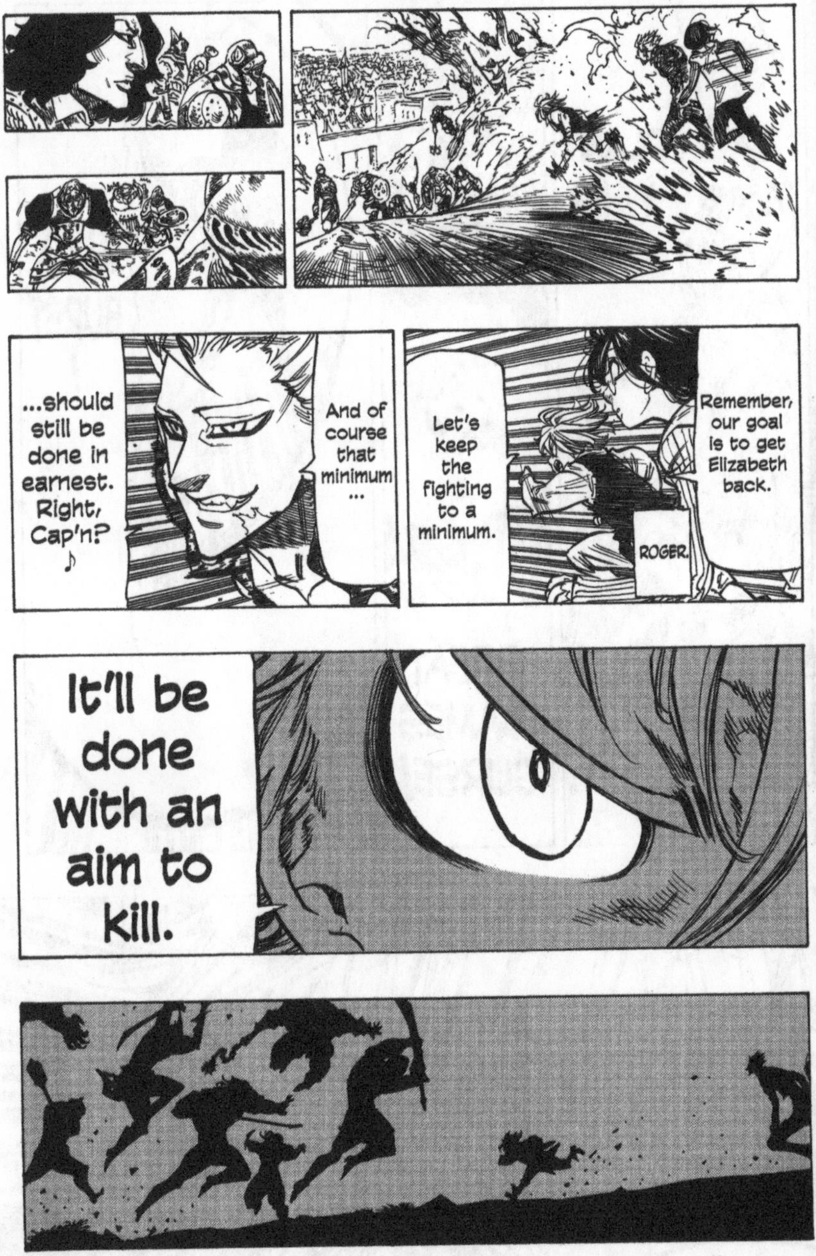
Remember, our goal is to get Elizabeth back.
Let's keep the fighting to a minimum.
ROGER.
And of course that minimum ...
...should still be done in earnest. Right, Cap'n? ♪
It'll be done with an aim to kill.

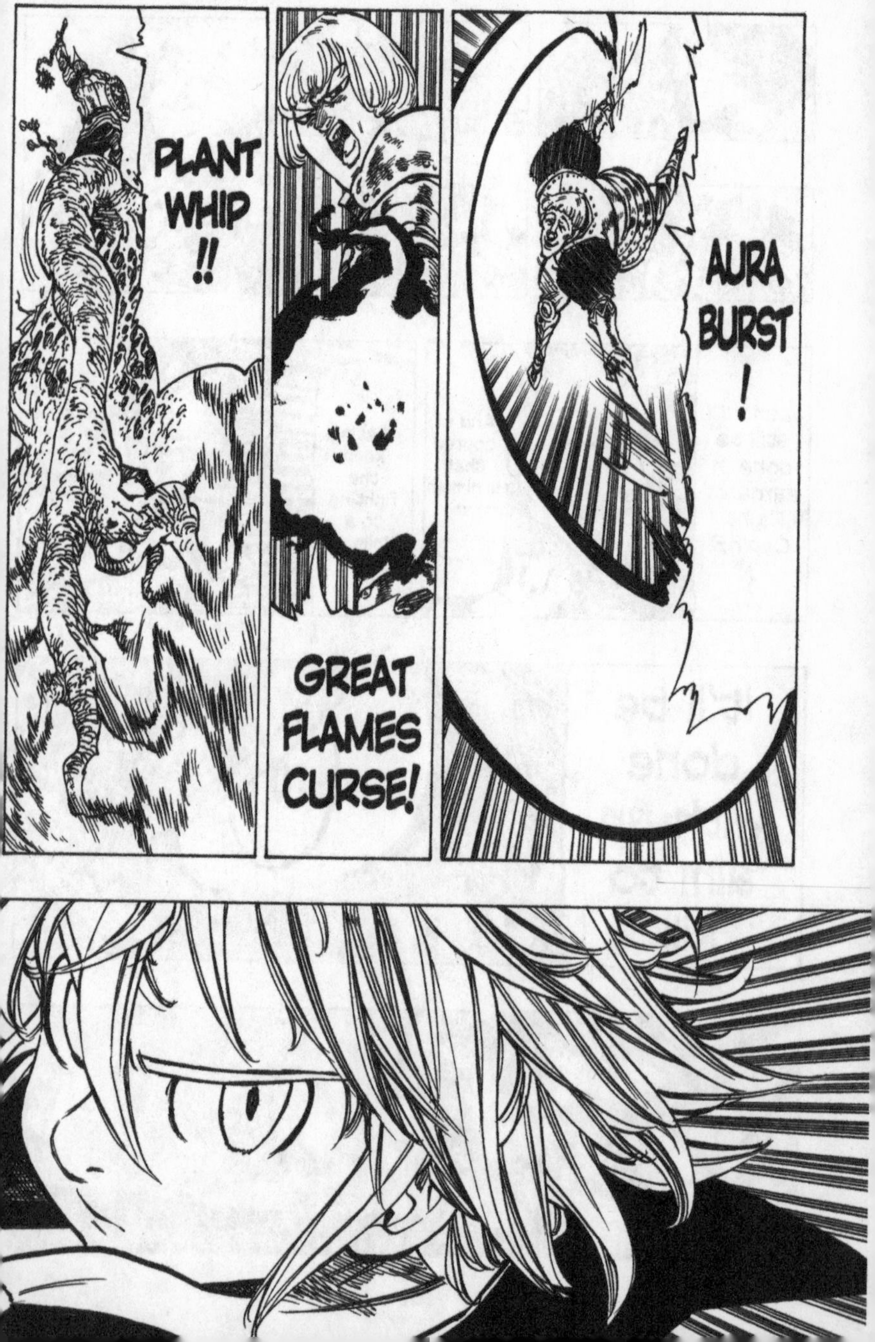
AURA BURST !
GREAT FLAMES CURSE!
PLANT WHIP !!

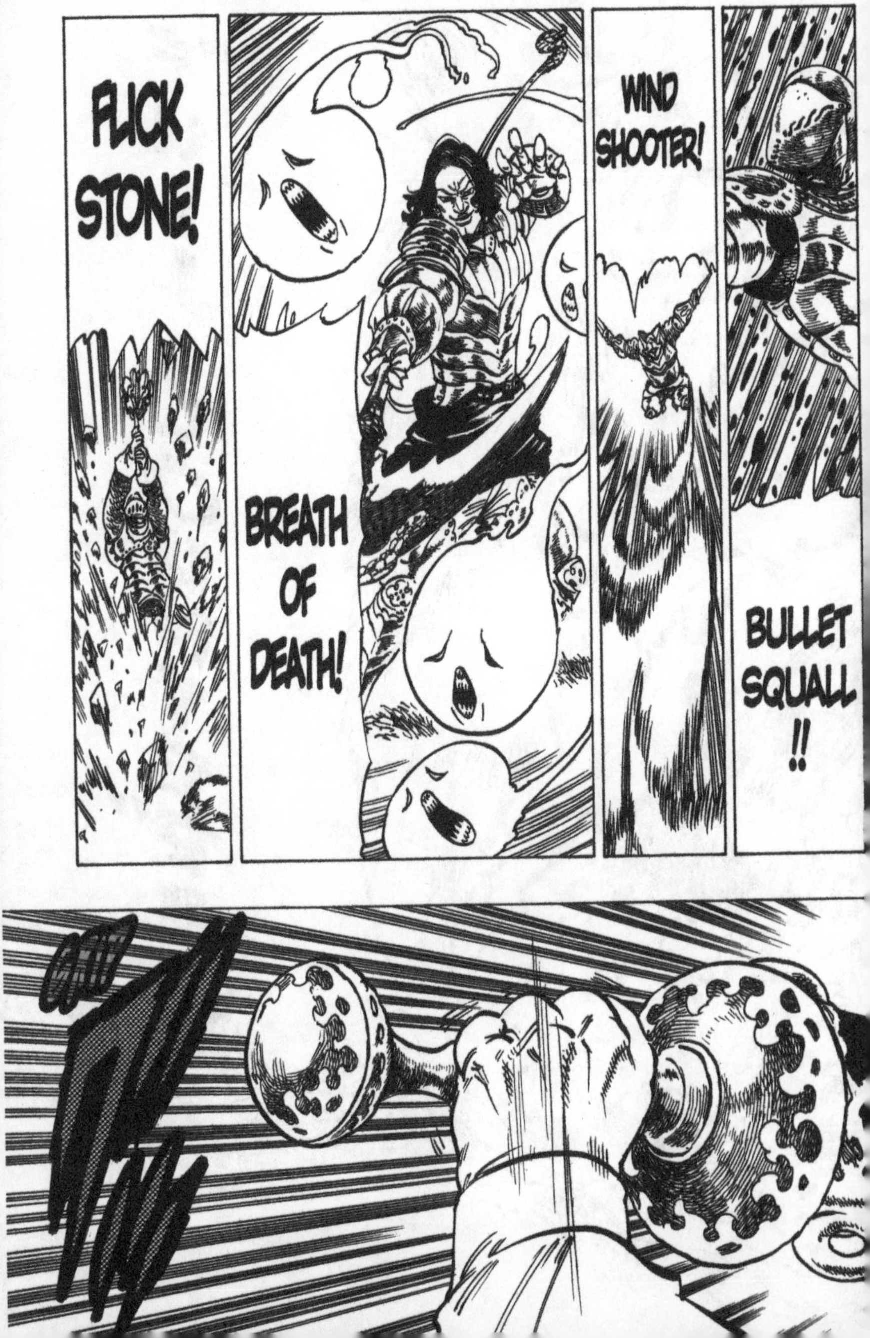
BULLET SQUALL!!
WIND SHOOTER!
BREATH OF DEATH!
FLICK STONE!

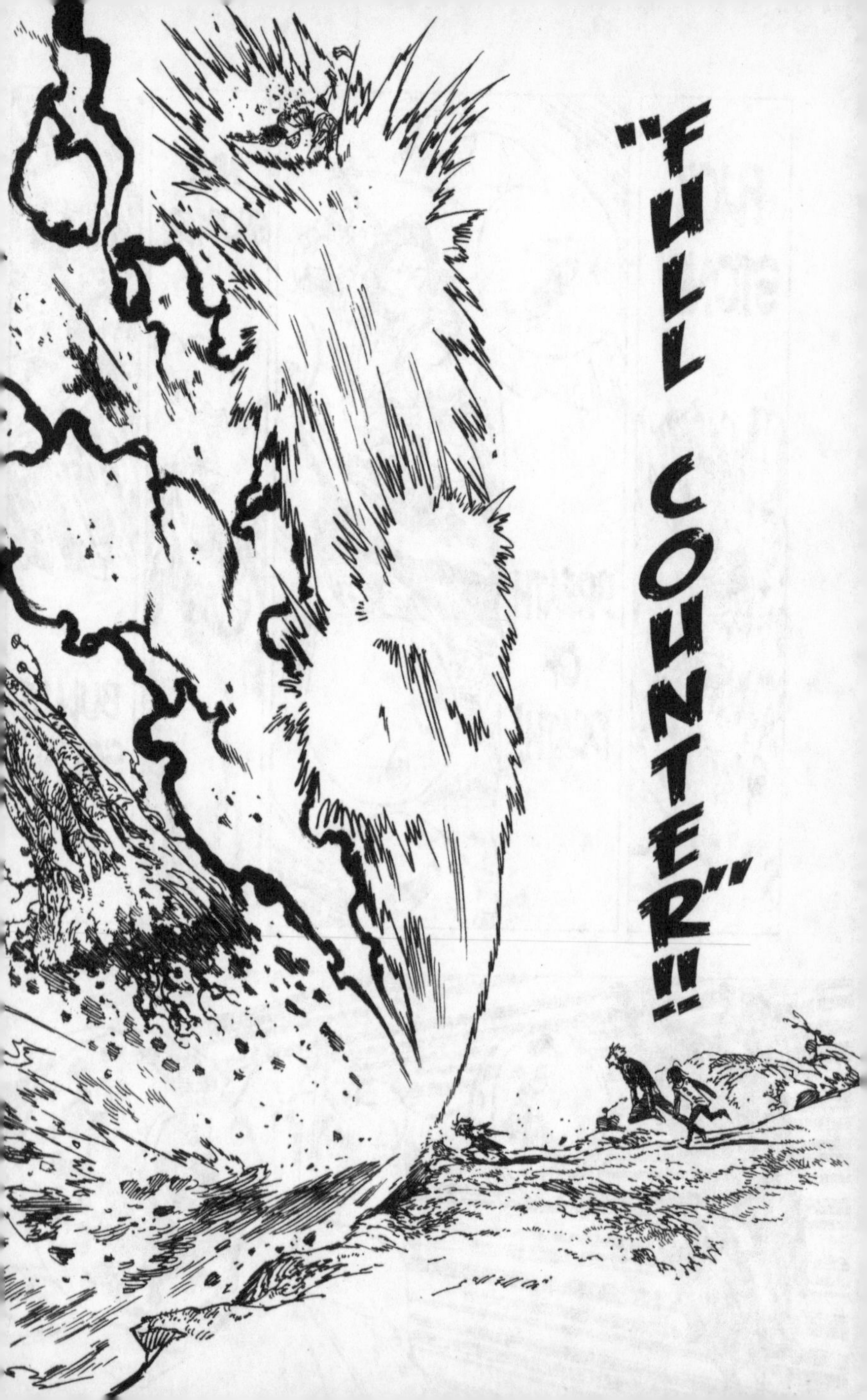
"FULL COUNTER"!!

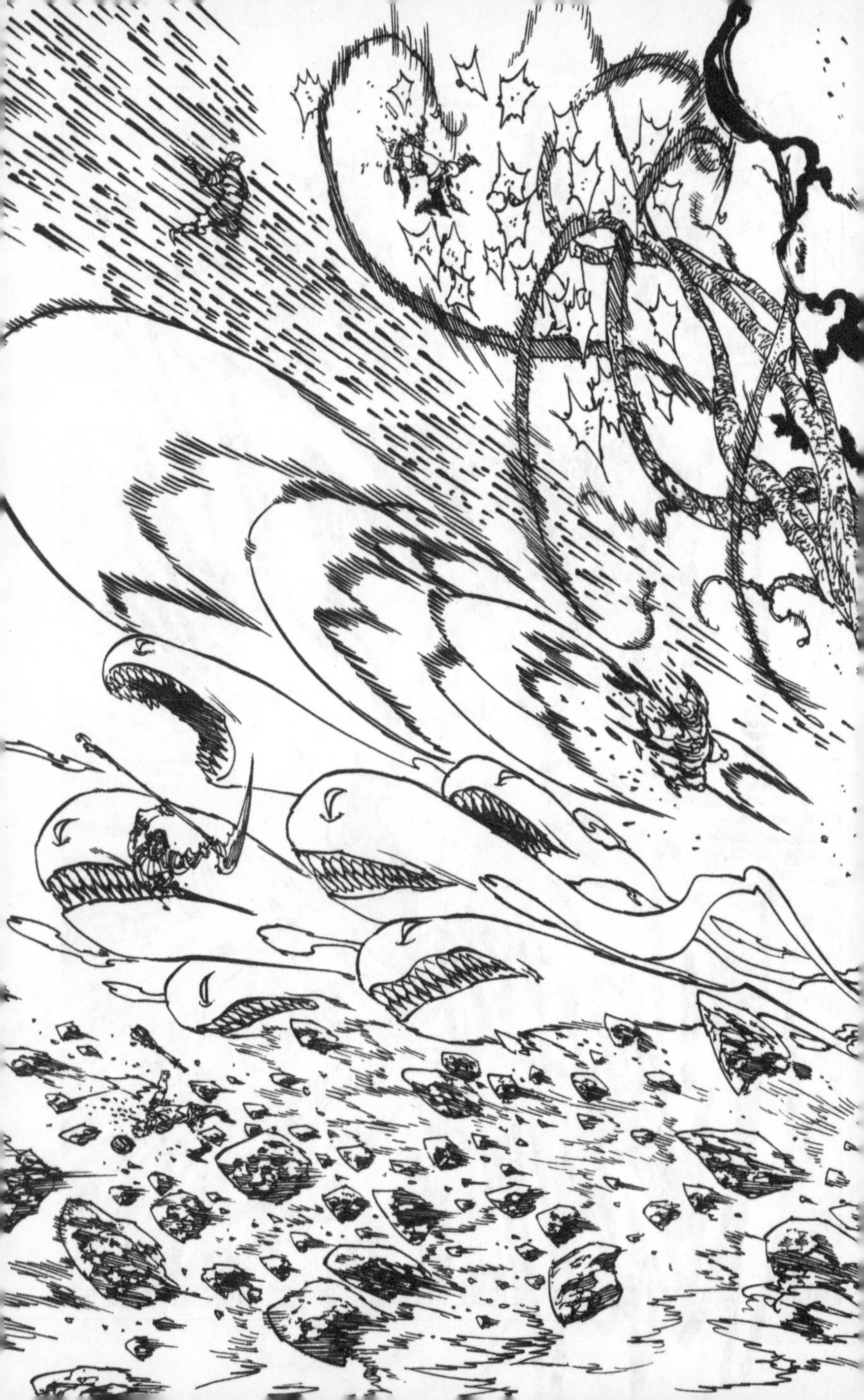

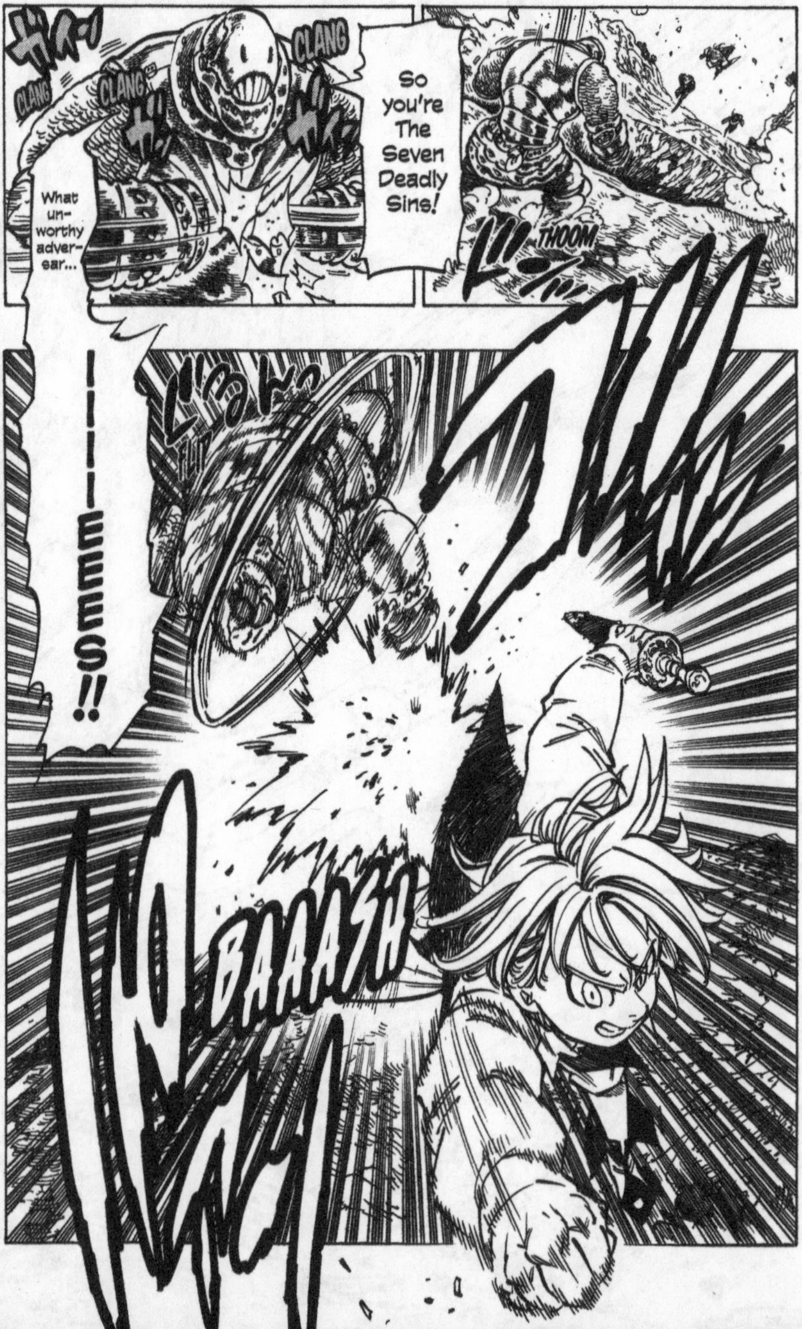

THOOM
CLANG
So you're The Seven Deadly Sins!
CLANG
CLANG
What un-worthy adver-sar...
IIIIIEEEES!!
FLIT
BAAASH

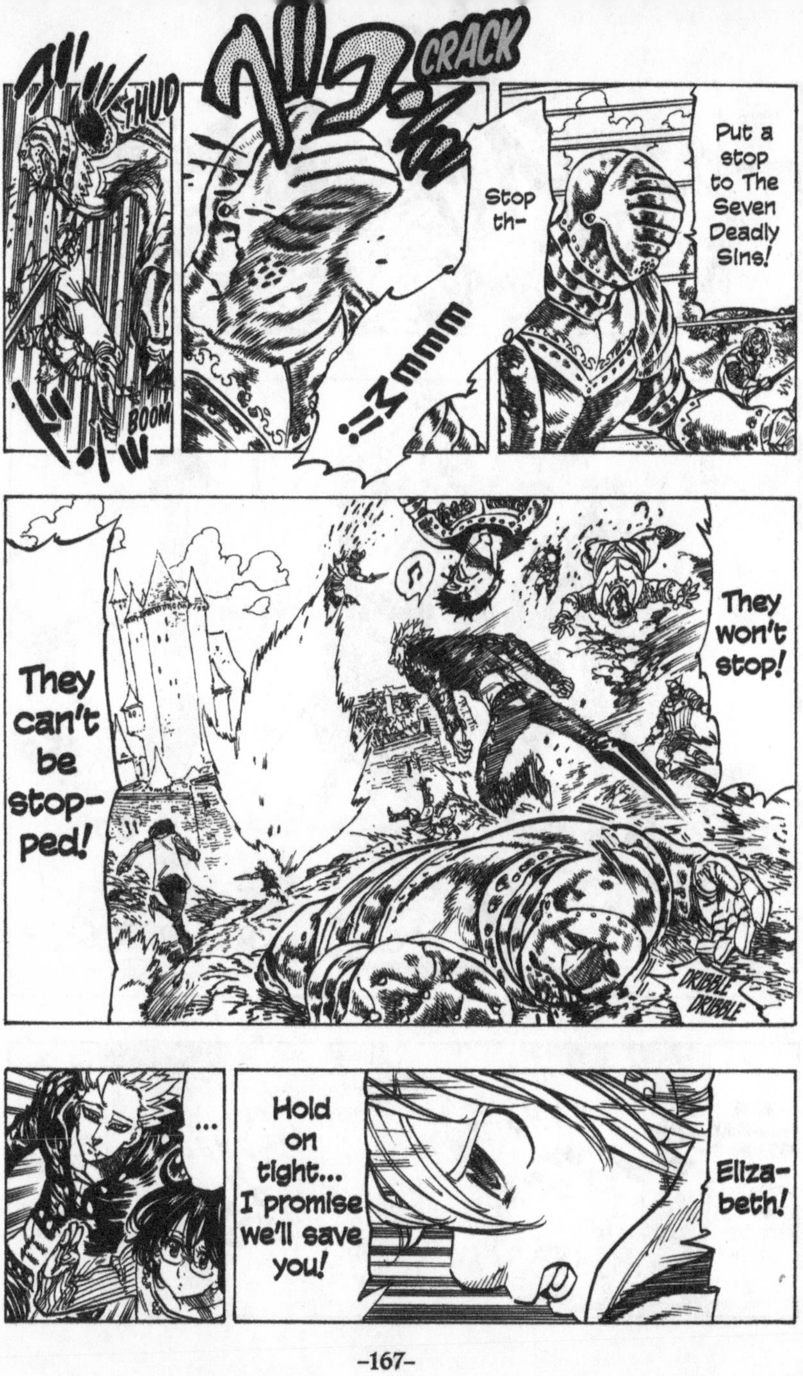

Put a stop to The Seven Deadly Sins!
CRACK
Stop th-
Mmmmm!!
THUD
BOOM
They won't stop!
They can't be stop-ped!
DRIBBLE DRIBBLE
Eliza-beth!
Hold on tight... I promise we'll save you!
...

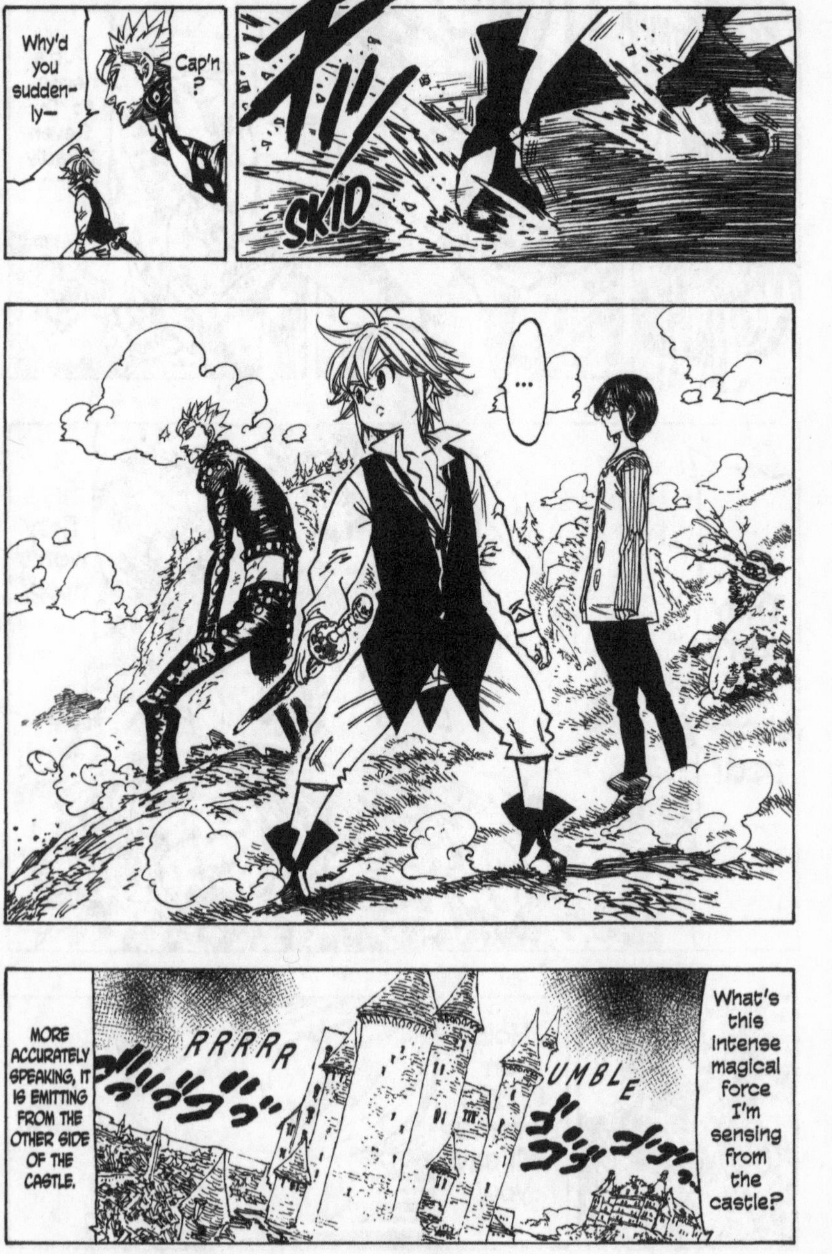
SKID
Cap'n?
Why'd you sudden-ly—
...
What's this intense magical force I'm sensing from the castle?
UMBLE
RRRRR
MORE ACCURATELY SPEAKING, IT IS EMITTING FROM THE OTHER SIDE OF THE CASTLE.

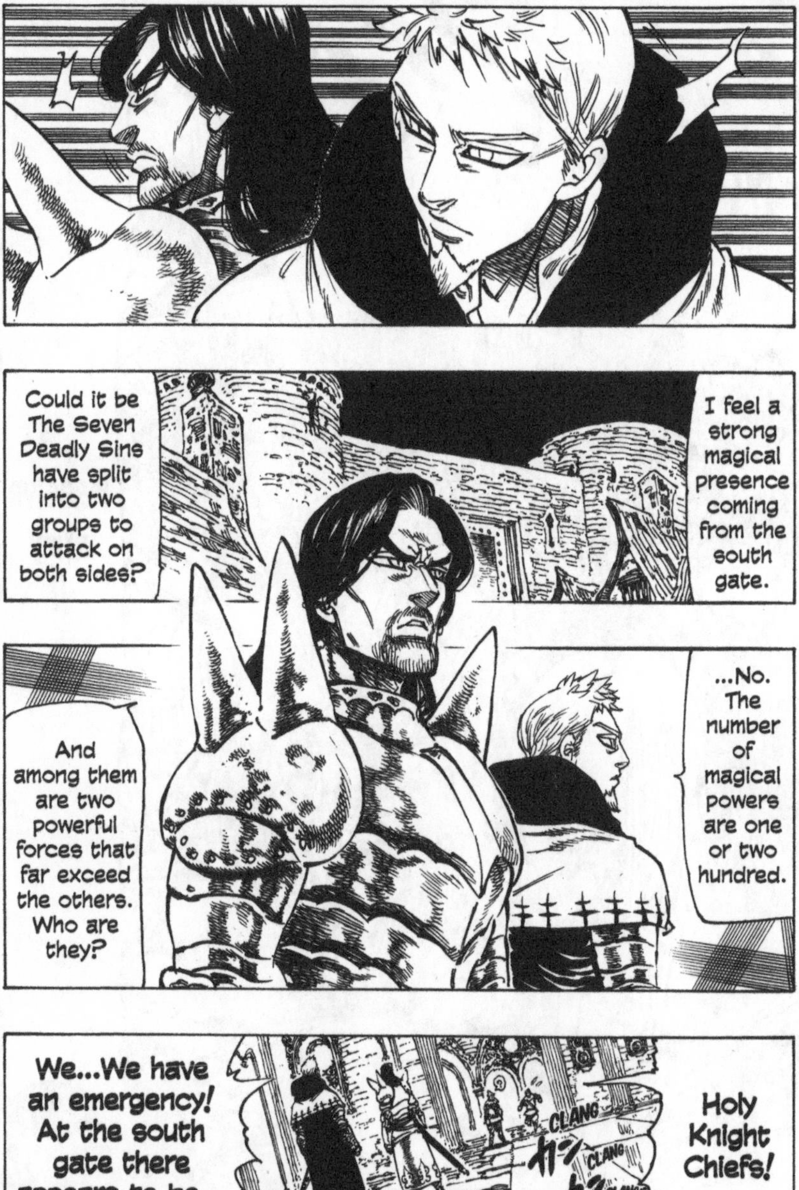
I feel a strong magical presence coming from the south gate.
Could it be The Seven Deadly Sins have split into two groups to attack on both sides?
...No. The number of magical powers are one or two hundred.
And among them are two powerful forces that far exceed the others. Who are they?
Holy Knight Chiefs!
CLANG
CLANG
CLANG
We...We have an emergency! At the south gate there appears to be...

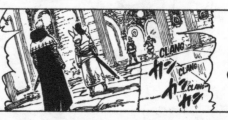

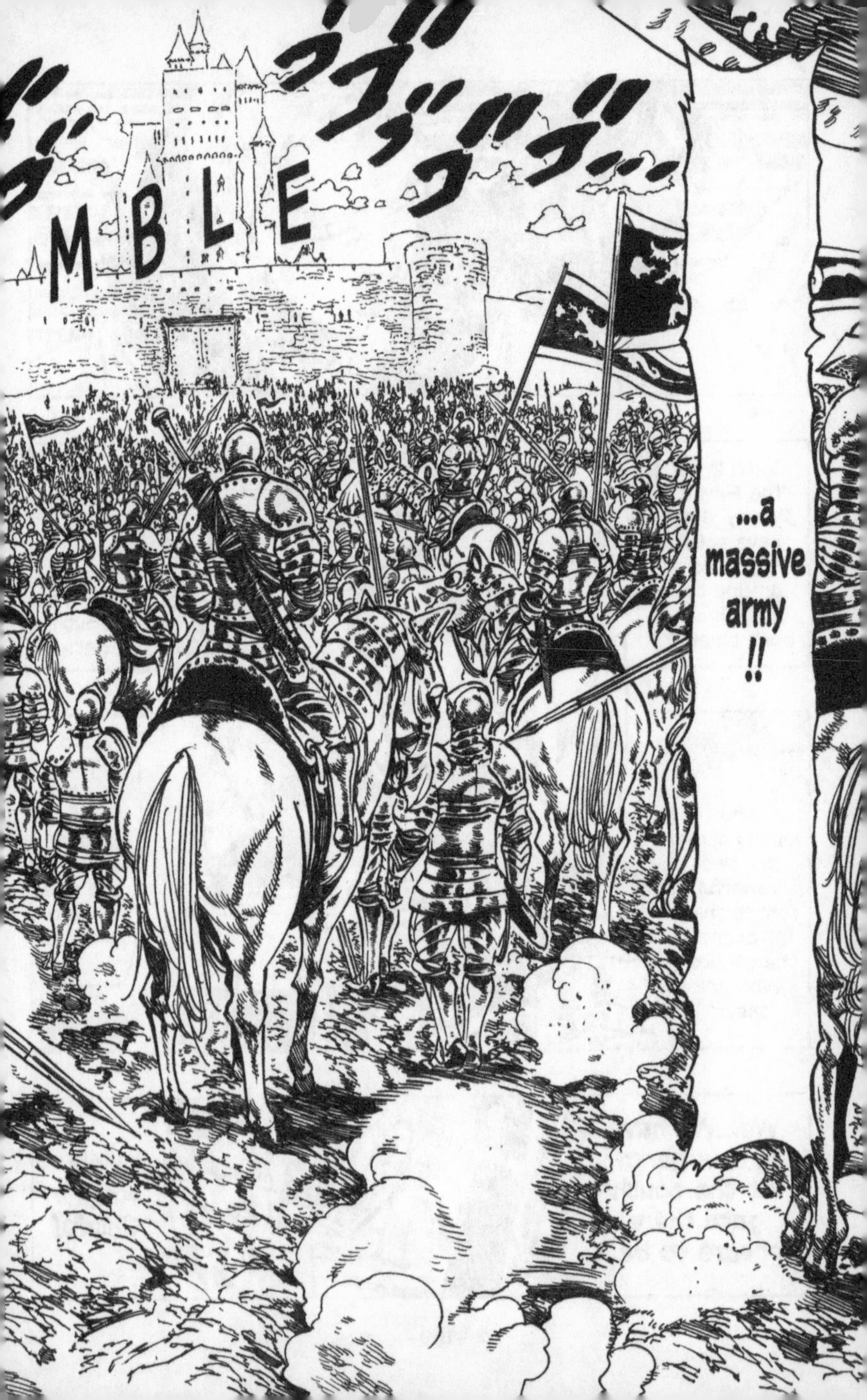
...a massive army !!
MBLE

Did you say... army?

From which nation?

Who is commanding them?

...Sir!

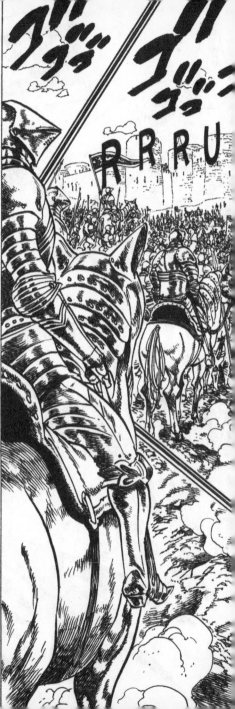

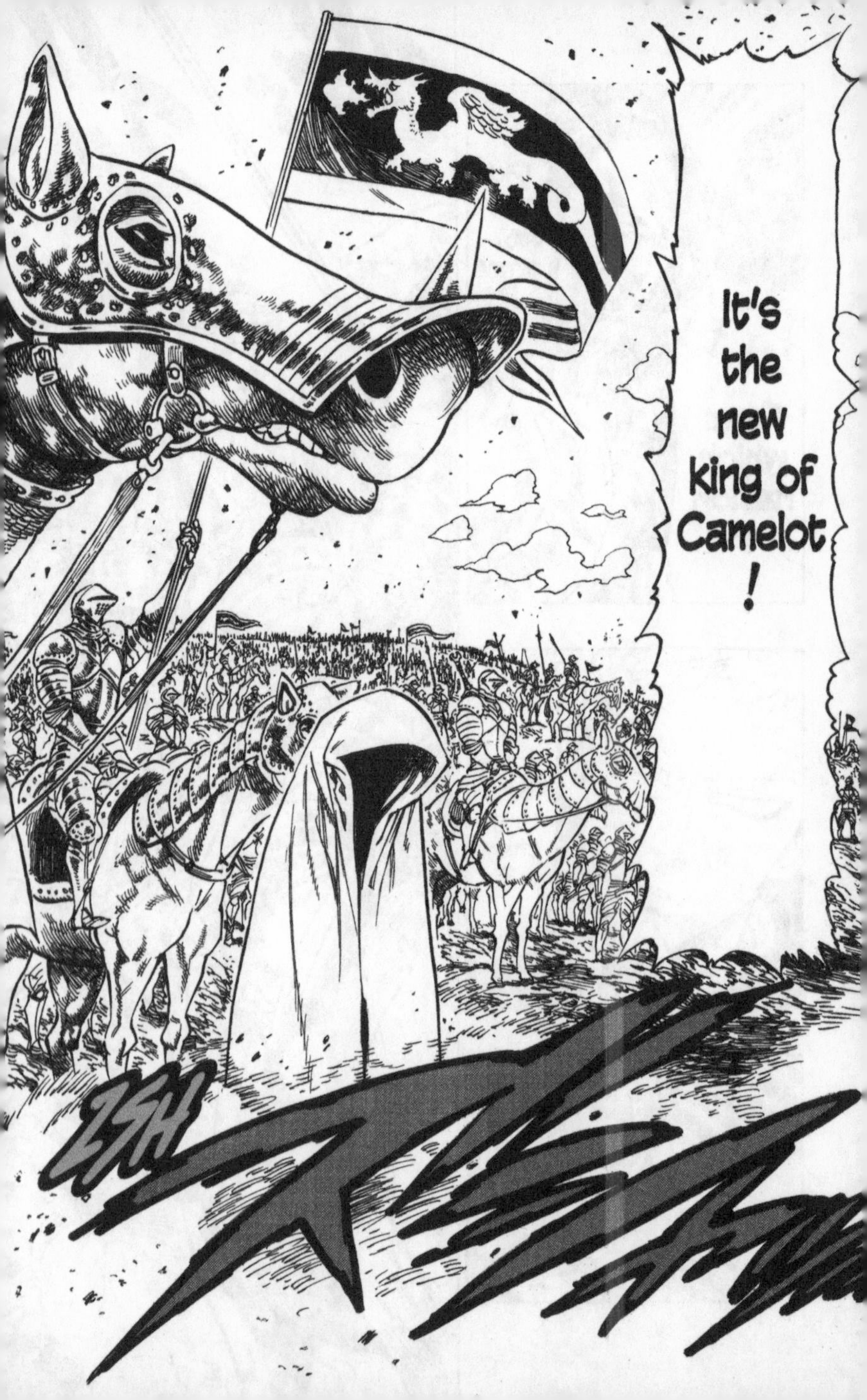
It's the new king of Camelot!
ZSH

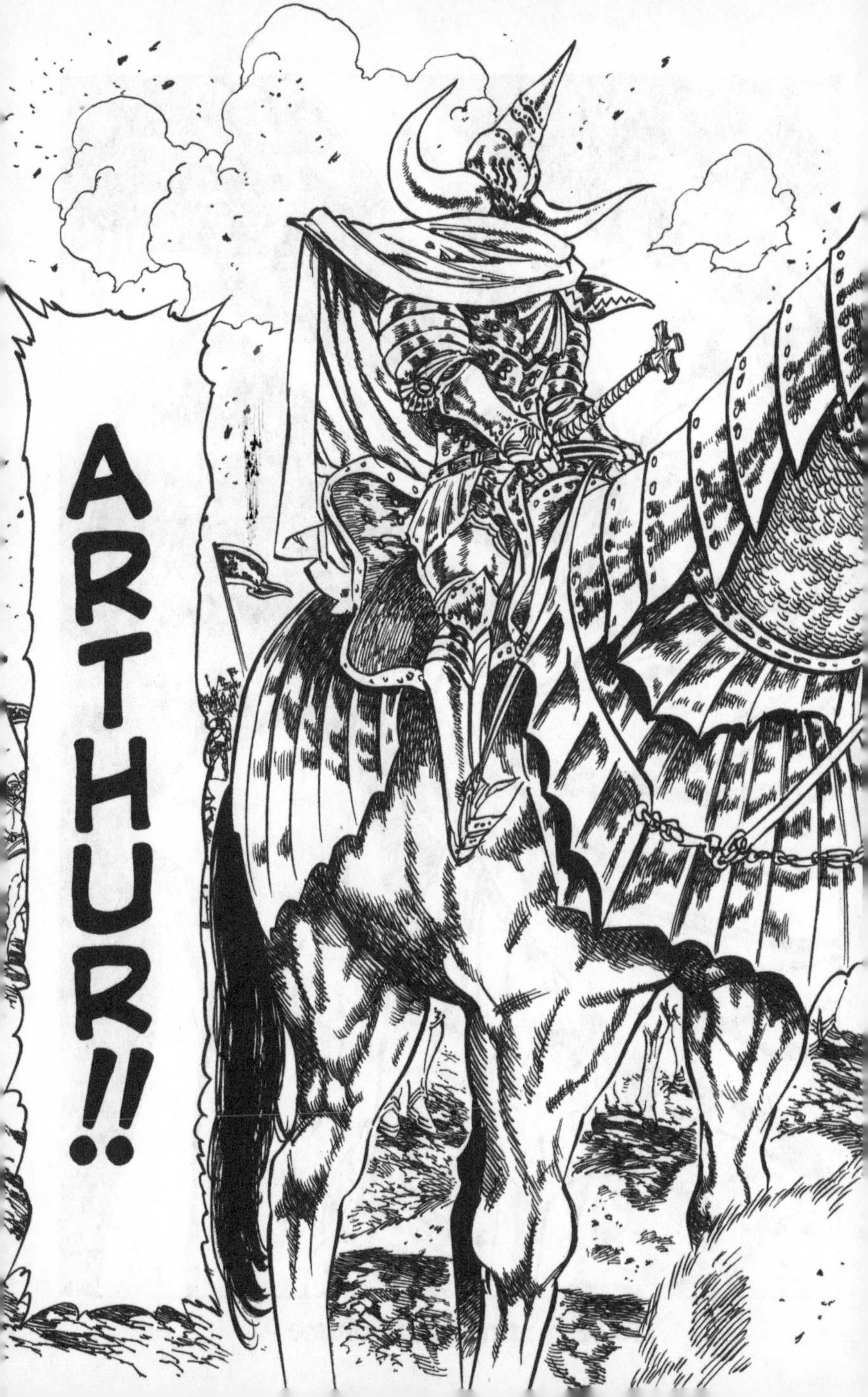
ARTHUR!!

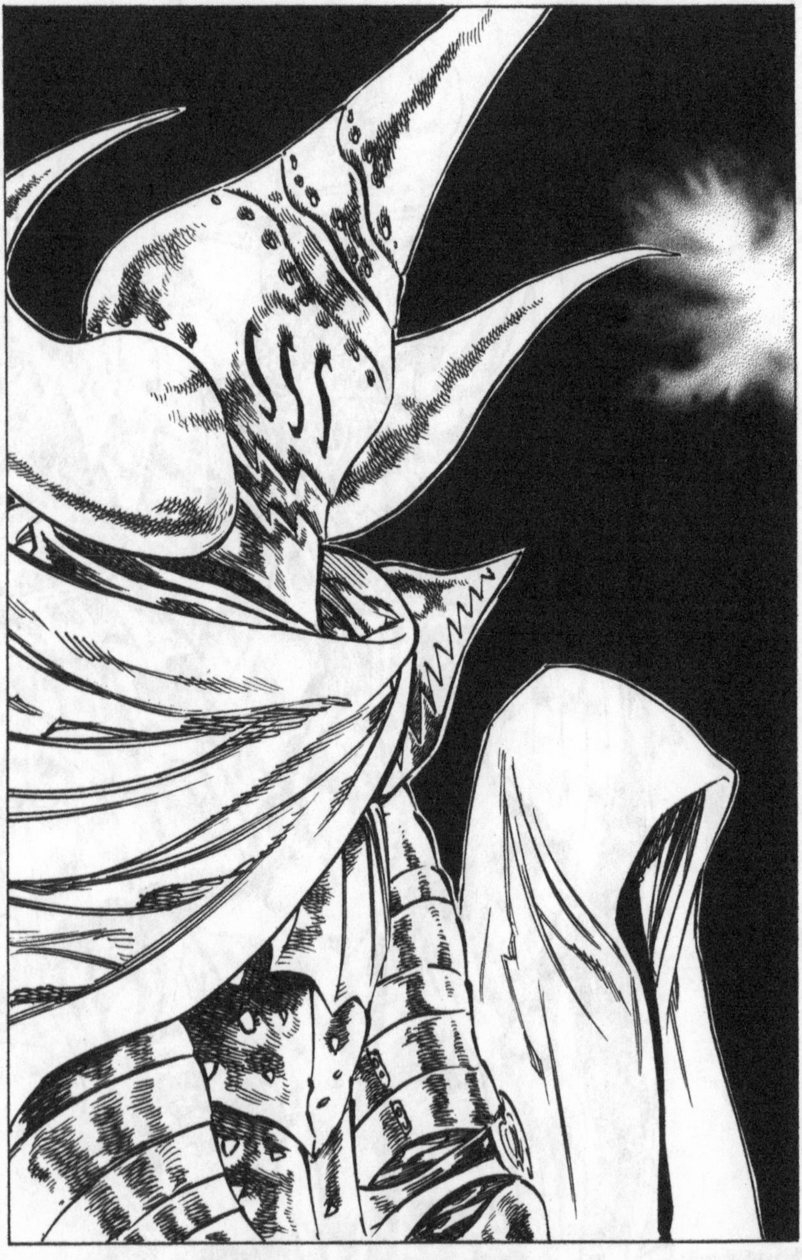

To be continued in Volume 9.

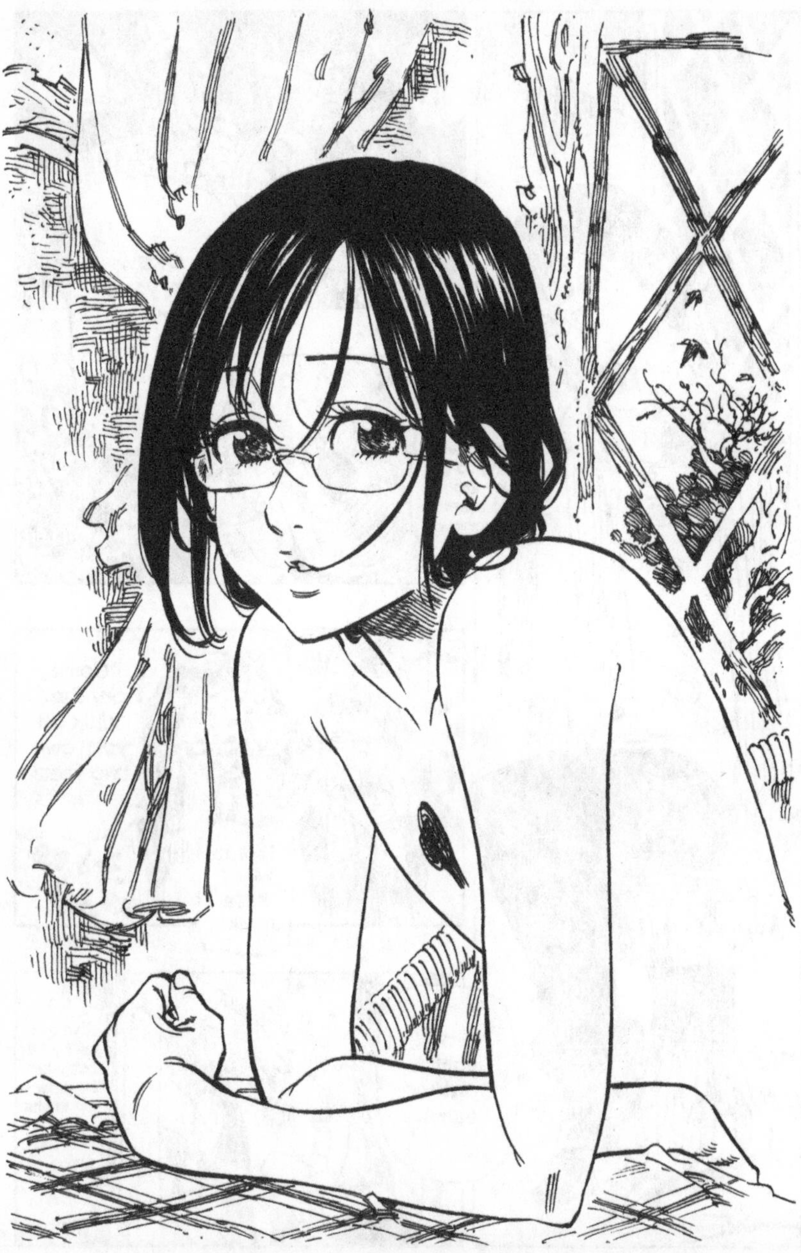

Bonus Story - Where He Belongs

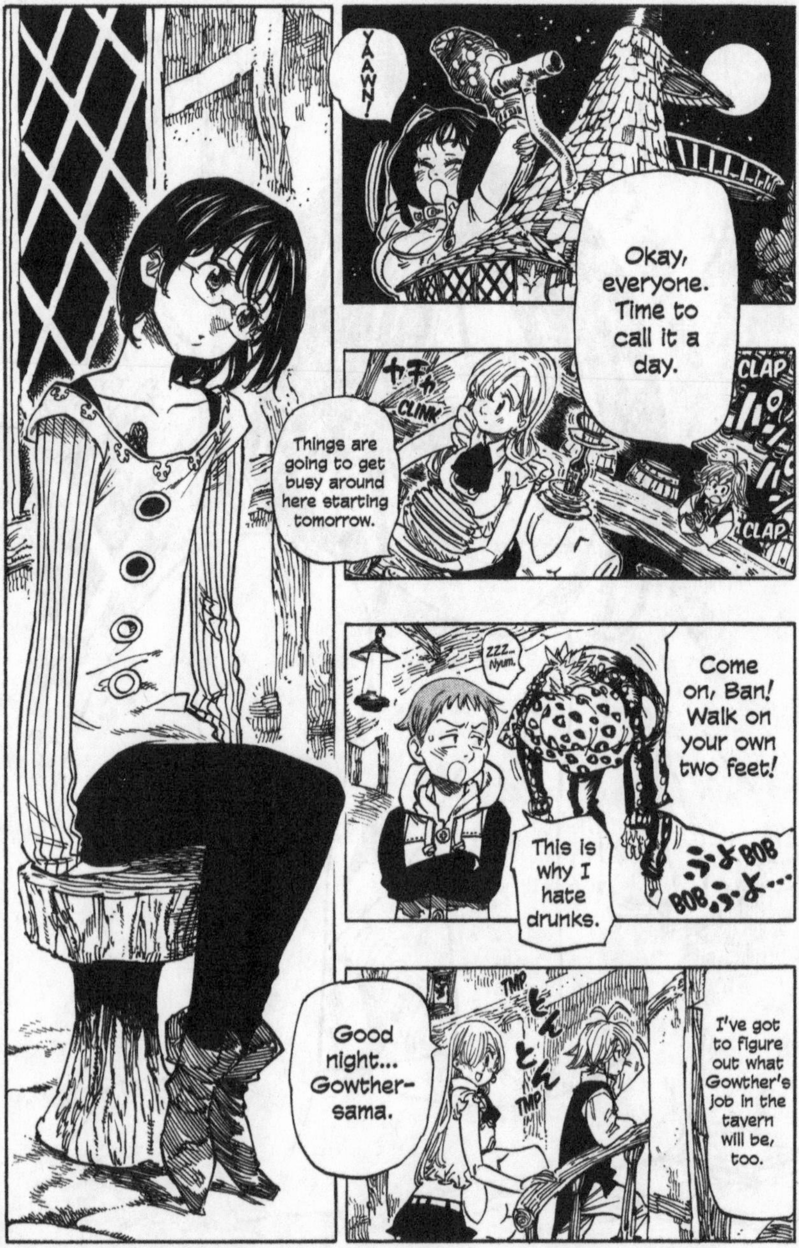
YAAWN!
Okay, everyone. Time to call it a day.
CLAP CLAP
CLINK
Things are going to get busy around here starting tomorrow.
Come on, Ban! Walk on your own two feet!
ZZZ... Nyum.
BOB BOB...
This is why I hate drunks.
I've got to figure out what Gowther's job in the tavern will be, too.
TMP TMP
Good night... Gowther-sama.

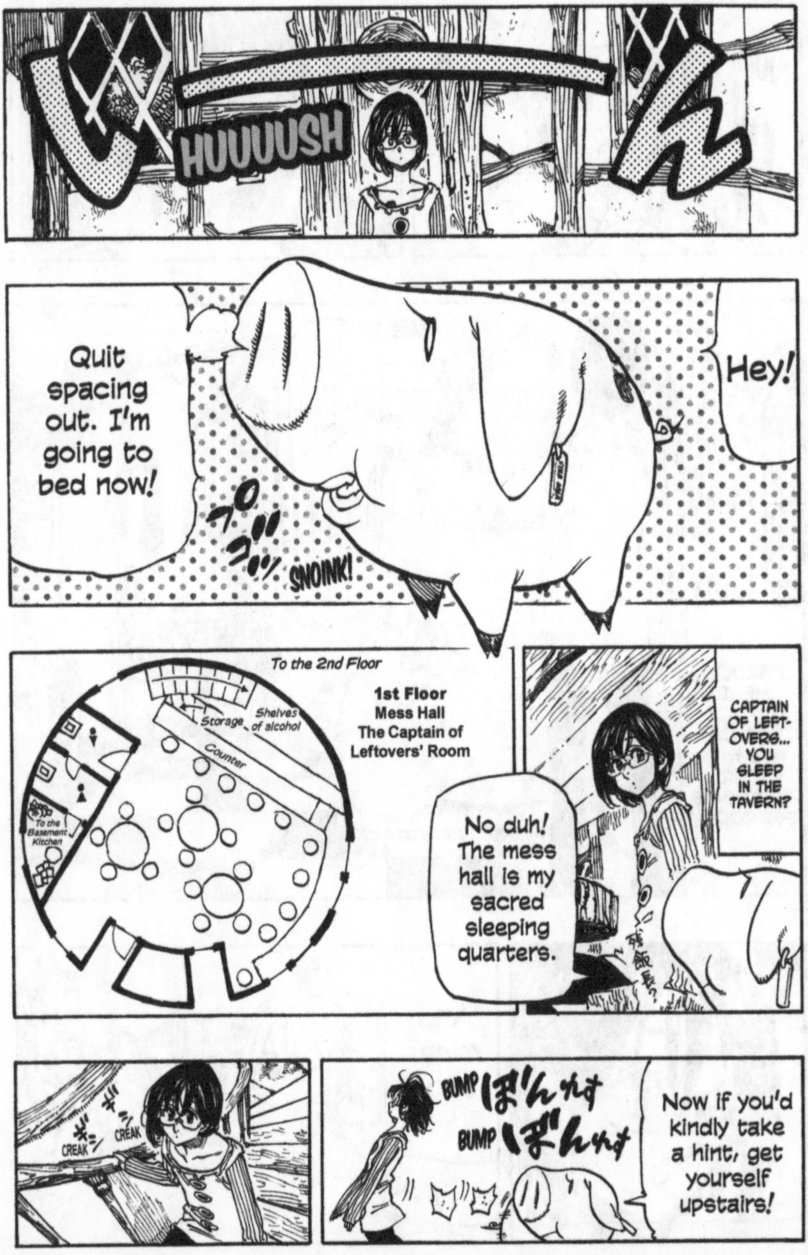
HUUUUSH
Hey!
Quit spacing out. I'm going to bed now!
SNOINK!
CAPTAIN OF LEFTOVERS... YOU SLEEP IN THE TAVERN?
No duh! The mess hall is my sacred sleeping quarters.
To the 2nd Floor
1st Floor
Mess Hall
The Captain of Leftovers' Room
Shelves of alcohol
Storage
Counter
To the Basement Kitchen
Now if you'd kindly take a hint, get yourself upstairs!
BUMP
BUMP
CREAK
CREAK

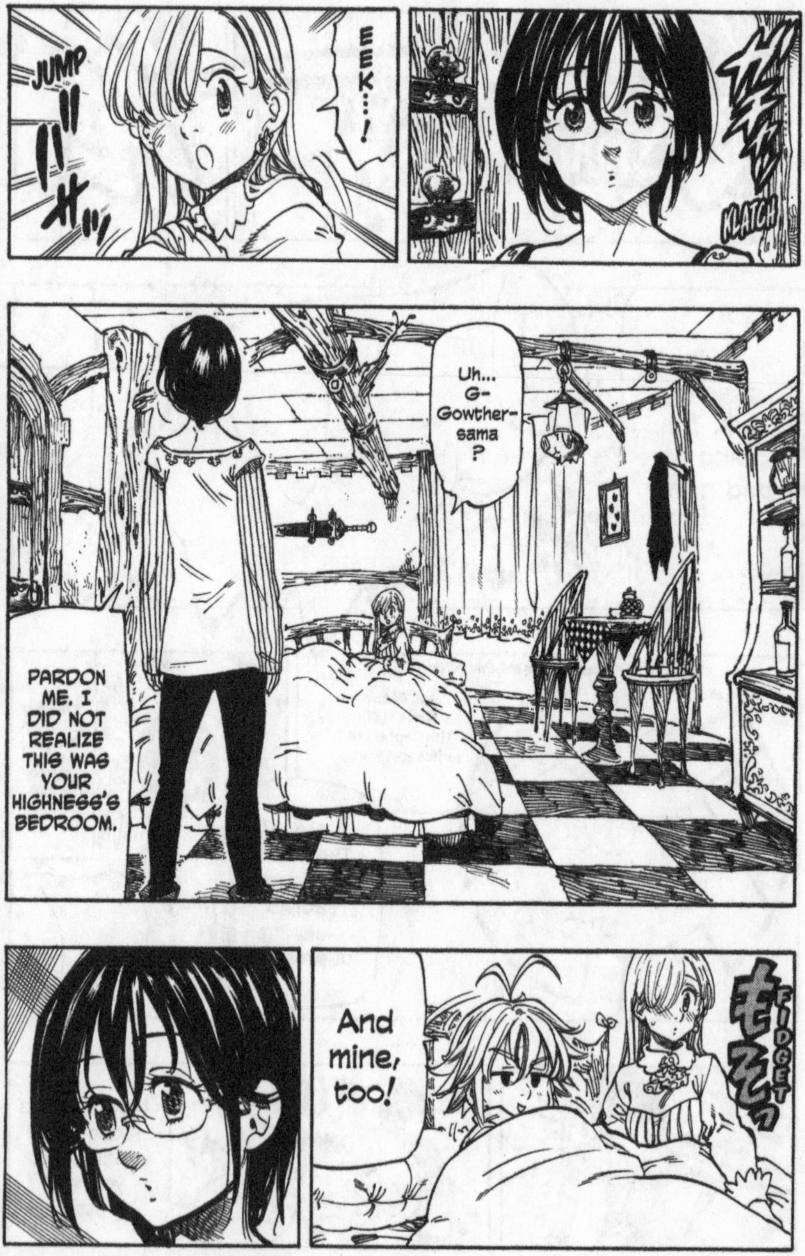
KLATCH
EEK...!
JUMP
Uh... G-Gowther-sama?
PARDON ME. I DID NOT REALIZE THIS WAS YOUR HIGHNESS'S BEDROOM.
FIDGET
And mine, too!

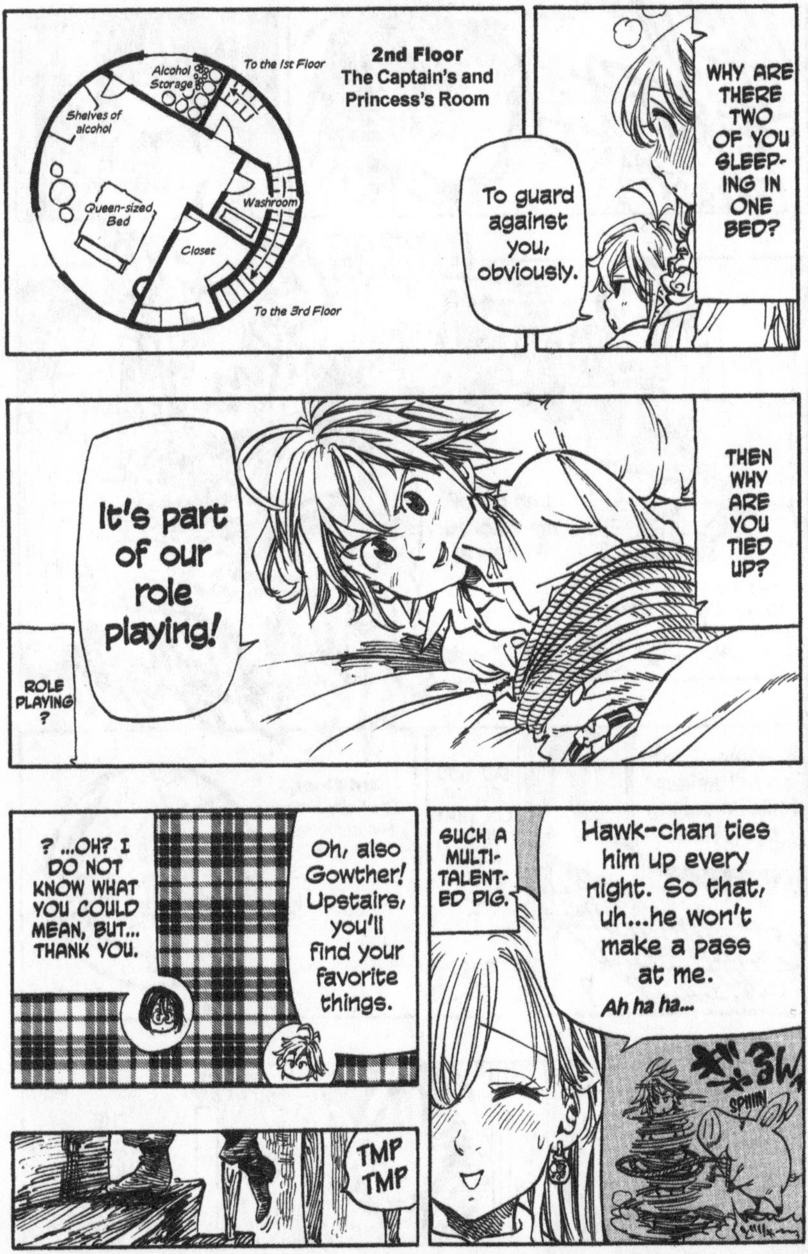
WHY ARE THERE TWO OF YOU SLEEPING IN ONE BED?
To guard against you, obviously.
2nd Floor
The Captain's and Princess's Room
To the 1st Floor
Alcohol Storage
Shelves of alcohol
Washroom
Queen-sized Bed
Closet
To the 3rd Floor
THEN WHY ARE YOU TIED UP?
It's part of our role playing!
ROLE PLAYING?
Hawk-chan ties him up every night. So that, uh...he won't make a pass at me.
Ah ha ha...
SUCH A MULTI-TALENTED PIG.
SPIIIN
Oh, also Gowther! Upstairs, you'll find your favorite things.
? ...OH? I DO NOT KNOW WHAT YOU COULD MEAN, BUT... THANK YOU.
TMP TMP

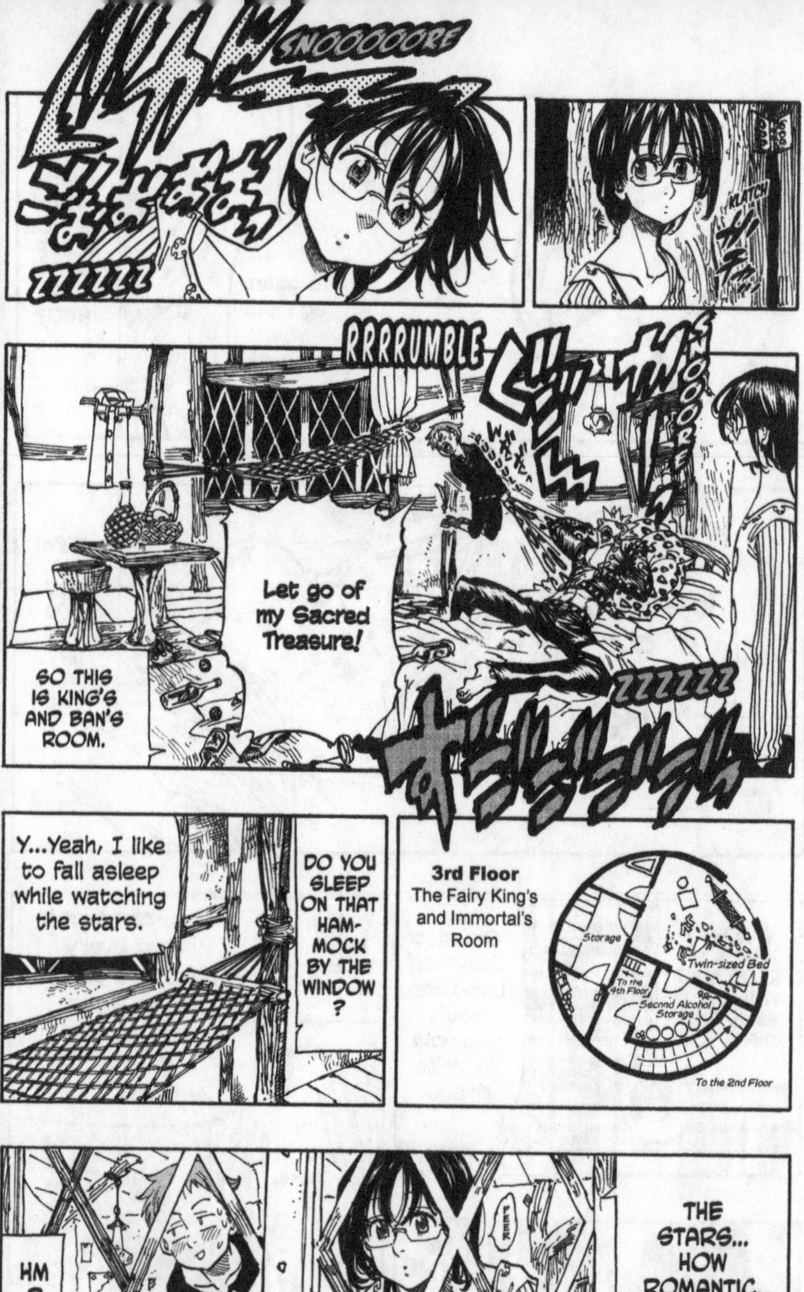
KLATCH
SNOOOOORE
ZZZZZZ
RRRRUMBLE
SNOOOORE
Let go of my Sacred Treasure!
ZZZZZZ
SO THIS IS KING'S AND BAN'S ROOM.
3rd Floor
The Fairy King's and Immortal's Room
Storage
Twin-sized Bed
To the 4th Floor
Second Alcohol Storage
To the 2nd Floor
DO YOU SLEEP ON THAT HAM-MOCK BY THE WINDOW?
Y...Yeah, I like to fall asleep while watching the stars.
THE STARS... HOW ROMANTIC.
PEER
HM?

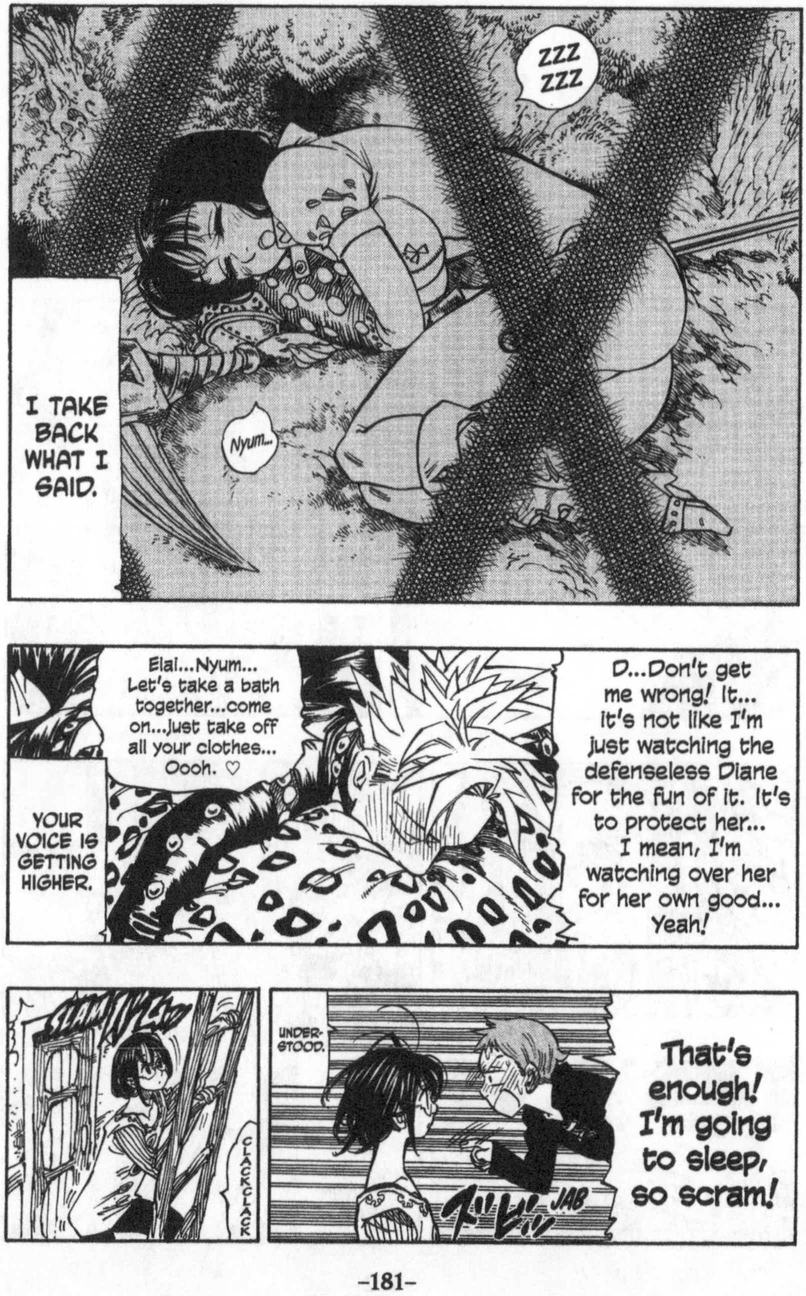
ZZZ
ZZZ
Nyum...
I TAKE BACK WHAT I SAID.
D...Don't get me wrong! It... it's not like I'm just watching the defenseless Diane for the fun of it. It's to protect her... I mean, I'm watching over her for her own good... Yeah!
Elai...Nyum... Let's take a bath together...come on...just take off all your clothes... Oooh. ♡
YOUR VOICE IS GETTING HIGHER.
That's enough! I'm going to sleep, so scram!
UNDER-STOOD.
JAB
CLACK CLACK

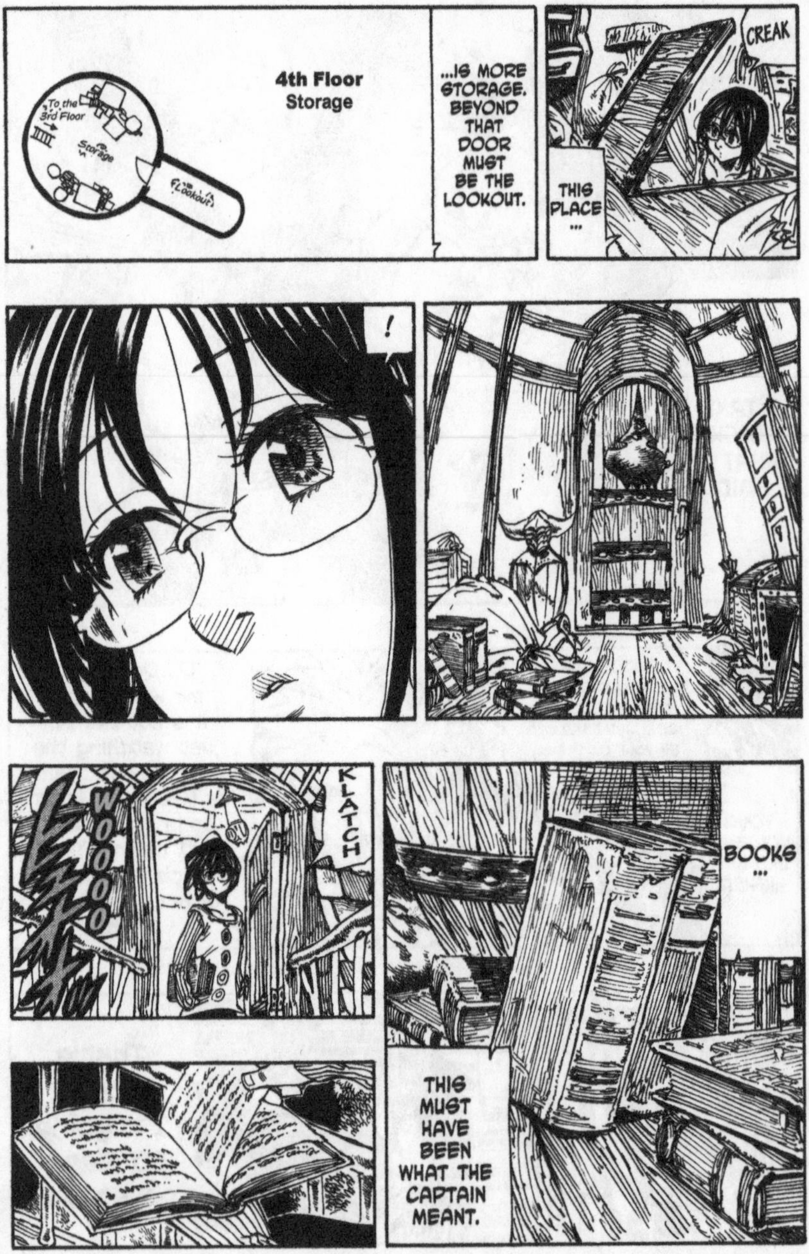
CREAK
THIS PLACE ...
...IS MORE STORAGE. BEYOND THAT DOOR MUST BE THE LOOKOUT.
4th Floor
Storage
To the 3rd Floor
Storage
Lookout
!
BOOKS ...
THIS MUST HAVE BEEN WHAT THE CAPTAIN MEANT.
KLATCH
WOOOO

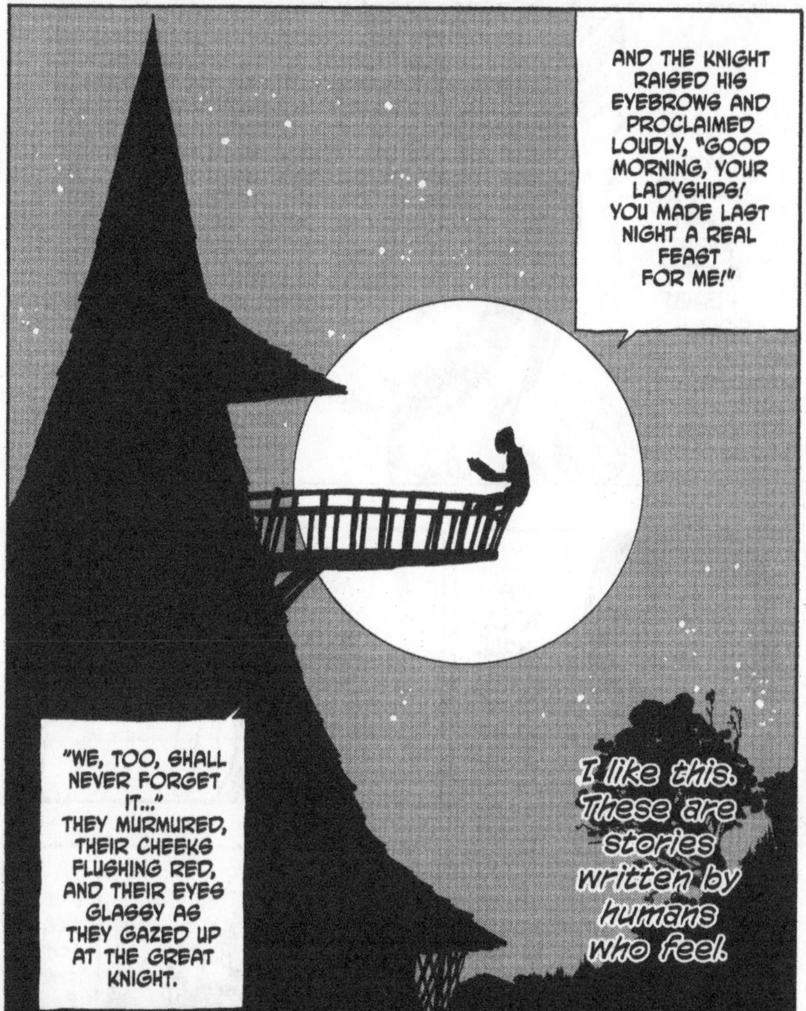
AND THE KNIGHT RAISED HIS EYEBROWS AND PROCLAIMED LOUDLY, "GOOD MORNING, YOUR LADYSHIPS! YOU MADE LAST NIGHT A REAL FEAST FOR ME!"
"WE, TOO, SHALL NEVER FORGET IT..." THEY MURMURED, THEIR CHEEKS FLUSHING RED, AND THEIR EYES GLASSY AS THEY GAZED UP AT THE GREAT KNIGHT.
I like this. These are stories written by humans who feel.

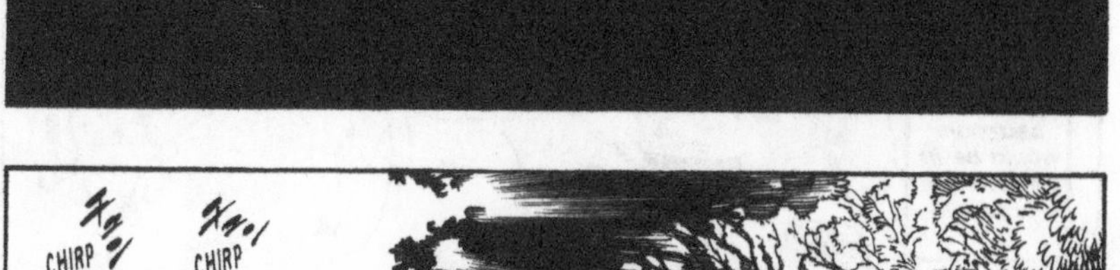
CHIRP
CHIRP

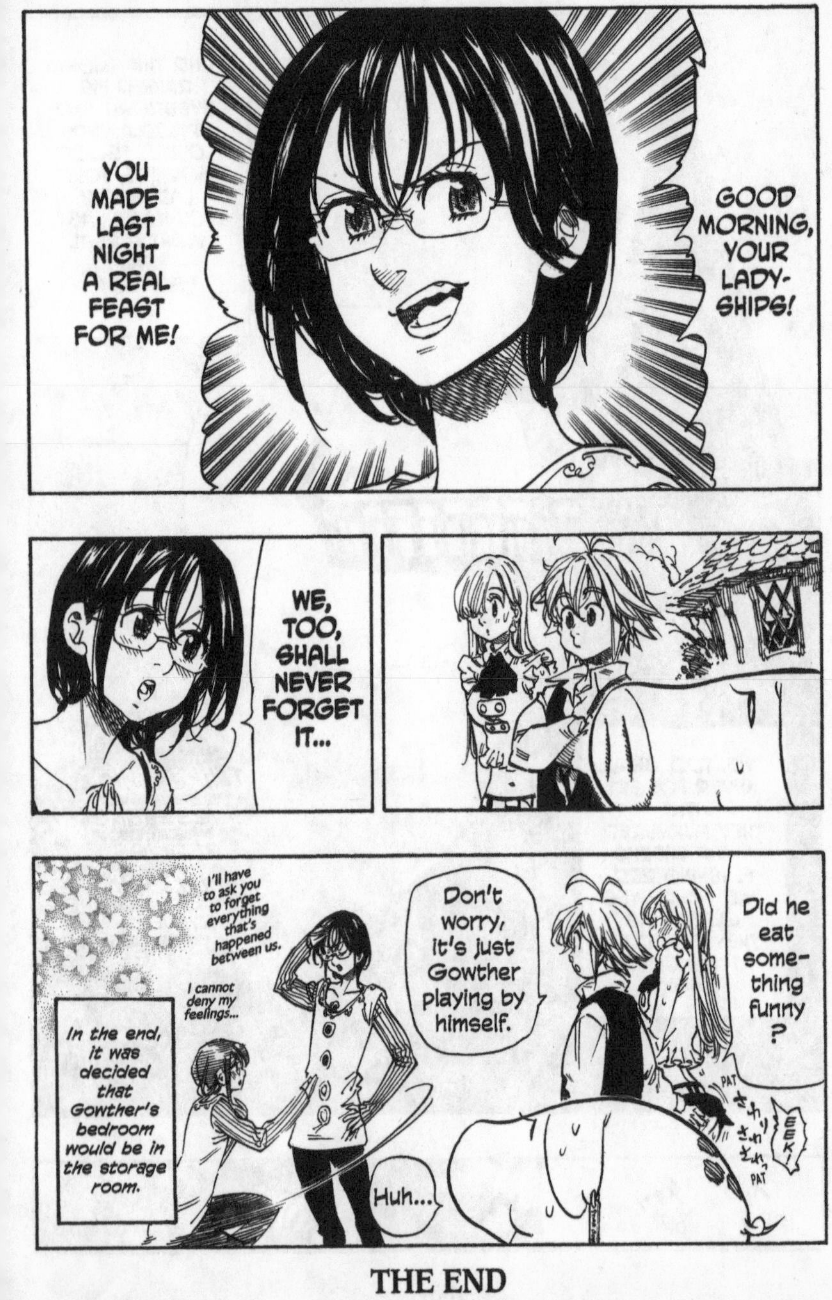
GOOD MORNING, YOUR LADYSHIPS!
YOU MADE LAST NIGHT A REAL FEAST FOR ME!
WE, TOO, SHALL NEVER FORGET IT...
Did he eat something funny?
EEK!
PAT
PAT
Don't worry, it's just Gowther playing by himself.
I'll have to ask you to forget everything that's happened between us.
I cannot deny my feelings...
Huh...
In the end, it was decided that Gowther's bedroom would be in the storage room.

THE END

"THE SEVEN DEADLY SINS" ILLUSTRATION CORNER

"THE DRAWING KNIGHTHOOD" SPACE

Be sure to include your name and address on your postcard!

M = H = E = D = B = K = G =

SPECIAL PRIZE

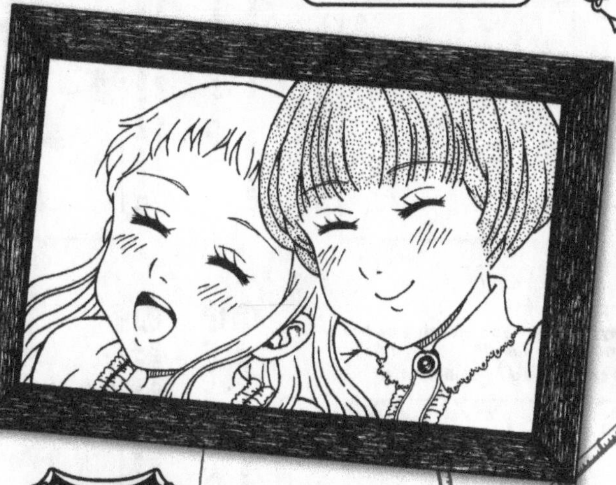

BENIKO-SAN / MIYAGI PREFECTURE

"Just you watch, Sister Veronica. I swear I'll get back our kingdom of Liones!"

"We won't give up!"

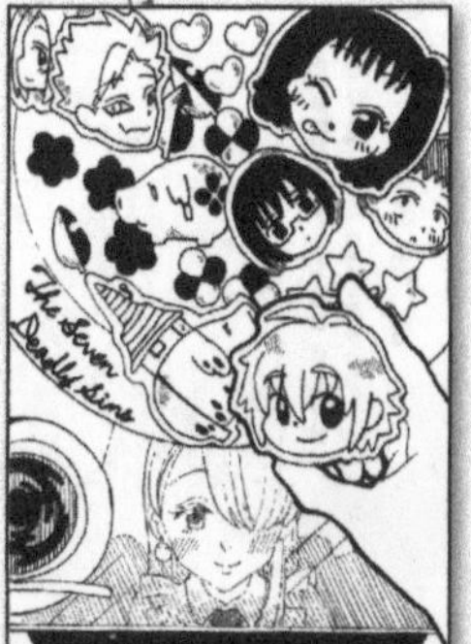

YUTAKA-SAN / GIFU PREFECTURE

E "I wouldn't be able to eat such cute cookies..."

M "The captain would taste like bitter chocolate and the Master would taste like fried pork cutlets." ♫

M "What kind of job do you want at the tavern?"

M "I want to be the girl that attracts customers inside."

H "But you're not a girl!!"

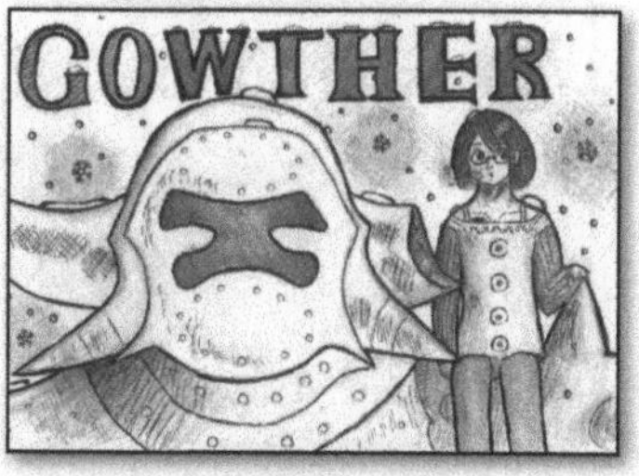
GOWTHER

ISHIPON-SAN / GUNMA PREFECTURE

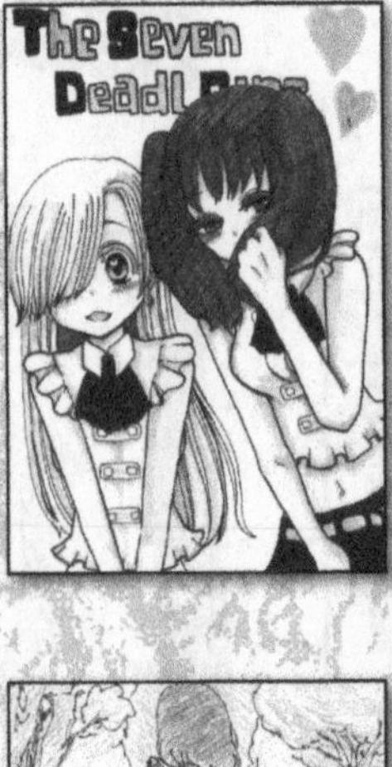
The Seven

GIFU PREFECTURE

D "We're the beautiful shop girl sisters from the rumors. Heh heh!♡"

G "I want to join you."

E "...You still won't drop that..."

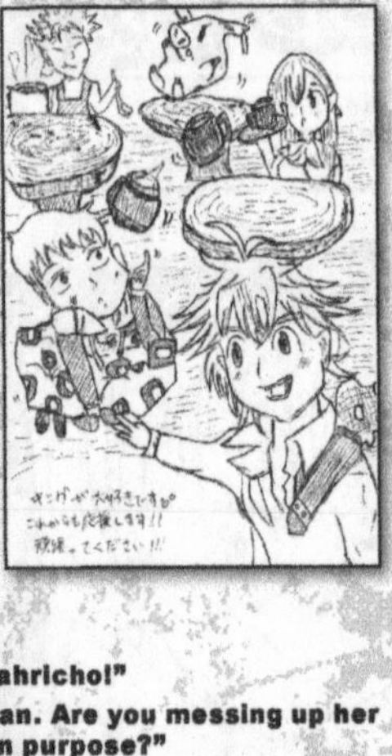

SHIAN-SAN / OITA PREFECTURE

M "King, quit goofing around."

K "But I've got nothing else to do."

M "I'll give you a hint: WORK!"

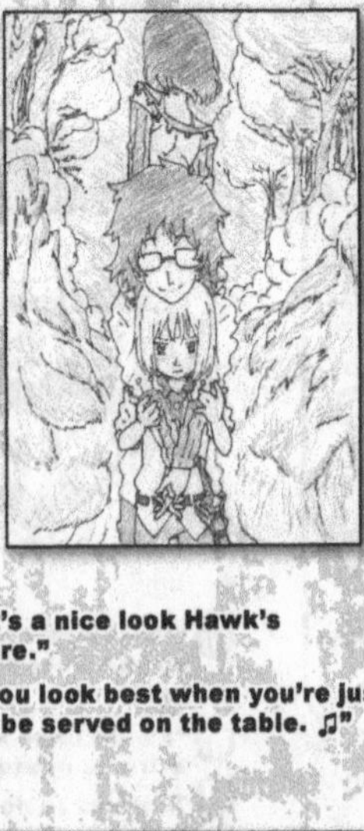

KUMAMOTO PREFECTURE

M "I still don't know what Gowther's thinking."

G "...Neither do I."

H "Well, aren't you the little enigma."

B "Hey, Jahricho!"

D "Hey, Ban. Are you messing up her name on purpose?"

B "Of course I am. ♪ Kah kah! ♫"

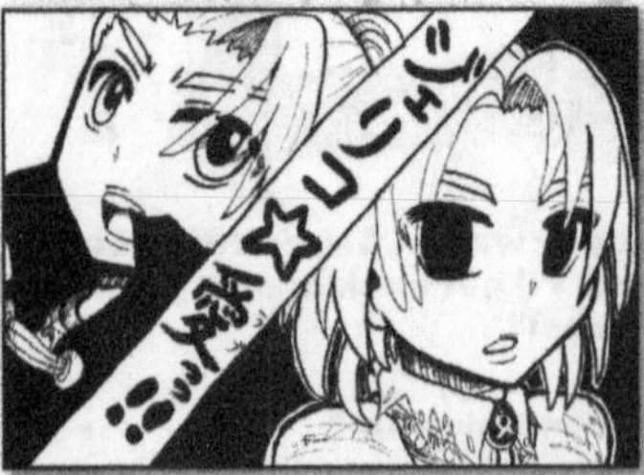

MOONLIGHT ☆-SAN / KOCHI PREFECTURE

M "Now that's a nice look Hawk's got on there."

B "Master, you look best when you're just rearing to be served on the table. ♫"

H "Snoink!?"

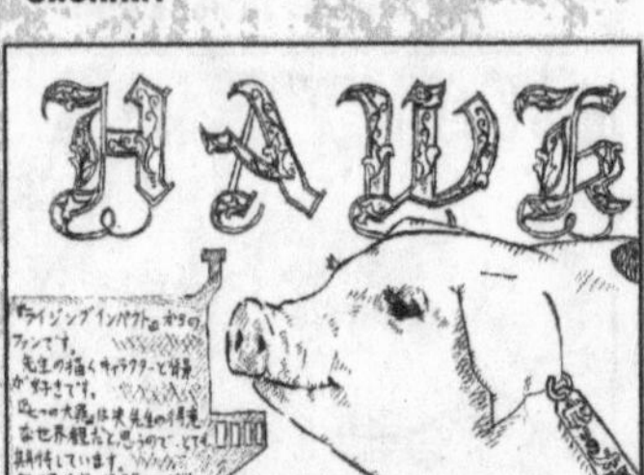
HAWK

SHINKAI-SAN / KOCHI PREFECTURE

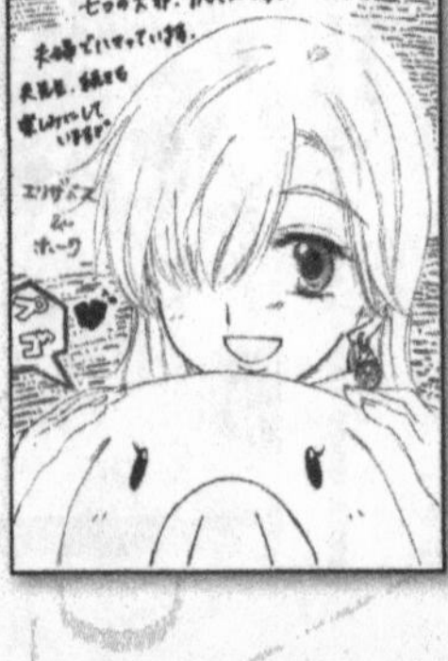
The Seven Dealy Sins

YUKIKO KUMATANI-SAN / WAKAYAMA PREFECTURE

M "Elizabeth, come come. I'll pet and stroke you."

E "Eek...! Ah! Uh...!"

H "That's her butt, not her head!"

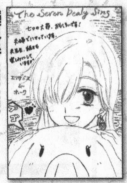

YUYA IKU-SAN /
OKUYAMA PREFECTURE

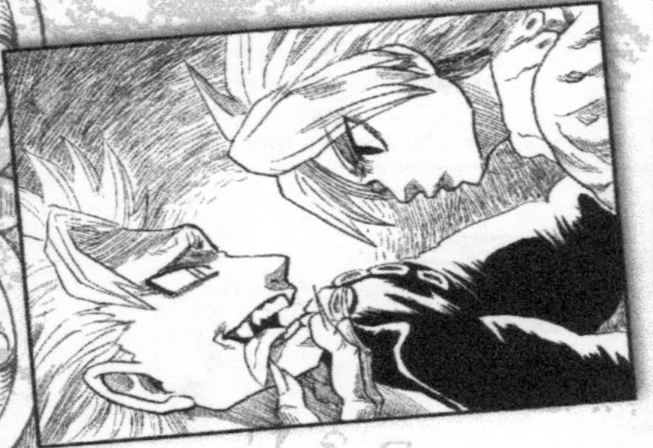

"Why's she always treating me like an enemy? ♫"

"If you really don't know, you just forgot."

YUME KUWABARA /
SAITAMA PREFECTURE

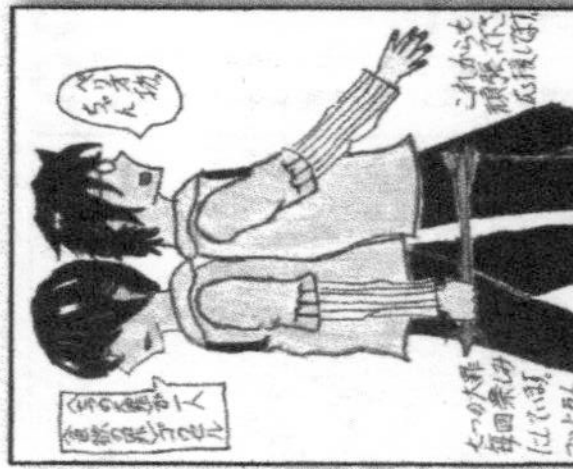

K "Hey, Gowther. Can you read our little piggy's mind too?"

G "It's awash in leftovers."

K "W...Wow!"

SHREK-SAN /
HYOGO PREFECTURE

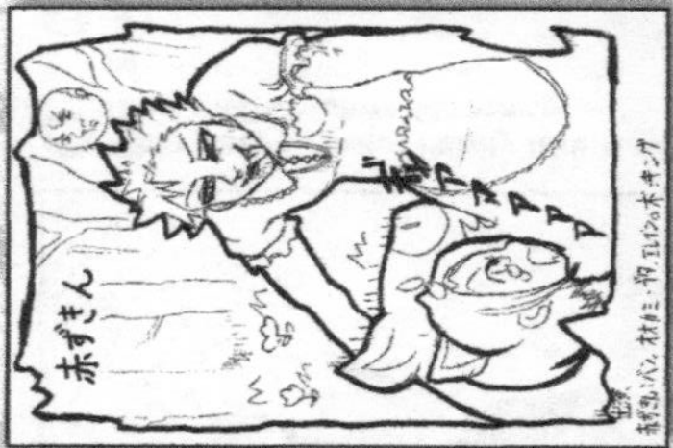
赤ずきん

B "Heh heh heh. ♫ You've got an awful lot of nerve if you think you can eat me. ♫"

EL "Y...Your threats don't scare me! Nip!"

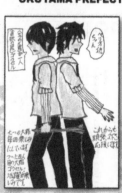

YUNA MORISAWA /
KANAGAWA PREFECTURE

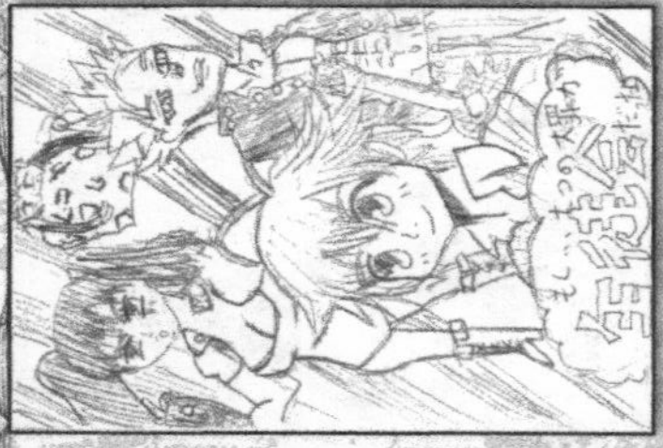

M "If 'The Seven Deadly Sins' were a student council...Huff! Huff! ♪"

D "Huh...? But everyone's clothes are just the same as always..."

MASASHI SUZUKI-SAN /
HIROSHIMA PREFECTURE

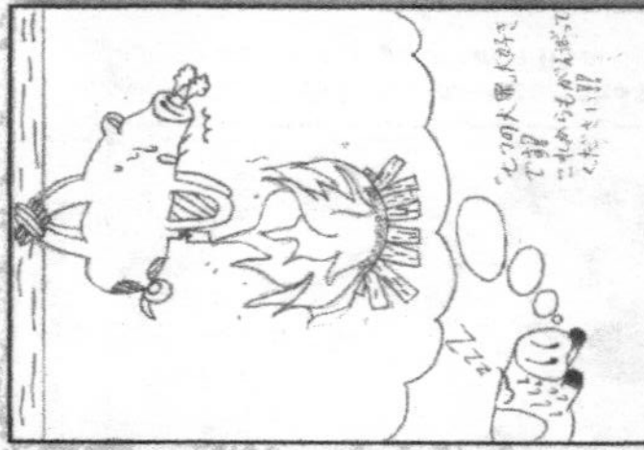

H "Uuugh, Uuungh...hot..."

B "Are you dreaming you're being boiled alive, Master? ♫"

M "I think he's being grilled alive."

B "I gotta say, Diane, you've got the most accurate aim when you launch your artillery!"

D "Heh heh! You flatter me. ♡"

H "...You're a beast."

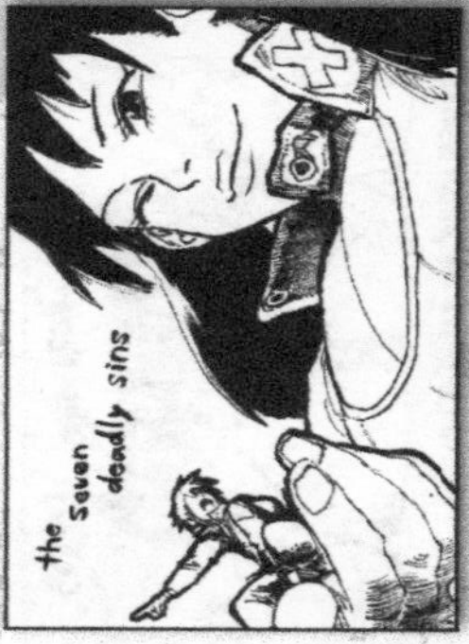
the Seven deadly sins

CHIAKI-SAN /
HYOGO PREFECTURE

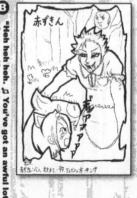

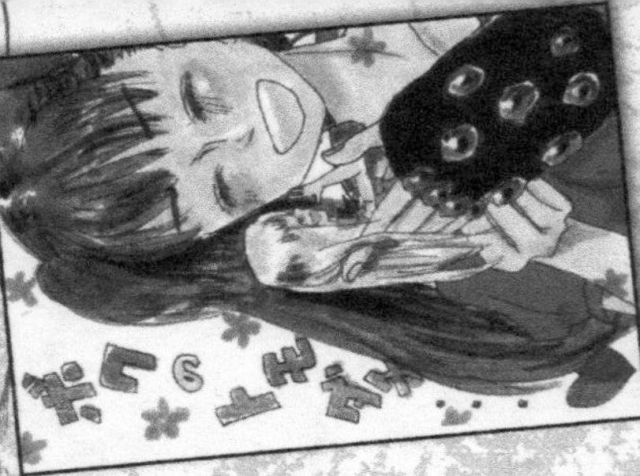
ボクのトモダチ…

PARAPARA-SAN / MIYAGI PREFECTURE

"I looove you, Elizabeth!"

"I'm happy, too. I've always wanted to be your friend."

"...You lucky..."

CHIHARU MITUOKA-SAN / IBARAKI PREFECTURE

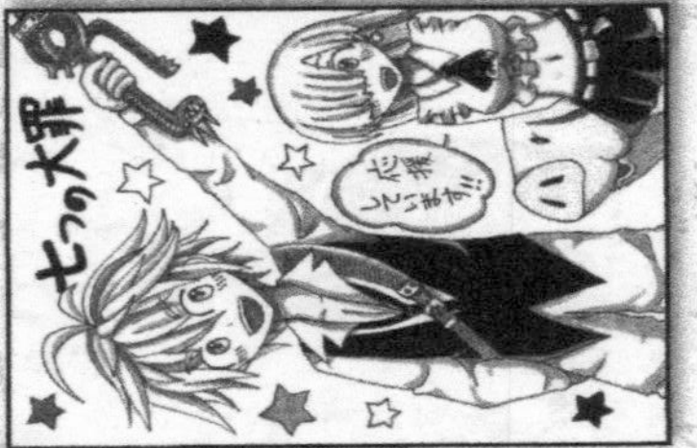
七つの大罪
応援しています!!

E "It feels like so long ago when it was just the three of us."

M "Let's keep working hard to gather our seven members!"

H "Yeaaaaah!"

NOGAWA-SAN / MIYAGI PREFECTURE

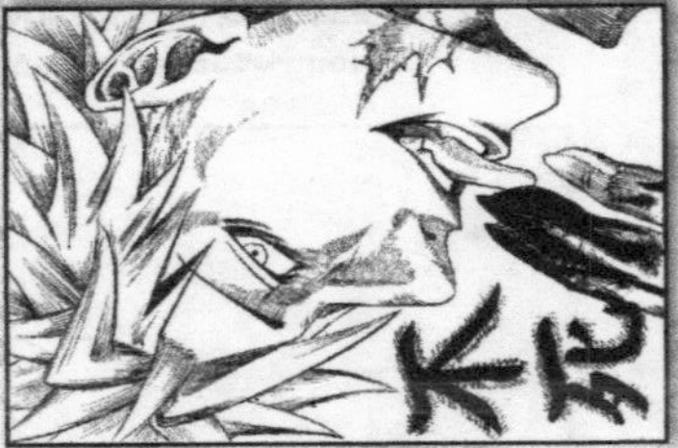
不死

K "When did you develop that bad guy face? Were you born like that?"

B "I don't want to hear that from you, you two-face."

K "T...Two-face...?"

KAIRI-SAN / KANAGAWA PREFECTURE

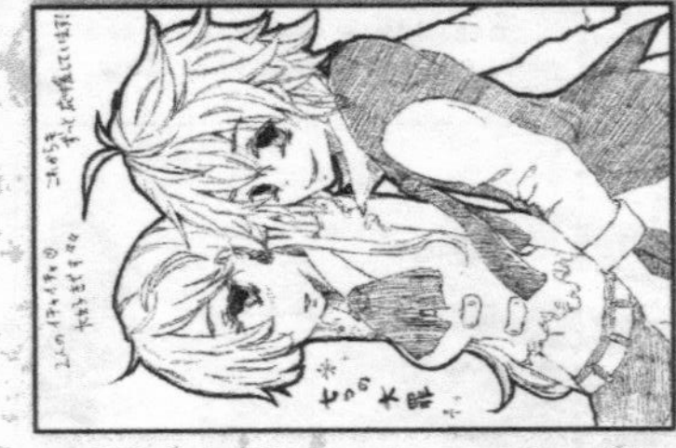
七つの大罪

H "Uh, I don't know if you can call that being 'lovey dovey'..."

K "Touchy feely?" B "Sticky fingers?"

M "Nah. It's 'soft and squishy'."

K "C...Can I eat one of the...Diane buns? Huff! Huff!"

M "Trust me, it'll lie heavy on your stomach."

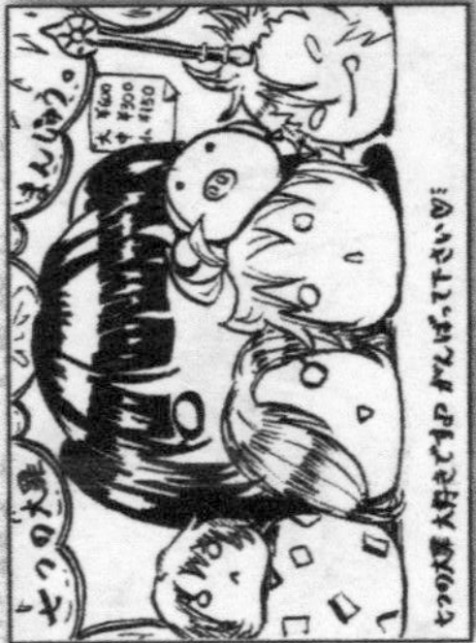
七つの大罪 まんじゅう。
大 ¥600
中 ¥300
小 ¥150
七つの大罪 大好きです♪ がんばって下さい♡

SAKI MITSUNO-SAN / TOKYO

I LOVE CHICKEN MANTANGO-SAN / SAITAMA PREFECTURE

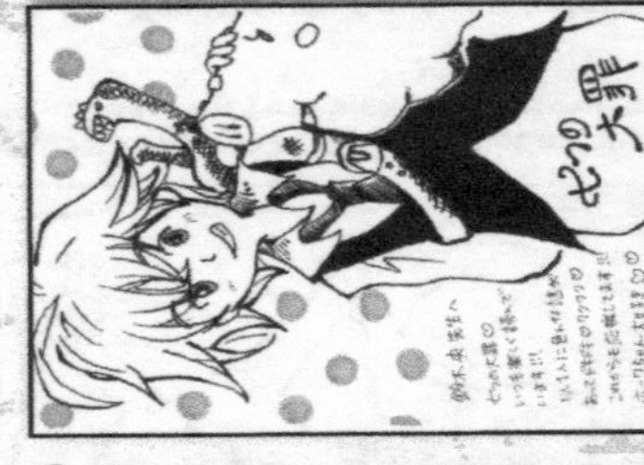
七つの大罪

E "This person must really like Hawk-chan and Chicken Mantangos."

M "To eat, you mean?"

H "How rude!"

the seven deadly sins

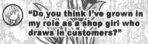

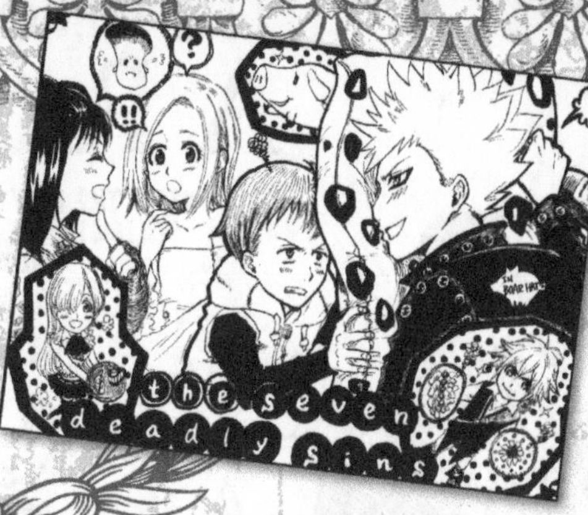

"Do you think I've grown in my role as a shop girl who draws in customers?"

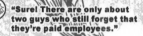

"Sure! There are only about two guys who still forget that they're paid employees."

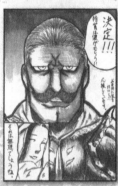

MIZUKI-SAN / HYOGO PREFECTURE

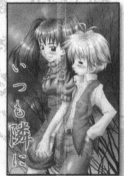

決定!!!

KUNIAKI AMANO / AICHI PREFECTURE

K "W...Who is this handsome man?"

M "You're the only one who would say something like that! Verdict!!"

いつも隣に

MATOROS-SAN / YAMAGUCHI PREFECTURE

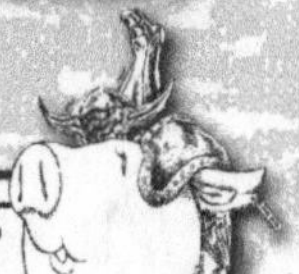

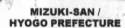

D "Next time I shrink down again, I'm going on a date with the captain. ♡"

H "I'm afraid the Chicken Mantangos will become an endangered species."

Now Accepting Applicants for the Drawing Knighthood!

- Draw your picture on a postcard, or paper no larger than a postcard, and send it in!
- Don't forget to write your name and location on the back of your picture!
- You can include comments or not. And colored illustrations will still only be displayed in B&W!
- The Drawing Knights whose pictures are particularly noteworthy and run in the print edition will be gifted with a signed specially made pencil board!
- And the best overall will be granted the special prize of a signed shikishi!!

Send to:
The Seven Deadly Sins Drawing Knighthood
c/o Kodansha Comics
451 Park Ave. South, 7th Floor, New York, NY 10016

* Submitted letters and postcards will be given to the artist. Please be aware that your name, address, and other personal information included will be given as well.